THE GEORGIAN
LITERARY SCENE
1910   1935

THE AUTHOR

THE GEORGIAN
LITERARY SCENE
1910   1935

by

FRANK SWINNERTON

WITH TEN ILLUSTRATIONS FROM BUSTS BY

JO DAVIDSON

RADIUS BOOK/HUTCHINSON

Hutchinson & Co (Publishers) Ltd
London Melbourne Sydney Auckland
Bombay Cape Town New York Toronto

First published	1935
Eighth Edition, revised	1954
This Edition, revised	1969

Printed in Great Britain on Antique Wove paper
by Balding & Mansell Ltd, of London & Wisbech
and bound by Wm. Brendon & Son Ltd, of Tiptree, Essex
09 028671 5   09 028672 3

CONTENTS

LIST OF ILLUSTRATIONS

PREFACE TO THE SIXTH EDITION

Somewhere about the year 1930, John Farrar, the American publisher, was inspired to suggest that I should write a book of anecdotes of contemporary British authors. It was to be personal and "intimate"; and he thought it would be popular in the United States, where I had a considerable following.

The reason for this suggestion was that from 1912, when I wrote a book about George Gissing, I had had considerable acquaintance with living writers. I knew several of my seniors extremely well, and met familiarly almost all of my own age. Also, as John Farrar knew, I was an easy talker, and I could tell about these men stories which to my hearers seemed extremely fantastic although they were strictly true. John Farrar believed that if I wrote as I talked I should amuse everybody very much.

However, my notion of the permissible, sometimes considered lax, prevented me from talking at large for strangers. I refused the proposed commission. I offered instead to do my best in what I saw as a conversational but critical study of contemporary literature. Mr. Farrar agreed to this counter-proposal; and for the next five years, in the course of other work, some of which was a help in the task, I polished up my familiarity with what had been written in recent times. *The Georgian Literary Scene* was the result.

I mention the origin of the book to explain why it reads as if it were being talked. That was the design. What I wanted to produce was a study expressing my own views on current literature which could be enjoyed by those without professional interest in the subject. Rightly or wrongly I believed, and believe, that taste cannot be taught by professors, and that what is taught by them is too often snobbery.

The Georgian Literary Scene accordingly did not please academic critics. Some of them proved the truth of what I had said about ill-manners by abusing it; the more dignified, doing their best not to flounce, looked the other way. But readers of a more innocent or practical turn received the book enthusiastically. It has had considerable popularity; and even the large sale of a version of it in Everyman's Library has not prevented a number of people from asking for a new library edition. Here is this new edition, reset and subjected to minor revisions, but not carried beyond the term of King George the Fifth's reign. I have left all I said largely as it was, in part because my interest in current literature has declined, but also because really to have brought the book up to date would have been a task beyond my present strength.

I want to write other things before I die, not endlessly to potter with something old. And *The Georgian Literary Scene* may even benefit in archæological interest from being, in a sense, "period." I have therefore left the verdicts as they were, deleted repetitions, and suppressed some explanatory references to myself which appeared in the earlier library editions. These references were merely candid, because I wanted not to pretend to be better informed than I was. They were sometimes misinterpreted by those who mistook candour for defensiveness.

For the rest, I add here the last two sentences from my original preface. "It is my opinion that writers detach themselves from their competitors less by their ideas or their technical performances than by a quality for which I find no better name than original talent. This assumption will explain why, although I refer to æsthetic theories, I make no attempt to judge all these contemporaries by a single æsthetic theory." If possible this attitude is still less fashionable than it was in 1935, when the book was first published. But I do not repent. Hazlitt said that fashion was gentility running away from vulgarity, which was a sign that the two things had much in common. There is neither fashion nor gentility, I hope, in *The Georgian Literary Scene*. There is instead a truthfulness not always to be found in our highly pretentious age.

I am greatly indebted to my friend Jo Davidson for a piece of characteristic generosity. He allowed my publishers to reproduce here photographs of ten busts modelled by him from life. Those who knew the men they represent will agree that these busts have extraordinary veracity as portraits; all will see that although Mr. Davidson's interpretations are his very distinguished own, so that he cannot be charged with endorsement of anything I have said in the text, the resulting decoration to my book is unique.

POSTSCRIPT added to this edition, of 1969. I have again been through the book, making verbal changes, but leaving the judgments as they were. To revise extensively, at the age of 84, when my preferred reading is of authors long dead, would be merely to cobble something which at the time of its original composition had organic life.

F.S.

Chapter One

INTRODUCTORY

i

A T the risk of beginning this book with a repulsive truism, I must remark that authors are born very untidily. They do not live, as they should do, from century to century, or from reign to reign, but rise as and when they will, and do their work unwinkingly regardless of the historian. Even Shakespeare himself— although Chaucer, who died neatly in the last weeks of the fourteenth century, might have shown him a better way—lived in two centuries and in two reigns.

But historians have their own methods of dealing with such rebels. They long ago decided that Shakespeare was an Elizabethan, and so he remains to this day. It is a convenient and justifiable assumption. Equally justifiable, it seems to me, for brief reference, is the description of Congreve, Farquhar, Vanbrugh, and Wycherley as "Restoration" dramatists; and equally convenient the term "Augustan" as applied to the characteristic literature of the reign of Queen Anne. "Commonwealth" and "Regency" are also pleasant and suggestive economies for the historian of manners. But two subsequent major labels, both misleading in themselves, give an arbitrary order to the births, deaths, and works of innumerable celebrated authors as diverse as the ills of mankind.

The first of these labels is that of the original "Georgian" period with which this book has no concern. England was ruled, from 1714 to 1830, by four successive kings named George. Anything built or written at some time in the eighteenth century was "Georgian". Johnson, Horace Walpole, Sterne, Cowper, Fanny Burney, Burke, Gibbon, and Collins were all "Georgian." You could also call Lamb, Keats, and Hazlitt Georgians if you wished. As for Queen Victoria, whose name forms the second of these labels, she lived (she was born in 1819) and reigned (from 1837 to 1901) so long that whole generations of writers came and went while she indestructibly occupied the throne of her country.

No wonder historians, triumphant at their success with Shakespeare, and misled by the overwhelming embrace of the Georges and Victoria, assumed thenceforward that centuries and reigns and literary types marched together. In face of Queen Victoria's long reign, we all know what a jovial person means when he indicates by a single word smugness, stuffiness, woolwork, industrialism, moral

I

straitlacing, or whatever it is he most dislikes. But the historian and the jovial person are alike making a grand mistake. Just as smugness was to be found elsewhere than in England during the nineteenth century, and just as it lived on in that very scorn of the Victorians upon which scorners set such value, so literary types fall with extraordinary diversity far outside the widest limits of the descriptive term. And individual writers, already smiling at the critic who arrives with an Aristotelian formula, become positively ribald if the critic begins to classify by era.

The reason of their mirth becomes clear as soon as we try to apply the Edwardian name with precision. King Edward VII had so short a reign—only from 1901 to 1910—that there was barely time in it for Bernard Shaw, H. G. Wells, Joseph Conrad, Arnold Bennett, and a few more Victorian-born writers to shoot into decided prominence; and their real fame has been post-Edwardian. Shaw's best-known work, for example, was written in Victorian days; his triumph at the Court Theatre (the audience there, he once retorted to a questioner, was not an audience but a congregation) was Edwardian; but his deification, after much fruitless abuse in 1914–18, has been entirely a matter for latter-day seekers after a new Grand Old Man.

Again, Wells conversed selectly with his uncle as long ago as 1895, and besides writing his greatest short stories and scientific romances before Queen Victoria's death he had reached "Anticipations" in 1901. Nevertheless, "Tono-Bungay," his masterpiece, was published in the very last year of King Edward's lifetime, and the height as well as the decline of his reputation as a novelist was purely Georgian. Bennett's "Clayhanger" was published after the accession of King George. And although his best work was done earlier, Conrad's success with "Chance" came as late as the Spring of 1914.

The word "Edwardian," accordingly, has no such general and acceptable meaning for any of us as the word "Victorian." When used—by those who were themselves, amusingly enough, Victorian by birth and Edwardian by first literary effort—as a term of discrimination and disparagement, it failed. But the object of its use was clear. The object was to suggest that Shaw, Wells, Conrad and Bennett were out of date. It would have been very convenient for those fashionable since 1920 to appropriate the Georgian name to themselves. It would have justified that exclusiveness to which they attached much importance. But all the same there was something juvenile in the plan, as if not very pleasant and nurse-bred children showed a familiar kind of ill-breeding. We saw the new little band of brothers and sisters crowding the windows and doorway of a first-class English railway carriage, and pretending that the carriage was reserved for them. "Full up, full up!" they cried, to Shaw and the other elderly and less elderly trippers. "Plenty of room for *you* in the old third-class, Edwardian, coach." Not very agreeable children; a good deal worried (like minor royalties) about precedence and congenital superiority.

ii

Now King George V ascended the throne in 1910. And it was in or about that year, you will remember, that (on the authority of a much-admired woman novelist) human nature underwent a remarkable change. Human nature, at bottom, had been recognizably similar under Victoria and Edward. Philosophers had gone so far as to suppose it unchangeable. One of them, indeed, wittier than the rest, had said that the more it changed the more it remained the same. But no sooner did King George come to the throne than (if we were to believe our novelist) human nature disobeyed every known law. It must have done this, I suspect, in order to give some friendly assistance—almost a nudge—a sort of preferential nudge—to the literary historian. For in or about 1910 we entered the period of time which is now universally described as, not "modern," but "modn."

I do not believe that human nature changed in 1910, unless it can be said to change every twenty or thirty years. Perhaps it does that? Or is it only fashion that changes? Modernity, at least, is almost as old as history; and there have always been two opinions of it. For example, and to take superficial details only, I find that in the eighties of last century, much as the discovery may astonish those who regard youth as an exclusively modn phenomenon, there was something widely known as "the revolt of youth." How "modn" that sounds! How almost incredible! Yet young women of the eighties shocked their parents by all sorts of uncouth doings, from fencing and boxing to travelling on the tops of omnibuses. In Mayfair at the same time the most fashionable accomplishment of all was the ability to play the banjo. Still in Queen Victoria's day, men and women of birth were "almost ostentatiously" going into trade, and noble ladies were opening millinery shops in the West End just as if they belonged to the new poor. Shortly before the end of Queen Victoria's reign, young women were using cosmetics for facial decoration; cigarette-smoking was notably on the increase; smart dinner parties were no longer given at home, but in hotels and restaurants; and the week-end habit was in full swing. All this seventy years ago, as a part of the normal development of fashion. Has there been, in manners, so abrupt a change since then as to constitute proof of a change in human nature?

It is true that the Georgian period had its own peculiarities. At the opening of it the general tempo of life everywhere was visibly quickening. The telegraph, the telephone, the automobile had all helped to break up old ways. Wireless telegraphy had been effectively used at sea; the moving picture was in being; the phonograph had given way to the gramophone; the whole world had with marvel begun to look up into the skies at machines that flew. These things were simple indications that the imagination of the human race had been captured for a time by the fruits of that scientific genius which had been increasingly active since the middle of the nineteenth century. They foreshadowed most of the preoccupations of later years. They seem in retrospect very threatening as well as very wonderful. But they were the result of earlier research, earlier experiment, earlier learning, and earlier irresistible movement towards the kind of world amid which we now live.

Nor was this all; for the successive Education Acts of 1870, 1891, and 1897 had produced in England a state of almost universal literacy which was then considered a step towards the democratic millennium. Halfpenny newspapers had made the reading of news and views a matter for every breakfast table in the land, a daily feast of excitement, hotter and hotter as competition forced editors and contributors towards ever greater licence. And there was news in these papers, even then, provocative enough to make men thump tables and lose tempers, and to make women argue and lecture and go to prison. Although education had not greatly improved their intelligence, it has without doubt increased group consciousness in these men and women; and popular newspapers were very powerful, not so much in initiating ideas or movements, as in spreading infection far and wide, and in agitating half-developed minds into a state of foaming anger.

In the political world, after a good many years of Tory rule (rule, that is, by those with possessions and privileges who none the less had their disinterestedness also), and after a humiliating war in which general after general had lost his military reputation, the Liberal party in 1906 had been returned by a tremendous majority of voters. The Liberals, or democratic reformers, were no longer politically the most advanced body in the House of Commons (there were a few Labour members), but they were a body which in Victorian days would have seemed revolutionary; and they used their power to propose greater taxation of the rich, health insurance for the poor, and other progressive legislation tending to equalize distribution of wealth in the British Isles. The measures thus introduced were rejected by the House of Lords, which represented in its own eyes national stability and in the eyes of eager partisans of the other side the well-nigh indestructible bulwark of privilege;

and the wildest feelings were roused throughout the country. In 1910, accordingly, another election was fought entirely upon the question of whether the House of Lords should or should not in future be able to check the designs of the people's elected representatives. This election also was won—not without loss—by the Liberals; but the Liberals—in turn—those defenders of the Rights of Man—were terribly assailed by advocates of Women's Suffrage who once and for all destroyed the legend that women were a mystical cross between angels and slaves. Tempers at this hour, the beginning of King George's reign, were unusually hot.

But these things again were only signs of the times; they were the open results of a general tendency which had been long maturing. What may for conciseness' sake be called the democratic idea had taken possession of men's minds. The idea was not merely political; it was social. The long moral acquiescence of a nation which took its good manners from a widowed queen and her circumscribed court had been ending in the last twenty years of Queen Victoria's lifetime; and at her death everybody realized that it had gone for good. It had been ending because the old dominance of the landed gentry in England had passed, because wealth had grown and spread to the middle classes, because the franchise had been extended so as to bring into the electorate all sorts of people who had earlier been excluded, because of the rise of compulsory literacy, and because of the fall of class barriers. Respect for the Upper Classes had been undermined; the self-complacence of the bourgeoisie had taken its place; in turn the self-complacence of the bourgeoisie was being attacked; and finally the dominance of man was being assailed by that new feminist arm—physical force.

In literature, since literature, when it is not actively leading that thought, reflects so much of the common thought of the time, the consequences of this unrest were profound. The Victorian tradition in letters was represented only by a few surviving old men and women. There were not many of them. George Meredith and Algernon Charles Swinburne had both died in the year before King George's accession. Alfred Austin, who had been chosen Poet Laureate in the "naughty nineties," according to the gossip of that time as "the least of evils," was one of Time's laughing-stocks.[1] Robert Bridges was still unknown to the majority. Thomas Hardy

---

[1] "Indeed, Austin's appointment is a ridiculous one, for, with the exception of three sonnets, Austin has never written anything in the smallest degree good. . . . He has floated in at last to the Laureateship on the strength of a prose volume about his garden in Kent. There really was no choice, however, for the post. William Morris refused, the Queen objected to Swinburne, old Patmore was a Catholic, the rest were, if possible, worse than Austin. He is better, anyhow, than Lewis Morris, the Liberal candidate, or than Watson, Dobson, Davidson, and the rest of the sons of their own penny trumpets."
—W. S. Blunt, "My Diaries," p. 261.

had just succeeded to the post of literature's Grand Old Man recently vacated by Meredith; and although he was still to achieve immense fame as a poet, so that his reputation may be said not to have reached its climax until about 1920, his work as novelist had been long done.

Professor Saintsbury and Edmund Gosse represented the elders in multifarious literary criticism, the one with gathering veneration, the other as a busy social figure, while A. C. Bradley represnted them in criticism on the loftier levels. Theodore Watts-Dunton survived, largely as one who had seen Swinburne plain (it was thought, none the less, that his oversight had been detrimental to Swinburne's poetic talent) and as one who had contributed many columns of material to *The Athenæum* in days when space was of no moment. His biography had been written in good time by James Douglas. Buried in the tomb which he had erected over the remains of Gladstone, the original Grand Old Man of English reverence, John Morley watched with gloom the decay of authority. Hardy was the only surviving "giant"; and although the legend of giantism persisted it did so with difficulty. The convention by which belittlement of great men was discouraged on the ground that we were "too near" to judge them wisely ("Stand away! Stand away!" cried the guards of fame) was yielding to a newer convention by which great men could at least be focused as soon as they were dead. Giants were smaller; and a small giant is an anomaly. It is also an anachronism, for although year by year some literary or political or economic figure is raised a little above the crowd by a few admirers, admirers quickly tire of supporting an idol, and when dropped the idol of a year or two looks positively dwarfish.

iii

THE true Edwardians, it seems to me, who represent the tumultuous charge of Liberalism passing over the country between 1906 and 1910, were G. K. Chesterton and Hilaire Belloc, with the Victorian William Watson as a sedate and unheeded singer of Liberal songs far from the battlefield. Chesterton and Belloc, both men of genius, were carried to renown by this glorious charge. With their colleague Charles Masterman, they spoke and wrote everywhere, cutting and slashing and waving large banners of purple and gold. But when the charge had spent itself, Belloc and Chesterton were somehow cut off from their fellows. They both worked indefatigably during the Georgian age. But they were not of it. Something happened to their bugles. Instead of sounding triumphantly a further charge, these instruments uttered nothing but the retreat.

It was accordingly left to others to lead both Liberalism and literature down steep places into the sea. Chesterton hoped to the end that he was right, and almost with his last breath announced that the true revolution is the counter-revolution; but he lost pace with the times and will become a classic rather than an influence upon our day. Belloc devotedly rewrote history. He will probably be "edited" in a hundred years' time, when his propagandism has become archaic, and when his genius will shine like the jewel it is.

So much for the truly pre-Georgian writers. These were the men who had their roots in the past. They were entirely surrounded either by Victorianism or by Medievalism. It was enough for them to picture their own fixed world, or to criticize contemporary history in terms of former history. Chesterton and Belloc demanded the return of Merrie England; Hardy lived most richly in Napoleonic or forgotten rural days; Morley was lost in Gladstonian grandeur; the critics I have named, having celebrated, the one his father, and the other his cellar, were happiest with old books. It was time that other voices should be heard. They were heard.

The voices said little of the past. They were very clear voices, and they spoke of the present in scathing terms, and of the future as an opportunity for shattering the world and remoulding it nearer to the heart's desire. The present, it appeared, was bad; and it must be changed. But England had had writers in Victorian days who had criticized the ugly and industrial present; none more strongly than Mrs. Gaskell, Charles Kingsley, Disraeli, and George Gissing. William Morris, alternatively, had dreamed of idyllic clodhoppers in endless medieval narratives and prophetic visions. All these writers were now outmoded; the new criticism was something different in style from all they had attempted. On the one hand it worked through irresistible raillery; on the other through what was at that time a quite shockingly fearless vein of speculation. "Shaw and Wells," said an old newspaper editor to me one day, "we've never treated as 'literature,' but always as cranks." It was the pre-Georgian voice that spoke. In pre-Georgian days, "literature" was "serious" or it was "light"; it was not effervescently destructive with a seriousness that shamed solemnity. Shaw and Wells came among the respectable with whips, scorpions, the extruded tongue, and an agitating suggestion that men and women were not wicked, but only stupid and smug. How unlike were these weapons to the Old Testamentary lamentation and exhortation of Carlyle. "Woe! Woe! Unless ye repent—." How unlike to the nostalgic buglings of Chesterton and Belloc. "Oligarchy! The Church! Medievalism!" It is not surprising that readers of plays and novels were disconcerted and rather annoyed by the new methods. But of course fascinated also, and drawn to attend to what was so indignantly denounced by the effete, and delighted by a sense of their own "modernity" in cultivating the latest frightfulness in moral criticism.

In those days the sociological play and novel were the chief recreation of those who consider themselves cultured. And at the beginning of the Georgian age it was the correct thing to see or read Shaw's plays and to read Wells's books. It was the correct thing, because it was, comparatively, a new thing. It was the fashion. The fashion had changed again. In the eighties it had been all for the now much-maligned three-volume novel. Having been replaced by the fashion of Stevenson and his imitators, and in turn by the fashion of the knowing and vigorous work of Rudyard Kipling, it had gone democratic. Besides Shaw and Wells, the public was attending to Arnold Bennett's closely-studied engravings of provincial society, to John Galsworthy's dramatic vignettes of capital and labour and the dying bourgeoisie, and to the work of young men and women who had been influenced, in chief, by the spirit of the time as exemplified in the work of these elder leaders.

But then, as now, the spirit of the time worked in more than the immediately observable and immediately popular way. Just as I have said that you cannot fit authors into centuries and reigns, so you cannot without distortion fit them into schools and groups. In the nineties of last century, for example, which are forever labelled with the names of Wilde and Beardsley, George Gissing was producing his sombre and powerful novels; Conrad and Wells were both active; Ibsen's plays had been translated and were being very widely read; Israel Zangwill and Kipling were the popular successes. In the nineteen hundreds, when Utopias were rife, and the present over-development of scientific education had already begun, Francis Thompson's selected poems were the success of their year, Granville-Barker wrote "The Marrying of Ann Leete" and collaborated in the writing of "Prunella," while Kenneth Grahame's "The Wind in the Willows" was published and a new poetic dramatist named John Masefield followed his historical novel, "Captain Margaret," with "The Tragedy of Nan." There was a stirring among young writers which made as much ferment as the current stirring of young writers appears to do. It may not now seem to us a stirring of pure gold, but at least there were bubbles of modernity in the crucible.

It may give some indication of the variety of writers whose work was watched with interest at the beginning of King George's reign if I mention what was at the time a periodical of great importance to observers of literary tendencies. This, *The English Review*, edited by Ford Madox Hueffer, was an impressively non-commercial monthly. It was first published as for the month of December, 1908; and during its life under Hueffer's control it was unquestionably the most valuable literary journal in the country. The earliest contributors to *The English Review* included some who will not come into our review of Georgian letters. But among the elders should be mentioned Thomas Hardy, Henry James, W. H. Hudson, R. B. Cunninghame Graham, Maurice Hewlett, Vernon Lee, and Lowes Dickinson. Bernard Shaw, as far as I know, was never a contributor.

In a generation rather younger, contributors included Joseph Conrad, John Galsworthy, Arnold Bennett, H. G. Wells, Norman Douglas, C. E. Montague, Violet Hunt, John Masefield, and H. M. Tomlinson. Conrad was not yet a success, in spite of the fact that his first book, "Almayer's Folly," had appeared in 1895 and "Nostromo" in 1904. Galsworthy was already the author of "A Man of Property," "The Silver Box," and "The Country House." Bennett's "The Old Wives' Tale" had been the talk of 1908. Wells's "Tono-Bungay" began to run as a serial story in the first number of *The English Review*. Norman Douglas and H. M. Tomlinson were quite unknown, unless some curious person had chanced upon Douglas's pamphlet, "The Herpetology of the Duchy of Baden," and unless readers of *The Morning Leader* had noted Tomlinson's articles in that newspaper. Parts of "The Sea and the Jungle" were published in *The English Review*. Montague was the chief leader-writer on *The Manchester Guardian* as well as the dramatic critic who wrote about Manchester theatrical productions; but outside Manchester he had no literary reputation until he published "A Hind Let Loose" in 1910.

To these names were gradually added those of writers still younger, the first of the distinctively "Georgian" names. I instance Harley Granville-Barker, who at the age of thirty was considered the hope of the English theatre, Walter de la Mare, W. W. Gibson, Gilbert Cannan, Edward Thomas, and D. H. Lawrence. The youngest contributor to the earliest numbers of *The English Review* was Percy Wyndham Lewis who wrote, he afterwards said, "from the standpoint of genius."

There are omissions, of course, both from my list and from the complete list of contributors to this excellent journal. No editor can be more than catholic. And any list of authors much admired at the beginning of the Georgian era would be partial which did not include the names of Hilaire Belloc, Maurice Baring, E. V. Lucas, and G. K. Chesterton. Rudyard Kipling was in the doldrums, partly because his politics were unpopular in the decade following the Boer War, and partly because his later work was inferior to the work by which he became famous. Arthur Symons was at the height of his reputation as poet and critic. Robert Hichens was a writer of importance. Sir Arthur Pinero was in those days always

called—rather defiantly, it seemed, and by those who were uneasy at
the rising Shaw—"England's greatest dramatist." J. M. Barrie was
the leading figure in the theatre. Hall Caine and Mrs. Humphry
Ward had become occasions for ribald comment. William de Morgan
had ceased to surprise as an example of reanimated Victorianism,
although he still published novels of notable volume. Sir Arthur
Quiller-Couch, who became King Edward Professor of English
Literature at Cambridge in 1912, stood out from the wreck of the
picturesque novel. Robert Bridges (Poet Laureate in 1913), Lord
Alfred Douglas, William Watson, Laurence Binyon, Stephen
Phillips, Alfred Noyes, and John Davidson were all well known as
poets, however much opinions might differ as to their gifts. Somerset
Maugham and Rudolf Besier were rising popular dramatists. Eden
Phillpotts, "Elizabeth," W. B. Maxwell, May Sinclair, Charles
Marriott, and John Buchan had all distinctive reputations in the
novel.

As will be seen at once from the enumeration, not all these
writers hold their high place of that hour in the literary opinion of
today. Fashion is always changing, and names go up and down
very oddly, even in the minds of those whose taste is catholic rather
than exclusive. If I were writing a purely critical study, I might
omit some of these names altogether. To do so would be to give a
wrong impression of the period which I am trying to sketch. In this
introductory section I want to show, however superficially, which
writers were "established" in the year of the King's accession, which
writers had still to make their reputations, and which writers were
as yet engaged in preliminary scrawlings at school and in the
nursery. The writers not named above were for the most part
preparing for the great assault. They had not been heard of outside
their own homes or their own small societies for mutual aid.

iv

BUT surely, it will be suggested, there were in 1910 at least dim
notions of some critical standards by which any writer whatsoever could be judged? There were. I have no doubt at all that there
were severities of judgment in the rising generation which could
equal those of the present day. I remember in particular that Gilbert
Cannan was demolishing all the older writers as they are still being
demolished; but some of these older writers are like the man in the
song, of whom it is said that "he's dead, but he won't lie down," and
they survived, dead but not forgotten, in some extraordinary
manner more alive than those who assailed them, more provoking,
more antediluvian, and at the same time more essential than ever as

Aunt Sallys to critics armed with ever new weapons of destruction.

For it must be admitted that the critics of to-day are provided with a more elaborate critical apparatus than any enjoyed by their predecessors. In 1910 there were cheap and easy translations of Aristotle's "Poetics," Longinus "On the Sublime," Lessing's "Laocoon," and Coleridge's "Biographia Literaria." But modern æsthetic criticism, with its new and baffling terminologies, was young. Benedetto Croce was on the horizon but no more; Professor Irving Babbitt did not publish his "New Laocoon" in England until 1911. A. C. Bradley was considered the last word in the criticism of poetry and of Shakespeare's plays; Professor Dowden was the last long word on Shelley; Georg Brandes the last word on everything. Psychoanalysis was unheard of by the majority of English writers, and accordingly the application of post-Freudian methods and terms to the study of the minds of writers was unconsidered. We had to make do, the youngest of us, as well as we could, and in spite of some very haughty Aristotelians, with the light of Nature.

Meanwhile all these writers were at work producing in excellent faith books which were felt to be more or less good, or more or less interesting. Not equally good, not equally interesting, but all possessed of some quality which justified their contemporary existence. Occasionally it was a social quality in the authors, more often it was an air of originality or profundity or just plain enjoyableness in the work. Some writers were fashionable, some were unfashionable; some had the suffrages of ordinary people (but most people were at that time ordinary), one or two greatly impressed those who pride themselves upon an exclusive taste. Is not that the history of books and their appraisement in all ages? There were "the few" and "the many" then, as now; and only the extremely democratic tone of the leading writers of 1910, who were democratic in manners and sympathies as well as in scholastic theory, kept literary snobbery at bay. The fight was then against professors who felt that "literature" had mysteriously ceased in 1850; it was waged by those who desired greater liberty for everybody.

Perhaps, most of all, they desired liberty for themselves, but what they wanted was freedom from library censorship and freedom from dramatic censorship. More than anything else, they wanted a distinction made between the possible unpleasantness of work that shocked because it was too literal and the approved pruriency of work that was shocking by innuendo. And they wanted the novel and the play to be taken seriously. They were not, they said, telling tales to keep old men from chimney-corner, but were all for the making of a better world by means of free criticism and prophetic vision. Finally, they insisted that art meant something more than pretty pictures and photography. Because they were entertaining, even when most serious, they captured the public. First of all, they captured the young, and then they captured the old. The stolid they never captured, because the stolid are always found in the last ditch, reading old numbers of *Punch* and playing follow my leader.

The young stood for seriousness. They stood also for iconoclasm. But the young have an endless capacity for reverence and a bottomless self-doubting, the first being the outcome of the second. And high above all fights, marked by everything that makes an author respectable in English life, sat one man. His years were many; his work was considered too rare for ordinary readers; his disinterested devotion to art had been lifelong. To read his books appreciatively was to prove oneself both intelligent and of fine taste; and to share his æsthetic ideals was to feel that one moved upon the same plane as a master-craftsman who was also a master-critic of the art he practised. Although crabbed professors who "taught" literature might fidget at an approach to their subject wholly different from their own, even they at last were forced to acknowledge that if literature was in truth an art the secrets of it were best revealed by an artist obviously too good for the multitude. For these reasons, and for the reason that he had a very distinguished irony and great dignity, the writer I have described rose slowly to extraordinary eminence. He could not be the Grand Old Man (the post was held by Thomas Hardy); but he could be, and was, appointed Grand Literary Panjandrum of the Time. His position was lofty; it had been unsought; and it was deprecatingly relished by its holder. In the early years of King George V no critical voice had as subtle a power as that of Henry James.

Chapter Two

ARTFUL VIRTUOSITY

i

" 'He makes it, somehow, such a grand, possible affair.'
'Ah, well, if he makes it possible!'
'I mean especially he makes it grand.' "
The Wings of the Dove.

HENRY JAMES was not born a Panjandrum. He became one as the result of longevity, taste, and sustained technical virtuosity, but especially of longevity. He hardly knew himself to be a Panjandrum, for he was very modest, rather a snob, and quite unreadable by many of his fellow-creatures. He was born at Albany, New York, on April 15th, 1843. His grandfather, an Irishman whose great commercial success in that city is still commemorated in the name of a street, left considerable estate to be divided among numerous heirs; his father—Henry James, senior—was an unworldly mystical theologian whose devotion to Swedenborg was such that he always travelled with his own set of the Master's works. Henry was the second son, a year younger than William, the philosopher, and the second of five children.

To dismiss the father of Henry James, as I have seemed to do above, as "an unworldly mystical theologian" would be very unjust to a man of abnormal mental ingenuity. The published portraits of him do not perhaps prepare us for the revelations of his son by which he becomes one of the most amusingly lovable characters outside fiction; but they do show the calm height of his noble head, the protrusive habit of his eyes (which seem not unlike those of his second son), and an unmistakable disinterested benevolence which shines from the whole countenance; and all these points mark him as an exceptional creature. He was a philosopher who was also a Christian; apparently, too, he was not only witty in himself, but the cause that wit was a natural activity in his family. The atmosphere of the James household was shot through and through, that is, with a gaiety and kindness allowing unlimited humorous reference to the father's "ideas" (it was supposed to be Mrs. James's word); while based, nevertheless, upon respectful affection. With what relish does his son, after referring to the senior Henry James's attachment to Swedenborg, add concerning this philosopher that "in reply to

somebody's plea of not finding him credible our parent had pronounced him, on the contrary, fairly 'insipid with veracity'!"

The little boy was much appreciated by his father, who took
him freely upon various journeys, even, on one occasion, to the
daguerreotyper's, where the two Henrys were photographed side
by side, the boy with his hand upon his father's shoulder, charming,
modest, and wondering, the man kind, bland, and confidently at
peace with his faith. But the education of the James children, if free,
according to Henry James senior's wish, was also, in formal par-
ticulars, irregular. As Henry describes his own share of it, in that
great autobiography, "A Small Boy and Others," it was so hap-
hazard, so much an experimental setting of the boy to tasks which
proved uncongenial, and taking him away from them, so much a
confusion of New York city and country life with impulsive travels in
Europe, that the reader wonders how in the world such a bewildered
child learned anything at all. And yet might not such an education
have offered a perfect development to a master-novelist? "Simply
everything," says Henry James, "simply everything that should happen to us, every contact, every impression and experience we should
know, were to form our soluble stuff; with only ourselves to thank
should we remain un-aware, by the time our perceptions were decently
developed, of the substance finally projected and most desirable."

No priggishness was allowed, for "we were bred in horror of
conscious propriety, of what my father was fond of calling 'flagrant'
morality" and "our father . . . only cared for virtue that was more or
less ashamed of itself"; but as time went on Henry James reached a
kind of philosophical justification of a trait which coloured the whole
of his life and work. "One way," he says, "of taking life was to go in
for everything and everyone, which kept you abundantly occupied,
and the other way was to be as occupied, quite as occupied, just with
the sense and image of it all, *and on only a fifth of the actual immersion.*"
Thinking of Henry James, do not forget the second way was his own.

From Albany to the city of New York, where the Jameses lived
down town, and where William and Henry haunted such theatres
as there were and endlessly attended the church services of every
denomination; and from New York back to Albany, where innumerable cousins, male and female, came to stay and play; and
from Albany to London and Paris, these children passed in a rich
process of picking up impressions. Here and there they acquired
some book knowledge, William, the elder, ever a leader in that
department, while Henry, given to what he frankly calls "pedestrian
gaping," and less pragmatically absorbed in rationalizing the
universe, made do with his sensations and intuitions. "I had but
one success, always—that of endlessly supposing, wondering,
admiring; I was sunk in that luxury."

ii

IN the evenings, while William made drawings—he was in the early stages of his artistic period—Henry also imitatively drew; but he did something else as well, which threw a long finger out towards the practice of the future craftsman. "I sacrificed," he says "to the dramatic form with devotion—by the aid of certain quarto sheets of ruled paper bought in Sixth Avenue for the purpose; . . . grateful in particular for the happy provision by which each fourth page of the folded sheet was left blank. When the drama itself had covered three pages the last one, over which I most laboured, served for the illustration of what I had verbally presented. Every scene had thus its explanatory picture, and . . . I thought, I lisped, at any rate I composed, in scenes. . . . Entrances, exits, the indication of 'business,' the animation of dialogue, the multiplication of designated characters, were things delightful in themselves—while I panted toward the canvas on which I should fling my figures."

And so the Jameses went to Europe; and for Henry the plunge into astonishing older lands was like a plunge into a dream. He had been acquainted with some of the aspects of England in much-conned pages of *Punch*, but the reality of a country so like and so unlike his home, and a city which was then, long ago, a world in epitome, affected him for ever. In later years he went through his period of impatience with the English, only, in the end, to take them permanently to his heart; but now he was the instinctive artist, the "votary and victim of the single impression and the imperceptible adventure, picked up by accident and cherished, as it were, in secret." He could only absorb and absorb, dreaming, listening, storing. "I recall in particular certain short sweet times when I could be left alone—with the thick and heavy suggestions of the London room about me, the very smell of which was ancient, strange and impressive, a new revelation altogether, and the window open to the English June and the far-off hum of a thousand possibilities. I consciously took them in, these last, and must then, I think, have first tasted the very greatest pleasure perhaps I was ever to know—that of almost holding my breath in presence of certain aspects to the end of so taking in. It was as if in those hours that precious fine art had been disclosed to me."

That precious fine art was to be still further practised a little later, when the party travelled to Paris and this inveterate gazer and wonderer learned more consciously the lesson of art which was to dominate his creative life. Here, "with plot thickening and emotion deepening steadily, . . . we mounted the long, black Rue de Seine—*such* a stretch of perspective, *such* an intensity of tone as it

offered in those days; where every low-browed vitrine waylaid us
and we moved in a world of which the dark message, expressed in
we couldn't have said what sinister way too, might have been 'Art,
art, art, don't you see? Learn, little gaping pilgrims, what that is!'
Oh, we learned, that is we tried to, as hard as ever we could, and
were fairly well at it, I always felt, even by the time we had passed
up into the comparatively short but wider and finer vista of the
Rue de Tournon, which in those days more abruptly crowned the
more compressed approach and served in a manner as a great outer
vestibule to the Palace. Style, dimly descried, looked down there, as
with conscious encouragement, from the high, grey-headed, clear-
faced, straight-standing old houses—very much as if wishing to say
'Yes, small staring *jeune homme*, we are dignity and memory and
measure, we are conscience and proportion and taste, not to mention
strong sense too: for all of which good things take us—you won't
find one of them when you find (as you're going soon to begin to at
such a rate) vulgarity."

After such saturation and injunction, and some less ecstatic
experiences in Switzerland and Germany, William James decided
to be an artist, and studied with William Hunt, in whose studio
John La Farge was the only other pupil, although Henry James was
also thoughtfully to be found there. And when William James
declared suddenly for Physical Science, and went to Harvard
University to study it, Henry had already reached a sense of his
artistic destiny. Law, which was put to him as a possibility, and
which he read for a year, had no lure. "I didn't want anything so
much as I wanted a certain good (or wanted thus supremely *to* want
it, if I may say so). . . . What I 'wanted to want' to be was, all intimately, just *literary*."

iii

HE became "literary," at first not venturing very far or high (his
first work seems to have been a translation from Mérimée, and
he never attempted poetry), but modestly, as at all times, under-
estimating the originality of his own mind. The James family moved
to Cambridge; acquaintance followed with Charles Eliot Norton, at
that time editing the *North American Review*; and Norton accepted
Henry James's first timidly-submitted manuscript. E. L. Godkin,
also, whose control of the newly established New York *Nation* was
a matter of international fame, encouraged the young writer by
printing his criticisms. Finally he had the fortune to make a lifelong
friend of William Dean Howells, who read his earliest fiction with
enthusiasm and bought some of it for *The Atlantic Monthly*.

He was launched; and he hastened to London, "drawn by the

sense of all the interest and association I should find." This was in 1869, when he was twenty-six. He settled at first in Half Moon Street, off Piccadilly, in a couple of dusky ground-floor rooms the walls of which were hung with glazed coloured plates from the Christmas numbers of *The Illustrated London News*, and he began in earnest to explore the town. The Nortons were then in London, and through their friendly aid he had a round of visits to the famous, from George Eliot, Ruskin, and Charles Darwin to William Morris and the Rossettis. But he was not, at this time or at any other, a "mixer." For choice, his company was imaginary. He was "more and more aware of the 'fun' (to express it grossly) of living by my imagination and thereby finding that company, in countless different forms, could only swarm about me."

Thus the dreaming, gazing little boy had become a dreaming, gazing young man who preferred the delights of his own mental labyrinth to those of general society. He was in the old world, upon "haunted, holy ground," remote, a spectator. He was happy. Thenceforward, his way of life was settled; and he was to know little change in it for over forty years.

He was "just literary." During a long stay in Paris he made the acquaintance of Ivan Turgenev, who was the grand third of his literary influences (the earlier influences had been Hawthorne and Balzac); and from Turgenev he learned in long conversations how Turgenev wrote novels, and how novels should be written. Crucial conversations. And when he published "Daisy Miller," which still ranks very high among short stories written in English, he achieved a distinguished reputation with the critical public. It was his most interesting and original tale in this period, the scenes laid in Switzerland and Italy, with which countries he was familiar, and the American type new, baffling, and presented with suggestive detachment.

"Daisy Miller" was first published in 1879, when Henry James was thirty-six. From 1874–5, in which years he wrote "Roderick Hudson," he was continuously productive. Book followed book with great rapidity, sometimes a novel, sometimes a volume of short stories, sometimes in a single year as many as three books of one sort or another. He was a critic, too; and it is a remarkable fact that when he was not travelling or writing novels he was in a style of the utmost grace describing the places he had visited, or analysing with much fastidious insight the qualities of some classic novelist, such as Balzac, or George Sand, or Flaubert, or Turgenev. What a happy manner of life for one who aspired above everything else to be "just literary"!

Nor were rewards wanting to encourage the rising author, and for some years everything went very well indeed—not sensationally, but in a manner to assure his income and maintain his reputation. He was fortunate in being able to serialize many of his earlier novels either in America alone or in both England and America; and his short stories, or long-short stories, of which there were many, were to be found in the magazines upon both sides of the Atlantic. He contributed two or three tales to *The Yellow Book*, when Henry Harland enthusiastically projected that famous publication; and the rest slowly but steadily appeared, as long as editors thought them readable, in more widely circulated periodicals.

In those days he was less impressive in appearance than he was to be in old age. He mixed, it is clear, with the select few whose main interests were in art and letters; but as a quiet, bearded man, his head ever slightly cocked, as if he were listening and reflecting, who came and went with an air of shyness and elaborate self-deprecating solemnity, and not at all as the literary "lion" he was afterwards to be. He was even considered a trifle portentous, and the memories of him which appear in such typical books as the autobiographies of Evelyn Sharp and Arthur Waugh are unflattering. Evelyn Sharp recalls a time in her friendship with Henry Harland when James came to tea, "and Harland, for once losing his sense of humour in the presence of one whom he always referred to as 'mon maître,' took me aside to say in an impressive whisper, 'He says he has *heard* of your fairy tales!' This was the occasion on which we sat in dumb humility while the famous American walked up and down the room seeking the word he wanted for the completion of his sentence. I am sure we all knew the word, but the sacrilege that would be implied in our intrusion upon his mental travail by mentioning it was un-dreamed of. It was, of course, an immense honour to have been invited to worship at the shrine; but the atmosphere cleared plea-santly when he left." Arthur Waugh adds to a wickedly mild account of an evening in which his cousin Edmund Gosse and James "sat over the fire and talked confidences in an undertone, while Mrs. Gosse showed [Waugh] an album of photographs" one characteristic touch. "I realized that it was fully time the great evening ended, since I had to get home to Blackheath. 'To Blackheath!' exclaimed Henry James; 'not, I trust, in a hansom-cab—an interminable under-taking!'"

Once, late in life, our author returned to the United States for the sake of writing an immense impression of the land he had deserted. But for the most part he was in London or the English country, in an apartment in town or staying at the Reform Club, or living in the beautiful old house which he had discovered in a corner of Rye. Here, in that charming little hillside town in Sussex from which the English Channel has drawn back a couple of miles in the last two or three centuries, he lived from 1897 to the end. He aged, he corresponded voluminously, he gradually received all those signs of respect which in England are accorded to literary survivals of the approved social variety, and his art grew ever more elaborate, more scrupulous and wordy and, for those who relish its quality, more wonderfully engrossing. He became a naturalized Englishman early in the First World War, and died on February 28th, 1916.

In those last years his position in English letters was unique. Thomas Hardy might be the Grand Old Man; but Henry James was the lawgiver to his juniors. His considerable critical gift and his disinterested devotion to the art of fiction set him above party. Only those to whom the art of fiction seems a triviality in a difficult universe scorned his devotion. Rude people might scoff at the elaborately parenthetical manner—a manner of successive alternatives—which marked James's later writing as well as his later conversation; they might also object that the themes of his most famous books were singularly unworthy of the delicacy and the bland copiousness of his treatment; but he had dignity and taste and style, and the rude, while they scoffed, were unwillingly still aware that such gifts are without price. The fine large head upon a body which, without being clumsy, was shorter and stockier than it should have been for perfect grace, was indication enough of the subtle spirit within; and the affectionateness, reserve, and timidity of his character caused those who knew him well to feel for him that curious mixture of admiration, respect, and protectiveness which is generally described, in brief, as love.

iv

IT was once irreverently remarked, by a non-Jacobean too-ready with historical analogy, that there were three Henry Jameses— James the First, James the Second, and the Old Pretender. That last, with its implications, was never true; but the suggestion held just enough malice to make it effective. Like other writers, Henry James had his three periods, in the first of which irony did no more than temper ingenuousness, in the second of which the emotional problems of travelling Americans were replaced by the doings of imaginary famous authors and other odd characters, and in the third of which every wizened theme was so dwelt upon, and turned, and manipulated, as to yield its last and finest shade of ironic meaning. The progress between these periods was natural, and in each of them the author was keeping pace with his own development. He was writing from young manhood until the age of seventy-two. During the whole, roughly, of that half-century he believed strongly that it was the finest thing in the world to be an artist and to write novels which were works of art.

I have used the term "works of art," and I want now to remind the reader that when Henry James thought of art he thought in terms of pictures, and not in terms of modern æsthetics. He was very much the professional artist, the man who assesses the value of a work of art according to the degree in which it may be said to be "done." When he spoke critically of novels he always used words such as one might hear in a studio when two painters were speaking intimately of a picture. But while, with a little study, he probably could have understood the phrases adopted by living æsthetes from Physics and Psychoanalysis, he would not have felt it necessary to use them. A book had "composition," "tone," "values," "colour," and "form." It might have had such qualities as "foreground" and "middle-distance." But it never had a moral; and it never took heed of such things as "rhythm" or "planes" or the "sub-" or "super-conscious."

He began by writing critical reviews, and his first fiction consisted, as Hawthorne's did, of short stories. The earliest novel of which he thought well enough to include it in his Collected Works was "Roderick Hudson." This is a book about a detached young American who conceived an admiration for the work of a young sculptor and offered him the chance of studying the antique in Rome. The sculptor, Roderick Hudson, jumped at his chance; but although he was engaged to a good girl in New England he fell in love in Italy with a wayward and enigmatic young woman of a kind always more fascinating to a novelist than to his readers. The young woman having been disposed of matrimonially—under the threat that if she did not marry the Prince Casamassima her mother and father would inexplicably disclose the fact of her illegitimacy—Roderick forsook his friends, lost his talent, and at last was killed in a mountain storm. The detached young American was in love with his protégé's sweetheart; but this young lady preferred to cherish her memory of authentic emotion, and the end of the book lies in shadow.

"The American," which followed, carries us a stage farther in the history of our author's development. It is the story of a man who had made a sufficient fortune in his own country, and who coolly determined to marry a beautiful French widow. The widow's relatives, including an all-powerful mother from the English aristocracy, at first permitted the suit; but presently they decided against the American, sent his young fiancée to a convent, and defied him when he threatened disclosure of a frightful family secret. He burnt the evidence of this crime, from pride, and all was as before.

The third novel is about a lovely young American girl who was enriched by her uncle's will. She was so simple-minded as to be led into marriage with a dilettante egoist, whom she ultimately left after discovering that the marriage had been "arranged" by her husband's former mistress, the mother of his daughter. There are two sick men who die in this book, both of them American, whimsical, wise, and kind; and there is a quiet, persistent, but unfailingly considerate American lover who turns up again at the end. The book is called "The Portrait of a Lady," and it is the first in which one of those beautiful, tranquil old English houses in the country the imagination of which James so adored makes its appearance.

The fourth novel was "The Princess Casamassima," one of the worst books by a good writer that I have ever read. It is about a youth of the lower orders (his mother had murdered a man, and he had been brought up by a sempstress and an old fiddler, both Thackerayan figures), who joined a revolutionary organization, was given some unspecified piece of assassination to do, and committed suicide. He was by trade a bookbinder, infatuated with the notion that he was of noble birth; and the Princess Casamassima, who first appeared as a *femme fatale* in "Roderick Hudson," still works her wicked will upon the young and impressionable, without so much as stirring a hair of the reader's head.

These four books may be said to represent James's first period as a novelist. They were essays in what Hawthorne called "psychological romance." They have in common the distinction of a very simple style of great dignity. They are about small groups of characters who are saved from insipidity by unusual conversational gifts and by a pervasive air of secret drama. In the case of the first three, the chief male character is a cool spectator of the events dramatized, not unmoved by these events, but powerless to stay them, hardly at all, effectively, a participant in the action. This was a device, but a significant device. The author deliberately chose to employ a single male character as chorus, in order to exercise his own peculiar combination of intimacy and detachment. He could thus be in the book and out of it, without in the least sacrificing his own independence. Later on, the bachelor chorus was to be discontinued; but a chorus, in the shape of a single abnormally sensitive person or a number of gossips who could speculate and scrutinize and comment at large, there was to be to the end.

The development of these early books is generally slow. A situation is indicated for us by means of a series of conversations between different people, aided by calm and revealing accounts of their antecedent doings. The characters are unpressed for time, and, in any convincing sense, for money. Most of them are extremely, almost too pointedly, well-bred. They are not marionettes, controlled by the author; and yet they do, as one remembers, most singularly forgather and group themselves, as people do in plays or in pictures, and while rational in talk behave in such a way as to seem unaccountable for their actions. Not one of them exerts himself or herself except by painting or embroidering or producing impressive sculpture or touring picture galleries or visiting the Colosseum. It is as if they were dream characters rather than real people.

I will not follow the ungracious and usually inaccurate habit of some critics, who speak of characters being lifted bodily from other books; but I cannot help believing that in these early novels of Henry James, exquisite to me as they are, the people *derive* (no more) from certain types in books by Hawthorne and Turgenev and Balzac. That, in fact, they are as much "just literary" as their author. The Bellegardes, in "The American," for example, are Balzac; but the travelling Americans, and in particular the constant Mary Garland, in "Roderick Hudson," might well have entered James's pages from corners of "The House of the Seven Gables," or from one of the exquisite tales of Turgenev with which the author must by now have been very familiar. They are not copies; the author's explanations of them have profundity; but the characters themselves are ethereal. Perhaps the books altogether were nothing but Henry James's lovely prolonged play; perhaps each of them was something of which he was the godlike creator and the happy, interested, tremendously aware and relishing spectator. "It is not my impulse," said a character in "The House of the Seven Gables," "either to help or to hinder; but to look on, to analyse, to explain matters to myself, and to comprehend the drama." And James: "My identity for myself was *all* in my sensibility to their own exhibition, with not a scrap left over for a personal show."

v

IN the composition of these books, as in the composition of many of Henry James's books, one notices a very odd circumstance. It is that the concrete is often a matter of great difficulty. I do not mean the sort of detail about which novel-readers write triumphantly to the newspapers, such as the right railway station for Paris, the right omnibus number for Richmond, and so on; for such matters interested Henry James not at all. "The station," "the omnibus," and "the train" would ever be sufficient for him. I mean points of greater moment. In the author's mind there was to be "a something" that forced Roderick Hudson's wayward young women to marry when so clearly she did not want to. There was to be "a

GEORGE BERNARD SHAW

something" in the history of the Bellegarde family which should enable Newman unavailingly to frighten them. There was to be some sort of secret society, and some sort of disagreeable job for the hero to fail to perform, in "The Princess Casamassima"; just as the mystifying divorces in "What Maisie Knew" had to be conducted "somewhere" and "some-when" outside the book's obvious theme, and (most amusing of all) some odd and unmentionable small article of commerce upon which the family fortune had been built had to figure in "The Ambassadors." Just what these things were, James's speculative intelligence, his endless habit of wondering and supposing, did not tell him. In his early books he tried to invent practicable "somethings"; and so we have in "Roderick Hudson" an illegitimacy, in "The American" a scrawled message from a dying man to the effect that his wife is killing him, and in "The Princess Casamassima" a desperate effort to give conspiracy a kind of tangible convincingness. But as time went on James either pooh-poohed the matter altogether, as he managed to do (with the aid of what Maisie could not possibly be expected to know) in "What Maisie Knew," or carried off his own ignorance with a high hand, as in "The Ambassadors," where there is an almost feverish questioning from which, although severely pressed, the possessor of the knowledge escapes with a promise—never kept—that he will reveal the nature of the article at a later date.

> "'Is there a business?'
> "'Lord, yes—a big, brave bouncing business. A roaring trade.'
> "'A great shop?'
> "'Yes—a workshop; a great production, a great industry. The concern's a manufacture—and a manufacture that, if it's only properly looked after, may well be on the way to become a monopoly. It's a little thing they make—make better, it appears, than other people can, or than other people, at any rate, do.' . . .
> "'And what *is* the article produced?'
> "Strether looked about him as in slight reluctance to say; then the curtain, which he saw about to rise [the two are in a theatre], came to his aid. 'I'll tell you next time.' But when the next time came he only said he would tell her later on . . . 'Unmentionable? Oh no, we constantly talk of it; we are quite familiar and brazen about it. Only, as a small, trivial, rather ridiculous object of the commonest domestic use, it's rather wanting in—what shall I say? Well, dignity . . .'"

And so on. Like his father, Henry James enjoyed "the strongest instinct for the human and the liveliest reaction from the literal." But James's great exemplar, Balzac, would have reminded our friend that such reaction from the literal may result in the vagueness of the bluffer. Balzac certainly would have explained the nature and use of the article; he would probably have gone farther and described its manufacture and its sales organization, and if he had done that he might well have supplied us in good faith with details of the firm's costs, earnings, and profits over a period of years.

The truth was that James did not know what sort of thing would force a spirited young woman into marriage with a man she despised, or what sort of secret might or might not frighten an old French family into permitting the marriage of their daughter and sister to an outsider, or how divorces were managed, or what kind of small article—or indeed what kind of large article, other than a literary article—might be manufactured with immense profit in the United States. These things did not interest him otherwise than as pretexts for psychological conflict or a gathering of people upon the stage of his imagination. He pretended not to care about inconvenient details; but in reality he could not be bothered to take any steps to find out what he should have known, because in all things he preferred to puzzle out explanations, rather than to step outside his study and into the world of practical affairs. "Something . . . the money comes from . . . somewhere . . ." There was an old kind of laborious and boneless picture-making known to artists as "stumping." This was done with an instrument of white washleather, resembling a cigar in shape and size; and shadow effects of much softness were obtained by working pencil dust about the paper with the stump. James at his vaguest is like a stumper. Not the enchanting poetic vagueness of a Corot was secured by his method, but a loss of verisimilitude. His experience of life was extraordinarily restricted.

As long as he could bring transatlantic types to Europe and show them the extreme gentility of the old world, full of princesses and other titled people, and lovely old English houses and good breeding, he had a distinct place among American writers. But when he grew tired of such things, and became absorbed in the purely literary life, he tended to write about writers and the occult—two difficult and unpopular subjects. Some of his shorter stories in this vein, it is true, are among his most famous, and one or two of them are very good indeed. But they are stories for a small public; and while the small public invariably thinks itself a choice public, most authors, however select, hanker after general applause. James was really, I think, at the end of his resources as a writer of long, straightforward stories of character when he published, without success, in 1890, at the age of forty-seven, "The Tragic Muse."

This book is very smooth, and, with the exception of a mother and daughter who have the air of being extensions of the Princess Casamassima and her mother, it is about English people of the leisured class. It is not very unlike a novel by Mrs. Humphry Ward. All the characterization is neat; the dialogue is accomplished; but although I have read "The Tragic Muse" three or four times it has never seemed to me other than dull. One gets an impression of artistic purposelessness, a mechanical aggregation of men and women going and coming without passion and without object. Titles, money, endless talk of art and the theatre; none of it important, all superficial; as lifeless as a copy. For some reason writers and artists and actors and actresses and musicians are terribly uninteresting in fiction. No wonder that Henry James at this period was in something like despair. No wonder he wrote to W. D. Howells—as late as 1895—that "I *have* felt, for a long time past, that I have fallen upon evil days—every sign and symbol of one's being in the least *wanted*, anywhere or by anyone, having so utterly failed. A new generation, that I know not, and mainly prize not, has taken universal possession. The sense of being utterly out of it weighed me down, and I asked myself what the future would be."

The future was to be brighter, for James must in those years have been feeling his way towards what proved to be his natural and ultimate vein. His later books may not have had any large sale; but within two years of writing that despondent letter to Howells he had published both "What Maisie Knew" and "The Spoils of Poynton." He had found—or had perfected—a new, highly characteristic manner. And the manner provoked comment. Was it, or was it not, due to his venture into the habit of dictation? He said that dictation had no effect at all upon his style; others said that it was responsible, at the very least, for increased verbal artifice. However that may be, the rise of Henry James to a peculiar and personal rank among novelists—that subtle ascendancy to which many distinguished writers never attain—began in 1897. His remoteness from common life ceased to hamper him: it became, instead, one of the literary miracles of the age. "The Spoils of Poynton" is still a contribution to the technique of prose fiction which can be studied with advantage. Until we reach "The Ambassadors," that fine flower of the Jacobean novel, it is his best work in the long story.

"The Ambassadors" was written before "The Wings of the Dove," although it was published later. It is superior both to "The Wings of the Dove" and to "The Golden Bowl." The former book is very long, and the author considered it a failure. "The thing in question," he said in a letter, "is, by a complicated accident which it would take too long to describe to you, too inordinately drawn out, and too inordinately rubbed in. The centre, moreover, isn't in the middle, or the middle, rather, isn't in the centre, but ever so much too near the end, so that what was to come after it is truncated. The book, in fine, has too big a head for its body."

More than that, it has a body too big for its substance. A

journalist—still a writer, you see!—is in love with a young woman largely dependent upon a wealthy aunt. He is too poor to marry, and the two meet in Hyde Park on the sly. A dove who is something of a pigeon, and fabulously rich, comes from America to England, and falls in love with the journalist. He is induced to pay some court to her, and his sweetheart goes so far as to assure the dove that there is no understanding between them. However, when the dove dies of a mysterious and almost operatic complaint (a sort of world weariness), and leaves the journalist a legacy, he and the young woman whom he loves fail to approximate their scruples over the result of what has been in fact a sordid deception, and the novel sinks. No amount of casuistry upon the author's part can purify the atmosphere of this degraded book, which is without spirit and point.

In the same way, if the story of "The Golden Bowl" were told of ordinary bourgeois people it would be seen to rely upon the practicable plot than an Italian sponger has married money, that his discarded mistress reappears and re-establishes her attractiveness to him, and that his wife, scenting the difficulty, manages to bring the husband back to her side. The symbolism of the golden bowl is adventitious; the manipulation by which the mistress of the young husband becomes her lover's mother-in-law is quite artificial. But whereas "The Wings of the Dove" has, as I see it, no redeeming feature, "The Golden Bowl" has great beauty in many of its aspects, and in particular in the relationship between father and daughter. No other novelist could so delicately and so entirely without mishap have created the illusion of a realationship unselfishly loving and protective such as Maggie and her father feel for each other. In some respects this relationship is the most beautiful thing in any of Henry James's books, illustrating, as it does, to perfection, his enchanting sympathy with the disinterested. As a piece of composition the book is marvellous; and as a presentation of idealized love it has nobility and exquisiteness. What a pity, therefore, that the tale upon which it is built should have been—and should have been allowed to remain—commonplace!

"The Spoils of Poynton" is similarly mean at its heart. It arose from a dinner-table anecdote; and is about the squabble between mother and son as to a houseful of art treasures collected by the mother and her husband before the latter's death. The son has become engaged to an obstinate and tasteless creature to whom his mother takes an instant dislike. Although she realizes that her son is legally the possessor of the treasures, the mother surreptitiously removes the bulk of them to her cottage. The struggle between mother and (by representatives) her prospective daughter-in-law is ferocious and prolonged; but in the end the daughter-in-law wins the battle, the treasures are restored, and the house which they thus readorn is immediately afterwards destroyed by fire.

The virtuosity of "The Spoils of Poynton" is extraordinary. The book is maintained by the smallest, most voluptuous hints of what the actual treasures are, and there are but five characters in it. But while these characters, presented with great brilliance, contribute with precision and in due proportion to the drama, coherence as well as richness is assured by a familiar Jacobean device. This device is the one by which a single character presents an abnormally sensitive mind, at times baffled (but that is for the further artful purpose of elucidation through clarifying analysis) and at times miraculously lucid, to the whole intrigue; and in "The Spoils of Poynton" the mind is the mind of a girl tempted into great concern with the matter by the prospect that she may herself hereafter possess the treasure by a reversionary marriage with the combative son.

Henry James, jubilant at his discovery of this theme, replies to possible criticism of his use of such a heroine as his prime co-ordinator. He says: "It is easy to object of course 'Why the deuce then Fleda Vetch, why a mere little flurried bundle of petticoats, why not Hamlet or Milton's Satan at once, if you're going in for a superior display of "mind"?' To which I fear I can only reply that in pedestrian prose, and in the 'short story,' one is, for the best reasons, no less on one's guard than on the stretch; and also that I have ever recognized, even in the midst of the curiosity that such displays may quicken, the rule of an exquisite economy. The thing is to lodge somewhere at the heart of one's complexity an irrepressible *appreciation*, but where a light lamp will carry all the flame I incline to look askance at a heavy."

The light lamp; the comic muse; James had no sort of gift for tragedy. He was an ironist, some will think from natural coldness of temper, but perhaps from a too-sensitive dread of personal suffering. If you live apart from life, as he did, you cultivate a delicious acuteness of mind (I noticed this with my own mother, who was inactive physically for several years before her death, but whose mental subtlety became terrifying and whose elaborate speculations regarding matters in which I was involved approached second sight); but you lose actuality. "The Spoils of Poynton" is rich comedy; but it is only tolerable so long as one regards it as artificial, as a marvellous *performance*. The assumptions upon which the performance is based are appallingly gross.

"The Ambassadors" is an entirely different case. A young American, son of a manufacturer of the unspecified article—"Unmentionable? Oh no, we constantly talk of it; we are quite familiar and brazen about it"—has been too long in Paris. His masterful mother has sent over her tame editor, who may in time be her second husband, to bring the boy home. The editor, in company with a rather morose friend, makes the trip. He convinces himself that the boy is living an entirely moral and admirable life in innocent relation with a French married woman. He lingers on in Paris. In this act he renews his youth, and is made to see the boy as fruitfully enjoying what he regards as his own lost opportunity. But the morose friend sends home messages less pacificatory than his own; a further detachment of the family arrives in Paris; there are many complications; the boy's relationship with the French-woman is revealed as less innocent than it has seemed. And our poor editorial traveller and ambassador is faced with the knowledge that his return to America and to his employer is both unavoidable and undesirable. He ruefully makes preparations to depart.

That is a very crude and over-simplified outline of the story told in "The Ambassadors." It does shameful injustice to a novel which I consider as of almost the first order in comic literature. It is consistently comic, and upon a high plane; rich in scene and dialogue, in atmosphere, detail, and implication. Technically it is the work of a master in his own craft; and unless one is very prejudiced against the arch and elaborate manner of Henry James, with its rather puffing alternative sentences and its persistent avoidance of the direct, I do not see how one can fail to admire it. It is the most excellent complete example of the Jacobean method as outlined in the abstract of his unfinished novel, "The Ivory Tower," where he says, in reference, of course, to "The Ivory Tower," and not to "The Ambassadors": "By the blest operation this time of my Dramatic Principle, my law of successive Aspects, each treated from its own centre, . . . I have the great help of flexibility and variety: my persons in turn, or at least the three or four foremost, having control, as it were, of the Act and Aspect, and so making it *his* or making it *hers*."

If a novelist could be great by virtue of his devotion to his art, Henry James would be a great novelist. He gave to the writing of novels a fastidiousness and a conviction of the importance of his task which was new and strange in English fiction although it was not new in France or to Turgenev. Whatever the great English novelists may have been, they had no conception of the novel as something to be executed within a frame, to be "composed" in the painter's sense, with what Henry James called "shades" and "the lovely art of foreshortening," and that impressionistic vagueness in the distance about which I have already written. James had this conception.

He had another excellence, which is explicitly stated in a letter which he wrote in 1884 to Alphonse Daudet. He there said: "J'estime pourtant qu'il n'y a rien de plus réel, de plus positif, de plus à peindre, qu'un caractère; c'est là qu'on trouve bien la couleur et la forme."

From character, in this specialist sense, which he regarded as the essential basis of the novel, and form, of which he was to become a master, the Jacobean novel springs. "Form alone takes, and holds and preserves, substance—saves it from the welter of helpless verbiage that we swim in as in a sea of tasteless tepid pudding. Tolstoi and Dostoievsky are fluid puddings, though not tasteless, because the amount of their own minds and souls in solution in the broth gives it savour and flavour, thanks to the strong, rank quality of their genius and their experience." And, finally, in revolt from Wellsian improvisation: "Any illustration of anything worth illustrating has beauty, to my vision, largely by its developments." "There is, to my vision, no authentic, and no really interesting and no *beautiful*, report of things on the novelist's, the painter's part unless a particular detachment has operated, unless the great stewpot or crucible of the imagination, of the observant and recording and interpreting mind in short, has intervened and played its part— and this detachment, this chemical transmutation for the æsthetic, the representational, end is terribly wanting in autobiography brought, as the horrible phrase is, up to date."

In these four quotations may be found the artistic theory of Henry James so far as the novel is concerned. Character, development, form and experience. His form was increasingly expert and satisfying; the development (he once deprecatingly referred to his own practice as "embroidery," and in his case "delightful dissimulation" was unquestionably among "the refinements and ecstasies of method") became virtuosity of an extreme kind. No novelist of the two generations which followed his was uninfluenced by him. I doubt if any novelist who loves the finesses of his craft can read a book by Henry Janes without a sort of triumphant relish. But, in the matter of character and experience, this great craftsman was much inferior to many of those whose stumbling efforts would have caused him desperate distress.

He was inferior, that is, at the very core of the novelist's art. His characters, although they were material for endless, and the most exquisite, speculation, and although he liked to imagine them as aristocrats of the spirit (as well as, sometimes, aristocrats by birth), were cheats, liars, adulterers, and simpletons without grandeur. One's final impression of them is that of commonness. James never knew this; he never guessed that they were otherwise than the ladies and gentlemen of his dreams; he would have been disgusted if anybody had told him that under the brocade of his magnificent stitching they were little pigmies of no account. But this was because he made a fetish of refinement, and was naïf enough to believe that if you called a person a lady or a gentleman (or a prince or princess) you gave that person, automatically, as it were, a distinguished personality. Many years ago I knew some little girls of a class far below James's recognition, who played with numbers of small dolls; and every doll, to my surprise, was "Lady Maud" or "Lady Angela." Yet the dolls were trumpery penny things with china heads, who behaved, as far as I could tell, exactly like dolls of no class at all. Just so, James pretends that his characters are wonderful, and with tremendous charm and mysteriousness allows us to peep ever farther and farther into their minds; but when we might expect a Hamlet or a Lady Macbeth we get nothing but a china doll taken from stock and of the penny variety.

The explanation of this, in my judgment, is that James was prevented by timidity from ever having more than a superficial acquaintance with men and women who were not writers. He had no practical experience of the world; for wherever he went upon its surface he was alone, and his thoughts were of art and artists, craft and craftsmanship. He could, and did, watch strangers; he had a delightful life of speculation as to the ways and thoughts of all except the poor and unrefined; but unless you are ready to suffer by and through experience you do, it seems to me, content yourself with the second-hand. James did not want to suffer.

Why, then, was he so powerful an influence upon the Georgian writers? I think because no writer who lives in England to a great age (no writer, at least, who is willing to cultivate the literary *ton* of his period) can fail to gather the prestige of continued practice in his craft. I think because James could never have been accused by any other writer of being false to his own artistic standards. But beyond and above these reasons I think he had his influence because nobody had ever done so well, and with such grace and elaborateness, such skill and such subtlety, the thing that he did. He took a little story and a small group of characters; he made a picture; he made a drama; he made a continuously developing narrative. The picture was for beauty's sake; the drama was for suspense; and the narrative was for all the artfulness and interest and delight he took in the practice of his craft. If only the people in these books had been interesting James would have been a great novelist; but as it is he is in every other respect the finest craftsman among Victorian novelists; and the man nowadays who could write novels as well as Henry James, after learning a little more than he did about what really goes on in the world, would stand a good chance of being canonized (in a literary sense) about the year 2000.

Chapter Three

TEACHERS

SHAW AND WELLS

i

"All that we have lived on up till now has been the remnants of the revolutionary dishes of the last century, and we have been long enough chewing these over and over again. Our ideas demand a new substance and a new interpretation. Liberty, equality and fraternity are no longer the same things that they were in the days of the blessed guillotine; but it is just this that the politicians will not understand, and that is why I hate them. These people only desire partial revolutions, revolutions in externals, in politics. But these are mere trifles. There is only one thing that avails—to revolutionize peoples' minds."

Henrik Ibsen.

WHEN, in 1895, Henry James complained to William Dean Howells that "a new generation, that I know not, and mainly prize not, has taken universal possession," he was saying what every writer who sees himself neglected by the fashion feels impelled to say. He was in the midst of literary movements with which he had, and could have, no sympathy. There were the romantics, such as Gilbert Parker, Stanley Weyman, and Anthony Hope, who were all for post-Stevensonian charades. There were the so-called Kailyarders, such as J. M. Barrie, Ian Maclaren, and S. R. Crockett, who were being arch about the Scottish scene and the Scottish character. There was Rudyard Kipling, of whom James despaired as he came "steadily from the less simple in subject to the more simple—from the Anglo-Indians to the natives, from the natives to the Tommies, from the Tommies to the quadrupeds, from the quadrupeds to the fish, and from the fish to the engines and screws." There was the Dead Sea Fruit School, sentimental and cynical, with which the nineties are now usually associated. And, finally, there was the New Drama.

The New Drama was as far as possible from Henry James's comfortable reticence. It was imported from Northern Europe, and was unpopular, but it aroused great controversy. Although in Victorian days English novelists and preachers had criticized the social system, they had never mentioned the unmentionable. The New Drama not only mentioned it, but insisted upon it. W. S. Gilbert had laughed at corruptions and hypocrisies in a dozen comic operas; the New Drama seriously arraigned corruption and hypocrisy and called men to judgment. It attacked the morals of the

31

respectable, and showed those in high places intriguing for power, sweating the poor, transmitting venereal disease, hiding sins and hushing up scandals. It announced that "all our spiritual sources of life are poisoned, and that our whole bourgeois society rests upon a soil teeming with the pestilence of lies." It went thoroughly into the question of the unmarried mother, offering her, not as a wanton and a shame, but as a problem of character and the product of social conditions. The woman with a past became a stock figure; the woman with a future not exclusively matrimonial and subservient was pictured as something other than a freak of nature. When one such woman was asked, at the end of the first act of a play by Ibsen, what *she* would do in our society, she brought down the curtain by answering "I will let in fresh air." Her words might have been taken as a motto by all New Dramatists; for in their plays all that was generally accented as good, proper, and desirable was brought into the light of day and shown to be considerably affected by moth. How could Henry James, to whose art a stable world of conventions and prosperity was an essential background, possibly approve of such boisterousness, such rawness, such ugly blurtings-out of things better hidden, better murmured? Fresh air was the last thing he wanted.

It is sometimes objected to the plays of Ibsen—and it was objected to them as long ago as the nineties—that they are provincial. But as a social critic the provincial writer has always an advantage over the writer reared in a great city. He has been a member of a society known as a whole; because a small society has few secrets, cause and effect are more easily to be observed and confirmed in it; the writer's practical acquaintance with the social system is a part of his nurture. To the metropolitan-born person, whose horizons are potentially wider, but whose conceptions of society, once he steps outside the life of his immediate circle, are vaguer, the provincial often appears crude. If his manners are rough, and if his taste in clothes is peculiar, there is no limit to the amusement which he may give the metropolitan; but it is usually the provincial writer who has something to say about society, while the metropolitan, who knows very little about any society but that of his own circle, perforce concerns himself with manners. James was a metropolitan by choice. When plays of the kind written by Ibsen in his last period are condemned as provincial it may be replied that they are criticisms of society, robust with knowledge gained in a provincial upbringing, and deliberately restricted in scene for the sake of dramatic economy.

Ibsen's plays arrived late in England. That they arrived at all is largely due to the enthusiasm of a young Scottish dramatic critic named William Archer and a young Irish dramatic critic named

George Bernard Shaw. Archer, who never grew old, but always looked rather parsonically Victorian, long-faced, and with thin, plastered hair, was one of those curiously non-priggish reformers who began to flourish in the eighteen-eighties (Havelock Ellis was another of them), and who did such disinterested work in the cause of what they believed to be truth. It was H. G. Wells who first referred to Archer's "unscrupulous integrity," and this variation of the common phrase pleased all who heard it. There was indeed so overwhelming an air of patient honesty about Archer that he might have struck a superficial observer as dull and half-dead. In the theatre, for which he had an inexplicable passion to the end of his life, he would very silently and absorbedly sit through the worst of plays; and in the intervals between the acts he would draw from his pocket a little book which he would read with similar absorbedness until the curtain rose once more. There used to be the wildest guesses at the nature of this little book; but I believe it was often a detective story. It used also to be said that Archer had the power to sleep through a bad play, rousing himself by inerring instinct when anything of importance occurred on the stage; but this was the surmise of those less conscientious than himself, who mistook immobility for slumber. His voice was low and nasal; his conversation (whenever I heard it) was rarely about the theatre, but was always on grave or preposterous topics, such as suttee or the incredible cheapness of taxicabs in New York; he was a Rationalist and ethnologist; he was constantly deceived by a third-rate play merely because it was solemn or because it dealt with an ethical theme. And yet he combined enthusiasm for Ibsen and indefatigable work for the New Drama (as it was called) with such open-minded friendship for those dramatic rivals, Shaw and Pinero and Henry Arthur Jones, and was so obviously able and wise and kind and honest, that although his translations were uninspired and his writing never lively he enjoyed the great respect even of his juniors. He continued to do this until his death in 1924. His one successful play, "The Green Goddess," did not survive the Georgian era.

The Archer translations of Ibsen were far from being the first or the only translations to be attempted; but it was Archer's persistent advocacy and disinterested waiving of rights in the stage versions that enabled progressive-minded English people of the eighteen-nineties to see performances of some of Ibsen's plays. That such audiences were astounded may be taken for granted; the epithets of contemporary dramatic critics survive to please us profoundly. But audiences, and still more dramatic critics, were then still gravely concerned with the original plays and adaptations of Sydney Grundy, the Lyceum antiques, and productions much more shoddy than these. Perhaps they are to be forgiven for being shocked. The truth is that there were Movements afoot. A new generation, in the phrase of the hour, was "knocking at the door." Another provincial (or perhaps he ought rather to be called a foreigner) had arrived in London, and was casting what afterwards he pretended was normal eyesight upon the city and the English. He had not heard of Ibsen when he arrived; but he was ready for Ibsen. He was ready for anybody and everything. His name was George Bernard Shaw; and he hailed from Dublin, where poets, dramatists, politicians, and inexhaustible talkers are common phenomena.

ii. George Bernard Shaw

"GLORIA (sweeping round at him again). What gifts were you born with, pray?
VALENTINE. Lightness of heart."

You Never Can Tell.

SHAW was born on July 26th, 1856. He was the youngest of three children, and the only boy. His father was a wholesale corn-dealer, and his mother was the daughter of a country gentleman named Gurly. Having quite early in life established his independence by a refusal to go to church, young Shaw had some schooling of the ordinary kind then available; and at the age of fifteen became a clerk in the office of a land agent, where he proved himself so clear-headed that he was soon made cashier and accountant. Clear-headedness, Shaw discovered, is rare. But he was so modest that his advancement seemed to him to be due to something else—something later remarked by Cleopatra:

"CLEOPATRA: No, no: it is not that I am so clever, but that the others are so stupid.
POTHINUS (musingly): Truly, that is the great secret."

It is the way in which genius first explains its own superiority to the rest of mankind.

Within a year, Shaw's mother and sisters left Dublin, the mother to teach music in London and the sisters to make their own careers. Shaw for a time stayed where he was; but when he was twenty he too left Dublin for London. He never recovered from this plunge; for he fell in love with the English (as Henry James did), and has been explaining them to himself ever since.

Shaw first noticed, and was baffled by, the fact that the English have a habit of ignoring everything but what they wish to see. It is the primary act of good breeding in England, and is disconcerting to strangers. Also, at that time, the English had not been shaken by a few events which have occurred since; they were calm, prosperous, perhaps rather complacent. Shaw's admiration was thus of the exasperated kind which shows him to have fallen in love with the people in spite of his better judgment.

His judgment told him that England was in a muddle morally and industrially. It told him that the English were smug, comfort-loving, half-asleep. Their terrible incuriosity affronted him. And yet from that day onward Shaw gave his life to the English, wooing them with all the blandishments of insult (of which he was a master) and the charm of his incessant wit; until the English, at first ignoring him, became successively amused by a jackanapes, stimulated by a humorous, truth-loving scourge, enthralled by an original dramatist beside whom all other dramatists were tame, annoyed by a schoolmaster who lectured while bombs were being dropped, eager to be friends again, in the English way, as soon as the row subsided; and at last reached a state of impatient pride in an octogenarian chatterbox and a nonagenarian classic. Shaw's wooing of Britannia was successful years ago; but he was too modest to believe it. While Britannia waited with reserved amorousness for his embrace, Shaw, like John Tanner, kept on talking. He never knew when to kiss.

But in his early days he was serious enough in his wooing. He was not merely the joke Irishman wrecked upon a strange coast and demanding of the first person he met "Phwat's the government of this counthry? I'm agin it!" The England to which he came in the eighteen-seventies was an England drowsy with prosperity, yet stirring with anarchy. Its typical citizens believed that the best form of government was one which interfered as little as possible with the world as it then was. Laissez faire. Let well (or ill) alone. The English were Christians or Rationalists and Utilitarians; but in any case they were largely materialists. Even young people of the day were engaged in reading John Stuart Mill, Malthus, Ingersoll, Darwin, Spencer, and Tyndall, all of whom, whether Christians or Agnostics, had conducted animal, vegetable, or mineral research, and all of whom, whatever they might say about the Primal Cause and the Unknowable, had unsettled the religious beliefs of their readers.

Shaw's religious beliefs, long his own, were not unsettled by what he now read. But when he was barely a man he had one or two shocks of another kind. First of all, he heard Henry George speak, and was converted to Socialism; and secondly he read the "Kapital" of Karl Marx, and was converted to revolutionism. He formed a friendship with Sidney Webb, who, although an unimpressive public figure and a poor speaker, possessed an acute and well-stored brain, and was able to see in Shaw an ideal intellectual foil and partner. He also made the acquaintance of Edward Carpenter and Henry Salt, whose idols were Thoreau and Whitman, and through whose influence he became a Shelleyan, a Vegetarian, and a Humanitarian. He learned to declaim against hanging, flogging, and anything known as sport. He began to dress as a Simple-lifer; he went without an overcoat and wore astonishing woollen gloves; he stood at street corners upon soap-boxes and harangued loiterers. From the point of view of the average Englishman, Shaw was in a fair way to become a crank.

In 1884 Shaw weighed 142 pounds. His height, without shoes, was six feet one inch. He was lean, pale-faced, bearded, rather ginger, with blue-grey eyes and small hands. Upon a soap-box he may well have looked eight feet tall, and of course far above the heads of such men as gathered to listen. To look down upon an audience is to feel mastery of it: hence the soap-box, the platform, and the stage. Shaw was always above his audience. He did not know what passed in the minds of individual listeners. He did not become a crank, because he had great humour and great shrewdness, and he was very ambitious. But he was confirmed by his soap-box altitude in a truly aristocratic contempt for democracy, "the last refuge of cheap misgovernment." He threw over the respectable bourgeois, agnostic, and materialistic thinkers who in adolescence had impressed him. Altruism, he found, had higher, colder reaches than theirs; and upon the whole he preferred the nobility of Shelley and the passionate economics of Marx to their philosophy of the merely good and useful. Also, whether by reading Samuel Butler at this time or not I do not know, he found reason to reject, not evolution, but the Darwinian theory that variation of species was due to blind accident. Lamarck, many years before, had suggested that variation arose from a "sense of need" or the impulse towards improvement; and this suggestion, so brilliantly reinforced by Butler in "Life and Habit," always had for Shaw an irresistible charm. Blind accident was the horror of his life; a world in which nothing was ever attempted because all was hopelessly evolutionary would have been, for him, intolerable. Since he, Shaw, wanted to make a new earth, that was proof that man had arisen through the desire of lower forms of life to "better themselves." He felt that even the amœbæ must have had their Shaws, working towards a higher excellence.

Another discovery he made was Woman. To his surprise, the young, consciously intellectual and revolutionary women of that era were greatly drawn—as they would be to-day, or at any time— to a handsome and talkative young Irishman, attractively rufous, and with a baffling habit of turning to nonsense any approach to a Very Serious Subject Indeed. They came closer, fascinated by his eloquence and charm; and Shaw, at first not quite understanding the possessive aim of these ladies (possessiveness being a non-Shavian trait, and thus outside his comprehension), kept on talking and edging away in perfect good humour. At length he was compelled to realize his own attractiveness; and, just as he had explained in Cleopatra's way clear-headed superiority to others, so now, in his modesty, he sought to explain biologically what most men would smirkingly have set down, in Gissing's phrase, to "sexual preful-gence." Shaw was a natural ascetic. Not himself, but some strange general necessity, he thought, must cause these women to mistake his laughing eloquence for wooing and come a-wooing in earnest. He began to long for the peace which equality of the sexes would give him; and so threw his weight into the campaign for women's rights and the development of women as rational creatures.

Shaw had started with a combination of Irish clear-headedness and English humour that made him different from all other men. He had inherited a love of music and an exceptionally accurate ear. He had discovered the revolutionary music of Wagner and the revolutionary theory of class war propounded by Marx. He was a Lamarckian or Butlerian evolutionist because any action not dic-tated by the intelligence was abhorrent to him. When, presently, he discovered the revolutionary drama of Ibsen, so vigorous, so critical, and so moral, he was again deeply impressed; and when at last (although this did not happen until much later) he read "Beyond Good and Evil," and found in that work the first expression of Nietzsche's doctrine of the Life Force, he felt that he really under-stood everything that was to be known about the world of men. The Life Force was the phrase he needed to crystallize his belief in purposeful evolution. It was the phrase he needed to explain the behaviour of those women whose intellectualism was but a prelude to courtship. He adopted it. To the roles of economist, vegetarian, revolutionary, musician, and reluctant lover he added that of prophet and philosopher.

While first living in shabby gentility in London he had written some novels; but although these novels are highly readable, and full of effective dialogue, they were neither overwhelmingly excellent nor acceptable to the publishers of the time. Accordingly they made no appearance in book form. The young Shaw, baffled to fight better, turned from novels to art criticism, music criticism, and finally to dramatic criticism. This was for the purpose of earning a living. For diversion and training, as well as for the love of argu-ment, he joined all sorts of debating societies, spoke in public, formed a large circle of acquaintances, and in his own words was "up to the neck in the life of his time." He should have said that he was in the life of his time "from the neck upwards."

iii

THE first time I ever saw Shaw was at a lecture delivered by G. K. Chesterton (from notes hastily made while the chairman "introduced" him) before the Humanitarian Society. Chesterton suggested cheerfully that Humanitarianism, like Charity, should begin, but did not begin, with one's next-door neighbour; and he embroidered this sound proposition with his own fancies until the meeting seethed with misunderstanding. I, a boy, sniggered with delight at the ferocious exclamations uttered all about me by the humane. Just as hysteria threatened to ruin the meeting, a tall, bony, energetic man with a brogue and a brain sprang to his feet near the low platform. With his hands upon his hips, his head back, his words full of subtle aitches and lovely variations of emphasis, he put everybody right. The lecturer was eclipsed; the audience was appeased; everybody clapped and glowed; my friends said "Well, that was Shaw." We streamed out of the hall filled with elation.

Shaw said he had nothing of a voice; but he knew how to produce it. When he spoke, his Irish accent, and still more his Irish intonation, captivated the English ear. He seemed to sing. Moreover, few men think as clearly and adroitly as he did or could express themselves as clearly and adroitly as he. He was a first-class debater. On that occasion, as on many others, he triumphed because he knew perfectly well what he was saying and doing. It is a rare accomplishment in a public speaker.

From the time when he first spoke to an audience Shaw lived in the eye of the world as few men other than leading actors and politicians do. He had little or no private life as the oridnary citizen knows it. His job was to reform mankind, and he went about his task day in, day out, from morning to night, from the day, back in the nineteenth century, when he first heard Henry George speak.

How did he do it? By means of plays, prefaces, lectures and pamphlets; by means of earnest sincerity presented with such a flow of nonsensical high spirits that it passed often enough for provocative folly. New readers, coming in these days to Shaw's writings, cannot possibly understand what was the effect of those writings at the time of their first appearance. "It is peculiar to original genius," says Coleridge, "to become less and less striking, in proportion to its success in improving the taste and judgment of its contemporaries." And Shaw's alleged love of paradox, now cheapened in its undergraduate gown of the inverted obvious, was in fact the disconcerting candour of the child in Hans Andersen's story of "The Emperor's New Clothes." It is no longer novel; some of the arguments which now pass for truisms seemed in those olden days, to the sedately muddle-headed, the sheerest acrobatics; and furthermore Shaw all his life belittled his own gifts. He did what Jack Point promised when he told Wilfred Shadbolt that he would "teach thee all my original songs, my self-constructed riddles, my own ingenious paradoxes; nay more, I will reveal to thee the source whence I get them." Shaw told the world that his ideas were derived from Wagner, Ibsen, Samuel Butler, and Nietzsche, and that his characters were stolen from Dickens. There is not a word of truth in all this. The cast of his mind, his mingling of kindness with an impatience of fools, his mingling of sense and nonsense, was altogether natural and peculiar. He had that intellectual simplicity to which all ideas are, as it were, foreknown. He wrote in the manner of Ibsen before ever reading Ibsen; Wagner was a fellow-revolutionary; Nietzsche merely gave him the formula, the phrase, necessary for the expression of his own views, Samuel Butler had almost privately written down thoughts long familiar to Shaw.

> "Whatever in those climes he found
> Irregular in sight or sound
> Did to his mind impart
> A kindred impulse, seemed allied
> To his own powers, and justified
> The workings of his heart."

It is necessary to mention these other writers, and no doubt it was necessary for Shaw to mention them, because otherwise some burrowing nonentity with a craze for parallels would almost certainly have accused him of plagiarism, and because Shaw, as a solitary phenomenon, would even now seem too good to be true. But once they are mentioned an explanation of Shaw's boasted indebtedness suggests itself. He was always a lonely man, both socially and intellectually; and he never wanted to be lonely. He said he "had not the great man feeling." Just as, when he found himself abler than others, he explained the matter by supposing the others to be very stupid, and just as he explained his unsought attractiveness to women by reference, not to himself, but to a mysterious driving power, the Life Force, which compelled women to take the initiative in love, so he never believed in his own originality, but proclaimed incalculable debts in order to escape the charge. Very vain he may have been; but no man ever tried to express a more modest estimate of his own talents.

It is true that Dickens—and also Bunyan—showed him how characters, to entertain, must have objective consistency, how they must be broadly outlined and self-explanatory (what E. M. Forster calls "flat"), and how if seen with exultant and exaggerative humour such characters are manipulable at will by the expert dramatist. It is true that Nietzsche at his best throws off ideas so instantaneously convincing that a superficial reader believes them to be his own inspirations, and a modest one the teachings of a master (but Freud and other great men have the same instant convincingness), and that the idea of the Life Force was due for revival when Shaw gave it dramatic expression. It is equally true that Ibsen, once his work was known, must have influenced any man already determined to express moral ideas in dramatic form. But Shaw's real impetus came from something else.

I said just now that Shaw was a first-class debater. I think the reason why he became a dramatist was that when as a young man he spent his evenings in debate he always found the opposition so weak that he longed to take both sides—all sides—himself, just to show how a case should be conducted. Most of his plays are dramatic debates, interspersed with farcical incidents. The brilliance of the conversation may at times blind us to some lethargy of invention; but we have often in retrospect a little discomfort when we realize that only a scuffle or some desperate turn has brought to an end arguments which, uninterrupted, might be going on to this hour. Shaw could always think of something more to say; he was never at the end of the matter, so that he had to write long and very eloquent prefaces to his plays to incorporate all that he was not able to say in the plays themselves, or all that occurred to him on kindred subjects after the plays were written; and he several times cruelly over-estimated, in prefaces as in the theatre, an audience's power of continuous attention. But in spite of all this the plays conquered because they were so much more amusing and interesting and stimulating than any other plays of their period; and it is necessary that this fact should be recognized before all others.

They did not conquer without difficulty. Although Shaw was known as a writer and pamphleteer and speaker, he was regarded by theatrical managers as a hopeless investment for them. Cursed as theatrical managers always are with the belief that only cretins pay for stalls in theatres, these men had marked him down as one doomed for ever to Sunday evening performances to the loud-voiced intellectual snobs of the Edwardian Stage Society. But they were wrong; and when the public, in disgust at everything associated in its mind with the humiliations of the Boer War, threw over its old literary favourites, the way was opened for Shaw and other new figures. They stepped forward.

Shaw was enabled to do so because a young actor named Harley Granville Barker and a young impresario named J. E. Vedrenne had joined forces in leasing the Court Theatre in Sloane Square, Chelsea.

Here were given some matinée performances of "Candida," with Barker in the role of Marchbanks; and here, too, other plays, by Galsworthy, St. John Hankin, John Masefield, and Barker himself, were intermingled with a host of plays by Shaw. Since Ireland was prominently in the news, Shaw's Irish play, "John Bull's Other Island," was given its first London production. It created a furore.

The play, which flattered and ridiculed English and Irish alike, made everybody laugh. It made everybody feel that he was thinking hard and wisely about politics and human nature. Instead of being "buffoon" and "charlatan," Shaw became with all the politically minded bourgeois—who are the really stupid English (the rest of the community being not so much stupid as ingeniously idle)—"a queer fellow—quite a genius in his way." He had reached the public. Young men and women, the modest equivalent in those days of our black-hatted or bare-headed devourers of whatever is the latest fashion in literature, had for years taken him very seriously indeed. They had discussed him, over nuts and barley water, over red ties and straggly beards; and had resolved long ago that it was proper to be "modern" in the Shavian way. But after the success of "John Bull's Other Island" there was little intellectual superiority to be felt by old-time Shavians. Quite conventional people came and went in a state of bewilderment as the result of contact with new emotions and new aspects of the social picture. I well remember walking home after a Shaw performance with one extremely conventional young woman, typical of the hour. She was silent for a long time. At last she said: "One really doesn't know *what* to think." The leaven was working: I fear she subsequently became a Positivist.

It was a new experience for English theatre audiences to see plays which presented, not a situation twisted for the sake of arousing superficial excitement or amatory prowess, or for the sake of driving home for the millionth time some creaky moral obsolete in every place but the theatre, but the fantastic world of a social and political revolutionary. Whatever the artistic faults of the Shavian drama, when these plays were new they did without any question change theatre-going from a habit to an event. At their worst they seemed endless; but at their best they roused and rewarded the audience as oxygen revives the cellar-dweller.

Shaw's fame grew and grew. He was more and more successful. True, even after the accession of King George he was arraigned by dramatic critics on the ground that he could not write a play; but he was generally admired as a man of extraordinary gifts. His more recent reputation, which has sometimes verged upon idolatry (but fashions pass quickly nowadays), demonstrates his virtual creation of the Georgian mentality out of nothing.

iv

"THE DEVIL . . . The truth is, you have—I won't say no heart; for we all know that beneath all your affected cynicism you have a warm one——"

Man and Superman.

THE plays seemed to the generation that first saw them the most ruthless of destructive humours. We, being more ruthless than Shaw (who could not hurt a fly, and who would hurt a man, even a fool and an opponent, only because he could not see or hear him), find them gentle. At first they emphasized the rentier's moral obligation to invest his money in untainted concerns, or laughed at the difficulties of a lover who in spite of every Shavian device could not get rid of a supplanted mistress, or showed what a shock a modern girl might have if she found that her mother, a self-made woman, lived comfortably on the proceeds of Continental brothels. Or they told the world that poets have their dreams and clergymen of upright character their mystical weaknesses, or that a supposed ne'er-do-well has his code of honour, or that a brigand would be as much a slave to Ellen Terry as any dramatist, or that you have only to put on a false nose and talk a lot of nonsense to bring sanity into a situation hitherto impossible. The first three of these plays were labelled "unpleasant." One of them was found by the British Dramatic Censorship so distasteful that its public performance was forbidden altogether.

But it was not the themes of the plays that upset all who objected to Shaw. It was their verbal irreverence. Not what they said, but the nasty way they said it. To a people accustomed since the death of Dickens to a serious treatment of serious matters, a mocking attitude towards morals, parents, and respectability was abhorrent. Few except the dramatic critics—and even to-day there are not half a dozen dramatic critics in England who can criticize a play—knew what the author was after. The public liked, and wanted to see, plays in which after a period of delicious suspense morality was sententiously triumphant. These were not such plays. The honour due to parents was mocked in them; indeed, the parents were made such crass humbugs that it would have been impossible to honour them. The poet, instead of being a defeated seducer, left the theatre without a stain upon his character. Dick Dudgeon seemed almost to have been ready to sacrifice himself because he had an idea in his head, and not because (which would have been quite comprehensibly in accord with stage convention) he was romantically in love with a married woman. They were queer stuff: were they "art"?

Art was a new thing in literature; it was usually associated with those who

"walked down Piccadilly
with a poppy or a lily
in their mediaeval hands,"

and there was nothing at all æsthetic in Shaw. Nor had these plays "dignity and memory and measure," in Henry James's sense. But then Shaw had said of James that "his intellectual fastidiousness remains untouched by the resurgent energy and wilfulness of the new spirit. It takes us back to the exhausted atmosphere of George Eliot, Huxley, and Tyndall, instead of thrusting us forward into the invigorating strife raised by Wagner, Ibsen, and Sudermann." He did not want to write like Henry James or Oscar Wilde. like Pinero and Henry Arthur Jones. Instead, he wanted, apparently, to make jokes in very bad taste at the expense of mothers and fathers, and rake up a lot of disagreeable stuff about slums and brothels, and libel young English womanhood. Such a man could safely be left to the dramatic critics.

But what then? The dramatic critics were in the position of all critics who are governed by formula and who are called upon to deal with a writer who acts upon his own assumption that "the golden rule is that there is no golden rule." They laughed in the theatre; and then—it is always done—they went away and announced that Shaw had written another play which (a) was not a play, and (b) was inferior to its predecessors from the same agile pen. In this way they kept the theatre sweet for adaptations from the Palais Royal and the lighter or heavier productions of others.

We cannot do what contemporary critics did, for Shaw cannot now be budged from his place among the stars. But we can at least agree that the earlier plays were less entertaining than the plays of Shaw's maturity, and that they were inferior in everything except genius to the plays that thousands of well-educated young writers of to-day can produce. But they were the prentice work of a born dramatist, a man to whom talking and writing (with him the acts are almost inseparable, so much has his writing the ideal conversational quality of emphatic lucidity) were the most enjoyable of all occupations. All the characters in these plays were bursting with talk. As characters they may have been rough and not unfamiliar; but when they talked they were reanimated with original life. The talk in "The Philanderer" is even better. It is fuller of high spirits. Moreover the play itself shows a movement away from mechanism and towards spontaneity. Shaw, willy nilly, was to have a brief flirtation with art. It was to last until he had written "Candida," "The Devil's Disciple," and "Arms and the Man."

The last-named, a farcical comedy, is the best of all his plays in the respect that it is the simplest and clearest of them. It is based upon a good comic theme, and it deals with that theme dramatically and without excursions. The scene is a house somewhere in the Balkans, a district which came into the news in the mid-eighties with the first Balkan War; and there are only half a dozen characters in the play. All of these characters are original, from the sentimental, untruthful girl Raina and her brave but self-deceiving fiancé to the practical Swiss who puts everybody and everything to rights and meets his matrimonial fate with philosophy. The whole play has a natural and happy development from its opening passages; and it is full of little surprises that are heightened because one sees them an instant before they occur. The play is in consequence extraordinarily effective in the theatre. It is more effective now than it was when Shaw, taking his call after the first performance, and in reply to a solitary booer, said politely: "I quite agree with you, sir. But what are we among so many?" Not only has it become more pointed, so that every point may be said to make itself, but its wisdom is more immediately appreciated. That is what emphasizes its classic quality and gives one the sense of enjoying and praising a work that has lived through its own generation and found continued life in ours.

"Arms and the Man" shows that Shaw had abandoned realism for ever. His sole connection with it henceforward was to be a persistent anti-romanticism. Where the realist coolly and fatalistically shows the inevitable sequence of events—Ibsen in his social plays is a realist,—Shaw leaps hither and thither among solemn follies and makes them ridiculous. He shows in this play, with a glee akin to that of Molière, the absurd impulse to lie and to pose which is dominant in men and women. And, instead of allowing the lie to persist, and even to triumph, as a realist might justifiably have done. he makes every lie achieve the ignominy of ludicrous exposure, That is an unmistakable mark of comic genius, and in the field of farcical comedy "Arms and the Man" remains unequalled in Shaw's work.

Bright and amusing though it is, "You Never Can Tell" has no theme to carry the delightful nonsense. Parents, those butts of Shavian and post-Shavian drama, are made to look absurd—the guying of mothers was a part of the campaign for youth the results of which did not please too well the author of "Too True to be Good";—children are pleasantly unruly and impertinent; young lovers quickly reach an understanding. But false noses, ludicrous discomfitures of the irascible, waiters whose sons are famous barristers, and fun about a dental chair do not quite carry the play beyond hotch-potch. Perhaps for the first time in his plays Shaw allows us to notice his inability to distinguish between what is good and what is not so good in his own work.

Much better and wiser, and more characteristic of the author's mind, are the two moralities, "Candida" and "The Devil's Disciple," in which the chief characters illuminate what Dean Inge calls the "absolute values" of goodness, beauty, and truth. They do right from a natural impulse to do right. The two plays illustrate another of Shaw's beliefs, comprehension of which is much overlaid in the minds of those who pride themselves on sophistication. This belief is in the power of virtue. Candida and Dudgeon are both —like Shaw—self-sufficient and self-sacrificing; but they are able to sacrifice themselves without weakness and without heroics because they are both above fear and temptation. Shaw is not a puritan (who wishes to impose his own strictness upon others), but a naturally virtuous man; and to the world a naturally virtuous man appears to be cold, through disinterestedness, censorious, through ignorance of the charms of sin, and superior, through excess of reason. Shaw never had a sense of superiority; he had merely a sense that all other men must be fools who humbug themselves. He was never censorious. But from the fact that his ideal life is the contemplative life one may gather that the object of his worship was always wisdom, of which, indeed, the majority of men have little knowledge.

"The Devil's Disciple" and "Candida" are not the plays by Shaw which have most impressed the public (although George Jean Nathan always extolled the latter, and many people piously suppose it an attempt of the Life Force to put Barrie's ink into Shaw's pen); but they show that behind all bravura his spiritual assumptions are quite as simple as those of his own Joan of Arc, and not unlike them. The machinery of both plays is adequate, but not inspired; both have some amusing sketches of character; both are still easy and agreeable to read or see in the theatre. But it is because they express with such veracity the positive Shavian conception of personal virtue and personal strength that they are important. In my opinion they are, with "Arms and the Man" (because of its classic quality) and "Man and Superman" (because of its richness), the best of Shaw's dramatic works. They have not had anything like the influence of "Man and Superman."

Owing to the fact that the whole of "Man and Superman" is hardly ever seen upon the stage, but only the more farcical flight of John Tanner, embodiment of his creator's coyness and garrulity, from the boa-constrictor Ann, many theatre-goers believe that the Superman is Woman. The fundamental seriousness of Shaw in this play, and the extraordinary beauty of the interlude in Hell, are alike ignored, and the play as performed is only a joke in three acts. Hence its popularity. Shaw, meaning to help along the mind of the race, roused in beholders of "Man and Superman" nothing but laughter and concupiscence. It is a misfortune, and one for which he cannot have been in the very least prepared. Among those who neither see plays nor read them, but who rely entirely upon hearsay for their news of wisdom, he contributed to the modern man's sense of helplessness before the predatory Female. That was not his design. Nor was it his design that "Man and Superman"should be thought of as a sort of Clo Graves farce, like "Mother of Three." But without the interlude this play, as performed, is hardly more than a feast of back-chat. What is it, indeed, but the picture of a lair and a gossip, a concealed marriage between two other young people, and a collection of discomfited elders? Ann Whitefield, resolved (at the bidding of the Life Force) to marry her true mate, John Tanner, succeeds in spite of his wild motor journey to escape her, his capture by brigands, and his protestation to the last that he will not succumb. To most people there is nothing more in the play than that. Was it not a weakness in Shaw that he should have had to supplement his farce with an explanatory play, a preface of great length, and a whole collection of maxims under the title of "The Revolutionist's Handbook"?

You could never have convinced him of that; and it is quite true that as a whole, with interlude, revolutionary postscript, and a brilliant jumble of preface which darts from Don Juan to the duel of sex, from Shakespeare to politics, from Bunyan to art for art's sake (art for art's sake does not stand a dog's chance), it is an epitome of Shaw's genius. If this were the only work of its author to survive a cataclysm it would still provide laborious delvers with materials for treatise after treatise concerning Shaw. The preface illustrates in perfection his belief that "effectiveness of assertion is the Alpha and Omega of style"; the four-act play betrays the beginning of his break-up as a dramatic craftsman; the "Revolutionist's Handbook," a medley of opinions, is in itself proof of the opulence of a talent calculated to stretch the covers of any book; and the complete work is so full of life, thought, argument, and eloquence that it shows the author (then at the height of his powers) as an original and creative genius of first-class importance in modern letters.

"Man and Superman" belongs to the twentieth century. It was published in 1903. Shaw followed it with many plays, one at least of them a very ambitious attempt to express the philosophy of his old age. This, "Back to Methuselah," is so long that one would have to emulate the ardent Wagnerite in order to see the whole of it performed in the theatre. I have not seen it. I can judge it only from the printed text, which is disappointing. The play begins in Eden, and it ends far in the future, when life has become as humourless as it always seems to do in imaginative pictures of an ideal state. In this play Shaw is very serious indeed. The brilliance of "Man and

Superman" is left far behind. But while the play is no doubt packed with wisdom it is less entertaining, and therefore less successful, than others which the author undertook with less serious purpose. Much more excitement was caused in the theatre world of London by a later, very slight, and extremely comic peep into the future called "The Apple Cart."

"The Apple Cart" was one of the author's most successful plays. It was successful in spite of a perfect rage of condemnation on the part of the dramatic critics. These odd persons declared that Shaw had betrayed the cause of democracy, and gone back upon all the lessons of his own earlier teaching. But they were wrong: Shaw had never been a democrat. He was always, politically, something of a realist. And if a dictatorship would give mankind a chance of escaping from the dead weight of democratic doctrine he would support a dictatorship, whether totalitarian or not. His question was "Will it work?" So in "The Apple Cart" he made a dictatorship work. He so much enjoyed the knockabout portions of the play that he affronted once again, as he had always done, the uncommonly serious. But he did once again what he had so often done—he made people angry; he made them argumentative; he stirred the sluggards by means of a little charge of dynamite. That was always his strength as a political thinker, and his strength as a lively dramatist—the power to make ideas amusing. With the ultimate truth or otherwise of his ideas the critic of his work, it seems to me, has no concern. It is enough that it is self-consistent and his own. I take the view of Arthur Symons, that "criticism is a valuation of forces: it is indifferent to their direction." If one is a politician first, one disagrees with this proposition; but one restricts one's approval to a small body of tendentious work and shuts one's mind to everything else and so to wisdom. Therefore I say that it does not matter to the critic of literature—although it matters, of course, to the polemist—whether Shaw's immediate teaching is acceptable or not: what matters in literature is the vitality of the work. And "The Apple Cart," although far below Shaw's finest work, has a life of its own. Not one of its critics has the talent to write anything a tenth part as stimulating.

Many Shavians believe that this "finest work" is to be found in "Saint Joan." I do not. The play is an admirable essay in the dramatic chronicle form invented anew by John Drinkwater with "Abraham Lincoln," and continued by him with "Robert E. Lee," "Mary, Queen of Scots," and others. It has many beauties. It is very exciting. It is shot through and through with Shaw's unsurpassed lucidity. But it owed its popularity to the fact that respectable people, long shy of a revolutionary who was also an irreverent, found as they thought a new seriousness, a new faith, in an author whom they longed to admire because he was getting so old; and it was praised by dramatic critics because the hour had struck and Shaw was due for acclaim. Such gratification as was felt at the thought that he had given up teasing arose from ignorance of the author's mind. If these same thankful stalwarts of conventional faith had studied "The Devil's Disciple" and "Candida," and if they had listened to William Poel's delightful performance of Father Keegan in "John Bull's Other Island," or better still if they had read with attention any large stretch of Shaw's criticism of other authors, they would have known that throughout his life, whenever he cared to do so, he employed an almost divine gift of understanding the good, the simple, and the unpretending. Because he was so much a propagandist he was forced to attack ideas the virtue of which he well knew, but he was never a blind man. Having been wound up, as it were, to talk for twenty-four hours a day, he had no opportunity of listening to anybody but himself; that was his public performance, and it is due to this public performance that his name is known to more human beings than the name of any other modern author, not excepting Wells. But nobody could talk so much as Shaw without becoming familiar with his own performance, and while still perfectly able to startle and anger millions of stupid people—merely by pressing the old button,—he did not reach great old age without the restorative refreshment of quietism. He could as well have written "Saint Joan" in 1903 as 1923 if he had wished; but in 1903 he was busy upon something else.

Shaw could not be a reformed character. He was always Shaw. And he recognized throughout his life the value of work by other authors, even though it was work antipathetic to him. He sat devotedly in the uncomfortable seats of innumerable theatres and perceived and remembered the talents of actors and actresses struggling with bad small parts. He was ever a chivalrous opponent. He was so kind to those less kind than himself as to be beset mercilessly by spongers and favour-hunters. He was modest, polite, and considerate to strangers whom he could have eaten (had he been omnivorous) out of hand. These traits are worth pondering in connection with his genius. They can be set beside his notorious self-advertising, which in comparison with the laborious and pointless self-advertisement of a hundred modern quack-authors was positively reticent, and which was always undertaken as publicity for his ideas as well as publicity for himself. And while it is true that he made his characters say and do many things upon the stage with the sole object of raising a laugh—as in my judgment he was entitled to do,—he never wrote any work with the sole object of exhibiting the wonders of G. B. S. As nearly as possible, he was a selfless, a disinterested author who worked for the destruction of error; and for him the whole business of any writer worth his salt (apart from those "artists" for whom he professed such contempt and had in fact such respect) has been that of arousing from sleep or lethargy the Good or the Will in mankind.

v. Herbert George Wells

"The Owner of the Voice you must figure to yourself as a whitish plump man, a little under the middle size and age, with such blue eyes as many Irishmen have, and agile in his movements and with a slight tonsorial baldness—a penny might cover it— of the crown. His front is convex. He droops at times like most of us, but for the greater part he bears himself as valiantly as a sparrow. Occasionally his hand flies out with a fluttering gesture of illustration. And his Voice (which is our medium henceforth) is an unattractive tenor that becomes at times aggressive. Him you must imagine as sitting at a table reading a manuscript about Utopias, a manuscript he holds in two hands that are just a little fat at the wrist. The curtain rises upon him so. But afterwards, if the devices of this declining art of literature prevail, you will go with him through curious and interesting experiences."

H. G. Wells: A Modern Utopia.

SHAW once described himself as a "revolted bourgeois." He might equally well have used the phrase "intellectual revolutionary," for his aim has always been to hold a bunch of carrots before the nose of civilization, and not at all to flatter workers into the belief that they are the salt of the earth. He was never a democrat. Wells, on the other hand, although never a believer in votes for all, was much more definitely a man of the people than Shaw. His father, instead of being a wholesale corndealer, was a retail shopkeeper. His mother for some years was a domestic servant, then lady's maid, and finally housekeeper in a big house in Sussex. Gardening, cricket, shop-keeping and service are the soil from which Wells's much more personal Socialism sprang in the first instance. As a boy he had to touch his cap to the idle rich; he listened restlessly (but with an excellent memory) to the unctuous conversations of ladies' ladies and gentlemen's gentlemen; and he and his brothers were all enslaved as apprentices to linen-drapers through his mother's pathetic wish that they might at any rate wear black coats and collars and look like second-rate gentlefolk.

He was born at Bromley, in Kent, now a London suburb, on September 21st, 1866. His birthplace was a small room over his father's persistently unprosperous shop (originally established for the sale of glass and china, but used also for the sale of cricket bats, balls, and other odds and ends); and before he was fourteen he was tried as a shop assistant. After one or two false starts he spent two years as apprentice to a draper in Southsea; and when desperation drove him to flight he was lucky enough to find a friend and employer in the headmaster of the Midhurst Grammar School. In 1884 he applied for and obtained a scholarship as a teacher-in-training at the Normal School of Science (afterwards the Royal College of Science) at South Kensington.

This meant that he would have just over a pound a week to live on while he explored the marvels of human knowledge. "He was a passable-looking youngster of eighteen, fair-haired, indifferently barbered," said Wells of Mr. Lewisham; "he wore ready-made clothes, his black jacket of rigid line was dusted about the front and sleeves with scholastic chalk, and his face was downy and his moustache incipient." And "he kept himself in London" (this is no longer Mr. Lewisham, but Hill, in "A Slip under the Microscope") "on his allowance of a guinea a week, and found that, with proper care, this also covered his clothing allowance, an occasional water-proof collar, that is; and ink and needles and cotton, and such-like necessaries for a man about town."

To the three years of active learning, arguing, and prentice writing which he enjoyed at the School of Science can be traced the experience upon which Wells drew in composing first of all his scientific romances, then his sociological criticisms and forecasts, and finally his novels of contemporary life. He was an ardent debater; he for a time edited the School magazine and wrote for it; and although in the examination finals for June, 1887, he was "slaughtered," so that he left without taking a degree, his active, incessantly curious mind had found its range and direction. He was to be the first scientific novelist in English literature.

Before he became a novelist he believed—wrongly—that he had "smashed a kidney at football, and lost the greater part of one lung." He had been nursed by his mother in the great house at Uppark, and had read an extraordinary variety of books. He had held two posts as assistant master, one of them under the father of A. A. Milne (who was one of his pupils). He had taken his degree as Bachelor of Science. And, at the age of twenty-four, he had married for the first time. Within five years he had found his marriage a hampering failure, had been divorced, and had married again.

This second marriage, to Amy Catherine Robbins, was a turning point in his life. Mrs. Wells was a great woman, small, very fair, pale, timid in manner, and in some respects curiously conventional; but she was a wit, she had exceptional sympathy, and to the end of her life was the staunch ally and helpmeet of her husband. Without her aid, as he more than once admitted, Wells could not have pro-duced anything like the amount of work he did. She was for years his secretary; she typed his manuscripts, corrected his proofs, did much research, dealt with difficult and disagreeable correspondents, and acted as hostess in both London and the country to a multitude of visitors of every kind and colour. With her encouragement,

Wells from the first wrote steadily and with increasing confidence and success. He began with journalism and short stories; then, as soon as he had written one book, he wrote as if by magic a dozen others. Actually in two years he published nine works of fiction; and from the nineties onwards not a year passed which did not see one, two, three, or four new books of his. No wonder that he was famous before he was thirty! And no wonder that although he was ten years younger than Shaw he seemed for almost the whole of his literary life to be equally a one-man arsenal of new and explosive ideas!

Apparently inexhaustible brilliance was shown in the rapidity with which Wells worked, in his extraordinary gift for assimilating facts, in the swift ease with which he communicated to the simplest mind the results of his observation and reflection. No contemporary can compare with him in this unceasing and always stimulating fertility. Although some of his books were less acceptable than others to critical judgment, he was always the champion surprise packet of the lierary world. And while, having written so many books, "mood after nood of the one mind within him," he fully revealed, long before his death, the entire range and degree of his intellect, no man could confidently prophesy, as long as he lived, what new aspect of cosmic activity he would next choose to analyse.

Naturally this versatility and fecundity resulted in great popular success. That proved unfortunate for his later fame; and at the present time he is seen too much as an author of yesterday alone. He was also charged with having been inconsistent. Nothing could be more untrue. He was, on the contrary, particularly consistent. He always wanted the World State and all that the World State involves. He wanted the abolition of kings and privileges. He wanted a new type of aristocracy, the severely self-disciplined Samurai. His views of details may have varied with the increasing awareness of different facets in the universal kaleidoscope; but in the main his constructive ideas were the same from quite early days to the end. That is noteworthy.

What gave critics the excuse for suggesting waywardness is that Wells from time to time took up different *instruments* and let them fall. He took up the Fabian Society; but when he found that the Fabian Society was more Fabian than international, and that it preferred its own Shavian corner in ideas to any ideas that he could bring in from outside, he dropped it. He took up the League of Nations; but when he found that the League of Nations was a thing of committees and compromises, and that it would do nothing to advance his own view of internationalism, he dropped that too. He took up the Labour Party, hoping that he could instil into it some of his knowledge and faith in a scientific future; but when he found that the Labour Party was a nest of private vanities and personal ambitions, wedded to class warfare, and incapable of non-political conceptions, he dropped it. He was never a political democrat. He was never, in the strict sense, a Socialist ("I was never at any stage a loyal party man," says Remington). But he was willing to take any path that might bring him to his goal; and only when he found the paths leading to dead ends did he retrace his steps in order to get once more upon his own road. There is no inconsistency here, but only an excess of faith in the power of the Wellsian mind to dominate the hesitations and self-importance of other men.

He was always a lively and vigorous host. His social contacts were innumerable. Scientists of every order, politicians of every party, his fellow-writers in every genre, philosophers, labourers, painters, actors, lawyers, and civil servants of every description all came within his immediate purview. Hence the thumbnail sketches scattered through his work of all sorts of odd types. He went here and there about the earth and in the air, always active, always alert, always storing observation with those quick eyes, that astoundingly rapid mind, and talking, talking with that witty, exaggerative tongue. There was hardly an Englishman of note whose personal experience Wells did not explore, whose character he did not assess, whose brain and temper he did not enliven. There is hardly a reader in the world to whom he has not opened new vistas of enter-tainment, understanding, indignation, and the millennium.

He had not Shaw's platform gift; he did not always enjoy the support of experts in this or that kind of learning which he sur-mounted with his seven-league boots. But after he had passed, and after the dust had settled, many an expert scratched his head, swept together the ruins of his hobby-horse, and (to adapt a popular advertisement) murmured "That's Wells, that was"; while many a common man hitherto baffled by jargon or old hypocrisy saw the world afresh as if by the brilliant passage of a meteor. To say that Wells was always right, or always fair, or always subtle, would be to risk exaggeration; but to undervalue the influence of so impetu-ous a force upon changing social conceptions would be the merest futility

vi

IT might be thought from this, by those who did not know him, that Wells personally resembled a hurricane. He did not. Shaw might bring with him a breeze of some force; but Wells entered any room, and shut the door behind him, as quietly as you or I would do. If you had been a very young and modest person, who had failed to catch his name, you would have seen a not very tall but rather stoutly built man with a brown face and very blue eyes. You would have heard a hoarse little voice which, although not at all like the solemn squeak of many English intellectuals, was pitched high and was not incapable of surprising shrillness. Your first impression would have been of a very friendly and easy manner. You would have noticed small birdlike jerks of the head. At last you would have seen that the very blue eyes were darting here and there with great quickness, and that they were full of amusement and mischief.

If you had quite distinctly heard the name of the newcomer, were conceited, and furthermore knew all and more than all about the celebrated Mr. H. G. Wells, your response would have been different. You would first of all have been surprised and possibly disappointed by the absence of glitter, carriage, *empressement* in so famous a man. All your preconceptions would have been disconcerted. You would have been paralysed by the feeling that what you had to say could not by any means be made to interest this all-knowing, restless, and unimpressible person. You would have felt helpless, would have said stupid things, would have fallen haughtily silent. Or you might have found yourself embarked upon a conversation amusing, indeed, but on your side strained, never comfortable, never quite natural because you could never overtake Wells' inventiveness and quickness of epithet, and on consideration a failure. Some people were absolutely unable to talk to him, not from awe, but from constraint. Sinclair Lewis, for example, otherwise hard to check, and in spite of almost idolatrous admiration, was tongue-tied. Lewis needs an evening: Wells gave nobody an instant.

The truth is that his quickness of mind carried him to the end of a sentence long before a tongue that required room in language could make the same journey. Really to converse with him one should have been as quick as he, as fluent, and as little devoted to those scrupulousnesses of verisimilitude which delay the lumbering talker. Perhaps one should have been a very adroit woman. Or, if less gifted, one might have trusted to his kindness, for Wells was a great sufferer of fools. He was so kind that one had but to be simple and receptive to evoke his affectionate consideration. But he was impatient of the long story or the aggressive or pompous manner.

At his best, he was the most richly amusing raconteur I ever met. He improvised; he invented; he mimicked (not with precise accuracy of intonation, for which his voice was unsuited, but with irresistible sense of character); and he laughed and teased all the time with the greatest spirit. He did everything with spirit. Whether he was dancing, or playing at cards or hockey, charades, or the many-ruled (and I may say constantly and even momentarily re-ruled) ball-game of his own invention, he was hotly and energetically active all the time. I think he began to write a book as if he were playing a game, and with the same enthusiasm; but there was this

difference between his play and his work, that the former was a re-
laxation, whereas the latter originated in a really passionate desire
to change the world, so that those born into it might be healthier,
wiser, and happier than any of their forerunners.

Change! That was the keynote of his character. He could not be
content with what is. I recall visiting the late Sir Harry Johnston
shortly after Wells had spent a week-end at St. John's Priory. Now
Sir Harry, although one to whom (as to the infant Nelson) fear was
unknown, had some of the idiosyncrasies usually linked with the
traditional old maid. Having quelled the fiercest of savage warriors
and penetrated the most intimidating of jungles, he spoke like a
little old woman and clung to rule and habit like a recluse. And when
I saw him he was still palpitating from the Wellsian week-end. He
had proposed, it seemed, a scrupulously unscrupulous game of
croquet upon his beautiful lawn. But to his horror he found the lawn
by no means sufficient for Wells's game of croquet. The entire
garden, thorough bush, thorough brier, had been called into re-
quisition. The word itself would not have been too wide for its
range. In two twinks Sir Harry's sedate game of croquet had
become a mixture of golf and steeplechase.

I instance this because it shows Wells's hatred of all that was
cramped. It also illumines his dislike of the petty viciousness of
croquet as that game is usually played. As Alice in Wonderland used
a flamingo and a hedgehog for mallet and ball, Wells took all spite-
fulness from the most quarrelsome of pastimes by letting air into it,
and converted the game into both an open contest and a planned
campaign. Change and plan; plan and change. Not without significance that Schema of Mr. Lewisham's! If he had not had this eager
desire for change, Wells might have remained a draper's assistant all
his life; and if he had not had this intense love of planning he might
have remained a writer of romances and tales without ever giving
the world new visions of sanity and order. Nay, without the desire
to make mankind healthier and happier by means of air and light
and space, education and hygiene, change and plan, he might long
ago have lost his own zest for life and gone without reluctance to his
quiet grave. As it is, he lived to be nearly eighty, and until illness
and pain and bitter disappointment broke his spirit he remained
vividly interested in the human scene and its rectification. Those
who knew him well found him at every turn the boy who suffered
the woes of Kipps and Polly; the chalky young schoolmaster of
"Love and Mr. Lewisham"; the waterproof-collared student at the
School of Science, arguing and spasmodically swatting and learning
to see Victorian men as but a stage in the progress towards something
more admirable; the novelist of escaping workers who in early days
took bicycles, and then cars, and aeroplanes, and at last trips to

H.G.WELLS

J. M. BARRIE

Labrador and Utopia, in order to get away from the distracting pressure of daily life; the novelist of careers and inconvenient passions; the novelist who breathed life into a history of the world that all could understand; and, within and above all these, the very natural, sensitive, nonsensical, affectionate, quick-tempered human being who was born in a little room above his father's shop in Bromley. He was many other things, as superficial strangers could tell you in detail, and indeed as his books will show; but behind the celebrated writer and the ready talker, the not perfectly cogent moralist, the publicist and the open conspirator, was a much more endearing person, full of fun, kindness, and simplicity, a man who, if he was not really Mr. Polly himself, was at least of the Polly clay and the lovable Polly fantasy.

vii

"I've read an average share of novels . . . and I've found the restraints and rules of the art (as I made them out) impossible for me. I like to write, I am keenly interested in writing, but . . . do what I will I fail to see how I can be other than a lax, undisciplined story-teller."

Tono-Bungay.

WHEN Wells wrote "The Time Machine," "The Wonderful Visit," "The War of the Worlds," "The Invisible Man," and their companions, he was doing something which had never been done before, and which has never been done since with the same vivid freshness. Picture to yourselves the shock to readers of those days of a rush of new inventions, simple to us now, but then so novel and so startling; and imagine how they must have roused the attention of the age. Here was a man who put posers—scientific posers—with the facility and enjoyment of a child; who said "Why?" "What if—?" "How?" "Suppose—?" about all sorts of things that people found they wanted to know. It was prodigious. Jules Verne had taken boys on conducted tours under the sea, and to the moon; but he had creaked as he did so. This new man's quickness allowed no time for creaks; he bubbled with new notions, and they were notions to which other minds jumped just an instant late. And, as they jumped, so Wells jumped again—in a different direction. He asked a thousand questions. He always asked questions—odd, irreverent questions, such as those that Uncle Ponderevo asked about history. Do you remember?

"'Don't want your drum and trumpet history—no fear! Don't want to know who was who's mistress, and why so-and-so devastated a province; that's bound to be all lies and upsy-down anyhow.

c

Chaps who did it didn't clearly know . . . What I want to know is, in the Middle Ages Did they Do Anything for Housemaid's Knee? What did they put in their hot baths after jousting, and was the Black Prince—you know the Black Prince—was he enamelled or painted, or what? I think myself, black-leaded—very likely—like pipe-clay—but did they use blacking so early?'"

I need not say that Ponderevo's point is one that Wells himself made about drum-and-trumpet history; or that Wells himself had an eloquent passage in "The World of William Clissold" to the effect that the scholars who so tidily arrange history into systems—the Feudal System and the Manorial System, and even the Capitalist System—are dealing in artificial lozenges with no relation at all to the casual sprawl of events as they occurred. That is not what I want to show. It is that Wells's mind was ever a questing mind, in eager search of the things that are not in encyclopædias. He was seeking this when he wrote the scientific romances. To him, any fact was a starting point for| speculation. "Why?" "What if—?" "How?" "Suppose——"

What if an angel came to earth? What if a man experimented with the fourth dimension and could as readily visit and contemplate the future as the past? What would he see? How would he make the journey? What if a man could make himself invisible? And so on. He could treat the subject seriously and at the full stretch of his mind, as he did in "The Time Machine," still the most striking, though not the most charming, of the books of this general type. Or he could treat it fantastically, as he did in "The Invisible Man," where the unfortunate creature who had discovered a practicable formula for invisibility could not retranslate himself to opacity, though he perished with cold and hunger. Or as plain farce, as in "The Stolen Bacillus," where an anarchist swallowed in mistake for cholera germs something that would bring out blue patches upon his skin. Or as whimsy, as in "The Inexperienced Ghost"; or as tract, as in "The Wonderful Visit"; or as sensational thriller, as in "The War of the Worlds." There seemed no end to the subjects or the approaches to them; and while it could be said with force that such themes were not strange to the mind of any boy born poor, who had only imaginings to set between himself and the dreariness of drab circumstance, the themes were given new vitality, they were made more novel, more credible, by the scientific detail, the bright inventiveness of a mind ruthlessly active and coolly amused at its own power.

Modern readers can dissect these books now, and show (as Wells has candidly done) that they were light-hearted, that they took no account of profounder difficulties, that in fact some of them are completely incredible. But no dissection can rob them of their charm, which is that of the fairy story, their excitement, which is that of the romance, and their originality, a characteristic never to be faked for more than a season or two, and more than ever visible in these books as one re-reads them for glimpses of the mind of their creator.

Concurrently with the scientific romances Wells was writing novels not very much outside the manner of his period, but noteworthy because of their personal humour and increasing richness. They were simple narratives, long and short, of events in the lives of very simple-minded people. The first of them was the tale of Mr. Hoopdriver, the drapers' assistant with a bicycle, who went for a cycling holiday and became for the time being a knight-errant. There was also the more autobiographical, but still indulgent, story of "Love and Mr. Lewisham," in which a boy, a schoolmaster, fell idyllically in love, became a student at the Royal College of Science, went to a fraudulent seance (so, you may remember, did Mr. Parham, in one of Wells's later fantastic tales), met at the seance his early sweetheart, married her, and had his trials and quarrels until a stronger feeling checked the strain and ended the book with a rosy glimpse. A little later there was "Kipps," in which a draper's assistant inherited money and entered society and ran away from his intellectual fiancée to marry the domestic servant he had always loved and build a house and lose his money and settle in life as a shopkeeper again. Finally, as the supreme example of this sort of book, there was "Mr. Polly," the story of a little shopkeeper who set fire to his shop, ran away from his wife, and found a nice cosy widow who kept an inn to which all sorts of odd visitors came, and lived happily ever after.

All these books belong to the same order. All are fairy stories, and all are about "simple souls." All were written, not merely as relaxations, but because one side of Wells's genius, the happiest side, had kinship with the comic genius of Dickens, his favourite author. Whenever Wells was amused, he was happy and inventive. The living figures in his books are all comic characters, fantastic, talkative, simple, phonetically colloquial, seen with what used to be called "open pleasantry," but seen none the less with keenness and precision. Teddy Ponderevo, Polly, Chaffery, Kipps, Chitterlow, having amused us as we read, persist in our imaginations. We love them. When Wells was serious, he was expository; he did not create. We lose the character in the exposition; and this, I think, is why, as novels, all but the two best books in the serious and discursive manner must remain unsatisfactory. That is not to be said of the simple soul novels.

What is to be said of them, and of the early romances, is something else. It is that they were all written in an easy narrative form untrammelled by those shackles to which the rising authority of

Henry James presently condemned romancers. In the nineties and early nineteen-hundreds, people who wrote books thought little of "art" and "form" and "composition." They found the writing of books "fun," and not a stern tussle with refractory material. We have changed all that now. We have even gone rather too far in the other direction, for any author who writes less to exhibit than to amuse himself is regarded from the distance, by the immaculate, as a prostitute. But when Wells began to write things were so different that he was allowed, unreproved, to enrich out literature with several artless works of genius which still give delight to all but the æsthetically unco' guid.

As a consequence, Wells never learnt how to write a novel which was a work of art. When advised of this, he bluffed after the manner of the defendant in an English Law Court charged with libel. This defendant answers the charge by saying that the words were never uttered, or alternatively that they do not bear the meaning put upon them, or again alternatively that they are in fact true, and legitimate comment. Wells, charged with being unæsthetic, replied that he never said he was, and alternatively that the æsthetes can't prove it, and anyway, Yah! This seems to me, coming from Wells, to be entirely justifiable. The rules of art need revision, so as to include the work of Wells. Any suggestion that they are as fixed as those horrid wire cages which are put over box trees in the shape of peacocks, foxes, and the like, seems to me to beg the whole question. The rules of art are not made by edicts; they are developed from the practice of artists; and if they cannot admit of provision for such a book as "Tono-Bungay" they ought to be stretched; for "Tono-Bungay." illustrating as it does the form and pressure of the time in which it was written, is one of the great modern novels, and will be so appreciated after a century's variations of æsthetic dogmatism. But I must not pause here to dwell upon "Tono-Bungay," for it belongs to a later stage in the author's development.

viii

"I see about me a great multitude of little souls and groups of souls as darkened, as derivative as my own; with the passage of years I understand more and more clearly the quality of the motives that urge me and urge them to do whatever we do . . . Yet that is not all I see, and I am not altogether bounded by my littleness. Ever and again, contrasting with this immediate vision, come glimpses of a comprehensive scheme, in which these personalities float, the scheme of a synthetic wider being, the great State, mankind, in which we all move and go, like blood corpuscles, like nerve cells, it may be at times like brain cells, in the body of a man."   *A Modern Utopia.*

Having written the scientific romances, and having begun to write novels, Wells at the turn of the century found himself working in a new field. He had been a young schoolmaster, a young scientist, a journalist, a writer of romances, and a novelist; and now his increasing range of knowledge led him ever farther into speculation. It was speculation directed by the schoolmaster and the scientist in him; for his interests lay in the everyday world of that time and the future. For him the first step in the "New Republicanism" of which he became the champion was "to reject and set aside all abstract, refined, and intellectualized ideas as starting propositions, such ideas as Right, Liberty, Happiness, Duty or Beauty." He was a Darwinian; he knew that the world was to be more and more dominated by inventions and practical ideas; and he wanted to breed good citizens who would create a world in which order replaced present chaos. First of all, therefore, it was imperative that he should make up his mind as to the most probable developments of the near future. He did this, and wrote "Anticipations."

I need not say that many of Wells's anticipations were proved accurate. The book exists to demonstrate the fact. From my point of view it is more interesting to realize that "Anticipations" was but a first step in the clarification of Wells's own mind. He went on to imagine what kind of world it was that he and his fellow-reformers were striving to create. He dared to formulate his idea of a practical Utopia. That was much more difficult. It was so difficult that he made a number of false starts in the writing of the book, and at last took refuge in a hybrid literary form—half essay, half tale—that excellently suited his gifts. And as a bridge between "Anticipations" and "A Modern Utopia" he wrote another book, called "Mankind in the Making," in which he discussed elaborately the problems of Eugenics and Education.

The three books, taken together, represent the character of Wells's interest in the world and the human species. Later books in the same vein—and here I include such works as "The Outline of History," "The Science of Life," and "The Work, Wealth and Happiness of Mankind"—were educational. And whatever their positive qualities they were undertaken deliberately as stop-gaps, with no pretence to much more than utilitarian purpose. They were written because Wells felt the instructional need of such books; and the "History" was written only after he had failed to persuade other men, whom he considered better qualified than himself for the task, to undertake it. But all exhibit what I believe to be the same character. They are concerned with a practicable civilization of the future, and a civilization which has grown directly out of our present ways. They concentrate upon inventions, social order, education; they have little concern with æsthetics or what is called the psyche. And they are so simply expressed that any man of ordinary intelligence can read them with understanding. That is a quality due to the journalist in Wells. He is readable. It was made a matter of reproach

against him. He was said to have betrayed culture to the Philistines,
It should rather be said that he introduced the Philistines to a culture
larger than that of the Dons.

It was the desire to teach, to expound, that lay behind all Wells's
serious work. He did not like a vague world, or one that had un-
explored beauties; and for him the scientific mind was the best
possible type of mind. By science and through science, he thought
we should get a world that better men and women than ourselves
could inhabit. For this reason his vision had its limitations. He did
not see what the poet sees and what the musician sees: I do not
think he could sit still for long enough to relish the pure contemplation which Shaw considered the highest intellectual state. He
must be turning the room, the world, the lazy mind about and
about, like a house-proud woman with a vacuum cleaner in her
eager hands. His heroes are not military men, not poets, nor
philosophers, but scientists. He said in "Marriage":

> "When the intellectual history of this time comes to be written,
> nothing I think will stand out more strikingly than the empty gulf
> in quality between the superb and richly fruitful scientific investiga-
> tions that are going on and the general thought of other educated
> sections of the community. I do not mean that the scientific men are
> as a whole a class of supermen, dealing with and thinking about
> everything in a way altogether better than the common run of
> humanity, but that in their own field, they think and work with an
> intensity, an integrity, a breadth, boldness, patience, thoroughness
> and faithfulness that (excepting only a few artists) puts their work
> out of all comparison with any other human activity. Often the field
> in which the work is done is very narrow, and almost universally the
> underlying philosophy is felt rather than apprehended. A scientific
> man may be large and deep-minded, deliberate and personally de-
> tached in his work, and hasty, commonplace and superficial in every
> other relation of life. Nevertheless it is true that in these particular
> directions the human mind has achieved a new and higher quality of
> attitude and gesture, a veracity, self-detachment and self-abnegating
> vigour of criticism that tend to spread out and must ultimately spread
> out to every other human affair. In these uncontroversial issues at
> least mankind has learnt the rich rewards that ensue from patience
> and infinite pains."

With such faith, how could Wells do anything but create
Utopias in which orderly but apparently unmerry people are identified by their thumbprints and dominated by a highly organized
State, what time they travel at immense speeds, do everything that
can be done by means of machinery, and so manage their sanitation
that with the fly and mosquito every familiar loveliness of our
world, the world of the poets and merrymakers, has been ex-

punged? It would not be true to say that, like other Republican theorists, Wells had banished laughter and beauty from the State; indeed, he specifically refers to these indications of the human spirit. But when he talks of beauty he never carries conviction, and his future world, in spite of every persuasive effort of his, and in spite of the fascinating ingenuity of parts of his analysis, remains, as all Utopias do, a place from which one hurries back to one's own fireside with relief.

Why is this? One explanation is that Wells had more courage than we, in that he was not in revolt against machinery, but was determined upon subduing it to the service of man. Another is that in spite of every gift he was deficient in that kind of imagination which even those of us who are not poets do strangely share with the poets. The truth is that Wells, with all his quickness, all his power, all his vivid inventive habits of mind, had no true sense of beauty in art or in life. Even love, in his books, never moves us; every one of his busy scientific heroes, interrupted in full flight of research or political activity by what he terms an "urgency," has an affair with a woman, but as to emotion there is no sign of it, and as to beauty of relation there is so little that we quite coldly estimate the duration of the urgency and the affair. Wells was interested in other matters. He was interested in getting things done. He would work for a cause, for the improvement of the world, for the instruction of mankind in essential knowledge. But save in so far as it is useful to one or other of those ends he was indifferent to beauty. That is the weakness of his "serious" works, which reach out to a greater synthesis than is possible in the world we know. He was a prose writer, at his best in books where he was nearest his own time and his own people. His best novels are "Tono-Bungay" and "Mr. Polly," which are both rich with the very texture of life itself. His best expository books are also novels—"The Undying Fire," "The New Machiavelli," and "The World of William Clissold";—and they are the best because the first is passionate and the two others are less expository than exploratory of the author's always original and interesting mind and experience.

ix

"Art is selection and so is most autobiography. But I am concerned with a more tangled business than selection. I want to show a contemporary man in relation to the state and social usage, and the social organism in relation to that man."

The New Machiavelli.

THE above quotation reveals the fact that by the time he wrote "The New Machiavelli" Wells had heard from Henry James. The two, indeed, had long been friends; and James was full of admiration (but never quite of approval) for the younger master. By now, James, Joseph Conrad, and Ford Madox Hueffer had all brought the gospel of art into Wells's life. They had all groped for the precise word with which to express the finest shade of thought and feeling and drama. But while Wells was impressed with the men and their gospel, his response to the cajolery of the artists was only fitful, and at last became less a response than an impatience. He wanted to write well. He had written well. The writing of "The Time Machine," for example, is full of quality. He had been quick to see and praise the talent of Conrad; he respected James; he must have been enter-tained—who was not?—by Hueffer. But what he wanted to do was to get *himself* upon paper; and the search for words and phrases that should have just so much value and meaning (kinetic and potential in Arthur Ransome's phrase), and not a hair's breadth more or less, seemed to him a waste of valuable energy and time. Where did it lead?

Furthermore, he was not interested—he never had been in-terested—in the novel of situation. All James's relish for situation, and all the delicacy of James's poise in dealing with situation, left Wells wondering why on earth any man should think it worth his while to tell so feeble a story at such length, and with such gloating. It was life, the life about him, in the busy streets, and in the little houses he had known, and in offices and laboratories and committee rooms all over the world, that had value for his mind. And even then only value in respect of what was being done with it all, and how the people were planning their lives and work, and making false steps and adjusting themselves to new jobs and new exciting conditions. When there was so much real life, and when so much needed voicing and changing, how could one sit down to write a made story, with however great a finesse?

Once he had finished "Kipps." Wells was done with fairy stories. He had no longer any need of them. In his own case, the story had come true. He was at the height of his powers, and his reputation was tremendous. His success was popular and un-questioned. And about him was this intricate and absorbing world of workers and employers, inventors and politicians, and a new generation of free-thinking men and women who were none of these things, and business men and advertisers and newspaper pro-prietors, and graft and drudgery and exploitation and opportunity, all waiting to be expressed, all waiting to be used as material for fiction. By 1908, so far as any man can be said to do such a thing, Wells was living more fully in the life of his day, and was more generally informed as to all its ramifications, than any other English novelist has ever been. No wonder "Tono-Bungay" is such a full book.

But, to return to the art of the novel, nothing but a full book could have served the purpose of this one. To use an artificial story would have been to waste all sorts of material in which Wells was deeply interested. Moreover any visitor to Wells's library must have noticed one row of books which bore all the signs of constant reading: it was the row of Dickens's novels. There can be no doubt at all that when he began to plan "Tono-Bungay" Wells thought "David Copperfield" was a very great novel indeed. He used the form of the pseudo-autobiography with deliberation, as the one in which most freedom was allowed for the introduction of innumerable details of contemporary life, and the one in which such details could best be related to a select group of characters and a *milieu* with which he was thoroughly acquainted. "I want to show," he said, "a contemporary man in relation to the state and social usage, and the social organism in relation to that man." While we may wish that largeness of conspectus could have been more intimately associated with fineness of concept, we cannot without eccentricity deny to "Tono-Bungay" its importance both as a social picture and as a development in the craft of novel-writing.

Henry James did not deny either of these things. Writing to Wells about the second of the great pseudo-autobiographic novels, "The New Machiavelli," he said: "I have read you then, I need scarcely tell you, with an intensified sense of that life and force and temperament, that fullness of endowment and easy impudence of genius, which makes you extraordinary. . . . . Your big feeling for life, your capacity for chewing up the thickness of the world in such enormous mouthfuls, while you fairly slobber, so to speak, with the multitudinous taste—this constitutes for me a rare and wonderful and admirable exhibition." But he added (and it is for the sake of the addition that I quote this passage): "I make remonstrance . . . bear upon the bad service you have done your cause by riding so hard again that accurst autobiographic form which puts a premium on the loose, the improvised, the cheap and the easy. . . . There is, to my vision, no authentic, and no really interesting and no *beautiful*, report of things on the novelist's, the painter's part unless the great stewpot or crucible of the imagination, of the observant and recording and interpreting mind in short, has intervened and played its part—and this detachment, this chemical transmutation for the æsthetic, the representational, end is terribly wanting in autobiography brought, as the horrible phrase is, up to date."

This criticism—for it must be admitted that James's mind was like the mills of God—sums up all or nearly all the objections to the Wellsian novel. The weakness of the method is better seen when one contemplates the repetitions or variations that followed "Tono-Bungay." The stories told in these books were different; and yet the more they differed the more they emphatically remained the same story—the story of the man with a job to do, a marriage, an affair, a flight, the whole involved in a richly and consummately sketched chiaroscuro of the social and intellectual life of England between 1860 and 1930. "Tono-Bungay" is the best of these books because it was the first pressing of the grapes. It is a really amazing picture, furthermore, of the change that occurred in English life between the author's childhood and his maturity. It is contemporary history. Its vigour never fails; its detail, both domestic and social, is exact and sufficient. It is absorbingly interesting; it was a genuine attempt to present a modern man at something like full length in spite of every moral convention of the time.

It is also the best, however, because of another feature, not apparent in its successors: it is the only sociological novel of Wells's in which there are comic characters in any way to be compared with those in the humorous novels. Not all the intellectual interest of "The New Machiavelli" and "The World of William Clissold" can compensate for the loss, the temporary loss, by Wells of his comic genius.

When that comic genius had free play, as in "Kipps," there may be—there is—the air of improvisation to which James objected in "The New Machiavelli". But although "Kipps" may stumble, it stumbles from point to point, from one comic invention to another, and is a feast of character. Even better is "Mr. Polly," which does not stumble at all (does it falter just once, almost into sentimentality, when Polly talks to the schoolgirl?), but has a poignance not elsewhere to be found in Wells's work. Wells was always most at ease in writing about poor and half-cultured people; he understood and loved the simple souls among them, and understood and loved rather less the cupidity, the inquisitiveness, and the bad manners of the not so simple. They were, so to speak, in the hollow of his hand. He perceived the significance of every gesture they made, and every glance they cast. He could be kind to them—sometimes mercilessly kind,—ribald, indulgent without sentimentality, Dickensian and more than Dickensian because more economical in illustration, beautifully suggestive in phonetics or in phrase. In dealing with poor people he was an artist. Personally, I think that in this field he had no equal.

x

> "Fashions change more quickly than manners, manners more quickly than morals, morals more quickly than passions, and, in general, the conscious, reasonable, intellectual life more quickly than the instinctive, wilful, affectionate one. The dramatist who deals with the irony and humour of the relatively durable sides of life, or with their pity and terror, is the one whose comedies and tragedies will last longest . . . Fashionable dramatists begin to 'date', as the critics call it, in a few years."
>
> *G. B. Shaw: Dramatic Opinions.*

BETWEEN them, Shaw and Wells did more than any other writers to create what may be called the modern attitude towards morals and civilization in general. Not towards æsthetics, because for both of them art was of less urgent importance than the propagation of ideas and opinions. Each stood upon his rostrum and said: "You're all wrong. You have a world in which there is disease, poverty, dishonesty, and a huge mass of filth and corruption. The way in which you are to cure this is not the way of religion as it is taught in any church, or by any existing party in the political world; it is the way of common sense, determination, and a planned future. If you want a better world, you must will it. Believe in no more humbug: it is all about you, and it is ruining the earth. I will show you that most of your accepted ideas are humbug, and I will mock at those ideas or flout them, so that they will be seen of no worth. I will show you what men are, and what they might be if only they would make up their minds to work for a better and wiser world in which all could share in the rewards of that wisdom and that improvement."

And so, while Shaw laughed sentimentality and romance off the stage in his plays, and teased the English for their slowness and pomposity and self-infatuation, and made parents ridiculous and only the young wise and bold, and demanded a new aristocracy of supermen, Wells, ever more impatient of levity than Shaw (whom he once, as a young man, described as "giddy"), looked ahead and planned a clean and orderly future in which certainly there would be no place for Shaw's unnecessary beard and Shaw's irrepressible, irrelevant brilliance, and celebrated the new youth and the open conspiracy to revolutionize the world, and demanded a new intellectual aristocracy of Samurai who would lead mankind by way of "love and fine thinking." And the chief thing about both of them was that they addressed millions of men and women never before educated by the State by way of plays and novels which all could hear and read with delight. In this lay their novelty. There had been novelist-teachers before Wells, but none with his grasp of general ideas coupled with scientific training and the eager brilliance of his invention and improvisation. Other dramatists before Shaw had dared to be outspoken (but that was long ago), and had shown the

world as something in which not all was love and adultery; but there
had been none to whom blue books were child's play and the
English simultaneously a laughing-stock. Ideas, ideas, ideas, they
were in the heads of all the young Edwardians and early Georgians.
Shaw and Wells, Wells and Shaw; Chesterton and Belloc and Wells
and Shaw—the seeds of disbelief in accepted morals and manners
were sown by Wells and Shaw, while Belloc and Chesterton fought
a gallant but losing fight against the forces of science and economics,
machinery and the future, incandescence and destruction.

I say "destruction," for Wells and Shaw had need to be de-
stroyers. "Let it burn," says Cæsar in "Cæsar and Cleopatra." And
when Theodotus cries wildly: "Will you destroy the past?" he
answers: "Ay, and build the future with its ruins." It may be that
the future will be built upon the ruins left by Shaw, and that it will
resemble the future planned by Wells—this remains to be seen;—
but it is the case, and naturally the case, that the generations influenced by the two men should first of all seize upon what was
destructive in their philosophies. The young, having learnt from
Shaw that their parents were fools, proceeded to treat them as fools.
The young, having learnt from Wells that young people should be
bravely and nobly free from restraint, became, as they believed,
bravely and nobly free from restraint. To humility in face of all
authority succeeded conscious defiance of every authority. To the
hypocrisy of romantic virtue succeeded the pretence of frank,
honest sincerity which is such a nuisance to others when it is
paraded. I do not think Shaw liked the new freedom. He may have
done so; but I do not think he liked it. He was himself too fastidious
to care for the spiritual vulgarities of the current hour, and he cried
out against them. But that he first spread in influential form the ideas
upon which they are based I have no doubt whatever. I do not think
Wells liked the new and self-constituted intellectual aristocracy.
He may have done so; but it has a very aristocratic manner, and is
not so much leading mankind to wise freedom as trying to corral it
for the political ends of slavery; so that I cannot suppose him to
have been content. But that he first spread in influential form the
ideas upon which this new intellectual aristocracy has consciously
based itself I have no doubt whatever.

Nor is this all, for memories are short; and the very men and
women who owe their enlightenment to Shaw and Wells have out-
distanced their teachers, and lost the power to respect them. One or
two foreign professors have appeared in our midst; the stars have
been brought very near; faith in the future of mankind struggles
hard with nihilism; and the general level of culture has so greatly
risen that, while wisdom is no more widespread than it was, knowledge of unnumerable imposed and parrot-learned facts has never

been so common. And so Shaw and Wells must have learned—if they needed to learn it—the truth of Shaw's own maxim, now half a century old. "What exceptional people do in one generation, average people are generally doing in the next." And again: "In so rapidly progressive a business as fine art now is in England, no mortal man can lead more than one generation." A true prophecy indeed! For Shaw and Wells, though their work is as great as ever it was, and though they will both be venerated in the future for their share in moulding the minds of twentieth-century men, no longer actively influence that "modn," that fashionable intelligence which Bonamy Dobrée gravely calls "the best thought" of the hour, and are condescended to by those who are incapable of inventing the very jargon in which their current glibnesses are expressed.

Chapter Four

CATHOLIC LIBERALISM

BELLOC AND CHESTERTON

i

"They looked backwards to old enlightenment and forwards to new prejudices.
. . . They hoped—but it may be said that they hoped for yesterday."
                        G. K. Chesterton: A Short History of England.

I HAVE called this chapter "Catholic Liberalism"; but indeed that
is a mere label, for I propose to speak of Belloc and Chesterton,
not as Catholics or Liberals, or as Catholic Liberals or Liberal
Catholics, but only as writers. If I felt I could so do without imperti-
nence, I should use that name, "The Chester-belloc," which Shaw
invented to cover the common identity of the two; but while there
are many liberties I will allow myself there is one, the use of a
stranger's Christian or nick-name, which I feel bound to leave to the
less squeamish. The truth is that I never had any personal acquaintance with these two ornaments of our age.

With Chesterton I once had an anonymous conversation, when
he called at J. M. Dent's office after hours with a Dickens preface,
and refused to leave it with me because (as a little boy) I could not
give him in exchange the agreed remuneration; with Belloc I once,
as an adult, shook hands. Yet when I was sixteen, and Belloc and
Chesterton, with Wells and Shaw, were all a single radiance in the
firmament, I heard Belloc deliver what I thought, and still with less
confidence think, must have been the most brilliant speech ever
made—to the Fabian Society, on the differences between Collec-
tivism and Co-operativism;—and at the same period I used with a
couple of equally devoted friends to tramp round London in order
to listen to Chesterton lecturing, as he was ready to do, upon every
subject under the sun, from the Dreadful Danger of Liberalism
(which was the persistence in the party of hereditary caste) to Puck.
So while Belloc and Chesterton did not know me, I knew them, and
can testify to their former grandeur in the eyes of the young.

Probably young people now can hardly imagine how these four
men, Shaw, Wells, Chesterton, and Belloc, stood out from their
fellows and argued among themselves for the enlightenment of
extraordinarily mixed audiences. Wells, being no speaker, largely
contented himself with printed argument; the others were as happy
face to face as they were in column. Sometimes Shaw would debate

68

with Chesterton, and sometimes with Belloc: once, I recall, he debated with Chesterton while Belloc took the chair and rang an infuriating bell: upon another occasion he met Belloc in the large Queen's Hall, when an audience of three thousand people heard these two discuss the question of whether a Democrat who was not also a Socialist could possibly be a Gentleman, and came away with the problem unsolved after two hours of resolute hard hitting. The admiration between these men was not that of the literary nest, but that of the battlefield or the ring; and I think it fair to say that if any one of them wrote or spoke of another it was as an opponent whose nose at all costs must be struck and struck hard. This was especially true of Belloc; for while all felt a tenderness for Chesterton, none— engaged in a battle for self-preservation—had the smallest tenderness for Belloc, and none, certainly, received quarter at his hands.

One reason for the love of Chesterton was that while he fought he sang lays of chivalry and in spite of all his seriousness warred against wickedness rather than a fleshy opponent, while Belloc sang only after the battle, and warred against men as well as ideas, for the love of fighting and the pleasure he took in what might be called the deployment of the intellect. Another was that Chesterton could be distracted by a joke or an absurdity, whether it occurred to his own mind or to the mind of his foe, while Belloc was a master of the divagation or parenthesis, and never lost his place in an argument. But a third, and very important reason, was that it was often supposed that Chesterton might have been convinced if only Belloc had not stiffened him with recalcitrance. As the front legs of a performing horse are supposed to be the leaders (for Front-Legs works the head and ears), so in the monstrous animal conjured up by Shaw's conception of the Chester-belloc Belloc had the teeth and claws, while the warm and jovial heart belonged to Chesterton. The public said "G.B.S." and "G.K.C.": it said neither H.B. nor H.G.W.

Belloc's aggressiveness may have been due to the fact that he had served in the French artillery before ever he went to the University; or it may have been due to the fact that his college at Oxford was Balliol, which at that time—I know nothing of the present day— produced men deeply assured of their own superiority to other men; or it may have been due to the fact that he is a casuist, to whom the views of others are the mere rough material for destructive analysis. Whatever the cause, however, he was a most disconcerting and angering opponent, who had ever an impudent answer for hecklers and a severe thrust for the one who stood nearest upon the platform. These were a few—by no means all—of the differences between Chesterton and Belloc as they were seen by those who disagreed with both; and they will serve to introduce us to some details of the life of the elder and more pugnacious of the two.

ii

"'No,' said I, 'I have no land, and not even the power of which you speak. I am really, though moderately, poor. All that I get I earn by talking in public places in the cold weather, and in spring time and summer by writing and by other tricks."

H. Belloc: Esto Perpetua.

JOSEPH HILAIRE PIERRE BELLOC was born on July 27th, 1870, at La Celle, St. Cloud, a suburb of Paris. He was the son of a French barrister, Louis Swanton Belloc; and his mother was Bessie Rayner Parkes, daughter of Joseph Parkes, an English politician and the historian of the Chancery Bar of England. I do not know at what date Belloc left France for the first time; but he was educated at the Oratory School, Birmingham (a city in which his maternal ancestor, Joseph Priestley, was once a dissenting minister). On leaving school he served as a driver in the 8th Regiment of Artillery at Toul, Meurthe-et-Moselle, and when he left the service in 1892 he went to Oxford. At Oxford he became a Brackenbury History Scholar, and in his final History Schools in 1895 he took First Class Honours. That is a fact which should be kept in mind.

He published his first book, a collection of verses, in 1895, and in the two following years he enriched the literature of nonsense with "The Bad Child's Book of Beasts" and "More Beasts for Worse Children." He then revealed another gift with a book called "The Modern Traveller," and began that series of historical and biographical studies which forms his greatest contribution to library catalogues with books on Danton and Robespierre. In 1902 he became a naturalized British subject. In 1904 he published the first of his satiric novels, "Emmanuel Burden." In 1906 he not only acted as chief book reviewer for *The Morning Post*, but was elected Liberal M.P. for South Salford. Four years later, although unsupported by Party funds, he again won an election for the same constituency (this time as an Independent candidate), but in the second election of 1910 he refused to stand, and from that time has had no further connection with official politics. His work on *The Morning Post* ceased in 1910; his most important political book, "The Servile State," was published in 1912; and for two years (1911–1913) he was head of the English literature department at the East London College.

At the outbreak of the First World War he acted as commentator upon military operations for *Land and Water*, and thus perhaps for the first time impressed the large reading public with his extraordinary powers of lucid communication. Week by week a sceptical and badly shaken public read Belloc and was reconverted to faith by his unfaltering certainty, his logic, and a literary skill in that department second to none. "However powerful, native, sympathetic to his hearer's mood or cogently provable by reference to new things may be a man's idea," said Belloc in 1889, "he cannot persuade his fellow men to it if he have not words to express it. And he will persuade them more and more in proportion as his words are well chosen and in the right order, such order being determined by the genius of the language whence they are drawn." Belloc himself persuaded the British public not only by the genius of their language but by the genius with which he used it. He gave them a weekly draught of new life, new clarity, new nerve. The period of 1914–1918 was the period in which his influence stood at its highest point.

iii

I STILL have very clearly in memory the appearance of Belloc as I first saw him. He must have been slightly over thirty, not very tall but very broad-shouldered and with that fine head cocked at its usual considering angle. He bent over a small table, smiling, his big white shirt-front bulging; and he surveyed the congregated Fabians as if they were simple-minded children to whom he was unfolding the wonders of the universe. In fact he was explaining, among other things, with much salt, a few of the fallacies which lay fatally behind the principles of their own movement. He was confident, gay, rich in lively asides or extravagant alternative phrases. He made everybody laugh—that was intended—as his tongue played with the words of triumphant ridicule; and having made them laugh he slew them. Never was there such a Fabian slaughter.

I recall him at another time, also at a Fabian meeting (and a public one, for I was never a Fabian), speaking rather quietly, and somehow less confidently, at the Memorial Hall in Farringdon Street. I think he had been severely attacked at a previous meeting: at any rate he had papers with him, and may have been reading or carefully speaking from notes. And so low did he hold his head that somebody, hoping to disconcert him, called from the back of the hall: "Speak up!" There was a hush at the interrupter's cheek; but Belloc, lifting his head, only smiled, and like lightning answered the affront. The fluty French voice, rather high-pitched but never otherwise than pure and fluent; the French "r" that is very nearly a "w"; the arrogance which his former modest demeanour had concealed— all rose. He called out: "It's all wight: I'm only talking to myself." The interrupter's brief advantage was destroyed; and the lecture proceeded with increased animation on the speaker's part.

Belloc did not continue the same young and triumphant man of those early days. He grew stouter, more preoccupied. The keenness of his face roughened, and his colour became deeper. Having grown a beard he looked less like the Belloc of old than a French parish priest. His black cloak and low-crowned black felt hat increased the priestly effect. I do not think that Belloc ever lost pride in the fact that he was born a Frenchman; but there was always, none the less, a good English look to him which gave his admirers great pleasure. He grew more considerate of fools. He read Trollope at nights, and remained in his home in Sussex; writing no more poems nor prose accounts of his journeys in France or North Africa and the Four Men who made such songs of good wine and good ale and the Sussex inns. Alas that it should have been so!

iv

"If you cannot find him, and Fleet Street looks lonely and forsaken, then be sure he has been spirited away to some solitary place by his wife, the keeper of his business conscience, to finish a book for which some publisher is angrily clamouring. For 'No clamour, no book,' is his maxim."

A. G. Gardiner: Prophets, Priests, and Kings.

GILBERT KEITH CHESTERTON's life corresponded with Belloc's in no particular. He was not born a Catholic; he was a convert. He was not born in France, but in the London district of Kensington, which is as much associated in the popular mind with respectability as Chelsea and Bloomsbury are associated with æsthetic affectation or Tooting with the inexplicable gibes of professional humorists. He was four years younger than Belloc, having been born in 1874. He went to St. Paul's School, London, and did not go to a University. Nor did he engage in any military training; but instead attended classes at the Slade School, tried office life without success, and first began writing for the press by reviewing books on art for Robertson Nicoll's monthly magazine, *The Bookman*. From reviewing books on art he passed to reviewing books upon all subjects; and in 1900, when he was 26, he passed from reviewing books to publishing them.

The earliest title-pages to bear his name were those of "The Wild Knight," a collection of poems which included a poetic drama notable for its brevity, and "Greybeards at Play," a collection of rhymes inscribed to "E. C. B." (long subsequently, of course, the author of "Trent's Last Case") after this fashion:

"He was, through boyhood's storm and shower,
    My best, my nearest friend;
We wore one hat, smoked one cigar,
    One standing at each end."

These books were followed in the autumn of 1901 by a collection of reprinted essays called "The Defendant"; and from that time Chesterton was what is called an author, in contradistinction to a journalist. But he remained a journalist. Many of his books are made up of material which first appeared in periodicals. Others were written because publishers insisted. At least one such book owes its existence to Chesterton's quixotry. He was invited to write a history of England; and he declined on the ground that he was no historian. Some time later, he agreed with the same publishers to supply a book of essays. Hardly had the agreement been signed before Chesterton discovered that he was bound to give this book of essays to another firm, and in great distress he asked if his newly-made contract could be cancelled. In return, he offered to write any book which might be considered an adequate substitute. The publishers, concealing jubilation, sternly recalled their original proposal for a short history of England. Shrieks and groans were heard all the way from Beaconsfield, but the promise was kept. The "Short History of England" was what Chesterton must have called a wild and awful success. It probably has been the most generally read of all his books. But while the credit for it is his he must not be blamed for impudence in essaying history, when the inspiration arose in another's head, and when in fact no man ever went to the writing of a literary work with less confidence. This story will explain one of his publications: the stories of others must be innumerable—as the books themselves are almost innumerable. To his constant lecturing I have already referred. His journalism was never absent from the London press, and it remained vigorous to the end of his life. What profligate expenditure of energy for one who was born a poet!

It was in *The Daily News*, when that paper was edited by A. G. Gardiner, that Chesterton made his earliest reputation. He used to write in its columns upon all manner of books and other pretexts. A single sentence would be enough to set him at work with an antithesis or proposition that brought the stars into Fleet Street and light into many dark places. Gardiner, his former editor, in an affectionate sketch printed in "Prophets, Priests, and Kings," pictures the young journalist as he was in those days. "You may track him," said Gardiner, "by the blotting-pads he decorates with his riotous fancies, and may come up with him in the midst of a group of children, for whom he is drawing hilarious pictures, or to whom he is revealing the wonders of his toy theatre, the chief child of his fancy and invention, or whom he is instructing in the darkly mysterious game of 'Guyping,' which will fill the day with laughter. 'Well,' said the aunt to the little boy who had been to tea with Mr. Chesterton,—'well, Frank, I suppose you have had a very instructive afternoon?' 'I don't know what that means,' said Frank, 'but, oh!'

with enthusiasm, 'you should see Mr. Chesterton catch buns with his mouth.'"

Charles Masterman, another friend, and one who in old days was as inseparably linked with Belloc and Chesterton as Athos himself was linked with Porthos and the priestly Aramis, once told me how Chesterton used to sit writing his articles in a Fleet Street café, sampling and mixing a terrible conjunction of drinks, while many waiters hovered about him, partly in awe, and partly in case he should leave the restaurant without paying for what he had had. One day— I do not know whether Chesterton was present or absent—the head waiter approached Masterman. "Your friend," he whispered, admiringly, "he very clever man. He sit and laugh. And then he write. And then he laugh at what he write." It was always essential to Chesterton that he should be amused by what he wrote, and by what he said in public. I have heard him laugh so much at a debate that he gave himself hiccups for the rest of the evening.

In early days he was very nearly as big as he afterwards became, but whereas, towards the end of his life, his much-thinned hair straggled untidily, like a blown wisp of steam, it was then solid and well-brushed. A feature of it was a Whistlerian white plume in the centre; and anybody who sees an old photograph of Chesterton will there find the plume as neat and trim as brush could make it. Presently he grew more like Porthos; then like Doctor Johnson; and at last like the famous portrait by Velasquez of Don Alessandro del Borro. His gigantic aspect became a matter of common reference. The story of the man who gave up his seat to three ladies was associated with him. Finally a serious illness contracted his figure and forced him to live less strenuously than he had done. He went to Beaconsfield, in Buckinghamshire; and there he remained until his death, blind to the greatness of Disraeli, who took the name of the town as his title when he became a lord, but by no means blind to the forces of tyranny and the mischiefs wrought in the modern world by stupidity and exactitude.

Upon the public platform he swayed his large bulk from side to side; but he did not gesticulate. His speech was prefaced and accompanied by a curious sort of humming, such as one may hear when glee singers give each other the note before starting to sing. He pronounced the word "I" (without egotism) as if it were "Ayee," and drawled, not in the highly gentlemanly manner which Americans believe to be the English accent, and which many Englishmen call the Oxford accent, but in a manner peculiar to himself and either attractive or the reverse according to his hearer's taste. As he talked, and as he invented amusing fancies, he punctuated his talk with little breathless grunts or last gasps of laughter, so that he gave the impression—what with the drawl and the breathless grunts—of speaking very slowly indeed. He also gave the impression of speaking without any effort whatever, without raising his voice, or becoming intimidated by his audience or by lack of material to fill the time allotted to him, or feeling anything but sweet charity towards all those—even Jews, politicians, and sophisticates—whom he felt compelled to denounce. To those, accordingly, who care more for character than for opinion, more for talent than for fashion, Chesterton remains one of the great figures of his time. For the rest, and for those easily made impatient by his habit—they call it "trick"—of antithesis, he was merely an ingenious and snort-provoking creature. He certainly fell far behind the times, and at the hour of his death was regarded as prehistoric; but whether this is a sin or only a misfortune of unbending genius I shall not now attempt to determine.

v

THE explanation of the failure of Belloc and Chesterton to impress younger sceptics is that both were, in a sense, defendants. They attacked the trend of modern society towards mechanization as severely as any other writers whatsoever. But they did so from the standpoint of the Catholic Church. They said that the world was in a very bad way; but they both insisted that it was once—in the Middle Ages—in a very good way. Belloc, in a really masterly short work called "The Servile State," published in 1912, established the fact that slavery is a familiar condition of European life. It is his argument that slavery was destroyed by Christianity, and that until the end of the Middle Ages it had ceased to exist in the West. He believed, and so did Chesterton, that all the ills of modern England arise from what followed the dissolution of the monsteries by King Henry the Eighth. If Henry, says Belloc, had done as he intended, and kept in his own hands—the hands of the Crown—the property taken from the clerical body, the country would have had a happy future. Henry was not strong enough to keep his appropriations; he found the rich men of his day too powerful for him, and was forced to hand over the greater part of the spoils. Hence the violent inequality of wealth and power in England out of which grew from the sixteenth century onwards the evils of Capitalism. Hence, in process of time, the inevitability of the servile state, to which all parties by one path or another have led and will lead the people of England.

It is not my business to comment upon the truth or otherwise of this theory; but there can be no question as to the clearness and power of the book in which it is outlined. And there can be no doubt, I think, that possession of such a view of history prevented

Belloc and Chesterton from capturing the imagination of generations increasingly influenced by scientific and mechanical theory and practice. It is one thing to say that the world is wrong—every reformer agrees that the world is wrong;—but when, instead of proceeding to say that the world can be set right by something new, a man says that it can only be set right by a return to something old, he is thrown into a defence of the past. And the past, as Chesterton admitted, is no easy subject. "I can make the future as narrow as myself; the past is obliged to be as broad and turbulent as humanity." Both Belloc and Chesterton had to rewrite history for purposes of propaganda amid incessant interruptions both from dryasdusts and from ribalds who did not believe a word of what they said. Men who attack the present are always sure of support; men who contrast the present with the delights of an improved future society may be scorned as unpractical idealists, but they cannot be confounded by texts or refutations; men who insist that at some past time an ideal state existed may be challenged by the proven inability of that ideal state to withstand aggression, and they will certainly be floored by extracts from some old charter or pipe roll or antique letter which demolishes the whole structure they have so ingeniously erected.

That is what happened to Belloc and Chesterton. Belloc deliberately, and Chesterton with misgiving, set up a version—in Belloc's case a series of detailed versions—of what happened in England long ago. It was not accepted by Protestants, scientific historians, or sceptics. Belloc went farther. He told us in several books how the French Revolution arose, succeeded, and failed (the early chapters of his "Danton" give the clearest exposition of the events preceding the Revolution which I have ever read, but I do not know if they are the truest); he in one book of "Miniatures of French History" told us what must have happened in France at various crucial points from 599 B.C. to A.D. 1914. He traced the history of warfare in England. His mind played over the entire history of Europe, and he expressed himself as to that history with a certainty and I imagine a consistency which ought to have satisfied every reader. But he did not satisfy every reader. Every reader could relish the style in which Belloc told his story; but every reader, in spite of the charm and certainty of the narrative, felt that Belloc was a partisan, bent upon proving a case. It is nothing new in historical writing; if the case is the popular case it will be swallowed gladly; but when it conflicts with the case as presented by every Whig and Protestant historian, or with the case as overwhelmingly demonstrated by the ironist Gibbon, it is suspect from the start.

Now Belloc adored Froissart. He owed much to the gargantuan historical method of Rabelais. He believed that legends and ballads are better authorities than pipe rolls. He used his imagination in describing battles (for which he had a peculiar gift and fondness), political intrigues, and religious and economic influences as to which there are or are not written records. The results have been controversial. I need not dwell upon the horrid pursuit of A. F. Pollard whenever Belloc wrote upon the Tudors; nor upon that description of the campaign of Evesham in 1265 for which he gave as his chief authority the chronicle of Matthew Paris, who died in 1259. All I need say is that in a scientific period a man who sets out to prove upon general philosophical grounds that such and such events must have been caused in such and such a way, and in that way only, must expect to be challenged by all to whom his major premiss seems arbitrary. And that a man who writes history as if it had just happened under his eyes, in a scene as familiar to him as the palm of his hand, and for the glory of the Catholic Church, must expect to be smothered with dust brought directly from the Record Office.

But how delightful Belloc's historical method is! Take the following short passage from a book that is only musingly a historical work at all. Notice the grand introduction, the apparent candour with which two opposed views are presented, the preference for legend declared in the last lines:

"It is a debate which will not be decided (for the material of full decision is lacking) whether since the Romans crowded their millions into this Africa, the rainfall has or has not changed. It is certain that they husbanded water upon every side and built great barricades to hold the streams; yet it is certain, also, that their cities stood where no such great groups of men could live today. There are those who believe that under Atlas, towards the desert, a shallow sea spread westward from the Mediterranean and from Syrtis; there are others who believe that the dry water-courses of the Sahara were recently alive with streams, and that the tombs and inscriptions of the waste places, now half buried in the sand, prove a great lake upon whose shores a whole province could cultivate and live. Both hypotheses are doubtful for this reason—that no good legend preserves the record. Changes far less momentous have left whole cycles of ballads and stories behind them."

Would you not rather read history written thus than as it is told by so dead a person as Freeman, learned though Freeman was, or by somebody as accurate as Samuel Rawson Gardiner, or J. B. Bury? I have no doubt of it. But you might feel it wise—if a student—to read a little more deeply?

Chesterton suffered from the same charge of presenting what may be called unduly simplified history. He also had a preference for the legendary. He says:

"Probably the rhyme which runs,
'When good King Arthur ruled this land
He was a noble king,
He stole three pecks of barley meal,'

is much nearer the true medieval note than the aristocratic stateliness of Tennyson. But about all these grotesques of the popular fancy there is one last thing to be remembered. It must especially be remembered by those who would dwell exclusively on documents, and take no note of tradition at all. Wild as would be the results of credulity concerning all the old wives' tales, it would not be so wild as the errors that can arise from trusting to written evidence when there is not enough of it. Now the whole written evidence for the first part of our history would go into a small book. A very few details are mentioned, and none are explained. A fact thus standing alone, without the key of contemporary thought, may be very much more misleading than any fable. To know what word an archaic scribe wrote without being sure of what thing he meant, may produce a result that is literally mad. Thus, for instance, it would be unwise to accept literally the tale that St. Helena was not only a native of Colchester, but was a daughter of Old King Cole. But it would not be very unwise; not so unwise as some things that are deduced from documents. The natives of Colchester certainly did honour to St. Helena, and might have had a king named Cole. According to the more serious story, the saint's father was an inn-keeper; and the only recorded action of Cole is well within the resources of that calling. It would not be nearly so unwise as to deduce from the written word, as some critic of the future may do, that the natives of Colchester were oysters."

After that, and taking into consideration all that the method implies, it is perhaps hardly surprising that there are some—including myself —who believe Belloc's province to be not history, but that exceedingly personal product, the essay, of which he is complete master; and Chesterton's province not history, but poetry, or that beautiful kind of fable which he created for the exploitation of Father Brown, the priest-detective. Belloc at large, sailing, tramping, debating with the reader, singing, observing the country and the people he meets, eating and drinking with gusto, and writing with triumphant relish both of himself and his language (which he handles as a steersman handles a small boat at sea when the wind is freshening); Chesterton taking a common story, ingeniously twisting it, and at last leaving the earth altogether with a style that suggests the upward soaring (never the graceless flap) of a children's kite; both bringing to their art a love of life so uncommon at the present time as to ravish us with a sense of what they mean when they speak of Merrie England and "that laughter that has slept since the Middle Ages"—do they not thus establish themselves as very important figures in modern literature?

vi

I AM sure that most of us would find the Middle Ages an occasion for—it is the "modn" word—disgust if we were transported back into them. Belloc and Chesterton would not have done so. Belloc would have been happy if he had been born in the days when disputatious scholars went from University to University upon the Continent and argued for their bread. He had the hardiness to sail his own boat across the English Channel in a fog; and a life that gave him wine to drink, brains to test, and a soul to shrive was ever the good life for him. Chesterton was less hardy, but he was one, nevertheless, to whom eating and drinking and good talk could be as well conducted from the floor as from a modern chair. Neither Belloc nor Chesterton had anything of the funereal sleekness of the modn æsthete, the silence, the self-engrossed aloofness, the lack of good fellowship, the pinched assumption that humour is not humour unless it is concerned with sexual symbols. Yet neither Belloc nor Chesterton had the dreary boisterousness of the boon companion. Each was an original.

When Belloc wrote "The Path to Rome" he was following a recognized literary road—the writer of charm going alone upon a trip among strange people, laughing, learning, and then posing a little before the world. Stevenson had done just such a walk through the Cévennes, and his book about the journey had greatly pleased the sentimentalists. Rather earlier in history, Laurence Sterne had also told the story of his travels in France rather better than Stevenson (but as I am going to speak presently of Chesterton I must beware of saying anything ill of one of his idols) and had pleased even those who were not sentimentalists. And so Belloc knew what he was doing when he took this path and set down his account of what happened to him en route. But, miraculously, he avoided sentimentality; there was in him a certain robust and boyish courage and simplicity which, although he could chaff the reader and at times do a little bragging of one sort or another, gave "The Path to Rome" a character of its own. It remains Belloc's best long book, and the one by which most of his admirers would wish him first to be known. It is a tale of dangers run, and fears acknowledged, of hours enlivened by nonsense and accidentally good or evil meals. It is a chronicle of moods, a picture of mountains and forests and small towns, a traveller's tale, an enchanting monologue, and anything else the reader fancies. And it is the early work of a man who could already do anything he wished with his pen.

That, indeed, was one of Belloc's weaknesses—that he was always so much a master of his pen. He was too versatile for the mind of a public that prefers repetition. And furthermore it was sometimes difficult to discover at what point the serious Belloc yielded to the extravagant Belloc; for in the grand manner which he often used an able and humour-filled writer must often check himself sharply lest he guy his own grandeur. Let any reader take Belloc at his most serious, and then turn to his satirical novel, "Emmanuel Burden": it will be found that "Emmanuel Burden" contains passages, despite its satirical character, which strongly resemble Belloc at his most serious, and barely exceed the sonorousness of his more rhetorical mood. That does not happen in so finished and consummate a work of irony as "The Mercy of Allah," of course; but "The Mercy of Allah" is extremely mature, whereas "Emmanuel Burden," being experimental, is particularly interesting to the student of Belloc as showing his mind more fitfully playing between anger and pity, and particularly informing as showing the danger to a stylist of the power to burlesque all styles, including his own.

Even so, Belloc is a more persistent and sustained writer than Chesterton, who was best in short flights. To take one single work of his as an example, "The Flying Inn" is a laborious and aimless extravaganza, spoiled by the author's inability to keep upon one plane and by his uncertainty as to the particular plane he is occupying. But the lyrics in it, and single episodes or paragraphs where inspiration caught up the pen and made it caper, are sufficient to make "The Flying Inn" a book known to every man of humour in England. It would seem to have been an effort upon Chesterton's part to write a modern Peacockian novel; but Chesterton's is a rambling wit and not an incisive one, and the resemblance between "The Flying Inn" and the scholarly Peacock's "Melincourt" is in favour of the older book in all except the poetical passages. Here, indeed, Chesterton was on his own ground.

But if we compare a book such as "The Flying Inn" with the volumes of Father Brown stories we can see how admirably the Chestertonian genius is fitted to colour the slightest tale with magic. Whether we observe how a crime can be committed by a postman because nobody sees a postman (or any other quite familiar figure) entering a block of flats; or hear the steps of the tall man who is a guest to the waiters and a waiter to the guests and uses his opportunity to steal all the fish knives and forks of the "Twelve True Fishermen"; or imagine the velocity of a hammer flung from a church tower upon a villain below, we are taken entirely away from the world we live in and into a world of dreams and strangeness. And we are taken, not because the events are strange in themselves, but because the author mesmerises us with the aid of the genius which he conceals up his sleeve. It is the literary genius, and nothing else, which effects the mesmerism; for the charm of "The Hammer of

God," for example, would vanish if the story were told by any other writer. Father Brown mounts with the criminal, a clergyman, to a stone balcony about the tower of a church:

> "Immediately beneath and about them the lines of the Gothic building plunged outwards into the void with a sickening swiftness akin to suicide. There is that element of Titan energy in the architecture of the Middle Ages that, from whatever aspect it be seen, it always seems to be rushing away, like the strong back of some maddened horse. This church was hewn out of ancient and silent stone, bearded with old fungoids and stained with the nests of birds. And yet, when they saw it from below, it sprang like a fountain at the stars; and when they saw it, as now, from above, it poured like a cataract into a voiceless pit. For those two men on the tower were left alone with the most terrible aspect of the Gothic; the monstrous foreshortening and disproportion, the dizzy perspectives, the glimpses of great things small and small things great; a topsy-turvydom of stone in the mid-air. Details of stone, enormous by their proximity, were relieved against a pattern of fields and farms, pigmy in their distance. A carved bird or beast at a corner seemed like some vast walking or flying dragon wasting the pastures and villages below. The whole atmosphere was dizzy and dangerous, as if men were up-held in air amid the gyrating wings of colossal genii, and the whole of that old church, as tall and rich as a cathedral, seemed to sit upon the sunlit country like a cloud-burst."

In such a scene, how could any man not exchange with Father Brown the glance which confesses to murder?

These two men, Chesterton and Belloc, were essentially writers and dialecticians. They sported with ideas and imaginings for the enjoyment of sport; for as Belloc says:

> "Human affairs have always in them very strongly and permanently inherent, the character of a sport; the interest (at any rate of males) in the conduct of human life is always largely an interest of seeing that certain rules are kept, and certain points won, according to the rules."

They had greater skill in dialectical writing than any of their contemporaries excepting only Shaw. They had the gift of writing with peculiar simplicity and beauty, and the utmost clearness. But when it comes to what they write, it must be said that Belloc was governed by his passion for propositions; and that Chesterton was governed by his passion for antithesis. Belloc said "I shall show; I shall prove; I shall establish." He would show that the French Revolution turned upon and was conditioned by its military history. He would prove that Robespierre, a weak man, did not create the Terror, but resisted it and was unwillingly driven to it by others. He would establish that the dissolution of the monasteries in England in the sixteenth century was the beginning of the industrial revolution and the Capitalist system. But he does not convince us about the French Revolution or about Robespierre or about the dissolution of the monasteries for at least three reasons. The first of these reasons is that we already hold other views (the basis for which he ignores in spite of all clamour) as to the events; the second reason is that his style, being authoritative, is unfitted for persuasion; and the third reason is that despite every ingenuity he is unable in the communications he makes to fulfil the promise he has given. The third reason is the fatal reason.

Chesterton in the same way made propositions; but they were less peremptory and less serious than Belloc's. He did not say "I shall show." He said: "There is one metaphor of which the moderns are very fond; they are always saying, 'You can't put the clock back.' The simple and obvious answer is 'You can' . . . There is another proverb, 'As you have made your bed, so you must lie in it'; which again is simply a lie. If I have made my bed uncomfortable, please God I will make it again." But nobody, reading these remarks, can fail to make sufficient retorts to them; and the soundness of Chesterton's opinion is lost in a fritter of nonsense.

Now what can we do about such men? All who enjoy debate and the flexible use of thought and language must delight in their adroitness. All who can stand outside the stream of current opinion must observe how many ideas of virtue and value continually appear in their work. But when all is turmoil, as it is to-day, it is too much to expect that the occupants of a backwater will receive the proper rewards of literary genius. That is what happened to Belloc and Chesterton. They were regarded as old gentlemen doing whatever is the nautical equivalent of fiddling while Rome burns. For this reason their gifts—finally separated for ever from their views and resistances—will not be fully realized and acknowledged until at least a century has passed. How great those gifts were, in my opinion, could be stated only in terms which would seem at this time extravagant.

Chapter Five

FANCY FAIR

BARRIE, MILNE, JAMES STEPHENS

i

"VENABLES . . . You Scots, Mrs. Shand, are such a mixture of the practical and the emotional that you escape out of an Englishman's hand like a trout."

What Every Woman Knows.

IT cannot have escaped the notice of those who have been commended by Desmond MacCarthy as "alert, original men and women" that, so far, the only true-born Englishman to find a place in this book is H. G. Wells. I emphasize the fact, however, in view of constant generalizations as to the English character. We began our sketch of the Georgian literary scene with an American who became an Englishman only at the end of his life. We then continued with an Irishman and two men who are half-French. As the chapters follow, it will be found that an extraordinary number of English writers are Americans, Frenchmen, Scotsmen, Irishmen, Welshmen, Jews, South Africans, Australasians, and Poles. Let us look at our first Scotsman.

I suppose that Scottish invaders are outnumbered by the Irish, but I have not counted the two classes, and I must not stay to do so. The most celebrated Scots authors, apart from two kings who belong to earlier times, have been Hume, Adam Smith, Smollett, Boswell, Burns, Scott, Carlyle, Macaulay, Susan Ferrier, Dr. John Brown, William Black, and R. L. Stevenson; and it must be admitted, I think, that with the exception of Boswell all these writers—some of them very wrongly—are at the present moment estimated less highly than they have been in the past. Hume, though recommended, is never read; Adam Smith (whose economics are too simple for our intricate days) has received his quietus; Smollett has always been underrated, except by Robertson Nicoll; Burns as an original writer was rather blown-upon in the Henley-Henderson edition of his works; Scott, to my horror, is found dull; Carlyle, that admirable dramatist and rhetorician, has been daubed with the stigma of sexual chilliness or worse, and has been buried in a six-volume biography; Macaulay is the most traduced genius in English literature, since every Jack-in-the-box feels safe in accusing him of mud-slinging; William Black (although Justin McCarthy once witheringly dismissed Hardy as his inferior) and Susan Ferrier are alike forgotten;

and Stevenson is waiting for romanticism to come round again. The truth is that Scotland is out of the literary fashion.

That does not mean, of course, that Scottish authors remain unread. But it does mean that their names are less freely canvassed than of old. For one thing, ours is a day when reserves are suspect; and we have it on the authority of a Scots writer that whereas "the bolder Englishman (I am told) will write a love-chapter and then go out, quite coolly, to dinner, such goings-on are contrary to the Scotch nature; even the great novelists dared not. Conceive Mr. Stevenson left alone with a hero, a heroine, and a proposal impending (he does not know where to look). Sir Walter in the same circumstances gets out of the room by making his love scene take place between the end of one chapter and the beginning of the next." But that is only half the story. The Scots, being fundamentally sensual people, who would go raging mad if they allowed free rein to their emotions, long ago imposed severe restraints upon themselves, and became grave, cold, and haughty. Their domestic affections have always been strong; between those affections and the world they have interposed a barrier of pride and silence. This defence is rarely pierced from without; but, from within, the old Scottish character may be said to leak in a kind of superficial tenderness and sentiment. I have seen my own Scots grandfather move himself to tears merely by singing affecting notes. The words he sang did not matter; he cried because his voice was so beautiful.

Furthermore, there is a complacency about the Scots which is curiously combined with modesty. It is less objectionable to others than Yorkshire and Lancashire self-satisfaction, because it goes quietly deeper. Some men are troubled at the thought that others may be cleverer than they; the Scotsman has no such qualms. If he is humourless, it does not occur to him; if he is humorous, he has such playfulness of mind and such ingenuity of tongue that the problem is immediately dissolved and dispersed. Self-righteous the Scots may be, and it is a fault; but they are among the few people in the world who perceive and are amused by their own complacency, and who make jokes about it for the amusement of others. If they also stuff their emotions into the dark cupboard of the mind, and laugh and cry over the few remnants which have escaped concealment, we who are not Scotsmen can always bring our ever-ready contempt to the scene and dismiss the Scots as thrifty sentimentalists who make fortunes out of these by-products.

It was Stevenson who began the last Scottish revival. He told the world about a little Scots boy, and about a young man travelling about the world and charming everybody, and about the delights of make-believe; and in his hands Caledonia did not seem as stern and wild as had been supposed. It seemed a place where delightful children fancifully played in bed, or by the fireside, or out upon the hills; and English readers, who are always made to cry by anything about Ireland, thought that Scotland was nearly as touching, and somehow less harrowing and melodramatic than the sister isle. So at the end of the eighteen-eighties booksellers could not circulate tales of Scottish life fast enough to please their eager patrons. At that time a critic named "A.B.," whom I take to have been Augustine Birrell (his mother was Scottish), wrote in a weekly review that "what has happened so often before is happening now. Everybody is reading 'A Window in Thrums' and 'Auld Licht Idylls.' The instantaneous popularity of these two books," continued A.B., "is a beautiful thing. It is Faith's Restorative, for if it does not annihilate the doctrine of the Universal Depravity of the Human Race, it goes a long way to justify a belief in their Final Restoration. The author has conceded nothing to the public taste. May he never do so! Of sentiment, that odious onion, not a trace is to be found in these sweet-smelling pages."

"A Window in Thrums" and "Auld Licht Idylls" were not the only Scottish tales of that era; but they were the first essays in a new kind of book that immediately became the rage. They made Scotland not only charming but quaint. They enjoyed the applause of such pundits as A.B., who as you have seen thought them free from sentiment; and they went nevertheless directly home to the bosoms of men and women who judged with their hearts. And the author of these two books, who, without expecting to do so, had set a new fashion and created a new literary genre—the "kail-yard" or cabbage-patch novel—was a very small, quiet, pale Scots journalist named J. M. Barrie. He was unknown in London, not yet thirty years of age, the first Scotsman to take the town since Stevenson, and even then not so long after Stevenson. The public was already familiar in Stevenson's work with the Scots tongue as printed. It had expected nothing more in that line. But it now learned, with enthusiasm that grew from year to year until it resembled worship, that another genius had taken the road which, according to Dr. Johnson, offers the Scot the finest vista he will ever see. And although there were soon imitators of the new fashion who drove it at last into commonplace, Barrie himself went on to show that he had learnt more at his mother's knee than old memories of Thrums.

ii. James Matthew Barrie

"The horror of my boyhood was that I knew a time would come when I must give up the games, and how it was to be done I saw not. . . . I felt that I must continue playing in secret."

Margaret Ogilvy.

JAMES MATTHEW BARRIE was born at Kirriemuir, Forfarshire, on May 9th, 1860. He was his parents' second son, but his elder brother died while Barrie was very small, and from that time Barrie was the apple of the family eye. Kirriemuir was a tiny place; the Barries were poor; and the little boy had plenty of occasion for story-making. He was quick to imagine himself any kind of character he created in his fancy; and that is a habit which lasted to the end of his life, when he spoke to audiences less as J. M. Barrie than as some ghost, or fantastic figure of the past, whose opinions for the time he had appropriated. And he began to write stories before he was twelve years old. His first full-length novel was completed and offered to a publisher in the year before he went to Edinburgh University. It was rejected, with the assurance, nevertheless, that the author was "a clever little lady." That was a shock. For a time the impulse to write novels was checked.

But a literary life was the one for which Barrie pined; and as soon as he was able to do so he obtained a position as leader-writer on a Nottingham newspaper; and while he was there he began to send sketches, articles, and stories to the London press. It took him eighteen months to get his work accepted; but at last the first of the "Auld Licht Idylls" caught the attention of Frederick Greenwood, editor of *The St. James's Gazette*, who took it and asked for more. "There came to me," said Barrie, "as unlooked for as a telegram, the thought that there was something quaint about my native place."

Something quaint! That was exactly the key for which this talent had been waiting. He hastened to get more and more memories of the Kirriemuir of past days from his mother. "Now my mother might have been discovered, in answer to certain excited letters, flinging a bundle of undarned socks from her lap, and 'going in for literature'; she was racking her brains, by request, for memories I might convert into articles, and they came to me in letters which she dictated to my sisters." And when the articles had been published in sufficient number there arose the thought that they might be collected together into a book, and so make a bid for wider fame and fortune. "Auld Licht Idylls" was the result.

There was a slight difficulty about this, because publishers did not share the view of Frederick Greenwood as to the merits of the sketches of Scottish life. But at last a brother Scot, William Robert-

ARNOLD BENNETT

SOMERSET MAUGHAM

son Nicoll, a man whose nose for talent was uncannily sure, "found a wy," and the book was published. So was "A Window in Thrums." So was "When a Man's Single." And so, two years later, was "The Little Minister." Now "The Little Minister" differed from its predecessors in having a really old-fashioned and melodramatic story. It was a tremendous success; and it was dramatized, and had another tremendous success as a play. By this time Barrie had already begun to write original plays; and after Toole had produced one small skit on Ibsen which he had written he became the author of "Walker, London." When a little over thirty he was well known both as novelist and dramatist, and equally successful in both fields. From that time forward he could do nothing but add and add and add to his fame. The novels ceased with "Tommy and Grizel," in 1900, although a few later pieces of fiction appeared. But the plays went on, from "The Professor's Love Story," in 1895; "Quality Street," "The Admirable Crichton," and "Little Mary" in 1903; and "Peter Pan" in 1904; to "Dear Brutus" in 1917, "Mary Rose" in 1920, and "The Boy David," an almost posthumous failure, in 1937. "Shall We Join the Ladies?" produced in 1922, was but the fragment of a play which nobody as yet has ever quite known how to finish.

Towards the end of his days Barrie amused himself by accepting a baronetcy and various academic honours. He took to speaking in public. And he was rigorously condemned to exclusion from polite literature for an attitude to life which exasperated the "modn" movement. I shall come presently to that criticism and its justification.

iii

MYSELF. I had a letter the other day from an old friend of mine. She said: "I don't envy you anything except knowing Barrie."
BARRIE (gravely). Then she'd better not meet him.

WHEN he was a young man, portraits used to appear at times in the press which showed a little pale face, a tiny moustache, and an enormous brow. I am under the impression that in those days brows were worn high; and Barrie's was both high and broad. As time passed his face filled out and grew less pale, more full of character, more full of melancholy; and the brow became somehow less conspicuous. But then Barrie's whole appearance was inconspicuous, for he was one of the smallest writers who ever lived. He gave the impression of being very broad in the shoulder; he cared nothing at all for dress; and his little figure in general passed unnoticed. Quite different from Shaw, who, being tall and thin, strode along in woollen gloves and without an overcoat as if he were in training for a London to Brighton race. Quite different from Wells, who radiated

D

a sedate cheerfulness and, when he saw you from afar, was immediately full of the mock insult he would deliver at meeting. Quite different from anybody else, as one would expect. Totally different from the impression which might be formed of the author of a Barrie play. Smoking a great big pipe, in winter wearing a half-buttoned great-coat and hard felt hat, he (unlike the late Hall Caine, who could not help being spectacular) expected to pass unnoticed, and seemed unconscious of his surroundings. He was not unconscious. He was merely not self-conscious.

In company he was silent—unless cricket was mentioned, when silence departed from him, and he was filled with great eloquence. On the subject of cricket he was invincible. I remember one cold day many years ago—an English cricket team was at the time touring Australia—that I felt a touch on my arm, and turned to find that Barrie had caught sight of me and stopped. We had barely spoken; and the cold was such that the tears in our eyes were far from being those of sentiment; when a newsboy passed, shouting "Test Match Clozer Play." With incredible alacrity, Barrie deserted me, drew a penny from his pocket, and grabbed a paper, into which he completely disappeared for several minutes. On another occasion, A. G. Gardiner was invited by another friend to join Barrie and himself at lunch. Gardiner did not know Barrie very well, and tried his hardest to find a topic upon which Barrie would open his mouth. At last, in despair, he spoke of something that interested himself—cricket. He had no further difficulty, except that (he was a loud-voiced man) of making himself heard.

In 1919, after arranging the publication of Daisy Ashford's "The Young Visiters," I thought that a preface by Barrie would mean a great deal to the success of that strange and delightful work. So, as Daisy Ashford did not know Barrie, I had her permission to show him the typescript and boldly ask for his help. I sent the script, and made the request. Barrie refused a preface. He did not even think the story would be a success in book form. But he offered to write an article round it, and to give Daisy Ashford all the money he received for his article. It was my turn to refuse. I assured him that "The Young Visiters" was to be published; and asked if I might call.

I found him a pathetically sick man. Our conversation was marked by slowness and hesitation upon his side, and promptness on my own. He said: "I can't write the preface." I said: "It would make all the difference to the book." He said: "You ought to do it yourself." I said: "Nobody would care tuppence." He said: "E. V. Lucas would write a good preface." I said: "A splendid preface; an ideal preface. But your name on the title-page would make all the difference." He said: "Anstey Guthrie would write a fine preface."

I said: "I have not a doubt of it; but three words by you would take the book into every household that will find it funny." He said: "——(I forget who this was) would be quite a good man to write a preface." I said nothing at all. Barrie quailed before that silence. He said, now very ill indeed: "I see I've got to write this preface." I left him.

Subsequently Cabinet Ministers argued as to whether Barrie or Daisy Ashford had written the whole book. One woman journalist, meeting me in the street, fixed me with a demoniacal eye and demanded: "Did *he*, or did *she*?" "The Young Visiters" sold over a hundred and thirty thousand copies in England alone, and nearly twice that number in the United States; Barrie received nothing for his preface; and Daisy Ashford became a small heiress, married, and lived to bless her sponsor. I tell the story to illustrate Barrie's diffidence and generosity; but I wonder whether it does not also a little justify that romantic view of life proper to the author of "Sentimental Tommy."

iv

"Sometimes his emotion masters him completely, at other times he can step aside, as it were, and take an approving look at it!"

Sentimental Tommy.

BESIDES being the first Scotsman, Barrie is the first sentimentalist to figure in our panorama of the Georgian literary world. It was all very well for the A.B. whom I have quoted to say that there was no sentiment in "Auld Licht Idylls" and "A Window in Thrums," for we know he meant that these books are free from gross appeals to our lachrymal glands. He could hardly have repeated his commendation after reading "The Little Minister" and "Sentimental Tommy." One either reads the later novel with an all-indulgent smile or tear, or one fidgets, or one breaks into stentorian curses. To explain why this is so I should have to write a great tome on the nature of life and the value of differing interpretations of human nature. I am sure that no reader wishes this.

But I will try to make a distinction. Shaw said that men are self-deceiving humbugs, and that women are the instruments of what he calls the Life Force. Wells said that in a clean and orderly universe men and women would lead sexually commonsense lives, but that the men of to-day who plan great advances in science have their work seriously interfered with by the intrusion of sexual affairs. He was never voluptuous in describing these affairs. If he had been, he would have had little trouble with watch committees and censors. It was because he tried to justify freedom of conduct on grounds that upset Christian ethics that he had his black and prosperous days of "banning." Henry James saw men and women as strange oblique minds—not bodies—touching each other, glancing off, endlessly swimming in extraordinary comprehensions which common readers do not share. Belloc and Chesterton hardly at all concerned themselves with men and women as men and women; both were born allegorists and dealers in fantasy. But to Barrie women were tender motherly creatures and men were their little boys.

To an age which has been taught to ridicule parents (I do not say that it is wrong to ridicule parents) this conception appears so thoroughly preposterous that Barrie's sincerity is suspect. A wrong conclusion. The book he wrote about his mother—it is called "Margaret Ogilvy"—is both affecting and sincere. The relationship pictured in it is quite sufficient (even without the Freudian gloss) to account for the turn of all Barrie's work. She was his sweetheart. It was a joke in his family that every heroine he drew was but another portrait of her; and none more teasingly and complacently accepted the identification than the mother herself. But few now wish to believe in the tender motherly woman; and most of us feel that the boy who will not grow up is a trifle emasculated.

That is one aspect; here is another. By some dispensation, each one of us carries in his heart a little ideal self-portrait. Whatever we do has somehow to be adjusted to this picture; and whether we are æsthetes who regard our taste as too fastidious for toleration of the second-rate, or whether we are proud of being amusing, or whether we picture ourselves as loving—and loved by—all dear little things, or as disillusioned, or as pillars of moral indignation, or whether (like myself) we are so clever that we get right round behind these fantasies and reach a state of what looks to others very much like nonentity, we keep the ideal portrait as a sort of model. Now to play to a model, or to imitate oneself, is sentimentality. It is self-complacency in action. We have a lot of it nowadays tricked up as intellectual anger, disgust, or contempt for the familiar; but in its simple form it is sentimentality as Barrie illustrated it in "Sentimental Tommy."

Tommy Sandys, you will remember, could move himself to tears by a kind of impersonation of somebody or something heroic or pathetic or romantic, and at other times could "step aside, as it were, and take an approving look" at his own emotion. Barrie's sentimentality was this sentimentality. To those who are sentimental in other ways it was and is a source of acute discomfort. But just as egoists are mordant observers of the foibles of other men, sentimentalists, while observing themselves with pleasure, do not entirely spare the rest of mankind. In his three best plays. "The Admirable Crichton," "Dear Brutus," and "The Twelve Pound

Look," Barrie was almost cruelly critical of those who were neither mothers nor little boys. It may be said that these plays are sentimental; they do not, it may be, go to the very bottom of the human mind. But they are amusing, astringent, and pointed. Each presents, in the guise of a simple situation, a parable from nature.

"The Admirable Crichton," the first of them, depicts the experiences of a small party wrecked upon an island without inhabitants. Immediately a change in the relationship of the various members of the party begins. The man who, in a state where privilege is all-powerful, is a butler, assumes command; the others find their own level. Only when rescue is achieved does the old order re-establish itself, and all, ironically, is as before—but not quite as before. "Dear Brutus," written some years later, collects a number of unsatisfied men and women upon Midsummer Eve, all of whom believe that if—something other than what they have— could be theirs they would be happy; and gives them, in a fairy wood, a chance to realize their dreams. The melancholy result—so salutary, so convincing, and so saddening to the beholder—is shown to be that if they could all have what they hanker for they would be no better satisfied than they now are.

> "The fault, dear Brutus, is not in our stars,
> But in ourselves, that we are underlings."

Finally, "The Twelve Pound Look" is about a professional typist, once a wife, who had left her vulgar husband years before, and had been divorced by him. In the play, she is by chance engaged by the quondam husband to type letters of thanks for congratulations upon a new honour, is recognized by her husband, and pressed by him to tell the name of the man for whom she has sacrificed her position. She answers that there was no man, but that her liberty was of more value than anything he could give her. When assured by the husband that he is now worth a quarter of a million pounds, she answers that he is worth no more than twelve pounds, the sum she has paid for her typewriter and liberty. Husbands are warned to beware of the "twelve pound look" upon their wives' faces; and indeed this same look is discovered before the end of the play upon the face of the wife's successor.

These plays were not the work of a man well content with the world as it is; they were the work of a man who demurely presented his ideas in the form of parables. They are not the work of a man with abounding energy, such as Shaw, but of one who sat quietly in his chimney corner turning over the disillusions of a lifetime and giving them this wry little twist to make them tolerable to himself. The same ideas, treated grimly or exuberantly, might be more impressive, but they would not be more profound.

Treated grimly, they would strike most audiences as fairly bitter; treated with fancy, as they are, they may appear more bitter still. Certainly, with all their fancy, they are not happy plays. Beautifully neat, so that in public performance every shade is retained and a wealth of what Pooh Bah called "corroborative detail" of the theatre is added, they read, especially with the acid introductory stage directions, as unsmiling comments upon a world that is past helping. If, as I believe, the charm and the stealthy and subtle humour are no more than superficial—the play of a mind that works best in the darkness; but a subtle mind, even where it avoids the full implications of its own discoveries—they illumine very particularly the nature of the talent, I think the genius, from which they rise.

This genius is expressly a Scottish genius, one which never dares to regard literature (I grant the exception of Burns) as a field for the display of emotion. Excepting for superb passages in "The Heart of Midlothian," I do not recall any Scottish prose writing in which the author's imagination is allowed to range free. Always, with Scottish writers, either timidity or restraint or some personal or thematic hobble keeps them from attempting grandeur or the grandiose. It is as if they all said "Let me first of all be safe." That is not what they say, of course; it is only what they seem to say; but the effect is the same. The effect is that there is always measure alike in the work and in our response to it.

I say this of Barrie's finest work, which I take to lie in the three plays just described. Only in the case of one play of his can the response be called unmeasured; and this play unfortunately is the one by which he is always judged. "Peter Pan," the children's entertainment which is less a play than a portmanteau of games and insights, has given the utmost pleasure to many children and many adults for more than half a century. Lines from it, remembered from the past, are as familiar to grown-up children as lines from the Gilbert and Sullivan operas. And yet as one recalls "Peter Pan," and its admitted charms for many, one does, I think, hesitate. Although there has been no entertainment for children which approaches it in popularity in the whole of modern theatrical history, and although it has contributed greatly, I surmise, to the decline and fall of the English Christmas pantomime, there is in "Peter Pan" something approaching an exploitation of the child mind. As it entertains, so it deceives. When Peter says that "to die will be an awfully big adventure," he becomes intolerable. When he demands to know whether the audience believes in fairies, and poor over-excited tots thunder out their applause, we may wonder whether Barrie was a human being or a demon. For Barrie himself never believed in fairies.

This you will say is a moral criticism. So it is. But surely it also suggests why "Peter Pan" has been the chief cause of Barrie's decline in critical esteem. It is to entertain the children; that is agreed. So was "Alice in Wonderland." And yet "Alice in Wonderland" contains not the smallest hint of sentimentality. It is genuine gold throughout. There is not the smallest hint of sentimentality in any one of the Gilbert and Sullivan operas, which are genuine gold throughout. "Peter Pan" is sentimental. For this reason Barrie's work is now seriously undervalued by many who, if they knew the major plays and the early books of Kirriemuir sketches, would recognize in it a positive contribution to modern letters.

v. Alan Alexander Milne

"In conclusion, I must distress my friend J. M. Barrie (who gave me a first chance) by acknowledging my great debt to him. It would be more polite to leave him out of it, but I cannot let him off."

A. A. Milne: Preface to First Plays.

IT would also be more politic on my part, in writing of A. A. Milne, to omit reference to Barrie; but I, too, cannot let him off. Barrie was here first, and Milne would have been Milne if Barrie had never lived (make no mistake about that); but there are such parallels between the two that I want to introduce Milne here and now, instead of waiting until, in a manner of speaking, he is old enough to enter the book as a full-grown author.

Alan Alexander Milne was born on January 18th, 1882. His father was the schoolmaster whose preparatory school in Kilburn has already been mentioned; and Milne's association with modern writers began early. Those who are amused by such accidents will be glad to know that there is reproduced in the *Henley House Magazine* a photograph which shows H. G. Wells as a wispy young assistant master, and Milne as a ringleted child of about eight years old. He later went to Westminster School, and then to Trinity College, Cambridge. At Cambridge he edited *The Granta*, and upon returning to London he immediately became a contributor to *Punch*. He was sub-editor of *Punch* for eight years, and left the staff to fight in the line during the first European War.

Punch, therefore, is the key to Milne (or it has been assumed to be the key by those who think keys are derisory symbols). In its pages he made his first reputation; and his initials were familiar during several years to every reader of the paper. They appeared week by week at the end of the lightest of trifles, in which nonsense had such wings that the solid-minded could not in those days entirely distinguish it from silliness. They did not appear in connection with the smaller quips filling each tiny corner, or in connection with his more arduous sub-editorial labours. Few people realized that the trifling A.A.M. was in fact a very hard-working journalist, with no time at all to indulge his fancy for the luxury of play-writing. But Wars, as we know, change all things; and between 1914 and 1918, while other subalterns forgot horrors in games of chance or by writing poetry, Milne began in leisure hours to produce the plays upon which his heart was set. He is thus a First World War and inter-War dramatist, and his second reputation was made in the inter-War theatre.

Now it cannot be denied that Milne had a delightful unseen collaborator in his wife, who belonged to a talented and much-confounded family of writers and scholars,—the de Sélincourts. She did not write his plays for him (although she sometimes wrote with much wit, I can testify, his letters to old friends); but she was in fact the essential audience for them, and it is to her equal relish for nonsense that they owe a continued and unfailing lightness of raillery. That raillery, so unforced and so unaffected, was natural in the Milne household; and those who judge Milne's work without knowledge of its spontaneity miss the fact that his was an easy and impulsive wit, just as those who judge it from a hostile viewpoint miss the fact that if he had written otherwise he would have been egregiously false to his own experience.

Finally, it is now many years since *The Times* announced that a son, described as "Billy," had been born to the Milnes. That name, Billy, must have been soon discarded; for the name of Christopher Robin Milne has long been as familiar to thousands of readers as that of Peter Pan himself. And having written, to please himself, a number of poems and stories for and about Christopher Robin, Milne presently published some of the poems in a book, and this made his third reputation, that of a writer of verses for and about the children of pleasantly circumstanced parents in two hemispheres. The verses were followed by stories which supported and supplemented the third reputation.

Three reputations made in twenty years—unless we call them four, on account of "The Red House Mystery";—and as many reputations, of course, to be assailed by all who find the combination of lightness of heart with love of virtue an anachronism in the modern sceptic world. I think it must be said that to the "modns" Barrie and Milne are the least acceptable of all modern writers. Why this is so I have shown in the case of Barrie, and I shall presently show in the case of Milne. Meanwhile I am going to ask what kind of man wrote "The Day's Play," "Michael and Mary," "The Red House Mystery," "When We Were Very Young," and "Winnie the Pooh"? Although some critics think that one should take no heed of the author in estimating the quality of his work, that is not my notion; and in Milne's case the relation of man to work is especially interesting. Our judgment of that work, I agree, should not depend upon the author's moral character; but whether we mean to do so or not we do react to the personality of any author whose work we read, and far too many critics believe that because they like or dislike a mental attitude they are in fact dispassionately assessing a talent. As a boy in one of Milne's plays puts it: "Why are you the devil of a fellow if you like drinking whisky, and the devil of a prig if you don't?" Or in other words, why are you the devil of an artist if you write about prostitutes, and the devil of a literary prostitute if you don't? "The gentleman," says C. R. W. Nevinson, "cannot be an artist." One of the half-truths; for an artist may be a gentleman. But even if it were true, it is equally true that art is no concern of that shoddy cynic, the man-of-the-world.

Milne was so far out of the literary fashion that he failed to detest his parents. His parents had previously failed to ill-treat and misunderstand him. He failed to detest his school and his school-fellows. He failed to have furtive adolescent sexual misadventures which left him with burning hatred of all females and an illicit love for some fellow male. He married early, and his marriage failed to be a failure. He had one son, who failed to disappoint or to hate him. And his life failed to be disagreeable in every particular, perhaps because he failed to be as unpleasant as possible to every person he met. As the same boy whom I quoted a moment ago tells his young wife: "I'm respectable. That's what's the matter with me really." And the young wife sympathetically adds: "Public School, University and M.C.C." If I may again add an interpretation: Not a social misfit. Therefore not a rebel. That is very important.

In appearance Milne was extremely, extraordinarily fair. He was of the middle height—perhaps a little above it;—and to the end of his life was as slim as he was when he first came down from Cambridge. His eyes were very blue, his face thin but not pale, and on meeting him one realized at once that he had an active and quickly—smoothly—working mind. There are authors who look stupid and angry; nobody could miss the intelligence of Milne's expression, and the ready but not especially effulgent kindness of his agreeable smile. An observer who knew nothing of his books and plays would have seen that the face was notably keen and handsome, free from any sign of malice or cruelty, but lacking in what I may call the lines of boisterousness. He would not at first have found it easy to understand what Milne said, owing to the inaudibility and little slurring quickness of his speech. He would have noticed that, like Barrie, Milne was devoted to the game of cricket.

Milne dressed with marked taste and care (I mean no more than that); and he walked at a considerable speed without looking very much at those who passed him. I do not think he was at all interested in the casual. Certainly he was not interested in manufacturing conversation with strangers. An American visitor to England was once left sitting with Milne on a log while the rest of a cordial houseparty went for a longish walk. Upon their return, the walkers found Milne and the American still sitting on the log, perfectly content, and still in the attitudes in which they had been last seen; and the American joined his hostess for the short journey back to the house. As they strolled, he said thoughtfully: "You English are a wonderful people. You convey so much. And yet you don't say a word."

Unlike the man whose mind is unoccupied, then, Milne did not tirelessly volunteer conversation. Nor, however, did he repress it in others, as do the haughty; a fact from which I draw an inference concerning Milne the writer as well as Milne the man. The inference is that while plentifully blessed (as Barrie was) with fancy, and even more plentifully blessed than Barrie with verbal adroitness (as witness his versification), he did not command that gift of the great romancers and novelists, a profuse fecundity of invention. Although by no means unappreciative of these traits in other men, he was deficient in vulgarity, in energy, in largeness of thought, and in exuberance of action.

Milne's first books consisted of reprinted pieces from *Punch*, the slight sketches to which I have already referred. They were delightful nonsense. His children's verses are familiar, innocent, arch, and charmingly turned; the prose tales for children, which I find less excellent, are full of happy fancies and agreeable sentiment. His one detective story stands high among the lighter examples of a popular craft. All these books have a polish and bubble iridescence that secure them large numbers of admirers. But it is by his plays that Milne has made his most ambitious claim to attention, and, finally, it is upon his plays that the critic must concentrate.

The first of them, apparently, was "Wurzel-Flummery," the story of a trick played upon two proud men by a dying eccentric who left each a fortune on condition that each changed his name to Wurzel-Flummery. A name, as those who have read Lamb's "Mr. H." well know, is not a strong theme for a play, and "Wurzel-Flummery," which began in three acts, is now printed in one. "Belinda," another trifle, remains in three acts, and is about an inconsequent woman, her daughter (newly returned from a convent school), a long-missing husband, and two absurd suitors—one of them a juvenile poet, the other a middle-aged statistician. Here again the theme is slight to tenuity. Here again the amusingness of the play lies almost entirely in the persiflage which passes between shallow and very pleasing persons until the curtain falls. Both plays were very much like *Punch* sketches written in dialogue form at greater length; both were extremely nonsensical; "Belinda" gave a delicious part to one of the most charming actresses the English stage has known; but neither play had what may be called an "idea." The story in each case was just sufficient to hold together the various nimble sayings of the actors, and no more. But "Belinda" held the first of those former or missing husbands who have figured so prominently in the Milne drama.

"Mr. Pim Passes By" was about another of them;—but this time the husband did not appear, and in fact he did not (at the moment of the play's action) exist. Another delicious part for the same actress, and a success for the author in the commercial theatre. From "Mr. Pim" onwards, a Milne play has been a recognized type of theatrical entertainment. I shall not at the moment dwell upon the minor plays, except to notice that former and either desirable or undesirable husbands figure in at least two of them—"To Have the Honour" and "Michael and Mary";—but shall go straight to Milne's most considerable dramatic work.

"The Truth about Blayds," an ambitious piece which had only a short run in London, is about an almost centenarian poet who has carried on a lifelong literary imposture. At the end of the first act he dies. And as he dies he whispers with his last breath to the daughter whose life he has spoilt the fact that he did not write the poetry upon which his tremendous reputation has been built. He has stolen the profuse work of a dead friend and passed it off as his own. The remaining acts turn upon the posthumous incredulity and dismay of his family, and their relief when they invent a formula with which to discredit the confession and when they discover a will by which they legally retain the fruits of the old man's shame.

The second play, "Success," is about a prominent and careerist Cabinet Minister who has old memories stirred, meets again the only girl he ever loved, re-lives (visibly, in an interpolated dream scene) the days of his childhood, determines to relinquish career for love, and then, just when the crucial moment arrives, is pulled back to the baseness of politics by the offer of the Chancellorship.

Both "Success" and "The Truth about Blayds" failed in the theatre; the latter not unexpectedly, the former through an error in popular judgment. "Blayds" began with a serious and deeply interesting first act; but as soon as the situation had been grasped the play ceased to amuse, and was even a cause of some discomfort to those who saw it. "Success," which I never saw but which I have read more than once, was badly received by the dramatic critics, who thought that Milne, by giving it that title, had dared to presume upon their favourable verdict and the public response. It was an injustice. "Success" had more feeling in it than any other play of Milne's, was extremely skilful, both as to plan and character, and was full of good, quick, effective dialogue. It deserved quite another fate than failure.

But both plays have the weakness which it seems to me is apparent in Milne's work whenever he is most serious; that is, they suffer from a kind of punitive zeal against wrongdoing. Milne had such a contempt for backsliders and materialists and sycophants that he could not withhold a moral foreclosure which affects the structure of his play. Barrie, after seeing "The Truth about Blayds" (the first play by Milne, I believe, of which he had not read the typescript), is said to have remarked, with a wise theatre man's laconism, "I should have kept the old man alive"; and this comment, by whomsoever it was made, is really, as one thinks of it, devastating. It is much more than a technical criticism. It goes to the root of the whole question. For "Blayds," which might have been a great comedy about an imposter, shifts its centre to the impostor's dependants, ignominious indeed, but of no significance. To castigate the meanness and hypocrisy of those who, after an earthquake, are trying to pretend that there has been a shower, is to bully the demoralized.

Similarly, in "Success," although the reawakening of Mannock is made credible with extraordinary skill (this is quite Milne's best play), and his downfall before temptation is exciting and convincing, a moral judgment—not a doom—hangs over the entire play. It is not tragedy, but an arraignment. I suggest that owing to his knowledge that Mannock was going to collapse, and his bitter dislike of venality, Milne was unable to allow Mannock as much character as he should have done. So the fall is not great enough, because Mannock has throughout flown too low; the failure of a bigger man would have been a greater loss to his true love, and would have moved us more.

I had in mind this criticisn of Milne's work when I said that he was deficient in certain qualities of the great romancers. At times his invention is meagre; it is always hampered by a lack of boldness, an inability to shake off the author's strict moral standards. Thus, while in every play the dialogue is fresh and full of life, the content of the play, where it is not a jest, is too often conventional.

I do not mean only conventional in the theatrical sense, and yet it is true that on the whole these plays of Milne's deal with a life peculiar to the theatre. I say no more as to the husbands who turn up or who refrain from turning up; but what of the wives to whom these husbands have in the past belonged? They at least are principals in the action. If their husbands come and go in this wanton manner, do not the wives also lose something of acceptable reality? A husband who is mislaid as if he were an article of jewellery may serve as a pretext for drama; but the wife, charming chatterbox though she be, who merely resumes her life as if she said, "Dear me, I don't seem to have a husband this morning; never mind, I expect he'll turn up again some time," does put a slight strain upon our credulity. Of course these ladies are before us: we see them, we hear them, we relish their wit. But when they leave the stage, or when we leave the theatre, we cannot help feeling that they have been only make-believe wives, make-believe women, like the dolls which little girls ask to tea-parties and forget as soon as they have been put to bed.

That is the character of the Milne drama,—make-believe. In a sense it is the character of the Barrie drama. Here are embodied whimsies, delicious fancies, nonsensical dreams, tender memories of play and young illusion, an enchanting aptness of phrase, sometimes a piercing revelation of unseen things, a charm that is not poetic but half-real, half-arbitrary, in the manner of a child's game. But neither Barrie nor Milne ever, it seems to me, goes quite the whole hog. Neither deals quite with the real world or quite with the world of faery. The real world is too harsh, or at least too stubborn, for fanciful treatment; the world of faery too incredible. Once we listen to the coaxing, winning "Let's pretend," we are at the mercy of both authors; but they know as well as we do that they are pretending. A time will come when they will put away the toys and return to reality as represented by the grown-up evening newspaper. They will not absolutely let go at any time of the pleasant normal circumstances of well-bred and easy-mannered society.

vi. James Stephens

"SHADBOLT: I am to lie?
POINT: Heartily. But thy lie must be a lie of circumstance."
The Yeoman of the Guard.

ONCE more taking advantage of the loose structure of this book for my own purposes, I proceed to illustrate the foregoing by reference to another writer who is not a Scotsman and who has no Scots blood. It could not be said that the inhibitions which check the Scots have any effect upon the Irish. Where the Scot bent upon a spree first counts his money, the Irishman never troubles. Where the Scot makes a point of catching his train, an Irishman will accept a shakedown for the night and may stay, regardless of any physical discomfort, for a week's fine talking. And where a Scotsman, who loves truth as a miser loves gold, will hesitate to tell any story which has not at least a substratum of truth and a somewhat strictly assessed degree of probability, an Irishman in unaware that his own truth has

any limits whatever. In this way Scottish writers have been economists, biographers, and historians, and when they have turned to
fiction have been often *historical* novelists (using the national bent
for the antiquarian); but Irish writers have been poets, dramatists,
and fabulists of the most luxuriant order, and when they have
essayed history or biography have never been able to command the
assent of their fellow-countrymen in such measure as to establish
permanent reputations for themselves or their works.

The writer who illustrates my remarks on the caution with
which Barrie and Milne leave the familiar is James Stephens; and
James Stephens, accordingly, is like Milne brought forward among
the older writers in spite of the fact that he, too, was born in the
year 1882. The place of his birth was Dublin, and the place of his
later residence was London. But if you look in the reference books
you will find no more than the date of his birth (if that) and the
titles of his works (or some of his works). I do not know what his
father was, or what were the circumstances of his early life. I only
know that when he was old enough to begin to earn money he
worked for a time in the office of a Dublin attorney, and that later,
through the intervention of Thomas Bodkin, one time Director of the
Birmingham Art Gallery, he was for a few years engaged in some
occupation requiring his daily attendance at the Dublin Art Gallery.

But he was not so much absorbed in routine as to disregard the
development of his own gifts; and I remember that in 1909 the
London newspaper, *The Daily Chronicle*, then a literary power,
reviewed at column-length a small book of what were considered
very bold poems entitled "Insurrections," the nature of which
review (coupled with the support rendered by quotations from the
book itself) was enough to send a friend and myself straight to the
publishers for copies of "Insurrections" and to keep us for an hour
busy in reading or quoting its more vigorous stanzas. When, shortly
afterwards, I noticed that a story called "Mary Make-believe" was
being serialized in some publication, and recognized the author's
name as that of the insurrectionary poet, I subscribed to the publication and thus read the fairy tale subsequently published in book
form as "The Charwoman's Daughter." In Dublin, no doubt (for
"Insurrections" was dedicated to A E), Stephens was already well
known. In London he had still to make a reputation.

"The Crock of Gold" followed in 1912, and established that
reputation. "Here are Ladies" came in 1913, and "The Demi-gods"
in 1914. Having thus made innumerable readers his toys, Stephens
visited America, lectured with something like triumph, making
many Americans his slaves, wrote and published further poems, and
at last for the time being abandoned Dublin. He settled in a London
suburb, and from this suburb he regularly descended upon the

West End for the sake of intellectual conversation with his peers, until one day he collapsed in a London Street.

In person Stephens was small and slight. His face was old with, I think, resemblances (but these may be solely those of brow and natural tonsure) to that of Oliver Goldsmith;—and a droll face, the face of one who dwells for ever in a world mocked and twisted by fairies. It has been said to me by the Irish that he was exactly like a leprechaun; but I have never seen a leprechaun, and I cannot say if the description was just. He was a talker. He talked more magnificently than any other person I ever met. He recited poetry better than anybody else I ever heard—better even than Desmond MacCarthy, who recited very beautifully;—and would embark upon an evening's monologue without the smallest hesitation. His mind was quick, rich, unhesitating; his interests so varied that he was never at a loss for illustration or metaphor. Across his droll face stole constantly a little dry, quiet, melancholy smile, as if the consuming laughter of his hearers, being long continued, at last, for an instant, had conquered his gravity. When he related something which might seem incredible to the listener he prefaced the narrative, and its chief wonders, with two small grunts—hng-hng—as if to give fair warning that he had something inspired to reveal. He did not monopolize conversation; but when he spoke it was from an original knowledge of art and life before which the accomplished wit of the sophisticate lost virtue.

His later work very slightly resembled the poems which were published in "Insurrections" (these, I admit, have in the passage of years lost something of their first pungency, but not all of it); and in narrative has all the whispered assurance of the folk tale. Indeed, it is of the character of the folk tale, reinforced by an intricacy of saying and allusion such as only a witty mind could invent and keep of a piece with the whole. First it is a tale, and then it is philosophy, and then it is nonsense; but all these qualities are so merged and, for the reader, confounded, that the effect is one of deep laughter. At no time is there a hiatus between what is thought and what is said; all is of the same relish.

This is a very rare quality. It is not found even in Chesterton's fantastic narratives, for in such a book, for example, as "The Flying Inn," Chesterton several times uses the word "absurd" or "ridiculous" in a conventional sense, as if imagination had failed him and he admitted his make-believe to be a fake. Stephens makes no such mistake. His imagining is unaffected by interruption from an outside and alien judgment. He never sniggers. For this reason he commands us entirely, as Lewis Carroll does, who for as long as a book lasts never interposes Kensington into Wonderland. Thus, where Chesterton's fairies are but figures of rhetoric, and Barrie's are little bells and flitting lights, Stephens's are as cunning as the elves in old tales, before cleverness came to quiz invention.

> "In the centre of the pine wood called Coilla Doraca there lived not long ago two Philosophers . . . Their faces looked as though they were made of parchment, there was ink under their nails, and every difficulty that was submitted to them, even by women, they were able to instantly resolve. The Grey Woman of Dun Gortin and the Thin Woman of Inis Magrath asked them the three questions which nobody had ever been able to answer, and they were able to answer them. That was how they obtained the enmity of these two women which is more valuable than the friendship of angels. The Grey Woman and the Thin Woman were so incensed at being answered that they married the two Philosophers in order to be able to pinch them in bed, but the skins of the Philosophers were so thick that they did not know they were being pinched. They repaid the fury of the women with such tender affection that these vicious creatures almost expired of chagrin, and once, in a very ecstasy of exasperation, after having been kissed by their husbands, they uttered the fourteen hundred maledictions which comprised their wisdom, and these were learned by the Philosophers who thus became even wiser than before."

That is the opening of "The Crock of Gold," and it is typical both of Stephens and of the Irish invention. I do not pretend to be able to explain why no Scotsman would write in that way; but it shows why Irishmen, who in general have no sense of humour, must frequently laugh as they con lists of great English authors, to find in those lists the names of so many of their compatriots.

Chapter Six

TRAVELLERS

R. B. CUNNINGHAME GRAHAM, W. H. HUDSON,
JOSEPH CONRAD, H. M. TOMLINSON,
NORMAN DOUGLAS

i

"Where are the Spanish Main, the Guianas, and the Brazils? . . . They are in Raleigh's *Golden City of Manoa*, in Burney's *Buccaneers of America*, with Drake, Humboldt, Bates, and Wallace. . . . We borrow the light of an observant and imaginative traveller, and see the foreign land bright with his aura; and we think it is the country which shines."

H. M. Tomlinson: The Sea and the Jungle.

EVERY division of this book is arbitrary; and by "travellers" I mean, not men who go to some country to observe customs and practices, flora and fauna, for the sake of writing scientifically about them, but men to whom the life of cities is as disagreeable as life in a cage must be to the wild bird. Also men who have crystallized their experiences into tales and personal narratives marked by style giving them interest as literature. The archetype of such men in modern letters is Herman Melville, traveller, romantic, and superabundantly eloquent writer. In some instances those grouped in this chapter were born free; in others they have escaped from conventional life and have wandered far; all, whether free or bound, have brought to contemporary literature the atmosphere of distant lands and what seems to ordinary citizens the romance of violent and exceptional adventure.

How have they been able to do this? For that re-creation of the strange is something very different from the re-creation of the recognizable which has proceeded simultaneously in the more typical fiction of the period. Well, it is probable that in the first twenty years of their lives the majority of men accumulate all the fresh personal experience they are ever to enjoy. They are young for just that period, and no more. The conventional age early; the scholastically trained do not age, but they tend to prefer books to adventure; those who are neither conventional nor academic may nevertheless find a sufficient range in the life of cities. When they are no longer young, all may learn consciously, and with effort, and perhaps with greater intelligence; they can still suffer, and thereby create a flying illusion of renewed youth; but for the creative writer nothing whatever can take the place of that impulsive, unconsidered susceptibility to experience which is unreflective and almost wholly emotional. For the creative writer, that is, a prolonged youth is Fortune's greatest gift.

The men I have called travellers have been bent first of all upon adventure, "seeing the world," and embracing its opportunities. They have been non-academic in education. They have been able to keep young for longer than other men. But, having seen the world, they have thought, in the manner of all men born to be writers, that they would like to tell the world what they thought of it. So they have taken to the pen with much of the enthusiasm they feel for life. They have not wanted to be "just literary." Most of them have thought of the literary world as a world of indoor dandies, none too wholesome, and of their own writing rather as a contribution to the good talk of travelled men of wit than as a contribution to the pleasure of fashionable readers. Here again they have shown a unique combination of youth and good sense, for most of them have had to wait many years before the general public took any notice of their work. If you ask me to explain this neglect, I can do it in a few words: travellers do not write much of women.

For one reason or another—sometimes for reasons of arrangement, and sometimes through incapacity—I make no attempt to discuss here the character and work of several traveller-authors whose names will immediately occur to the experienced reader. Charles Doughty, for example, stands outside my period, a commanding figure of the pre-Georgian era. So, in a different category, does Sir Hugh Clifford. T. E. Lawrence, whose great book "The Seven Pillars of Wisdom" is much more than a work of travel, is beyond my praise. Nor shall I speak otherwise than briefly of others who should figure here; if I were to write of them, this book would be an encyclopædia. I will only briefly mention Sir Harry Johnston.

Sir Harry wrote much about the lands he visited; his novels, beginning with "The Gay-Dombeys," were widely read in his lifetime; he was adventurous to the end. But although a great personality he was not a good writer. His books communicated information, not all of it perfectly accurate, but all of it suggestive; they could not fail to illustrate the range of the author's interests and speculations and the extent of his curious memory; they were full of personally ascertained details—for example, when writing his sequel to Shaw's "Mrs. Warren's Profession" (which stunned Shaw into silence), Johnston elaborately pretended to be a possible tenant for an empty flat in order that he might by clambering obtain the view which Vivie Warren must have seen from her windows;—but when one thinks of Johnston it is as a man, not a writer.

In person he was very short, plump, round-faced. He had a

charming smile in which sweetness and roguishness were united. He had the soft voice of a breathless little girl, and the eyes of a lion. If he spoke on the telephone without mentioning his name he was always addressed (to his amused mystification) as "Madam"; but he once admitted to me that he had never known what it was to be physically afraid. Until almost the end of his life he looked like a chubby man of middle age; and when he was twenty-four he appeared so extremely juvenile that Ferdinand de Lesseps, the creator of the Suez Canal, on seeing him for the first time, exclaimed in excitement: "What a country! Where even the babies are explorers!"

Johnston began life—in London, in 1858—with a passionate desire to achieve greatness. He was a painter and a naturalist; a politician, a linguist, an antiquary; and both a great explorer and a great administrator. His interests were unlimited; and his conversation, so inexhaustible, so incessantly entertaining, was filled with the social gossip of three reigns. He had known everybody, from kings to Civil Servants, and he always took his dress suit into the jungle in case it might be needed. If one asked him to lunch at one's club he had to sit with his back to the room, because otherwise he saw about him too many men with whom he was not on speaking terms. The most amiable of men, modest, busy, gossiping, never bored, completely unshockable, he lost his identity when he took pen in hand; and even his memoirs give no impression at all of the raciness of his speech.

No; the first traveller-author who belongs by right to this chapter is Robert Bontine Cunninghame Graham, the aristocrat Socialist, the rebel against society who ornamented Society, the man who is said to have provided Shaw with at least an external model for the character of Captain Brassbound, and an author privately and singularly "discovered" for themselves by probably more people in different quarters of the globe than any other British writer of his period. It is of Cunninghame Graham, accordingly, that I shall now speak.

ii. Robert Bontine Cunninghame Graham

"To my Friend
R. B. CUNNINGHAME GRAHAM
('Singularisimo escritor ingles')
Who has lived with and knows (even to the marrow as they would themselves say) the
horsemen of the Pampas, and who alone of European writers has rendered something
of the vanishing colour of that remote life."

W. H. Hudson: Dedication of El Ombú.

R. B. CUNNINGHAME GRAHAM, of Ardoch, was born in 1852. Upon his mother's side he was of the Elphinstones, an old Scottish family of soldiers, sailors, and royalists. Having been at school at Harrow, he became a Socialist, a political candidate, and finally a Member of Parliament from 1886 to 1892. He was the colleague of M. H. Hyndman and John Burns, and in 1887, when the Life Guards marched up Whitehall to drive unemployed demonstrators from Trafalgar Square upon "Bloody Sunday," he had his head cracked and was arrested as one of the ringleaders of the riot. For some years after that he continued to play an active part in the Labour struggle; but after 1892 he was unsuccessful at election times, and the first of his published writings appeared in 1895. That his appetite for political adventure was unappeased to the last was shown by his active concern with the demand for Scottish Home Rule. He and Compton Mackenzie gave that inexplicable activity the fervour of a new Jacobite rising.

I do not know who first used the word "hidalgo" to describe Cunninghame Graham. It may have been Morley Roberts. But there was a pride, an elegance, and a nobility in his carriage such as we associate with the grandees of Spain in other centuries than this. He was always a very handsome man, a magnificent horseman, and a picturesque figure altogether. Even in advanced age his vitality, the grandeur of his manner, and the intellectual command of his mind were superlative. He was an aristocrat. And there is much of the aristocrat in his writings. It is this quality, combined with the fact that they have what perhaps I may call a static rather than a social interest, which prevented them from becoming popular. One does not read them feverishly to see what happens; one cannot zestfully embrace the proud and critical view of life which they express; they are not for the soft-minded; their chief admirers, I judge, are men of a mental detachment akin to Cunninghame Graham's own.

They have one extraordinary quality. Whatever scene they describe, whether it be laid in the desert, on the South American pampa, in Scotland, at sea, or upon the West Coast of Africa, they catch the very atmosphere of the place and the very mind of the people with whom they deal. The author is at home everywhere.

In a single ironic sentence he will communicate all that a lesser man would tell at interminable length. When we read what he has written we are for a dozen pages—the extent of his sketch—in baking heat, in snow, in Yorkshire, in Menteith, among the gauchos, or travelling to Mecca to find why there are no old women in Paradise. The effect is not obtained by a total immersion in memory; it is constantly heightened by comparisons which suggest themselves to a mind richly endowed with humour and imagination (those two requisites for true irony). It is irresistible.

"So quiet the garden was, that when the lizards chased each other through the dead grass, the noise they made was as distinct (in its degree) as if a troop of cavalry had passed. A scent of mint and of decaying orange blossom filled the air; all was old-world and still; and the bare-footed, white-clothed people passed about among the trees, as they were shades of some old life, making one feel, in looking at them, as one feels in looking at some pre-diluvian footstep, stamped in the rock, which once was river mud.

"'Yes,' said the Angeri, 'once Allah let all animals both speak and pray to him in Arabic, so that men, listening to them, could understand their speech.' A dreadful time it must have been, if with their speech they also enjoyed reason, and could accuse us to our faces of all our crimes against their kind. Who that could contemplate their speech and not go mad, with thinking upon all that they might say? But as it happened, God having let them all speak (once upon a time), and as the God the Angeri knew was Allah, the merciful, compassionate, capricious, envious, the invisible, and therefore unapproachable, except by prayer, that smoke the human mind gives off under its fire of cares, the animals had to pray, or else to lose their speech."

That is the beginning of a tale in a volume called "Progress," which explains why a certain small kind of lizard is known as "el Khattaia-es-salaa"—for the gift of speech was suddenly withdrawn from birds and animals, and this lizard, forgetful of the passage of time, missed its last opportunity for prayer.

"Running, back downwards, on the ceilings of the mosques, all day it chased the flies, basked in the heat, flattening itself against the white-washed walls, its feet expanding flat, like paddles, and its slim tail acting upon the air to steer it as it whisked through horseshoe arches, and shot out upon the vine leaves which grew up outside the holy place. Chasing its fellows in the sun, and catching flies, the sand ran through the glass and, at the mogréb, when the last quavering 'Allah' died away, only the lizard, in its joy of life, did not give thanks to God.

"Despair fell on it, and its tiny grief shook its prismatic sides, whilst little tears stood in its beady eyes. Its tail hung quivering, and its head bowed miserably, as it stood silently and without power to glorify the Lord. Then, darting to the mosque, it flittered up the walls, its little feet showering down lime upon the worshippers. Just over the mihráb it stopped, and, as the faithful in the mosque below looked up at it, scratched 'Allah Ackbar' with its claw upon the roof, and, scurrying back, was lost beneath the eaves.

"'So,' said the Angeri, 'it saved itself from Allah's wrath, and showed its faith'; and from that time we know it as *Khattaia-es-salaa*, that is, the prayer-scratcher; praise to His Holy Name!'"

Readers of the above will have noted several peculiarities of style. They are to be found—they and their like—through Cunninghame Graham's work. His ear was sometimes faulty; he was not aware that "old-world" is an estate agent's term; his grammar was his own (unless the printer helped him); he was sometimes obscure, and sometimes—it was his humour—slightly affected. Those are small blemishes. More interesting—and I should like to understand the cause of that omission—is the fact that he nowhere essayed a longer fiction. What he did instead—one of the things he did, and the most notable of them—was to write a superbly rich and amusing account of a journey in Southern Morocco, under the title "Mogreb-el-Acksa." In this he was exultantly humorous, instructive, eloquent, and sardonic by turn, and altogether at his best as a writer. In this, also, he was at his most characteristic, doing with glorious gusto exactly what he set out to do. What is that, you ask? Cunninghame Graham himself gave the answer. He said:

"Writers, I take it, firstly write to please themselves, if not 'tis ten to one their writing pleases nobody. Following my postulate I have set down that which pleased me upon my pilgrimage, hoping that it may please at least two or three who, like myself, have wandered. Therefore in this, my modest book of travels, I have tried to write after the fashion that men speak over the fire at night, their pipes alight, hands on their rifles, boots turned towards the blaze, ears strained to catch the rustle of a leaf, and with the tin mug stopped on its journey to the mouth when horses snort; I mean I strove to write down that which I saw without periphrasis, sans flag-wagging, and with no megrim in my head of having been possessed by some great moral purpose, without which few travellers nowadays presume to leave their homes.

"I fear I have no theory of empires, destiny of the Anglo-Saxon race, spread of the Christian faith, of trade extension, or of hinterlands; no nostrum, by means of which I hope to turn Arabs into Christians, reconcile Allah and Jahve, remove the ancient lack of comprehension between East and West, mix oil and vinegar, or fix the rainbow always in the sky so that the colour-blind may scan it at their leisure through the medium of a piece of neutral-tinted glass; and generally I fear I write of things without a scrap of interest to right-thinking men: of humours, sayings, proverbs, traits of character; little of eating, drinking, or night alarms of vermin, as travellers will; but, on the contrary, of lonely rides, desolate camping places, or ruined buildings seen in peculiar lights, of simple folk who pray to Allah seven times a day, and act as if they never prayed at all; in fact of things which to a traveller, his travels o'er, still conjure up the best part of all travel—its melancholy."

The thought did not, of course, enter Cunninghame Graham's head—or if it did enter it immediately escaped—that some men make a trade of writing books; it did not enter his head to believe that smaller men tell at inordinate length of their little love affairs and the stoves of life in studios and suchlike airless places. If he had thought of these things, he would have wondered fastidiously that they should occur, and would have turned again to more delightful themes, ignoring superbly all that ill befits the life of a free man. For him a city was a compound for slaves, and the world an open space for every adventure. For him the theorist and the miser, the stay-at-home and the preacher who does not practise his profession were all ridiculous anomalies. He was for action; and for action with humour. The assumption is at the heart of all his work. And so, when he wrote, he thought nothing of what the public might want, but only of setting down his account of an episode, or a scene, a reminiscence, a tale, with the grace and manner of a free man who, by the gift of the gods, was also an original artist. Diversely, he told with an air what befell him upon a journey; but it was not all or by any means all that befell him, only what amused him, or what it amused him to tell. When he had related what he liked, he passed on, indifferent to the reader's unsated curiosity, and greatly amused by his own private reflections. That is why he was always the grandee, and never the humble suppliant for public favour. It is also why he keeps his admirers.

For the rest, when this great man wrote at length it was the biography of some notable Spaniard otherwise little vaunted in English, or the tale of an exploration which he thought should be better understood and which it interested him to recall from the past. In these excellent books the same descriptive and ironic gift to which I have referred were displayed; but they were not sensibly augmented. It is therefore in "Mogreb-el-Acksa" and in his original sketches and brief stories that he is best read. Here his work has an edge and colour, a salt, a noble ease, which makes it seem like the lesser performance of a master to whom even greater triumphs were denied only because he did not seek them.

iii. William Henry Hudson

"A field-naturalist is an observer of everything he sees—from a man to an ant or a plant."

W. H. Hudson: A Hind in Richmond Park.

THERE is all the difference in the world between Cunninghame Graham and W. H. Hudson. The one was born in Scotland and from a natural love of adventure travelled much, fearlessly, in other continents; the other was born in the neighbourhood of Buenos Ayres, had his heart ruined by rheumatic fever when he was fifteen, and from the age of twenty-nine, when he came "home," as he called it (although his father and mother were both citizens of the United States), never again left the British Isles. In their writings the one had an air of scattering odd fragments of his mind and genius as fancy prompted; and the other, the "field-naturalist" of his own phrase, observed, remembered, recorded, but scattered nothing.

William Henry Hudson was born on August 4th, 1841, and although he lived until August 18th, 1924, he was never a strong man. His father, who was of English descent, was originally of Marblehead, Massachusetts, and his mother was a New England woman; but before any of their children were born these American parents, for reasons of health, settled in the Argentine. Hudson, accordingly, was born and reared among the pampas. From the age of six he was given to stealing away from his brothers to a little wood where he could watch the animals, snakes, birds, and insects common to the country; and after his great illness, which followed a terrible experience of driving cattle through a blizzard, he was more than ever a solitary. When doctors announced that he could not hope to live long, he was faced at the age of sixteen with despair so great that he made no effort to fit himself for adult life. He idled, he read; and his passion for nature remained in effect the one solace of his mind.

Time passed. He began to keep a journal of his observations. Then he became a corresponding member of the Zoological Society, and sent overseas a few slight papers recording what he had seen. When his father died in 1868 he left South America and came to England, where he remained for more than fifty years, always a semi-invalid, always aloof, silent, and in some degree a stranger. His first years in Hampshire and in London remain mysterious; all that is known of them is that he managed somehow to subsist until 1876, when he married a boarding-house keeper fifteen years his senior.

From that time onward nothing but failure attended Hudson. Three boarding-houses proved unprofitable; Mrs. Hudson earned but little money by giving singing lessons; Hudson wrote descriptions of South American birds and South American scenes which few editors would print. He had only his observations of nature to write about, and in the last decades of the nineteenth century nobody wanted them. When he tried to write a conventional novel, "Fan," it was as great a failure as the more typical "Purple Land," but more deservedly a failure. Only the bequest of a heavily mortgaged house in West London, which was let out into flats, saved the Hudsons from starvation.

This life continued for some years. At times the two would creep away to the country for fresh air, and Hudson had a few literary and other friends with whom he visited the coasts and southern counties of England. His books show that he was as closely interested in English beasts and birds as he had been earlier in those of his first home. Both "Idle Days in Patagonia" and "Birds in a Village" were published in 1893; "British Birds" followed in 1897, "Birds in London" in 1898, and "Nature in Downland" in 1900. In the latter year Hudson became a naturalized Englishman. Subsequently he received a Civil List pension of £150 a year; but by this time his fortunes were slowly improving, and with the aid of influential critics he was presently to have a valuable success with the long-prepared novel, "Green Mansions." In the last twenty years of his life this success was translated into money.

I first saw Hudson some time before the publication of "Green Mansions." He came into the office of J. M. Dent when I was reception clerk there, on some business connected with his two books, "A Naturalist in La Plata" and "Idle Days in Patagonia." These books had been taken over by Dents from another firm of publishers, and had so little sale that the bound copies still bore the old firm's imprint. The author of them, I found, was a very tall and thin man of middle age, in a very long overcoat which seemed to reach his heels. His head looked remarkably small at the top of this cylindrical enclosure, and his face tanned and shrunken; but his ears stood out from under a black hard felt hat. He was already grey-bearded. When I realized who he was I no longer wondered at Hudson's power to stand and watch unconscious animals and birds; for he was extraordinarily silent in all his movements, and he sat on the edge of a table, glancing at a book, without ever shifting his position. He had very bright eyes which my recollection makes as black as blackcurrants; the brows were thick to bushiness; the nose hooked. That he resembled a bird I felt sure; but he had not the malignance of the hawk or the solemnity of an owl or the satisfied vanity of the parrot. These were the only ruminative birds I knew. He was extremely courteous to the boy who ingeniously—he knew not how ingeniously—negotiated his interview with J. M. Dent.

Of a later occasion when—perhaps in 1914—I met him at lunch with Edward Garnett I recall only one incident, which is that in parting Hudson raised his hat in the foreign way. It was the early meeting that impressed me; this second one, although we must have conversed, is a speck in memory. I saw never him again.

Of his work I continue to think "A Naturalist in La Plata" and "Idle Days in Patagonia" the best examples. The former is a collection of essays reprinted from magazines now of an obsolete type; the latter a narrative presumably based upon journals kept at the time. The material is authentic, and the manner plain, clear, and attractive. And though the English books are full of good observation, curious incidents, and excellent quiet writing, the freshness of his early first-hand acquaintance with nature is never quite recaptured. His autobiographical "Far Away and Long Ago" is informative, charmingly written, and full of reserve; the work of a really old, sick man, looking back to childhood through a mist. It was influenced by Aksakov's memoirs, for which Hudson felt great admiration.

"The Purple Land," a rambling romance of a man's adventures in South America, which I have only read in the revised version of 1906, and which, in the earliest draft of all, was a well-nigh endless "History of the House of Lamb," has many beauties and vigours, and if Hudson had known better what he was intending to do with it, it might have been very distinguished indeed. Unfortunately he did not know what to do with it (except go on writing), and the book remains what publishers and reviewers, when they are forced to describe highly unsystematic inventions, despairingly miscall "picaresque." Cut and revised though it is, "The Purple Land" remains a broken and spasmodic book.

The style in which it is written, however, is much less studied than that drenching his other famous novel, "Green Mansions," which took him several years to write, and was a rage with the reviewers of 1904. Here again the scene, the strange and haunting scene, is South America; and here again forests, prairies, birds, and the naturalist's observations provide the basis for a romantic but ill-knit story of love and adventure. "Green Mansions" begins enchantingly, first with that little device by which Conrad and others sought to heighten romance, or perhaps only to disclaim autobiography, the encounter with a mysterious stranger, and then with the stranger's own narrative. Abel, elderly and sad, has had his hour of life. He has sought gold, and met sorrow: we hear his tale. Now as long as there is still a mystery in the tale; as long as the warbled notes which he hears in the fairy wood can be imagined as in some way supernatural, the book is odd and interesting. But from the moment when Rima is seen as a young girl the magic declines. It might have been otherwise; it ought to have been otherwise; there is no reason other than the poverty of imagination, why Rima should not captivate us as much as a woman as she does as a spirit. Unfortunately she can only chirp; the wonderful knowledge she possesses is uncommunicable. Her talk is leaden stuff. True, when she discovers Abel's inability to understand her chirrup she enjoys our sympathy, although we feel that a few lessons might have been attempted, and thus suspect the whole affair. True, there is a shock of horror at her revolting end. But as soon as Abel finds her no spirit the movement of the book becomes mechanical; its invention grows feeble; it is contrived.

That is the penalty paid by a naturalist turned romancer. His ability to imagine character with continuous power is insufficient. While in the case of both Rima and Dolores (the deceived but amorous young woman in "The Purple Land") the romantic note is pitched very high indeed it is not supported by any spontaneous play of emotion. Instead, there is a reaching up to literary beauty. Hudson knew painfully well the effect he wished to achieve— indeed, I suspect that both Dolores and Rima were dream heroines with whom he had long been preoccupied;—but the very fact of knowing paralysed his talent. It is one of the misfortunes of self-conscious literary art that the creative gift cannot be forced to work for a master. Hudson was an observer, strongly susceptible to the moods of Nature; but he was emotionally and imaginatively cold. Hence his failure as a novelist; for his coldness, which at first has charm, produces in the end an impression of labour. His best work outside the record of observed facts and inferences from those facts is to be found in the book of four short stories or sketches called "El Ombú," the first of which, the title story, if mannered, is fine and full of suggestion. He was not really a writer of fiction.

What he was, in a high degree, was just that "field naturalist" which he called himself. The close and absorbed observation of nature, begun in his earliest years, and continued even when he thought himself dying, runs through every page of his work. It is never sentimental, always humane and in a sense philosophic, and of rare excellence. He had to leave the town and go fifty or sixty miles into the country to find almost all he needed for happiness. The sight of a moral struggle between a draggled blackbird and a relentless chaffinch, or even that of the sensitive movement of a hind, which he thought betokened an interest in the world about her not inferior to his own, would start him upon a train of reflection; thoughts upon eyes, on the curious friendship of pumas towards the human species, on his favourite flower, the evening primrose, on a pair of scarlet flycatchers in lands far away, give every book its thoughtful and thought-evoking quality. He is not a Gilbert White; he has hardly any kinship with White. Indeed he says:

> "One of the books I read then for the first time was White's *Selborne*, given to me by an old friend of our family . . . I read and re-read it many times, for nothing so good of its kind had ever come to me, but it did not reveal to me the secret of my own feeling for Nature—the feeling of which I was becoming more and more conscious, which was a mystery to me, especially at certain moments, when it would come upon me with a sudden rush."

It may be asked what this feeling was; and Hudson answered the question himself in another book by calling it Animism. He said:

> "It must be explained that *animism* is not used here in the sense that Tylor gives it in his *Primitive Culture*: in that work it signifies a theory of life, a philosophy of primitive man, which has been supplanted among civilized people by a more advanced philosophy. Animism here means not a doctrine of souls that survive the bodies and objects they inhabit, but the mind's projection of itself into nature, its attribution of its own sentient life and intelligence to all things—that primitive universal faculty on which the animistic philosophy of the savage is founded. When our philosophers tell us that this faculty is obsolete in us, that it is effectually killed by ratiocination, or that it only survives for a period in our children, I believe they are wrong, a fact which they could find out for themselves if, leaving their books and theories, they would take a solitary walk on a moonlit night in the 'Woods of Westermain' or any other woods, since all are enchanted."

But if Hudson has no kinship with White, he has neither the emotionalism of Jefferies nor the vanity of Thoreau. Like Borrow, whom he does not otherwise resemble, he has a power to encounter strange people and converse with them, so that his books teem with tantalizing episodes. But he never obtrudes his own figure; there is a striking impersonality in all that he relates. That is his virtue, a coldness which many might link in their minds with inhumanity; it is in his style, which is quiet and without warmth, and which by some is thought too careful, or, in the case of "Green Mansions," too conscious; it is in his relations with other men, to whose natural ebullience he would oppose silence or at most a monosyllabic abruptness. At their moment of farewell in 1869 his younger brother, whom he loved deeply, was forced to say, in the warm candour of parting, "Of all the people I have ever known you are the only one I don't know." He never forgot the words.

Hudson was cold; his emotions were much buried under pride.

He had thought much of death since his sixteenth year, and he had felt much of poverty since his coming to England. He could perhaps have written—as his friend Gissing did—of the sufferings of those who live in poverty; but he did not do so. Instead, he stood very still and very quietly, watching wild birds, noting what they did in happiness or peril, and in love or war. The only living creatures he hated were full-feeders, publishers, stoats, weasels, and ferrets. Towards the rest of the animal kingdom he felt unique powers of understanding, based upon knowledge of and reflection upon the vicissitudes of all sufferers from the inhumanity of man; and it is in the quality of this understanding that his work attains distinction.

iv. Joseph Conrad

". . . But the Dwarf answered: No; something human is dearer to me than the wealth of all the world."

Grimm's Tales.

WHEN Hudson visited the English coast with Morley Roberts and other friends, it was his custom ritualistically to scoop up a handful of sea water and drink it as soon as he could reach the water's edge. Just why he did this was never explained, and it is not clear from any writing of his that the sea had any special claim upon his affections. But the case was different with Joseph Conrad, to whom the sea—at least in boyhood—was a passion.

Conrad's two passions were the sea and the human species; the sea in boyhood, and then, as he grew up and met them in the course of his voyages, men. To these two passions he added in time a third, that of language which should express richly and eloquently the passion he felt for men and the sea. When he was a boy, Conrad would pore over maps, and, putting his finger upon every large open space he found, he would say "When I grow up, I shall go there." And as soon as he was old enough to do so he went to sea, where he stayed for twenty years, until he had written his first novel and until, in despair of getting another ship, he one day sat down to write a second. From that time, almost by accident, he devoted himself to novel-writing, and after some years—I make the distinction deliberately—he became a professional novelist.

Teodor Josef Konrad Korzeniowski was born in Berdiczew, in Poland, on December 3rd, 1857. His mother was a woman of family, his father an energetic and enthusiastic revolutionary of literary gifts who was not shrewd enough to escape exile, hardship, and early death as the result of his sanguine love of freedom.

"A man of great sensibilities" (said his son); "of exalted and dreamy temperament; with a terrible gift of irony and of gloomy disposition . . . His aspect was distinguished; his conversation fascinating; but his face, in repose sombre, lighted all over when he smiled."

Before Conrad was twelve years old he had lost both father and mother.

He first saw the sea, at Venice, in 1873. In the following year he went to Marseilles determined to become a sailor, and in 1875 he actually took a brief voyage. But it was not until 1878, after some of the strange doings recorded in "The Arrow of Gold," that he went to sea and stayed at sea. In that year he sailed in three ships: first the *Mavis*, in which he visited the Sea of Azov and returned to Lowestoft, second the *Skimmer of the Seas*, in which he learned to speak English and plied between Lowestoft and Newcastle, and third the *Duke of Sutherland*, in which as a common sailor he made the voyage to Australia. In 1881 he was second mate of the barque *Palestine* (the Judea of "Youth"); and in 1887 went out to the east as first mate of the *Highland Forest*, left the ship at Samarang through illness, and joined the *Vidar*, in which as second mate he made a number of voyages between Singapore and Borneo. These voyages were crucial. In the course of them he met the originals of several of his most famous characters; and he also obtained that first-hand knowledge of Malaya which afterwards supplied so much material for his fiction.

In 1889 he was back in England, already with a pen in his hand; but before he could do more than begin a book he determined to go to the Congo, where he thought that through certain family influence he could obtain command of a Belgian river steamer. Some of the details of this exploit are to be found in "An Outpost of Progress," most of them in "Heart of Darkness"; but he did not get his command and he soon returned to London ill and discouraged. It was not until two years later that he was offered the post of mate in the *Torrens*, "one of the most successful ships ever built, one of the fastest and for many years the favourite passenger ship to Adelaide"; and it was during one of the trips made by the *Torrens* that he formed his first literary friendship—with John Galsworthy.

Galsworthy, at that time a sanguine young man, had been upon a pious pilgrimage to Samoa (which he did not reach); and when he joined the *Torrens* at Adelaide he very soon observed with interest one of the officers of the ship.

"Very dark he looked in the burning sunlight, tanned, with a peaked brown beard, almost black hair, and dark brown eyes, over which the lids were deeply folded. He was thin, not tall, his arms very long, his shoulders broad, his head set rather forward. He spoke to me with a strong foreign accent."

The officer not only spoke to Galsworthy; he entertained him on the voyage home with yarns and expositions. He quite enchanted the young traveller, who recorded that

> "Fascination was Conrad's great characteristic—the fascination of vivid expressiveness and zest, of his deeply affectionate heart, and his far-ranging, subtle mind. He was extraordinarily perceptive and receptive."

The strong foreign accent remained with him throughout life. Illness made him yet thinner, his hair grew grey, he aged early; but what he was then he continued to be until the end of his life. The subtlety, the perceptiveness, the receptiveness, and the love of yarning were all a part of the novelist's temperament. And when in 1893 Conrad left the *Torrens* (and also, although this was far from his intention, the sea) he gave himself entirely to the task of completing a written yarn which he had begun five years earlier. The book, "Almayer's Folly," was finished by the end of May, 1894, was then sent by messenger to the London publisher, Fisher Unwin, and by Unwin was immediately accepted for publication.

That was the beginning. It might have been the end; for Conrad still thought of himself as a sailor. But Edward Garnett, a young reader at Unwin's, who happened to be precociously the greatest discoverer and encourager of literary artists English publishers have ever known, took a hand. He said to Conrad: "You have the style, you have the temperament. Why not write another?" Conrad, enchanted by this simple suggestion, proceeded to write "An Outcast of the Islands." He then married (on March 24th, 1896) an English girl, on his honeymoon began a third novel, and at the same time tentatively experimented with the kind of writing for which, without any question whatever, he had the greatest talent—the long short story, or narrative, sometimes of an episode or series of episodes occurring at sea, sometimes of a situation arising among men who live remote from civilization in the tropics, but always of a problem of character or conduct. To this period and type belong "An Outpost of Progress," "The Nigger of the 'Narcissus,'" "Youth," "Heart of Darkness," "Lord Jim," "Typhoon," and "Falk." All were written by 1903. He never afterwards wrote anything as fine.

Besides being much delayed by illness, Conrad was a desperately slow worker, for it was his ambition to be what he called "an artist in words." His literary aim was "the just expression seizing upon the essential." Almost all his stories were published serially, but they appeared in magazines with relatively small circulations; and in book form, despite the applause of reviewers, they had no popularity. Consequently Conrad remained poor. If it had not been for the help given to him by his agent, J. B. Pinker, he might have starved. By his own admission, once he had re-created those seascapes and those pictures of the Congo and Malaya, he felt there was nothing left for him to write about. In vain, having exhausted his first strength of inspiration, did he try new styles. He was tempted, in this hour of difficulty, to the difficult and treacherous craft of collaboration; and at first in extravaganza and then in a joint rewriting of a sentimental romance conceived and partly executed by his friend, he worked with Ford Madox Hueffer. Finally he settled to the composition of a long and elaborate novel about silver mines in a South American state. The result was "Nostromo."

At the time of its publication and for long afterwards it was usual to say that this was Conrad's greatest book. In the infection of the moment (for I had discovered Conrad at the age of seventeen, and was then at the height of admiration) I too thought it was a masterpiece, and so it may be; but I should not now hold to that opinion. "Nostromo" was the first book of Conrad's to be built or manufactured. For the first time he departed from the imaginative reconstruction of lives and episodes drawn from the fibre of his own experience. He invented a whole *milieu*. From a single paragraph in a book of reminiscence he derived the hint for a tale involving many lives, and he planned this with the most profound seriousness and wrote it with scrupulous care. Unquestionably the result was a disappointment to him, for "Nostromo," however highly praised, was a failure with the public and always remained a comparative failure. I think I can understand why. The book is very elaborate; it is as rich as can be in comprehensions and in diverse characters; but its movement is extremely slow, the detail of its intrigue is not always intelligible, and it does not quite escape dullness. In vain does one dwell upon its qualities; the truth is that in place of that concentrated intensity of imagining which gives Conrad's finest work its thrilling dramatic force there is a generalized interest which the reader admires only at the bidding of his sense of literary duty. He knows that he should admire whatever is very difficult or very elaborate, whatever has cost the writer great pains or great ingenuity, and he admires most manfully, the more so as he is conscious that if the book were not so good he would yawn his head off. But since "Nostromo has never been intended for the hero of the tale of the Seaboard" and "silver is the pivot of the moral and material events, affecting the lives of everybody in the tale," it is perhaps allowable to say that for once Conrad forgot that motto of his to the effect that "something human is dearer to me than the wealth of all the world," and paid accordingly for his forgetfulness.

For ten years after this (1904) his fiction was the least interesting part of his writing, and only "The Mirror of the Sea" and a gradual absorption by the public of novels and tales written earlier maintained a position which had seemed to be assured upon the publication of "Lord Jim." His health was poor, and that choice of subjects which in a couple of melodramatic tales brought complicated ingenuity to bear upon Terrorism was unfortunate. He had lost his way. His fortunes were at their lowest. In 1911 something like a sensation was caused among strangers by the news that Conrad had been granted a Civil List pension of £100 a year.

And then, quite unexpectedly, everything was changed. A book which was to have been published in the Autumn of 1913 was held over until the Spring. It appeared at the very beginning of 1914, and created a furore. The book was "Chance," in which for the first time he romanticized the character of a woman; and from that moment he was a prosperous author. The reintroduction of Marlow, the imaginary self, the penetrating seer of life and character who narrated intricate tales to other men as he sat unseen in the darkness; the return to the yarn which was Conrad's happiest medium of expression; and above all the accidental use of a theme— the theme of what may be called deferred or doubtful consummation —which has led to so many fictional successes in the past, was irresistible. The book has charm, fluency, suspense, a few vividly-drawn persons, and a great deal of that singular probing beauty which was a chief cause of Marlow's (and Conrad's) fascination. "Chance" was a tremendous success. Everybody read it and praised it. Sidney Colvin, I remember, who spoke always of "My Conrad' as he had been used to speak of "My R.L.S.," led the way with an ecstatic review in *The Observer*, but he was quickly followed by a dozen more, by hundreds, by thousands, all of them as eager as he to proclaim their joy in the minor work of a master. If an author, for whatever reason, has been long neglected, there seems no end to the enthusiasm which accompanies the turning tide. In this case the tide led on to fortune. And when for the theme of his next book Conrad went back to the East, a further fond blurring of the critical faculty and a further rejoicing among all who had long admired the work of a distinguished artist followed his journey. Though the old glory was diffused, success had warmed his memory, and "Victory" rounded off the tale.

Prosperity continued until Conrad's death. He did not write anything more which can be compared with his best work, and his health slowly declined until 1924, when he died, was saluted with

E

dignity by his own generation, and in some slight measure was forgotten. His immediate juniors, Wells, Bennett, Galsworthy, had
long been profound admirers of his work; and Wells—in days when
he was a reviewer—had been among the first to proclaim its worth.
Those of the younger generation, and particularly Hugh Walpole
(who wrote a little book about Conrad), had given their admiration
and passed to newer gods. I think that writers still younger than
these must have viewed some of Conrad's close pages with distrust,
even with impatience. Moreover, he had lived almost continuously
in the country, near Ashford, in Kent, and he was socially little
known to his juniors. Few anecdotes were told of him; his features
were so unfamiliar to the public that on the night of the first performance of a dramatized version of "Victory" I myself was greeted
with applause by a mistaken group in the pit, which mistook me for
the master. His wife's book about their married life shows him to
have been difficult, irascible, and almost a chronic invalid. He sought
no publicity and was the least vulgar of men. If, therefore, the name
of Joseph Conrad now arouses less enthusiasm than it did before the
First World War it is because the novelty of his manner has gone and
because we have not yet had time to rediscover it. But his best work
is still better in its own way than the best work of his successors,
and a re-reading of it is very reassuring to those who recall with
misgiving an enthusiasm of the past.

This I say notwithstanding the fact that "Lord Jim," which is
his most interesting novel, loses its authentic quality in the middle
and drops to a quality not wholly beyond the range of a lesser
writer. It is a book about a sailor whose nerve failed in an hour of
crisis, who was arraigned and punished for his failure (while the
greater criminals escaped), and whose subsequent life, haunted by
something more than his own memory, was a series of misadventures. "Lord Jim's" quality lies in the curious intricacy and subtlety
of the method by which we are made aware of all the circumstances
of failure and discovery, and the beautiful delicate sureness with
which two scenes, those of the inquiry and the failure of nerve, are
so pictured that our imaginations are quickened to the highest pitch
of understanding, to positive complicity in the scenes themselves.
By contrast with such scenes, the rest of the book, although it is
vivid, is of lesser importance. What stirs us is the evocation of those
crucial moments.

The evocation is attained by means of Conrad's oblique method
of narration. He does not tell the story himself; that would be too
simple. He does not tell it as a straightforward tale; that would be
too crude. He tells it in the form of a yarn in which the subtle and
omniscient narrator has power to hold hearers as the Ancient
Mariner held the wedding guest, diverging, doubling, speculating,

bringing to his elucidations all sorts of other yarns, in one moment as near to his subject and in another as far from it as he pleases, as exact or as vague at all times in any detail as will best suit the dramatic emphasis he desires, as colloquial or as eloquent as the author thinks fit for his purpose. What an elastic method! How intimate and how pictorial! How reflective and how dramatic! Its impact, when it has the sea and seamen perfectly within grasp, is breathtaking.

It would be interesting to trace the history of this method, and to know how Conrad came to make use of it. The yarn, of course, was natural to him as to other travellers, and as a kind of informal literary form it was used considerably during the nineties by Kipling and Conan Doyle and several more. Henry James, further, had in "The Spoils of Poynton," "In the Cage," etc., allowed one subtle mind to reconstruct and so dramatize a whole series of significant circumstances. But Conrad took the method farther. Where James was content with subtlety in itself, the thing "done," Conrad wanted to explain the thing—whatever it was—quite down to its ethical basis. While James hummed and faltered over the small domestic object which in "The Ambassadors" could not be mentioned, Conrad very anxiously probed to the occasion when Falk had eaten human flesh, and why he had done this, and indeed must explain just how everything came about. Yet he too had his irony, and "Falk" is brimming with it; and there is no doubt in my mind that if it had been told in any other way but this "Falk" would have been either trivial or disgusting.

The simple explanation of this difference probably lies in the fact that Conrad was a traveller and James was "just literary," that Conrad had known Falk and James really could not be bothered to bring his mind to a definition of the object. "So-ome small thing," he said, waving a hand; "it doesn't matter what." But there is more in the contrast than that. James enjoyed the mystification. Towards the end of his life, rather than be definite he would take refuge in an ejaculation—"She's wonderful"—or a vagueness. But Marlow, who "had sunken cheeks, a yellow complexion, a straight back, an ascetic aspect, and, with his arms dropped, the palms of hands outwards, resembled an idol," was in despair at his failure to ascertain and reproduce every delicacy. When his host on one occasion murmured "You are so subtle, Marlow," Marlow answered in melancholy: "Who? I? Oh, no! . . . Try as I may for the success of this yarn I am missing innumerable shades—they are so fine, so difficult to render in colourless words!" James was absorbed in the exquisite ingenuities of his craft; Conrad in his search for the very essence of truth. "But do you notice how, three hundred miles beyond the end of telegraph cables and mail-boat lines, the haggard utilitarian lies of our civilization wither and die, to be replaced by pure exercises of imagination, that have the futility, often the charm, and sometimes the deep hidden truthfulness, of works of art?"

There is some difference in æsthetic theory here, surely? James did not perfectly comprehend and approve Conrad's work. One understands that. It interested him by its gratuitous embrace of difficulty, and perhaps he could see no point in it. Here, however, is Conrad, and he too has a point of view:

> "The moral side of an industry . . . is the attainment and pre-servation of the highest possible skill on the part of the craftsman. Such skill, the skill of technique, is more than honesty; it is some-thing wider, embracing honesty and grace and rule in an elevated and clear sentiment. . . . The attainment of proficiency, the pushing of your skill with attention to the most delicate shades of excellence, is a matter of vital concern. . . . But there is something beyond—a higher point, a subtle and unmistakable touch of love and pride beyond mere skill; almost an inspiration which gives to all work that finish which is almost art—which *is* art."

Conrad objected to the general belief that he was a writer of sea stories. He said: "It seems to me that people imagine I sit here and brood over sea stuff. That is quite a mistake. I brood certainly, but . . ." He regarded himself as a psychologist. "I insist not on the events but on their effect upon the persons in the tale." And again, "In everything I have written there is always one invariable in-tention, and that is to capture the reader's attention, by securing his interest and enlisting his sympathies for the matter in hand, whatever it may be, within the limits of the visible world and within the boundaries of human emotions." Those remarks, coupled with his criticisms of the work of his friends, show what acuteness Conrad could exercise. He worked at all times well within the range of his talent, and did not deceive himself as to its nature and limitations. Nevertheless, it may be added here without depreciation of that talent that he was most at home when he was writing of sailors and the sea, and that practically all his best work dealt with them. As he grew older he sought for greater subtlety and for finer shades, but his true gift was for the reproduction of scene and atmosphere, not for analysis.

Norman Douglas, perhaps thinking of "Lord Jim," ingeniously suggests that the worth of Conrad's psychologizing was nullified by very strict standards of conduct and an irrelevant conception of "honour." Douglas knew Conrad, which I never did; but the novelist's concern is with what Conrad called "the matter in hand," and even Douglas, I presume, would not deny that it is legitimate to show standards of conduct, however conventional, operating in simple minds. On the larger question of whether there were heights and depths beyond Conrad's recognition, or beyond his sympathy, there may be room for debate. His positive performance remains. Using for the sake of its simultaneous intimacy and detachment the free form of the yarn, and sometimes, to the horror of purists, the quoted yarn within a yarn, Conrad brought sea and tropics more immediately home to the minds of men than any other writer has ever done. Captain Whalley in "The End of the Tether" and Captain McWhirr in "Typhoon," Lord Jim as long as he is a sailor, are palpable. The scenes in which they move lend such stimulus to the imagination that we experience them as we read. To myself, this conjunction—some may call it stereoscopic—of intimacy and detachment represents the highest achievement of realistic art. It preserves the picture; it rouses the emotion; we see and understand all; and when the spell is withdrawn we are again, without shock and without disillusion, in the life we know.

That Conrad lacked the apocalyptic grandeur of Herman Melville is true; he also lacked Melville's fustian. That he nevertheless at times used melodrama for his own ends, and did not always carry the reader with him in distaste for scoundrels (or even interest in them), seems to me to be equally true. His earliest literary master, whom he met in his father's translation of "Les Travailleurs de la Mer," was Victor Hugo, and if one speaks of Hugo's extravagance one lets him off very lightly indeed. On the other hand, melodrama has been used by some of the greatest novelists; and I think it only offends us in Conrad because he does not relish it. Also, because, subsequent to Hugo, his one serious instructor in the art and craft of fiction must have been Henry James. I have already hinted at an acquaintance (before Conrad began to write) with the work of Kipling; but of this I shall say no more. From the moment he concerned himself with the short story or short narrative he was deliberately an artist, and quite undeliberately an original writer who brought to the writing of fiction new qualities of perception, sympathy, and irony.

v. H. M. Tomlinson

"Bates actually arrives at his destination in the first sentence. He steps across in thirty-eight words from England to the Amazon. . . . Well, I did not. I say it is a gross deception. . . . How Bates got over to his wonderful blue butterflies in those forest paths under a tropic sun in thirty-eight words I do not know."

H. M. Tomlinson: The Sea and the Jungle.

I SHOULD have liked to dwell at some length, here or elsewhere, upon two writers who deserve celebration in the pages of any such book. They are Morley Roberts and David Bone. Roberts, the

friend of Gissing and Hudson, and a novelist and short story writer
of merit, claims mention in particular on account of "The Western
Avernus," one of the best records of a man's travel experience ever
written; while Bone produced, in "The Brassbounder," a glorious
picture of life at sea in the days of sailing-ships. But Roberts must be
excluded because nearly all his non-scientific or non-medical work
belongs to its time, which is long pre-Georgian; and Bone's total
literary product is so small in bulk that when I have expressed
admiration for it and the reader's complaint that Bone should have
continued to be a practical and ageless traveller almost to the end of
his life there is little to add.

David Bone was born in Glasgow in 1874. He was one of three
famous brothers (a fourth, less famous, also published some account
of his adventures), of whom one, Muirhead, was artist and etcher,
and the third, James, was London editor of *The Manchester Guardian*.
James was a writer and character whose part in the Georgian literary
scene is unseizable, though at the same time beyond question. I have
in mind the picture of all three of them, Muirhead the gayest of the
party and the quickest-moving, with an ever-ready smile; James
lean, with the droll, dry face of a comedian; David, by contrast,
stocky, serious, and with the great dignity that becomes a captain of a
giant liner. They are looking attentively at me—evidently I have
demurred to some invitation;—and David speaks. He says, in a rich,
melancholy, impressive voice: "You don't often get the chance of
dining with all three of us at once." The others nod. The invitation
becomes irresistible. You would have thought David could never
smile.

But what a mistake that would be! His was a humorous eye;
a great yarner, he had such a sense of phrase that there is not a
spare word in "The Brassbounder" or in "Merchantmen-at-Arms,"
but only a mastery by which scenes are brought to life and given
their original colour and movement. It was the same whether he
spoke or wrote; sense was so exact, voice so rich, pen so unfaltering.
I had never been at sea upon a ship commanded by Captain Bone,
but if I had done so I know that I should have arrived punctually
after an experience of all the beauties and braveries that the sea can
offer, and with a memory fit to last for ever.

That must be a sufficient testimony to a fine sailor and a magnificent writer. My business now is rather with a landsman, but a
landsman who has been to sea a number of times, and into the
jungle, too, taking with him a mildness of manner, a warmly
coloured pen, a dry yet fluty Cockney voice, and an eye and sensitiveness rare among professional writers. His Christian names were
largely unknown, for nobody ever dreamed of addressing him by
one of them when an abbreviation of his surname was so obviously

all that was needed. I have already identified this man at the head of the section. He was H. M. Tomlinson; and I suppose that I have been longer acquainted with his work than most people, for when I was very young indeed my mother used to cut from the columns of a London morning newspaper, *The Morning Leader*, descriptive articles of his which she carefully stored—I should have said by the hundred. And so when Tomlinson was "discovered" by the quid-nuncs as the result of his first book, "The Sea and the Jungle," that was for me an old story. I knew all about Tomlinson. My mother, who had taste, and who knew the difference between a writer and a man who pushes a pen, had told me.

Nevertheless, Tomlinson was duly discovered by the literati; and his discoverer, round about 1911, was Ford Madox Hueffer, then editing *The English Review*, as I have previously told. Prior to that, Tomlinson, having escaped from an office job, had at the age of thirty or so (he was born in 1873) joined the staff of *The Morning Leader*. He was later to work as War Correspondent for Dickens's old paper, *The Daily News*, under A. G. Gardiner, and then for the weekly review, *The Nation,* under Henry Massingham; and like Massingham he could not write the smallest paragraph without stamping it with his own personality. But his books began in 1912 with "The Sea and the Jungle," and "The Sea and the Jungle," which was not at the time a popular success, remains still his most characteristic production. You will find in its luminous pages all the various Tomlinsons who have since expressed themselves so picturesquely upon the subjects of the sea and the War and the politicians and other matters.

In that book he gives an account of his participation in an exploratory journey from Wales to the Amazon and farther up the Amazon than any ship of such draught (23 feet) as the *Capella* had ever previously been. He had a friend who was chief engineer on this ship, and he was engaged nominally as purser for the voyage. There are no lies in "The Sea and the Jungle." It begins at the beginning, with our author finding his way aboard in darkness and rain. It continues with an account of a storm, not as a sailor sees it, but as we ourselves (who are not sailors) would see it and feel afraid and very uncomfortable. And we then see and feel the at-mosphere of Para and other Amazonian features. It is an experience. We actually sail in the *Capella*. Although our vocabularies may be smaller than that of our guide and companion, we share all his sensations. Here is Tomlinson mildly ironic at the moment preced-ing the start of his journey:

"I have a clear memory of the newspapers as they were that morning. I had a sheaf of them, for it is my melancholy business to know what each is saying. I learned there were dark and portentous matters, not actually with us, but looming, each already rather larger than a man's hand. If certain things happened, said one half of the papers, ruin stared us in the face. If those things did not happen, said the other half, ruin stared us in the face. . . . You paid your halfpenny and were damned either way. If you paid a penny you got more for your money."

That is one mood. Here is another, describing the hour of storm:

"I turned up the dull and stinking oil lamp, and tried to read; but that fuliginous glim haunted the pages. That black-edged light too much resembled my own thoughts made manifest. There were some bunches of my cabin-mate's clothes hanging from hooks, and I watched their erratic behaviour instead. The water in the carafe was also interesting, because quite mad, standing diagonally in the bottle, and then reversing. A lump of soap made a flying leap from the washstand, and then slithered about the floor like something hunted and panic-stricken. I listened to numerous little voices. There was no telling their origins. There was a chorus in the cabin, whispers, plaints, creaks, wails, and grunts; but they were foundered in the din when the spittoon, which was an empty meat tin, got its lashings loose, and began a rioting fandango on the concrete. Over the clothes chest, which was also our table and a cabin fixture, was a portrait of the mate's sweetheart, and on its frame was one of my busy little friends the cockroaches; for the mate and I do not sleep alone in this cabin, not by hundreds. The cockroach stood in thought, waving his hands interrogatively . . ."

Finally, as the ship reaches land,

"The *Capella* continued to stand in, till America was more than a frail and tinted illusion which sometimes faded the more the eye sought it. Presently it cast reflections. The islands grew into cobalt layers, with vistas of silver water between them; they acquired body . . . Curtains as black as bitumen draped to the waters from great heights. Two of these appalling curtains, trailing over America, were drawn a little apart. We could see beyond them to a diminishing array of glowing cloud summits; far through those parted black curtains of storm we saw an accidental revelation of a secret and wonderful region with a sun of its own. And all, gigantic clouds, the sea, the far and frail coast, were serene and still. The air had ceased to breathe. . . . We went slowly over a lower world obscurely lighted by phosphorescent waves."

It has been said that Tomlinson had a studied style. That is not the case. His style was a natural product, resulting from Tomlinson's lifelong habit of mind and ear. The sentences formed themselves in his head as he wrote; they were not laboriously reshaped after being set down. Any reader who knew the author will recognize every cadence they contain, and every word, even when it seems conscious, as if it were uttered as part of the conversation in that hoarse little undertone. He will see Tomlinson's surprisingly tall, bony head, and a hand at the ear to catch whatever reply is made, the almost anxious gravity of Tomlinson's expression, the sad, dry smile preceding a story, never afterwards forgotten, which sets the party in a roar, the thoughtfulness, the honesty, the convulsed silent laughter, and above all the scepticism which ran through his mind like a whisper.

He began by taking to heart the ways of two writers who were always his favourites. Two meditative writers who lived in a simpler world than ours and who seem to me a little less good than Tomlinson found them. His pen and his speech were alike the pen and speech of a lover of Henry David Thoreau and Ralph Waldo Emerson. For Thoreau, in particular (a writer whom I regard as a poseur), he had a feeling that approached veneration. That is because he believed what Thoreau said; he was too honest to do anything else. He was by temperament half a philosopher—one who turns over and over in his mind the nature of man, his needs and his errant civilization,—and half a journalist. Also, having seen the action of much humbug, he was socially indignant, so that when he wrote or spoke of suffering or of what he believed to be injustice or villainy he was often moved, as cold-hearted people are not moved, to emotion. Cold-hearted people, accordingly, or those who fear the display of emotion lest it should break down altogether too many restraints, suppose Tomlinson to be sentimental; whereas he was in reality so simple that he ever believed in the opposition of virtue and vice. He believed that the rich are unscrupulous, and that the very poor never have a chance. But unlike so many of our self-righteous rentier-communists of the latest literary movement he had experienced the life of the very poor, and knew what a slum was like, so that some indignation, however unsophisticated, should be permitted him. Besides, the doctrine preached by Tomlinson is old-fashioned Liberalism, and whatever he may have called himself he was an old-fashioned Liberal.

All his journalism was done for periodicals appealing to socially-indignant Liberals of the reforming kind—*The Morning Leader*, *The Daily News*, *The Nation*. These papers are gone, as Liberalism is gone. The more sentimental Liberals of the middle class, to whom they appealed, have taken a farther step to the Left; those who wish to maintain the world as they knew it have moved for safety to the Right. Tomlinson's views are anachronistic. Very well, he wrote several novels (the novel offering itself as a convenient receptacle into which a man may put his ideas and his emotions, his experience and his literary gifts), and some of them were widely and appreciatively read. But Tomlinson was not a born novelist. The books were written less as novels than as testimonies to the author's view of life; and he was never able to master a craft that seemed easy and was very difficult. True, "Gallions Reach" was a better book than many novels written by professional novelists. As long as it was descriptive, as long as it was personal, authentic, "felt," it had magnificence. But it had no construction. In a single book, that is a trifle. When, however, this book was followed by a much more ambitious novel called "All Our Yesterdays," the very title of which was charged with a kind of indignant pessimism, the failure in composition, as well as in what may be called the more human elements, was striking.

He subsequently produced novels of which the form was better, such as "All Hands"; but not one of them recovered the popular enthusiasm so warmly given to "Gallions Reach". The reason for this is clear. It is that the one prime need in a novelist is power to create characters interesting to us for their own sakes, irrespective of their political, social, and moral significance. This may be an old-fashioned definition; but it explains why many writers of considerable literary ability and much intelligence fail to stir the imagination of their readers and produce fictions which in fact are without life. It explains why some of those who cannot write novels nowadays declare that the novel is an exhausted form. In Tomlinson's case there was great experience of life and scene, all of which has its value in making a book readable or important to the reader. But I doubt whether Tomlinson had the detachment to be either a good critic or a good novelist. He had too many, or too strict, moral notions. They got in the way. He saw other people from the outside, trusted or distrusted them, liked them or disliked them, but never amused himself by imagining them as enchanting labyrinths, as fiery particles of flesh and spirit, as children, as human beings. To him, in a sense, they were all moral ideas.

That is not to say that he was a prig, or uncharitable, or humourless. On the contrary, his literary enthusiasms of later date were for writers of a mordant and sceptical cast, for Lucian, for Anatole France, for Norman Douglas; and his own patient and yet scornful humour had an acid bite that never contradicted his astonishing charity. But he did not relish character as character; and he did not create character. His gift was for writing. He was reflective as Thoreau and Emerson were reflective; and he was a natural descriptive writer. When he had something to describe which deeply moved him his writing was genuine communication, and as such ranks high in our time.

vi. Norman Douglas

"A man who has tried to remain a mere citizen of the world and refused to squeeze himself into the narrow methods and aspirations of any epoch or country . . ."

Norman Douglas: Alone.

MY last traveller is one who strayed not only far and wide upon a part of the earth's surface but also a considerable distance into the heart of the mystery of life. Rightly to appreciate Norman Douglas one should be a Scotsman, a student of antiquity, an epicure, a wit, a naturalist, and an amoral philosopher. He was all these things, and more. He was not solely a Scot, for his mother was half German; but the Scottish element in his nature prevailed over any other. He was at school at Uppingham and in Germany, was in the diplomatic service, was sub-editor of *The English Review*, a teacher of French to American soldiers in Paris, and many other things. His written books include "The Herpetology of the Duchy of Baden," "London Street Games," "Old Calabria," and studies of the private lives of Gods and other prehistoric persons. He lived to be an octogenarian; and if there was ever any mystery about his age it is because he wrote of his own Mr. Keith:

"Mr. Keith was older than he looked—incredibly old, in fact, though nobody could bring himself to believe it; he was well preserved by means of a complicated system of life, the details of which, he used to declare, were not fit for publication. That was only his way of talking. He exaggerated so dreadfully. His face was clean-shaven, rosy, and of cherubic fulness."

To this kindly description D. H. Lawrence adds the gloss:

"D—— was decidedly shabby and a gentleman, with his wicked red face and tufted eyebrows."

But Mr. Keith, who, although "a perfect host," was at the same time "an egoist, a solitary, in his pleasures,"

"disliked funerals. For all his open mind and open bowels, Mr. Keith displayed an unreasoning hatred of death and, what was still more remarkable, not the least shame in confessing it. . . . Mr. Keith was in love with life. It dealt fairly with him. It made him loth to bid farewell to this gracious earth and the blue sky overhead, to his cooks and his books, his gardeners and roses and flaming cannas; loth to exchange these things of love, these tangible delights, for a hideous and ever lasting annihilation."

To which I shall add two quotations from Orioli's "Moving Along," in which there are charming glimpses of Douglas. The first:

> "Norman said he felt quite at home here. He was really in Old Calabria now, and I could see he was enjoying it. We could sit round the brazier all night, he said, getting our clothes dry gradually, smoking our pipes and drinking wine. What more could anybody want? As to sleeping—damn it, if one cares to sleep, one need only rest one's elbows on one's knees and put one's head into one's hands, and there you are. Delicious!"

And the second:

> "Norman ate more than the rest of us put together and then regretted that he could eat no more; he said a man could not expect to have a proper appetite at his time of life."

Lawrence, less kindly:

> "D—— always grumbled about the food . . . D—— always poked and pushed among the portions, and grumbled frantically, sotto voce, in Italian to the youth Beppo, getting into a nervous frenzy."

You have the impression from these quotations of one who is interested in good food—an epicure. By his own account, given in the autobiographical "Looking Back," he retained much interest in other corporeal matters. He loved life, women, boys, food, drink, and knowledge. And he quoted with approval the story of a Leontine philosopher who, when asked "how he had managed to attain a hundred years with such glowing health and jollity," "was wont to shake his hoary locks and roar out 'Because I never went a step out of my way to please anybody but myself.'" Like so many Scotsmen he was born an antiquary, and like his own Mr. Keith again he "knew too much, and had travelled too far, to be anything but a hopeless unbeliever." That is, he was not merely a sceptic, but one wholly without the ordinary human need to justify himself to others. For this reason his work has been unpopular, and has sometimes inspired disgust in squeamish readers.

Not because the work itself has ever been pornographic: far from it. Merely because those who regard themselves as most emancipated from convention are usually most conventional. Rationalists comport themselves with a kind of glee in conscious blasphemy; and the very ironists of recent fashion do not care to endure the irony of others and in fact fear it. Douglas, they feel, might—so remote is his soul—laugh even at them. Horrible!

Horrible! "An egoist, a solitary," said Douglas, speaking of Mr. Keith. Yes, entirely selfish, no doubt, and a hedonist; an utterly irreverent mind beside which the incredulities of others are but the self-conscious waywardnesses of youth. And yet a writer who puts other writers to shame, "a perfect host," and a man of whom Lawrence, never sanguine regarding the virtues of his friends, was forced by candour to say "D—— has never left me in the lurch." Rather an interesting person, you would suppose.

You would be right. Douglas, whose literary work was ever fitful because he cared less for literary fame than for life, wrote several books in a style to make all who care for right expression envious of such perfect skill. And these books are packed with original observation and research presented so allusively and with such a damping of irony that one must love wit for its own sake to appreciate all the learning out of which it flows. If Douglas, with his reading of saintly biographies and his curious enjoyment of human idiocy, had kept to the narrow path of scholarship, he would have received the rewards of dignity. Or if he had been less intent upon knowing the details of the past, and had given his time to verbal decoration, he would have had the shallower sort at his feet to hear a flow of ridicule and invention such as his conversation afforded. But he was not ambitious. He wanted to enjoy himself. He wanted to learn, not for the sake of exhibiting his own splendours, but because the whole business of life seemed to him to be very odd and interesting and worthy of exploration.

Having his own pleasure in view, he never sought to teach others. That is the worst feature of the Scottish kind of humour; it is self-sufficing. Having no belief, he had no ambition to breed disciples or scatter his faith abroad. And that, too, proved a mistake. The young and ardent, always looking for assurances of immortality, or at least of importance, have found him negative. Only to lovers of classic civilization and literature has he afforded the spectacle of a modern Ancient Greek, too wise for illusion, and not in the least bothered by his lack of credit.

It is to "South Wind" that most readers of Douglas turn for pleasure; they would do better to read and re-read "Old Calabria," which is his masterpiece. By comparison, "South Wind" is a light record of the extraordinary life led by dwellers upon the island of Capri. We assume that it is a work of irony, and that no such fantastic creatures could ever be gathered together in a single spot (I am not sure, by the way, that "South Wind," in this aspect, is not the begetting cause of many artificial gatherings lately popular with novelists of hotel life, liner life, tenement life, and so on); but Francis Brett Young, in his preface to the English translations from Cerio's "Aria di Capri," says that it is but a transcript from life made in all simplicity. It embraces a little mock hagiology, some doubtful geology, a plot (Douglas is firm as to the plot, and also the moral, which many have missed), and some delicious writing. It is full of entertainment, and without doubt, in company with the equally delicious works of Thomas Love Peacock, has served as an inspiration to Aldous Huxley, among others. But it is, beside "Old Calabria," a by-product, a holiday, a nonsense-version of many-sided truth. "Old Calabria" is the real thing, and a work of unique character. It is a travel book, a history book, a system of philosophy, and a self-portrait, all in one. Too rich a diet for some minds? No; the difficulty is one of concentration. The sweep and toughness of Douglas's curiosity is greater than any we can summon, and we put the book aside for reflection. Sometimes we do not take it up again. That is true of all Douglas's work.

"Old Calabria" is the best of his books because Douglas always felt at home in Calabria. For one thing, he persuaded himself that it must have looked, in ancient times, much as it looks now; for another it is full of news for the antiquary who is also of a scientific turn and a collector of legends. He had his own method of acquiring knowledge, and a simple one. Orioli says:

> "Norman gives chocolates to the children. . . . He never travels in the less frequented parts without sweets in his pocket for the young ones, and without snuff for the old ones. He says that they are the only people worth talking to; all the middle generation in this country is useless for his purposes, too worldly and material, no legends, no poetry. How many hearts has he not conquered with sweets, and how many stories has he not collected with snuff! I have seen him giving snuff to old women of eighty, and then talking to them for hours and hours."

Well, the hours and hours are not wasted; and they were not wasted when he was gathering the material for "Old Calabria," for he was well-grounded in natural science, he already possessed much out-of-the-way knowledge, and he loved travelling and seeing and knowing so dearly that no discomfort or danger could possibly deter him from making every necessary investigation. Nor did he hesitate to buy and read masses of saintly biography with a solemnly mischievous attention that never became merely derisive. The book was a labour of love. Hills, villages, saints, critical asides, curious facts, and the author's personality all jostle each other in its pages. It is fit reading for sage and ribald, for ethnologist and the student of comparative hagiology.

Douglas had his views upon civilization, too; and these he imparted with customary calm:

"Nearly all the Mediterranean races have been misfed from early days; that is why they are so small. I would undertake to raise the Italian standard of height by several inches, if I had control of their nutrition for a few centuries. I would undertake to convert them from utilitarians into romantics—were such a change desirable. For if utilitarianism be the shadow of starvation, romance is nothing but the vapour of repletion.

"And yet men still talk of race-characteristics as of something fixed and immutable! The Jews, so long as they starved in Palestine, were the most acrimonious bigots on earth. Now that they live and feed sensibly, they have learnt to see things in their true perspective —they have become rationalists. Their less fortunate fellow-Semites, the Arabs, have continued to starve and to swear by the Koran— empty in body and empty in mind. No poise or balance is possible to those who live in uneasy conditions."

Half-concealed in a note is this other characteristic saying, which helps to indicate something of Douglas's attitude towards his fellow-creatures:

"By placid I do not mean peace-loving and pitiful in the Christian sense. The doctrine of loving and forgiving one's enemies is based on sheer funk; our pity for others is dangerously akin to self-pity, most odious of vices. Catholic teaching—in practice, if not in theory —glides artfully over the desirability of these freak-virtues, knowing that they cannot appeal to a masculine stock. By placid I mean steady, self-contained."

But wherever one turns in this book there are characteristic things, some of them beautiful, some of them shrewd, some of them—to say the least—debatable; and since it has, to speak roughly, one reader for every five hundred readers of "South Wind," it may justly be described as undervalued to the point of neglect. Yet it is one of the richest of modern books, and for all who care to acquaint themselves with a mind as odd and varied as that of Samuel Butler (but more adult than Butler's mind, according to our author, ever was) should first possess "Old Calabria" as its essential expression.

The lesser books, such as "Siren Land," which is similarly notable for what Douglas calls "that (characteristic) veneer of erudition," and "Fountains in the Sand," have much virtue as monologues; and the queer autobiography, "Looking Back," which is built upon an array of visiting cards used by the author as stimulus to memory, and which brings us closer than any other to his conscienceless temper, will be read as long as books are read at all. But only by the few. And when I say "the few," I am not using that term in the snobbish, or even the Stendhalian, sense, for

I do not share the genteel notion that what other people like must be contemptible, but solely "the few." Perhaps a greater and less self-sufficient man could have brought scholarship less desultorily and more universally to book.

Now, having ended my travellers with an explorer, I shall leave them for some whose interests have lain nearer home, right under their noses, and in the hearts and doings of common or, at least, normal town-dwellers such as we believe ourselves to see every day of our lives.

Chapter Seven

BLACK AND WHITE

GEORGE MOORE, ARNOLD BENNETT, JOHN GALSWORTHY,
SOMERSET MAUGHAM

i

"Every artist goes to real life for his matter, and from its chaos brings us an idea. . . .
The specific difference of the realist is that, having extracted his idea, instead of further
distilling it (as the Classicist does) or disguising it with mysterious essences (as the
Romantic does), he endeavours to restore to it the flavour of reality. He endeavours to
manifest the very texture and illusion of Life itself. Having unravelled a thread, he
shows it us with a new artful tangle of his own.

George Calderon: Preface to Two Plays by Tchekhov.

THE realist is inveterately plain, and not coloured; and the fact
that the lives of wealthy people are so rarely treated with
realism has led many to suppose that realism is pure squalor.
But English realism is undoubtedly as old as Thomas Nashe, and
while it has come to modern readers tinctured by French and Russian
influence we have no more realistic writer than Neil Lyons, who was
a humorist. I wonder whether George Calderon, in the extract I
have quoted above, was right in his belief that realism is a technical
matter: may it not, rather, be a personal matter? As a rough division
of men, it may be said that there are some who, like Stevenson,
think every action the better for a bit of purple, and some—not
Quakers alone—who shun colour. Purple was used by Stevenson
figuratively—as a synonym for bravery, or display; and his heroine,
Catriona, who is rather like Stevenson, after saying that she ought
to have been a man child, goes on:

"In my own thoughts it is so I am always; and I go on telling myself about this thing that is to befall and that. Then it comes to the
place of the fighting, and it comes over me that I am only a girl at all
events; and then I have to twist my story round about, so that the
fighting is to stop, and yet me have the best of it; . . . and I am the boy
that makes the fine speeches all through, like Mr. David Balfour."

Stevenson and Catriona were both romantics. They saw themselves, as Pyramus did, in heroic parts, triumphant parts, fine
costumes, speaking grand words, doing glorious deeds. Stevenson's
books are the echo of romantic ambition, and his stage is a toy
stage.

And there are those others who, while they cannot deceive them-selves with the stuff of charades, are yet chiefly delighted at the thought of appearing a little noble or brilliant, self-sacrificing, brave, enduring, arch and sensitive; and they are the sentimentalists, to whom we owe the bulk of our fiction. They have quick emotions, none too genuine when one comes to take stock of them, but of a special fluency and address quite sufficiently apt to persuade readers that something real lies behind. Others again, and these are inverted sentimentalists, are never satisfied with life, but must show it as something more bitter and testing and less heroic than we had hoped, a terrible disillusion for those who will not swim with the tide and run with the mob. They cry "Woe! Woe!" but in reality it is their object that we should admire them for what they refuse to do and say; and it is quite true that we are often impressed with their castigations of society and human nature.

But if we all have our favourite rôles in life, and wittingly or un-wittingly play them in our books, there are some who, for one reason or another, do not wish to take the lead, and do not wish to impress by the display of their own brilliance or courage or dis-illusion. These are the realists or potential realists, for whom the scene is complete if it be played by others, so long as these others are human (and not dolls), and so long as *they* can but watch and relish all that happens, and gratify vanity (it may be), or compensate themselves otherwise, by setting it down without adornment but with satisfying precision. Their preferred rôle is that of spectator, recorder, critic, not protagonist or participant; and their wear so sober that it will attract no notice at all from their fellow-creatures.

That is only a suggestion. You could say, if you liked, that these were men in whom what used to be called the feminine element is very strong. Or that they are without passion; or that their minds are too strict to allow passion its rein. Or that there is some physical reason, such as the stammer from which both Arnold Bennett and Somerset Maugham have suffered, or Galsworthy's shyness, or that curious accident of George Moore's childhood which he thus describes:

"It is difficult for me to believe any good of myself. Within the oftentimes bombastic and truculent appearance that I present to the world, trembles a heart shy as a wren in the hedgerow or a mouse along the wainscotting. And the question has always interested me, whether I brought this lack of belief in myself into the world with me, or whether it was a gift from Nature, or whether I was trained into it by my parents at so early an age, that it became part of myself. I lean to the theory of acquisition rather than to that of inheritance, for it seems to me that I can trace my inveterate distrust of myself back to the years when my father and mother used to tell me that I would certainly marry an old woman, Honor King, who used to come to the door begging. This joke did not wear out; it lasted through my childhood; and I remember still how I used to dread her appearance, or her name, for either was sufficient to incite somebody to remind me of the nuptials that awaited me in a few years. I understood very well that the joke rested on the assumption that I was such an ugly little boy that nobody else would marry me."

But whatever the cause it seems to me that there is more force in an argument for negative qualities in the realist than for any belief in a determined choice of realism as against any other ism whatever. "This craving," says Moore in another place,

"This craving for observation of manners, this instinct for the rapid notation of gestures and words that epitomize a state of feeling, of attitudes that mirror forth the soul, declared itself a main passion. . . . With the patience of a cat at a mouse-hole I watched and listened; . . . and though I laughed and danced, and made merry with them, *I was not of them*."

I do not wish to labour this point, but if it is true that men are realists because of an attitude of mind natural to them, and not by any choice, no scolding or praise of their ways will avail us. All we can do is to point to characteristics and the excellence of their work in its own genre. This, without further preamble, I shall proceed to do. And the first realist with whom I shall deal, who was not less a realist when he roved in archaic fields, is one who died believing that he had slain the conventional novel and created the style of Synge (neither of which things had he done), who execrated the work of most of his rivals and sometimes vilified them, along with his friends, in print, and who wrote in a manner which progressed from a sing-song abruptness to exquisite and mellifluous simplicity.

ii. George Moore

"I came into the world apparently with a nature like a smooth sheet of wax, bearing no impress, but capable of receiving any; of being moulded into all shapes. Nor am I exaggerating when I say I think that I might equally have been a Pharaoh, an ostler, a pimp, an archbishop, and that in the fulfilment of the duties of each a certain measure of success would have been mine."

George Moore: Confessions of a Young Man.

GEORGE MOORE was the son of a landed Irish gentleman who became a Member of Parliament and who bred and raced horses. He was born in 1852. His childhood was spent partly upon the paternal estate in the West of Ireland and partly in London, and neither in Ireland nor in London was he able to learn anything at school. Although the son of Roman Catholic parents, he became very early, through his private reading, an agnostic; and although to please his father he agreed to be a soldier he really wanted to be a painter. Finding military training excessively disagreeable, he soon abandoned it for the companionship of not quite excellent artists, actors, and their free-living friends. He "cultivated with care the acquaintance of a neighbour who had taken the Globe Theatre for the purpose of producing Offenbach's operas"; and when once he had done this he was in the true Paradise of all coldly sensual young men. "Bouquets, stalls, rings, delighted me; and of all, the life of the theatre—that life of raw gaslight, whitewashed walls, of doggerel verse, slangy polkas and waltzes, interested me beyond legitimate measure. . . . My mother suffered, and expected ruin, for I took no trouble to conceal anything; I boasted of dissipation. But there was no need of fear, for I was naturally endowed with a very clear sense of self-preservation; I neither betted nor drank, nor contracted debts, nor a secret marriage; from a worldly point of view, I was a model young man indeed."

Still, however, his mind had no positive direction; only a bent towards pleasure and the arts. As soon as he was of age (his father died when Moore was eighteen, and Moore inherited the estate) he set out for Paris. There, continuing his interest in painting and literature, stage and opera, he established himself among rather more excellent artists and writers than those whom he had known at home, and, while he soon gave up painting, lived for ten years the life of a dilettante, deep in the æsthetic fashions of an age already drawing to its close. Not until near the end of his stay in Paris did he awaken from a kind of strolling complacency of self-indulgence; and then a manifesto by Zola in praise of realism shocked him into new and positive literary faith. He knew at last what he must do with his talent, and the genre for which his temper had prepared him.

But in the middle of the dream and at the very moment of Moore's awakening to direction news came that his estate was in difficulties, and he was forced to leave Paris. In London he lived twelve years in comparative poverty before wealth returned and he became again independent. During those years he wrote art criticism, and consorted, as he has amusingly told, with a group of men who gathered round Tinsley, the publisher; and he began to produce his earliest realistic novels.

The first of them, written when Moore was thirty, was "A Modern Lover"; the second that landmark in modern literature, "A Mummer's Wife." Acquaintance with poor artists and actors, then and in the past (a fellow-lodger was an actress, and the wretched

Alice in "A Mummer's Wife" began her downfall by an effort to be sprightly in the part of Serpolette), was invaluable to him. Boyhood memory of his father's racing stables and the social ways of the Irish gentry and the Irish peasants was always at his call. And, having embraced the realistic method, he pursued it unremittingly. Nothing was lost upon him. He used to talk with a hard-pressed and illiterate maid-of-all-work at his lodging house, and later with his charwoman in the Temple; and he says that while the charwoman "didn't inspire the subject of 'Esther Waters,' she was the atmosphere I required for the book, and to talk to her at breakfast before beginning to write was an excellent preparation." Excellent indeed; for Moore explained that he had used another model "without shame or stint, as I have used all those with whom I have been brought into close contact."

When the Boer War broke out at the end of the century Moore found himself much opposed to the British Government in that matter, as many English people did; and he was inclined to shake the dust of the accursed oppressor from his foot. He therefore went to Ireland for two years, where he met Irish writers and had a good deal to do with the founding of the Irish Theatre, a scheme sponsored by his friend Edward Martyn and by W. B. Yeats. He was a severe critic of all that was done, and he did not find himself completely in accord with his countrymen, with the result that he left sore memories behind him in Dublin, and did not improve his relations with the Irish when he came to write, many years later, his memories of that period.

At last, however, early in the new century, he was back again in London; and by then matters had so much improved with Moore that he left his garret and took a flat in Victoria Street; and later he went to that house in Pimlico with which his name will always be associated. Ebury Street, where he lived until his death, is a long, rather featureless thoroughfare; but after the First World War it became both inglorious and glorious in London history as the scene of the assassination of another Irishman and the pursuit and capture of the murderers by an unarmed mob. It is also immortalized in the title of one of Moore's works. I was going to say "one of Moore's most characteristic works," but they are all, either in themselves or in relation to his work as a whole, highly characteristic, for he was an original. He always wrote the kind of book he wanted to write, and it was a kind of book peculiar to himself. It is because he was an original, and not because of his realism or his later style, that he will survive in memory; and no writing about him could possibly equal his own writing about himself, which was marked with so much curious detail, and was so precise, so candid (where he wished to be candid), and at all times so illuminative of his personality.

There exist paintings of Moore at several ages, and the best portrait of him is the famous one by Manet. But for those who wish for a verbal picture it would be difficult to improve upon that given by Susan Mitchell. This first appeared in a volume of "Irishmen of Today" which was published in 1915, and of course it represents its subject as he was at the beginning of the century. I will only add that the Moore whom I saw in 1920 corresponded well to Susan Mitchell's account, excepting that his hair was white, or appeared so by artificial light, and that he stooped somewhat. Here is the picture:

"Moore, who everyone said was a very wicked man, had the rosy face and innocent yellow hair of young virtue, kindness was on his lips, though his eyes were not quite so kind, a little slow in following the lips. . . . George Moore seemed to me then to be a man of middle height with an egg-shaped face and head, light yellow hair, in perpetual revolt against the brush, a stout nose with thick nostrils, grey-green eyes, lips thick in the middle as if a bee had stung them. He had champagne shoulders and a somewhat thick, ungainly figure, but he moved about a room with a grace which is not of Dublin drawing-rooms. . . . George Moore's is a face dear to the caricaturist and in itself at times a caricature; the yellow hair, the fat features, the sly smile, the malice, the vanity. But as has been said to me, let some-one begin to discuss an idea and in a moment the contours change, the fat shapelessness falls away, the jaw lengthens, the bones become visible, the eyes darken, the brows straighten, a hawk-like keenness is in the look. One does not caricature this Moore."

"The sly smile, the malice, the vanity": one sees them all in Moore's more personal writings, "Confessions of a Young Man," "Memoirs of My Dead Life," "Hail and Farewell," "Avowals," "Conversations in Ebury Street." At first, until the attention is caught, they may seem the outstanding characteristics of his work; but no writing as limpid as his could escape insipidity if it were not that every sentence has been overseen by a mind both keen and clear. One thinks one is listening to Mr. Woodhouse, Emma's father, whose conversational style might almost have been Moore's model. But in fact one is listening to a man in whom slyness is but the gentle handmaid of scarifying and tenacious judgment.

I said just now that Moore was candid when he wished to be candid; and I meant that in his printed discussions it is always he who chooses the ground, just as it was always Socrates, another deceptively simple casuist, who chose the ground upon which he could discomfit other spirits more generous in assertion. Moore's criticisms of Thomas Hardy, to take one instance, are based upon isolated passages or single poems, and they take no heed of Hardy's work as a whole or of Hardy's character as a writer. It is true that

Hardy's poetic preoccupations are often with death and decay. It is true that Hardy's prose style is occasionally clotted. One could catalogue other faults. But if preoccupations and faults and single paragraphs were to settle a writer's calibre, some of Moore's own shortcomings could be made to damn him for ever. I also meant that his confessions sometimes swear with his professions. The wicked Moore of Susan Mitchell's phrase is not to be reconciled with Moore's own "I am as timid in life as in literature," "I was naturally endowed with a very clear sense of self-preservation," "Within the oftentimes bombastic and truculent appearance that I present to the world, trembles a heart shy as a wren." He was a greater lover on paper than in reality, and the tales he told of himself were coloured to please, because if they had been plain they could never have gratified his own malice. It was an Irishwoman, Miss Sarah Purser, who said: "Some men kiss and tell; Mr. Moore tells but doesn't kiss."

The truth is that there is coldness in all Moore's writing. He was never more cold than he was in that tale of love, "Evelyn Innes." His realistic novels set down a series of facts which one accepts or rejects according to one's own experience; and I rate them lower than other commentators have done. They have a wooden, unleavened literalness which takes no heed of surrounding colour and movement. They have no humour. Not only has the author no passion, but his dramatis personæ kiss without conviction—one seducer enchants his love by dilating upon the qualities of Balzac as a writer, and, having had his offer of horses refused, is more successful with a set of the Comédie Humaine. By comparison with books written since in the same order, they are one-syllabled and one-toned. But when read in relation to the history of the novel, as pioneer works in a stage of fictive literature which otherwise was largely sentimental or decorative, they are outstanding. While other writers of the eighties and early nineties were being "just literary," or witty at the expense of others (few can be witty, of course, at their own expense; but still fewer make the attempt), or romantic, or ingenious, Moore and Gissing alone, or almost alone, were trying in the published novel to tell the world something about life at first hand. And in Moore's case it was quite extraordinary how the choice of detail and the continuous succession of plain incidents produced both an effect of nature and a progressive interest. Where Gissing showed his personal grievance and rebelliousness, Moore recorded. He was detached. He did not explain or expound (as Gissing did), but refrained from all personal comment, leaving to his characters any reflections which had properly to be made upon such situations as seemed inevitably to arise in the course of the tale. To me these books miss a thousand shades;

but that is their strength, for they are as firm as engravings. No wonder they impressed themselves, and still impress themselves, upon candid minds as very striking reproductions of reality. There is no question that they gave rise, towards the end of the nineties, to a new school of naturalistic writers, Edwin Pugh, Arthur Morrison, Somerset Maugham, and others. We know that a reading of "A Mummer's Wife" drew Arnold Bennett towards that re-creation of life in the Five Towns upon which his lasting fame depends. Merely to record the facts is to establish Moore's importance as an influence upon his age.

But he gradually moved away from tales of poor artists, maidservants, and travelling actors. Already, in 1886, he had passed across the Irish Sea to his own land, when he painted in "A Drama in Muslin" his picture of husband-hunting in rural Ireland, a book which in spite of crudities has beauty and sympathy and a quality of its own; and though he returned after this to the rigorous simplicity of "Esther Waters" he dwelt in that book for the last time upon the ways of very poor people. In "Evelyn Innes" and "Sister Teresa" love and theology and the arts were his themes; and in "The Lake" and "The Untilled Field" the consequences of his long visit to Ireland were to be seen. These books were very much better written than their predecessors. Those short paragraphs, as wearisome as couplets, in which "A Modern Lover" was written gave way to a more sustained prose which has enchantment for the ear. The Irish books, in particular, showed his advance in skill; for while they appeared literal they were approaching the colloquial simplicity which he was later to perfect. But "Evelyn Innes" and "Sister Teresa" betrayed a thinning of direct inspiration from life. He was in truth at the end of mundane experience; and had reached the condition of sedentary debate and literary inspiration in which the remainder of his life was spent.

From that time onward (that is to say from the comparative affluence which came to him with the new century) he was less a novelist than an editor, talker, and commentator. He began to re-write his earlier books. The mood revealed long before in "Confessions of a Young Man" took complete control of him. He was ready to confess all and more than all about himself and his friends. Seeking for material upon which to exercise his gift, he found only the past, in men and in books. He was over fifty when he related the "Memoirs of My Dead Life"; the great trilogy "Hail and Farewell" followed; for the rest he re-presented what had been written before. His own novels, the story of two medieval lovers, the story of two lovers of antiquity, and at last the New Testament itself, were all rewritten with a most cunning mastery of language and a strong and artful, rather than a subtle, intelligence.

It is interesting to recall that when Moore was writing his early novels they were the cause of fierce combats with the libraries and the moral censors of their day, when in reality no more rigidly moral novels have ever been composed; and that whenever he wrote of Ireland he was the centre of noise and argument inseparable from all discussion of Irish affairs; and that as he took up the life of Christ similar discord marred the acceptance of his work and averted its neglect. These excitements are now stale. Like other Irishmen, he enjoyed exasperating his fellows; and nowadays, when passions are concentrated upon more contemporary matters, he has lost the benefits of exasperation and fallen into oblivion. The realistic novels were not, in the sense in which Henry James used that word, "done"; the fury aroused by his pictures of the Irish scene is local; and "The Brook Kerith" is a discreet and polished work, the continuous interest and beauty of which testify to the author's genius. His other rewritings are of little interest. I doubt if they will continue to be read. The same may be said of "Aphrodite in Aulis," which has no more vitality than "The Well at the World's End" or "The Water of the Wondrous Isles." What will survive is the personality of Moore.

Not a creative personality; a critical, discomfiting personality, malicious, relentless, much-considering, cold, and with no capacity for self-surrender. Not without sympathy, for otherwise he could not have written novels such as "Esther Waters" and "A Mummer's Wife," but as shrewd as he was vain, as teasing as he was unhumorous. When he was summoned to Ireland to his mother's deathbed some peasants wailed that they had bad news for him. But Moore said to himself, "Not altogether bad news; my mother is dead, but I have been saved the useless pain, the torture of spirit I should have endured if I had arrived in time." That is a very candid statement; but a very revealing one: "I have been saved." It might have been a little disagreeable for him; his place as observer would have had to be vacated for a time; he might have suffered. I think he took his own comfort very seriously. He did not take quite as seriously the mental comfort of those about whom he wrote.

And yet what an interesting personality it was! And is! How excellent a book he wrote about his young days, and how full of malicious quality is the trilogy which he wrote about his Irish friends and associates! When he describes a person—the young, black-coated Yeats as a rook, for example—the reader can see that person as if the few inevitable words held magic; not only the features, but the spirit, the tone, the movements of hands and eyes,—all are portrayed. Our judgment of Moore is imperfect if we neglect two qualities in him, his observant quietness and his scrupulousness. Though his perceptions are tinged with cruelty, they are untinged with sentiment; they are referred always to his sense of truth, and what he sees he expresses with a fidelity as fine as it is beautiful. What he sees . . . It was not a generous mind, but though full of treacheries to friendship it was unwavering in strict loyalty to itself. I say, not a pleasant person, but a deeply interesting mind and one of immeasurable value in its time and place.

iii. Enoch Arnold Bennett

"I cannot conceive that any author should write, as the de Goncourts say they wrote, 'for posterity'. An artist works only to satisfy himself, and for the applause and appreciation neither of his fellows alive not his fellows yet unborn. I would not care a bilberry for posterity. I should be my own justest judge, from whom there would be no appeal; and having satisfied him (whether he was right or wrong) I should be content —as an artist. As a *man*, I should be disgusted if I could not earn plenty of money and the praise of the discriminating."

Arnold Bennett: Journal, Jan. 28, 1897.

ARNOLD BENNETT, the son of a solicitor, was born on May 27th, 1867, thirty years before the words I have quoted were written. As a boy, he suffered a serious nervous shock (its cause has been conflictingly explained), which led to a stammer that nothing ever cured. As soon as he was old enough to do so, he worked in his father's office, but in 1893 he left the Potteries and came to London. Like his own "man from the North," he felt himself to be "a certain kind of youth of whom it is said that he is born to be a Londoner. The metropolis, and everything that appertains to it, has for him an imperious fascination."

At first Bennett was in a solicitor's office; but while there he gave everybody the impression that he was potentially a literary light, and as, like his own Denry Machin, he was always sensitive and responsive to the expectations of others, he took heed of so complimentary a view. A parody of a sensational serial first brought some prize guineas; then he essayed brief articles and stories; and by the time he was twenty-five he had obtained by what he called the grossest kind of "influence" a post as sub-editor of a paper for women. Later he was editor of this paper; and it was while he was editor that he recklessly engaged himself to write for a provincial syndicate a sensational serial better than anything else of its kind. That was Midland bounce; many people were deceived into thinking it Arnold Bennett. But it was not Arnold Bennett. In those early years he was incessantly studying the great French novelists, and he was also writing an entirely serious, unpretentious, and still readable novel about a young provincial in London, which he published under the title of "A Man from the North." Out of this book, on its first appearance, he made a profit of one pound. The sensational serial paid better than that.

Bennett did not therefore embrace the career of sensational serial-writer. It is not without significance that "The Grand Babylon Hotel" and "Anna of the Five Towns"—the fantasia and the realistic study—both achieved book publication in the same year. He had found an enthusiastic admirer in Andrew Chatto, the publisher; and Andrew Chatto continued to publish for him (at a loss, it must be said) until 1905, when, having very unwillingly suffered "Sacred and Profane Love," he allowed Bennett to go to another firm, and so lost "The Old Wives' Tale."

In 1902, having established his ability to earn a living by means of fiction and journalism, Bennett did what George Moore had done thirty years earlier: he went to Paris. Either there or at Fontainebleau he busily wrote novels, short stories, plays, and many articles and reviews for London literary papers. And when he was forty he wrote a very long novel indeed, so long that the publishers who had contracted to publish it shivered at the prospect of a colossal printers' bill and—for at that time Bennett did not earn the £75 advance which he was in the habit of receiving—a small sale insufficient to cover costs. The book was "The Old Wives' Tale." It was at once hailed as a work of importance, and while its sales were not at first as large as everybody imagined (Bennett once told me that they did not in England pass six thousand), it established him as one of the leading novelists of the time. In America it gave the author, slowly but surely, a standing unsurpassed by any modern English writer.

Meanwhile Bennett had married a Frenchwoman, and under the pseudonym of Jacob Tonson he contributed to A. R. Orage's weekly political review, *The New Age*, a letter about books which was so much the best thing of its kind that it became the talk of bookish London. While Wells was publishing "Tono-Bungay" and "The New Machiavelli," and Bennett "The Old Wives' Tale" and "Clayhanger," these two men were the heavenly twins of literature and wonders of the age. The young men of 1909 and 1910 felt that with Shaw and Barker and Galsworthy in the theatre, Bennett and Wells and, in a lesser degree, Galsworthy in the novel, and Chesterton and Belloc in the press, there was thrilling life in the intellectual world; and they were right. There never has been so much life since.

Presently Bennett determined to leave Paris and live in England. He returned for a time in 1911, and very soon bought an elderly house in Essex, which was made habitable under the care of his closest friend of that day, E. A. Rickards, the architect, and to which from the first he invited not only his older English literary friends but those of the younger generation—J. C. Squire, Hugh Walpole, Robert Nichols, and others. He was established in this house early in 1914, and as he was able to keep the *Velsa*, his barge-built yacht, at Brightlingsea near by he seemed, in those peaceful days, to be assured of a long life of good work and literary eminence.

But in the summer of 1914 came War. Bennett was swallowed up in it, as husband (for Mrs. Bennett, being French, was at once tragically agitated by the fate of her country), as journalist, and finally as an active force in the Ministry of Information (or Propaganda), to the directorship of which he was in the end appointed. For Bennett the war years were years of intense pressure, literary, political, and social. From the first (and for the first time in his life) he was surrounded by military officers, politicians, and busy men of affairs generally. Strange and exciting as the emergency was, it completely changed the course of his life. He had been a novelist; he found himself an active publicist. He had been devoted to the arts; he found himself called upon to "sustain the morale of civilian populations." That seemed to him to be a wonderful experience. He flowered under it, never too busy for his friends and beneficiaries, but absorbed perpetually in the demands of the hour, like a banker or a Cabinet Minister, "winning the War." Cabinet Ministers, indeed, welcomed his company and his views. He had some power; he knew men who had more power and who would use it at his request. At the Ministry of Information he was brought into close contact with Lord Beaverbrook, a Canadian financier and newspaper proprietor whose influence upon him was immediate and irresistible. By Beaverbrook he was led more and more into the great world of affairs, until his novels looked to him, and became for others, smaller than life, instead of equal to it in size and worth. His other acquaintances were innumerable; his days full; his importance once and for ever after less that of a creative writer than that of a public character and oracle.

All these excitements had their due effect upon a nature which, under an air of strength, was sensitive to excess. The War was an overwhelming blow to Bennett. His experience in meeting what must be called the fashionable society of that time shocked deeply all the fundamentally rigid and "decent" notions of his bourgeois upbringing, from which he had been delivered only in his own imagination. Those people who objected to "The Pretty Lady" as pornography did not recognize that it expressed a loathing on Bennett's part for what he had been seeing. It was not a realistic book by a man-of-the-world; it was a cry of horror by one whose standards of conduct had been outraged. The levity and folly and recklessness portrayed in "The Pretty Lady" were seriously abhorrent to him. True to his new character as man-of-the-world, which had insensibly replaced that of the all-seeing and all-pondering artist, he pretended that these things were, and that they must be faced; but in my view he was never socially or politically an easygoing moralist, and I believe his will was then shaken, and his credence in a progressive world wrecked.

After the War, in 1919 and 1920, Bennett was so tired that he was in danger of serious illness. His closer friends noticed this, and several of them were greatly alarmed. It has been suggested that the unquestioned decline of his work in fiction was due to the fact that he was spoiled by success; I think it was due to physical exhaustion and the strain of the War. He continued to write steadily and regularly, because writing steadily and regularly was his habit, and he could not live without writing (I went with him in the early months of 1920 to Portugal, on the understanding that as a holiday was necessary to save his health he was to do no work at all; but on the third day following our arrival at Mont Estoril he confessed that he had written six hundred words before breakfast. When I said "Oh, no; *that's* not what you're here for," he answered: "I know. I had to."); but nothing he wrote after the War was equal to what he had written earlier.

Let me try to present him as he appeared to those who saw him in the flesh. He was stoutly built, and about five feet ten inches in height. He held himself very erect and his shoulders very rigid, so that his body had no natural swing as he walked, but rather swayed stiffly from side to side. He always walked slowly and with great seriousness. His brow was square, and rose straight from eyes that looked tired, because of rather heavy eyelids, to the small flourish of hair which latterly replaced the famous coif made fun of by caricaturists. His cheeks were clear and showed a faint colour. His mouth was irregular, and his upper teeth were also irregular. The eyes, once the first impression of tiredness was passed, were a warm brown, and smiled. Bennett was a master of the wink. When some effusive stranger buttonholed him to express admiration, Bennett was at all times courteous; but, if he caught a friendly eye beyond his enthusiast, one of those heavy lids would irresistibly quiver.

In repose his expression, I should have said, represented calm melancholy. But his smile was very sweet, and the aura of kindness which surrounded him was such that he was extremely popular with children. Odd as it may seem to some, he could converse with children very effectively. But he was a shy and sensitive man, who normally talked little. He talked more towards the end of his life, from politeness, to "make things go," and he did this very well, though sometimes with exaggeration of his own mannerisms. His voice was rather harsh, and gave the impression of being high-pitched. As far as his writing was concerned, although to strangers he professed to be very well satisfied, he was excessively modest, and if some of his work received great praise he would naïvely repeat the praise to me, and add, "It's . . . extraordinary." That was because he was very simple-minded.

That simple-mindedness, that naïveté, was what made Bennett many and devoted friends. When he was alive they teased him and were teased by him. They contradicted him and were contradicted by him; and nobody a penny the worse. He kept a strict eye upon the grammar of his friends, and they in turn rebuked him for eccentricities of phrase or judgment. One day some of them joined in protesting against the word "motivated," which he had used. He said "What else can you say?" Suggestions were made; he was assured by a classical scholar in the company that such a word was shocking. Undaunted at the end of ten minutes, he said: "Damned if I don't use it again next week." If he had again referred to the matter he would have said: "A-and . . . I *did* do."

It is the simple-mindedness of Bennett that causes those who like to regard themselves as European to call him "provincial". He was in many respects the young man from the Midlands. Whereas Gissing, also a provincial, had condemned the foul ugliness of cities, and Moore had hardly seemed to know what they looked like, so interested was he in clambering like an ant over the lives of wretched people, Bennett was delighted to embrace the beauties as well as the disfigurements of urban civilization. He not only saw the town, but he could see what it represented in the creative life of man:

"Bursley, the ancient home of the potter, has an antiquity of a thousand years. It lies towards the north end of an extensive valley, which must have been one of the fairest spots in Alfred's England, but which is now defaced by the activities of a quarter of a million people. Five contiguous towns—Turnbull, Bursley, Hanbridge, Knype, and Longshaw—united by a single winding thoroughfare some eight miles in length, have inundated the valley like a succession of great lakes. Of these five Bursley is the mother, but Hanbridge is the largest. They are mean and forbidding of aspect—sombre, hard-featured, uncouth; and the vaporous poison of their ovens and chimneys has soiled and shrivelled the surrounding country till there is no village lane within a league but what offers a gaunt and ludicrous travesty of rural charms. Nothing could be more prosaic than the huddled, red-brown streets; nothing more seemingly remote than romance. Yet be it said that romance is even here—the romance which, for those who have an eye to perceive it, ever dwells amid the seats of industrial manufacture, softening the coarseness, transfiguring the squalor, of these mighty alchemic operations. Look down into the valley from the terrace-height where love is kindling, embrace the whole smoke-girt amphitheatre in a glance, and it may be that you will suddenly comprehend the secret and superb significance of the vast Doing which goes forward below. Because they seldom think, the townsmen take shame when indicted for having disfigured half a county in order to live. They have not understood that this disfigurement is merely an episode in the unending warfare of man and nature, and calls for no contrition. Here, indeed, is nature repaid for some of her notorious cruelties. She imperiously bids man sustain and reproduce himself, and this is one of the places where in the very act of obedience he wounds and maltreats her. Out beyond the municipal confines, where the subsidiary industries of coal and iron prosper amid a wreck of verdure, the struggle is grim, appalling, heroic—so ruthless is his havoc of her, so indomitable her ceaseless recuperation. On the one side is a wresting from nature's own bowels of the means to waste her; on the other, an undismayed, enduring fortitude. The grass grows; though it is not green, it grows. In the very heart of the valley, hedged about with furnaces, a farm still stands, and at harvest-time the sooty sheaves are gathered in."

That, which is taken from one of Bennett's early novels, "Anna of the Five Towns," represents his view of urban life. "As squalid as you like," he says in effect; "but none the less full of grandeur, full of the proper stuff of romance." It is a view which may be called bourgeois; but it is a view which the realistic novelist may quite properly take. Nor was it anything but Bennett's natural attitude; for while he was as sensitive to ugliness as any man I have ever met he was quite definitely a townsman. The countryside was pleasant, fascinating to paint, exquisite to see; but there were not enough men and women, not enough houses, not enough of the movements and conflicts of human beings, to satisfy him. It was in people that he took all his interest; people who set their wits against each other, people who set their wits against the world, people who got on with their jobs, people who came to London and conquered it.

He enjoyingly laughed at such people in some of his books, of which "The Card" is the best and the best-known, and lesser examples, "A Great Man," "The Regent," "Mr. Prohack." He made them grotesque in such books as "The Grand Babylon Hotel" and "Hugo" and "The Gates of Wrath," which are well-written shockers. He made them horrible and piteous in "Riceyman Steps," a study of misers. In "The Old Wives' Tale" and "Clayhanger" he made them real. "The Old Wives' Tale" and "Clayhanger" are by far the best of his books. Into them he put without stint his humour, his scrupulousness, and his old knowledge of Midland life. In them he was completely an artist, if that means, as I take it to mean, that a man sacrifices everything to his conception. These books have not the peculiar excitingness that Balzac alone imparts to the fictitious mundane; they are lighter, less intense. But they are full of character and truth to character; the scene is clearly set; one reads with the sense of being taken not only among individual human beings but into the homes and shops and hearts of the Midlands and the Midland people. Above all, the books and the people in them grow, not arbitrarily, but organically. If it is true that they remain small, as small as human beings are in real life, that must be set down as a deficiency in the realistic novel itself, for in that genre only Balzac's and Dostoevsky's people are larger than life, and Balzac's live in a world altogether fabulous, while Dostoevsky's are so large as to be fantastic (or it may be only Russian!) to the verge of the gigantesque. In Bennett's best books one is still among the normal. It was his object to deal with the normal. That was what absorbed him.

I have never agreed with those who set "Riceyman Steps" on a level with the author's major books. Beside them it is tired and meagre; two misers and a servant girl and a certain deliberately observed *milieu*. He went daily to Clerkenwell while he was writing it, to gain knowledge; but the district was not in his blood as were the Five Towns. Some others of his novels, however, have not yet had enough credit given to them. There is "Whom God Hath Joined," which had a curious history, being published by a firm hitherto specializing in legend and folk-lore. Along with C. F. Keary's "Bloomsbury," a long book in the Gissing tradition, it looked strange in such a list, and as it had been printed in a foreign country the first edition was disfigured with extraordinary misprints. It is with difficulty recovering its place in the canon. There is "The Price of Love," to which at all times critics have been less than fair, so that it is supposed to be a twice-cooked pudding, when in fact it is, though minor, only just minor. There is the latter part of "Lord Raingo," a book which suffered from some confusion of mind in the author and some confused criticism from eminent publicists. This book was supposed to deal with the life of a real person; and I have been told that the daughter of the real person felt bitterly towards Bennett for lampooning her father. But the book is in reality an extraordinarily sincere portrait of Bennett himself, in late middle age, and in pain and fear of death. It should not be overlooked by the student of his work, although the political passages are incredible.

All the books in which Bennett tried to reproduce the artistic temperament, or the abnormal—for examples, "Sacred and Profane Love" and "The Glimpse," are very unsatisfactory. The hardness of the former is due, perhaps, to the fact that he was trying to be French; the hardness of the latter lies in the fact that he was doing something in which he did not believe. He was never at his best unless he could be both humorous and humane, unless he could be amused by his people as well as devoted to their representation. That is the success of "The Old Wives' Tale," that the two sisters and Mrs. Baines and Mr. Povey are within his heart as well as his head. He liked nice people; they need not be good, but they must be simple and they must be honest; they might lie or be grandiose (for that sin he had some kindness), but they must not be treacherous or cruel, or anything but the plain people who grow rich or keep poor, who do their best towards those whom they love and who certainly do their best towards what they believe to be the truth. There are millions of such people in England, and all over the world. They continue the work of civilization; and Bennett is their historian. Only when he went away from them, and tried to picture what is vicious or vulgar in itself, did he give away the secret of his own innocence. He was not sophisticated.

But he was attracted to grandeur as a moth to a lamp. That is made a cause of complaint against him by some; to his friends, who loved him, it was ever a matter for amusement. His clothes, his knowingness, his gaping wonder at gilt restaurants, have all been over-emphasized: my own belief is that he unconsciously yielded in later days to what he found to be a general belief in his love of the baroque. I do not deny such a love; I merely say that it figures in his lesser works, at first, in fun, because it amused him; latterly, in blindness, because he felt it was expected of him. Being tired, he grew lazy, and caricatured himself. The caricature was never conscious or deliberate, but it represented what was almost a mechanical act on the part of one who desperately needed rest and who could not, and was not allowed to, enjoy that rest.

Now let us take a final look at Bennett's work as he left it. There are plays, as to which I have said nothing. "Milestones," in which he collaborated with Edward Knoblock, had a great success, and was called by Bennett himself "a neat enough trifle." "The Great Adventure," which he wrote alone, had similarly a great success, and owed much to two pieces of magnificent acting, on the part of Henry Ainley and Wish Wynne. "The Title" had some success. The rest were not successes; and were never more than trifles. Of course, "What the Public Wants," that skit upon the vagaries of great newspaper proprietors, was extremely amusing and full of cheek; but the others lacked form and growth. They were too easily written for fun, to show that he *could*: . . . but he couldn't, or rather would not take the trouble to do something that was well within his power.

In his best novels, "The Old Wives' Tale," "Clayhanger" and "These Twain" ("Hilda Lessways" was never equal to its companions), he brought urban England to life and gave it significance. In the lesser serious books he only failed to do as well because the themes failed in importance or the method in

F

freshness. In the good humorous books—"The Card," "A Great Man," "Buried Alive"—he amused himself and others consumedly, for these books, too, were authentic Bennett, escaping from seriousness and enjoying himself. In the lesser books, the so-called pot-boilers, he amused himself and some others, but with "The Ghost," "The City of Pleasure," "The Regent," and "The Strange Vanguard" he hardly communicated the joke. In the thoroughly bad serious books—"Sacred and Profane Love" and "The Glimpse"—he paid the price for applying the realistic method to matters of which he had no real understanding. In the books which are called his "pocket philosophies" he gave a helping hand to the self-improving, which is enough to damn them with the cultured; but they did in fact help many, and while they consist of truisms expressed with all the emphasis created in Bennett by his stammer, that is enough to show that they were nor superfluous. They were certainly sincere.

Henry James, in criticizing Wells and Bennett, objected that they regarded life as a gigantic orange, to be squeezed indefinitely for the purpose of their fiction. He thought that they did not select, compose, "do" the job of art, concoct a situation or a picture and lavish all care, in the Jacobean way, upon its treatment. He found Wells so abounding in vitality and richness of experience that he winked often enough at what offended him and what he regarded as a squandering of wealth to no artistic end. Wells was a prodigal. Bennett he admired, but condemned. He said:

> "We confound the author of 'Tono-Bungay' and the author of 'Clayhanger' in this imputation for the simple reason that with the sharpest differences of character and range they yet come together under our so convenient measure of value by *saturation.* . . . Our argument is that each is ideally immersed in his own body of reference, and that immersion in any such degree is really among us a new feature of a novelist's range of resource."

However delicately expressed, that was a charge of "No art"; for the objection raised by Henry James was to the seeming assumption of both writers that memory and experience could all be poured out upon the pages of a novel, and made something significant in itself. Well, there is, certainly, this problem to be encountered in assessing the realistic or quasi-realistic novel; which is, the point at which virtue is its own reward and truth its own touchstone; and Bennett would have admitted that a literature entirely composed of "Clayhangers" would soon be an enormity. That book did give rise to a number of works of an autobiographical or semi-autobiographical character which in turn have resulted in further books of the same nature. But Bennett did not intend the sequel: his notion was that *he* would write in three volumes a history of a man and his wife from their childhood to their advanced age. He thought it worth while to show them in their environment, which chanced to be the environment with which he had been familiar. The artistic object may have been remote, in the sense that what he proposed was a highly detailed fresco, instead of a concentrated piece for the easel. But the object, in Bennett's case, was there. The surface was to be large, precisely because he wanted to "do" the job thoroughly. Not grandiosity was his aim, and not detail for its own sake (an absurd assumption), but thoroughness. Therefore, to me, James's criticism loses validity. Having failed to appreciate a large design, executed or to be executed with some copiousness, he mistook the nature of the work. If the work as a whole is a failure, that is another matter altogether.

iv. John Galsworthy

"For that is, my dear Jack, what you are—a humanitarian moralist. . . . This fact which you cannot help and which may lead you yet to become the Idol of the Public— if I may so express myself—arises as the greatest danger in the way of your art. It may prevent the concentration of effort in one single direction—because your art will always be trying to assert itself against the impulse of your moral feelings. . . . A moralist must present us with a gospel—he must give counsel, not to our reason or sentiment, but to our very soul. Do you feel in yourself the stature for that task? That you must meditate over with great seriousness—because, my dear Jack, because it is in you to be a great novelist."

Joseph Conrad to John Galsworthy, in a letter.

I INCLUDE John Galsworthy in this chapter, less because he was in any sense a realist than because he gives me an opportunity to draw a distinction. Whereas the two writers mentioned previously in this chapter owed much to French models, Galsworthy was I think the first English novelist to turn for what may be called technical inspiration to Russia. And whereas French realism always directed its attention towards an objective presentation of life, Russian realism was always tinged with philosophy (that is to say, with ethics and metaphysics) and with politics. The same is true of Russian literary criticism. In Galsworthy's case it was never denied that his earliest books were written in direct imitation of the novels of Turgenev; and his whole work was coloured by that humanitarian moralizing to which Conrad—always an acute critic—refers in the letter quoted above. Galsworthy thought as much of the moral of everything as Alice's Ugly Duchess.

Another point to which I wish to refer is that Galsworthy was the first genteel novelist of the Georgian scene, and only the second genteel novelist in English literature. Unlike his predecessor, he was no snob, though he too was a critic of snobs. He was a man of independent means, and was educated at Harrow and Oxford. Born in the year after Wells and in the same year as Arnold Bennett (1867), he was prolonging his adolescence while his two contemporaries were already biting hard at life. Their culture was personal, original; his the culture of a class. To him, honour, justice, breeding, and self-sacrifice were first principles; he represented all the virtues of what is called in England the public school spirit. Nobody could ever have thought Wells or Bennett "public school"; nobody could ever have imagined Galsworthy as anything else. He never quite caught up with his two great contemporaries in practical acquaintance with all classes except his own; and I think his fastidiousness in the matter of breeding, dress, and deportment prevented him from wholly enjoying either their company or their confidence. Bennett rather scoffingly liked him very much; I imagine that Bennett constantly set Galsworthy's teeth on edge. Wells certainly missed in him that malicious camaraderie which sets all at ease. He once impulsively said in my hearing: "Galsworthy makes one feel such a *cad*!" He did not mean morally a cad; he meant "personally uneasy." Galsworthy was very fastidious, very shy, and probably very timid. It was a timid face.

It was also a very serious face, full of kindness, but ever thoughtful. He was very short-sighted, and the glasses he wore were thick. He was obviously a gentleman, not only in his modest speech and bearing, but in Hillcrist's sense of "a man who keeps his form and doesn't let life scupper him out of his standards. . . . I assume, of course, that he's honest and tolerant, gentle to the weak, and not self-seeking." While Wells's quick blue eyes saw everything at a single flying, michievous glance, and while Bennett's brown ones wisely paused in scrutiny for perhaps two pulse-beats, Galsworthy looked patiently and gravely for quite a long time through his glasses, and behind the glasses the eyes were, I believe, a cold grey. You might have thought him a lawyer (as he had been); you certainly would have realized his kindness; but you would not—or I should not—have been very confident of his power to accept teasing. Nevertheless, he had great sympathy; and only a lack of humour and self-confidence, probably, prevented him from achieving an air of geniality.

Having been born, as it were, to plenty, he made a romantic marriage and lived happily ever after. He could not have passed Gissing's test of the good writer, for Gissing, upon hearing that a new light had appeared on the literary horizon, used always to ask, "Has he starved?" Galsworthy had not starved. All his sympathy with poor people was the sympathy of a sensitive and highly strung humanitarian who tries to put himself in the place of those whom he does not understand; those between whom and himself there can be no intercommunication. Whether lambs or horses, dogs or gutter-snipes, social outsiders or performing seals, all who did not belong to the English affluent middle class—the Forsytes—were in a sense dumb animals. He suffered their pains a thousand times over; but the last plumbing degrees of insight, of identification, were beyond him. As in the case of Gregory, in "The Country House," it was to his "reforming instinct a constant grief that he had been born re-fined. A natural delicacy *would* interfere . . ." That is why, when one has been poor, one never quite accepts Galsworthy's poor people, who are poor before they are human.

He started, in the vein of Turgenev, with tales of lovers; and many of his books are tales of lovers, some of them better tales and some of them less good tales, but always sensitive, marked by a kind of trembling emotion, and always about well-bred idealists who do wrong with the best motives, or from instability, or who avert wrongdoing by reason of some strong call to duty or virtue. In these books he took from Turgenev's method what he needed —measure and delicate precision; and he shared with his master a thrilling sense of beauty, irony, and an extraordinary feeling for tragic young love. Galsworthy often returned to this theme, trying to pitch the note high but always decorously, to catch a pure ray of emotion and at the same time woo reality and escape the namby-pamby. He did not always escape, and he did not catch the pure ray, which comes unsought to genius but may not be laboured for; while as to reality it has evaporated in the passage of time and is no more to be found in the tender pages. "Jocelyn," "Villa Rubein," "The Country House," "The Patrician," and "The Dark Flower" all belong to the same order; and if these books now seem to us to be sentimental, while Turgenev's "On the Eve" and "A House of Gentlefolk" continue to shine in memory as things of beauty, the explanation may perhaps lie in the fact that while Turgenev was at bottom a poet Galsworthy was at heart a gentleman, "born refined," as he has said, and forever constrained by his natural temper to make his characters "nice." If you are born refined, you cannot *allow* yourself to see everything or to write of everything; not only "good form" inhibits you, but a lack of moral courage.

Having begun to be a writer (he used the pseudonym "John Sinjohn" for his first three books), Galsworthy very soon revealed his moralizing impulse. He had been born into a comfortable class, and he found members of that class intolerably less sensitive to the evils which he saw all about. Like every other English moralist, he cried out upon the English hypocrisy. He arraigned his class for using every advantage which wealth and the British legal system provided. When he first went into the theatre it was to draw a pointed contrast between the lot of a young man of good family and a working man, both of whom, when drunk, had committed theft. He went on to show how one-sided any strike or lock-out may be, owing to the innate power of Capitalism to live upon itself while the unemployed workers starve. But while he arraigned, he could not bring himself to portray the rich as deliberately evil, and so he was again forced into the use of types and symbols, all of whom stood for their own point of view, for pride, for obstinacy, for selfishness, and for suffering. He was too modest to be severe; and as he painted in low tones it was thought that he was a realist, pointing out to the world candidly and with moderation where it was wrong. That was not the case. He was uneasy, uncomfortable, unhappy; and the cause of his unhappiness was an imagining of the pain and injustice which the world held and to which the world paid no heed.

It must have been a knowledge of this preoccupation on the part of a friend which caused Conrad to write his words of warning; for that horror of pain and injustice runs through the whole of Galsworthy's work, and affects its ultimate importance. The artist may rightly see and protest against injustice; but if he does this too narrowly, if he is but a fabulist, he may well miss truth for the sake of his moral. Galsworthy suffered from a cramping of the imagination. He had constrained his lovers; he now constrained his sinners and strikers and class-conscious neighbours and clubmen. He could not forget the claims of niceness; he could not forget the fact that a man was poor or rich or stupid or dishonest or a Jew. Not a human being, but the embodiment of a state of mind or a state of body. Any writer who has such strict notions of what is good and what evil, and who dare not let his principals stray outside a rigid code of conduct or behaviour, keeps them very short of character. And so while Galsworthy's plays (for in this section of his work the plays form a large proportion) are excellent as moralities they are exceedingly narrow moralities. Suffering as he did from that emotional sympathy with the loser in any fight which is the mark of humanitarianism, he unconsciously distorts both sides of a wrangle in order to produce his plea for the unfortunate, the weak, the dumb. He was a pleader.

But he was not only a pleader. Quite apart from the fact that he had an altogether exceptional sense of the theatre, which makes his plays very effective pieces, and a sure and delicate hand in the presentation of a story, which makes even his inferior novels readable, he had in one instance a mastery of family history and family psychology too notable for oblivion. I do not think the later instalments of the Forsyte Saga show anything but a decline;

but the first Forsyte book, "A Man of Property", was and is an original and vital contribution to the modern novel. In that book is embalmed for all time a departed way of life. The characters in it, although not full of life, are full of type. The moral prejudice which hampers Galsworthy elsewhere is lifted, and a romance is unravelled. Probably some who have come to maturity in the past few years may not realize how new "A Man of Property" was at the time of its publication: the plan of that book has produced a thousand imitations. But it was new, original, deeply interesting as a period piece, deeply interesting as a sign that a modern novel could be as rich in three hundred pages as anybody pleased. I think "A Man of Property" will continue to be read when most of Galsworthy's other work has passed into dust; just as I think that some of his plays will continue to be performed as long as there are repertory theatres in the world. Their freshness may go—it has already gone from the lesser plays; their interest as comments upon social conditions will assuredly lessen; but they are such good theatre, and they still read with so much life, that they will survive fashion and enter history.

Galsworthy had ceased long before his death to be a young man's author; he was either too wise or too tender for the modern world. He had no scorn and no impatience; but a great deal of sentiment. He was at his best with old men—old gentlemen—for example with old Jolyon, old Anthony, and the hero of "The Stoic." They were welcomely static; they had taken their stand, and they remained set to the end. The first of these, gradually dying in loneliness; the second holding grimly to his own will and losing his last battle; the third, defeated, ending his days with a feast which only a man who relished good food and drink could have devised. They were members of the older generation whom Galsworthy had seen at close quarters and admired. They had the old standards, the stiff upper lip of the aristocracy; he could appreciate them. Besides, they were quiet; they were not forever restlessly changing and shouting and darting hither and thither at useless, agitating speed. They were pathetic. He could love and pity them, and they would respond to his pity; whereas however much one may pity the young and futile they will not humbly lick one's hand for the treat. On the contrary, they bite, and Galsworthy did not like people to bite. His dream was of a world of ladies and gentlemen, very well behaved, very peaceable, ready to compromise grievances; no wolves, but lions and lambs living in perfect amity.

Nor had he the vigour which would have enabled him to carry a crusade for peace at white heat into the hearts of men. He was in a great difficulty, for a novelist who preaches, unless he attacks, must have a positive creed to expound. As Conrad said, "A moralist must present us with a gospel—he must give counsel, not to our reason or sentiment, but to our very soul. Do you feel in yourself the stature for that task? That you must meditate over with great seriousness." What, at the end of his life, was Galsworthy's conclusion when he so seriously meditated upon the counsel he could give? We must, I think, reach for ourselves the view that he had neither the intellect nor the fire for the job.

His strength was in his love of beauty, which was rare. It was greater than his love of men (from whom he shrank unless they were as fastidious as himself). He could pity men and animals, and wish to better their lot; but for men *as* animals he had an aversion. When he could turn his eyes back, away from conflict, as he did when he wrote of old and dying people, he could still see the world as a lovely viceless thing for the eye to rest upon. He could still believe in peace, leisure, and acceptance.

"It was quite shady under the tree; the sun could not get at him, only make the rest of the world bright so that he could see the Grand Stand at Epsom away out there, very far, and the cows cropping the clover in the field and swishing at the flies with their tails. He smelled the scent of limes, and lavender. Ah! that was why there was such a racket of bees. They were excited—busy, as his heart was busy and excited. Drowsy, too, drowsy and drugged on honey and happiness; as his heart was drugged and drowsy. Summer—summer—they seemed to be saying; great bees and little bees, and the flies too!

"The stable clock struck four; in half an hour she would be here. He would have just one tiny nap because he had had so little sleep of late; and then he would be fresh for her, fresh for youth and beauty, coming towards him across the sunlit lawn—lady in grey! And settling back in his chair he closed his eyes. Some thistle-down came on what little air there was, and pitched on his moustache more white than itself. He did not know; but his breathing stirred it, caught there. A ray of sunlight struck through and lodged on his boot. A bumble-bee alighted and strolled on the crown of his Panama hat. And the delicious surge of slumber reached the brain beneath that hat, and the head swayed forward and rested on his breast. Summer—summer! So went the hum.

"The stable clock struck the quarter past. The dog Balthazar stretched and looked up at his master. The thistle-down no longer moved. The dog placed his chin over the sunlit foot. It did not stir. The dog withdrew his chin, quickly, rose, and leaped on old Jolyon's lap, looked in his face, whined; then, leaping down, sat on his haunches, gazing up. And suddenly he uttered a long, long howl.

"But the thistle-down was still as death, and the face of his old master.

"Summer—summer—summer! The soundless footsteps on the grass!"

That is the end of old Jolyon's life, and it is peace. The story was written in time of war.

After the war while he still wrote novels and plays, he found a congenial task which gave him great satisfaction. He became the first President of that international society for writers which is known as the P.E.N. Club. He became a considerable figure in foreign countries, and except for those who regard English gentlemen as the least of God's creatures he satisfied all legitimate conceptions of what an English gentleman is. He had that "ingrained tenderness of soul, that forbade him from exposing his emotions, and recoiled from the revelation of other people's" (which the hero of "The Island Pharisees" also possessed); and he was a man "who kept his form and didn't let life scupper him out of his standards." He was "honest and tolerant, gentle to the weak, and not self-seeking." That is the man's own definition of gentility; and by that definition he filled the rôle to perfection. He was a great success as President of the P.E.N. Club. He was given the Order of Merit, which is the greatest official honour that can be paid to an English writer (it was never offered to Shaw, Wells, or Bennett). And he presented the original MSS. of such parts of the Forsyte Saga as had been preserved to the British Museum, where they will be kept in perpetuity.

v. William Somerset Maugham

"*Et ego in Arcadia vixi:* I too have been a highbrow. . . . I could not help noticing that a play produced by the Stage Society did not lead to very much. After the two performances they gave it and the notices in the press it was as dead as mutton. I felt a trifle flat after the production of *A Man of Honour*. I looked reflectively at the Thames and was conscious that I had not set it on fire. I badly wanted to write plays that would be seen not only by a handful of people. I wanted money and I wanted fame."

W. S. Maugham: Preface to Plays, Vol. I.

ANYBODY less like John Galsworthy than Somerset Maugham it would be hard to imagine. Both wrote good novels and plays with equal success; both also wrote works which were neither novels nor plays (but Maugham, if he attempted verse, cautiously refrained from tempting the reviewers by publishing it); and there the likeness ends. Maugham was born in 1874, and after attending King's School, Canterbury, and the University of Heidelberg, he studied medicine in London, at St. Thomas's Hospital. He was both a Member of the Royal College of Surgeons and a Licentiate of the Royal College of Physicians. But he began to write books when he was in his early twenties, and from 1897 to the end of a very long life he was a professional author. Like George Moore and Arnold Bennett he lived for some years in Paris, and first met Bennett there; the two men were friends until Bennett's death.

Many readers of Maugham's most famous novel, "Of Human Bondage," must have assumed—for it is usual to make all sorts of assumptions regarding authors, on the strength of what seems to be an autobiographical book—that Maugham, like Philip, suffered from a club foot. He did not. In fact it is never safe to believe a word an author says, whether he speaks in the first person singular or writes about a young man's growing pains. Not a word of "Of Human Bondage" must be taken literally, for all its deceptive directness of statement. Maugham is not Philip; but I will not deny that he seemed at times to resemble Ashenden. He was not a very tall man, was very dark, and had small, extremely dark brown eyes which one immediately noticed. He was very slim, and one's first impression was of a small head, a gentle manner of great modesty, and a slight hesitation in speech. One then discovered that all his remarks were unusually brief. And that when he told a story it was in so few words, and with such point, that there was time in his company for a considerable amount and range of conversation. Nor was the conversation merely brief; for Maugham was so quick-witted that he stimulated others to similar un-self-conscious brevity, and, whether the effect is one of imagination or not I cannot say, one left him with the sense that everybody—including oneself—had been very amusing. This is a rare and highly complimentary talent, and it deserves mention in a period—among English writers of any pretensions to intellect—of meagre, highly superior, and discouraging talk.

Readers of Maugham's books will immediately appreciate the brevity which is a part of his method. Not only was he a dramatist the speeches of whose characters are rarely longer than fifty words (he did not rival Noel Coward in snip-snap), but when he wrote a novel his sentences would have seemed abrupt if they had not combined in an unusual degree quickness and continuity. He had the ruthlessness of perception which goes with clear thinking. As to his literary manner, he said of himself that

> "In my strenuous youth, in order to learn English, I spent part of each day in copying out certain classical writers whose style pleased me, reading a little and then trying to write it from memory; and in this way I went through some of Dryden's essays, much of the *Holy Dying* of Jeremy Taylor, and the whole of Swift's *A Tale of a Tub*. It was tedious, but it enabled me to express my thoughts, such as they were, with facility. I hasten to add that there is no particular reason why the dramatist should have a literary training, and besides the ease it gives him in writing, an acquaintance with literature is perhaps chiefly useful in helping him to avoid the literary."

In those last words speaks the man who once gambolled upon the heights of Chelsea and Bloomsbury and who either slipped (as some would say) or found a path leading to reality. I think he found a path. But is it not a strange coincidence that George Moore used almost exactly the same tone in his "Conversations in Ebury Street"? What Moore, speaking also of plays, said was:

"Literature is never literary. And the manager is duped by the highbrow, and the highbrow in turn is duped by the disagreeable: Else I should drop, he says, into the commonplace."

Maugham was fortunate in that he had work to do which did not long allow him to be literary. He was a medical student; and "he found the work of absorbing interest." Of the hospital he says:

"There was humanity there in the rough, the materials the artist worked on: . . . the directness of contact with men and women gave a thrill of power which he had never known. He found an endless excitement in looking at their faces and hearing them speak; they came in each with his peculiarity, some shuffling uncouthly, some with a little trip, others with heavy, slow tread, some shyly. Often you could guess their trades by the look of them. You learnt in what way to put your questions so that they should be understood, you discovered on what subjects nearly all lied, and by what inquiries you could extort the truth notwithstanding. You saw the different way people took the same things. . . .

"To the others men and women were only cases, good if they were complicated, tiresome if obvious; they heard murmurs and were astonished at abnormal livers; an unexpected sound in the lungs gave them something to talk about. But to Philip there was much more. He found an interest in just looking at them, in the shape of their heads and their hands, in the look of their eyes and the length of their noses. You saw in that room human nature taken by surprise, and often the mask of custom was torn off rudely, showing you the soul all raw . . .

"There was neither good nor bad there. There were just facts. It was life."

These words are taken from "Of Human Bondage," and may be regarded with justification as expressing Maugham's own experience. Upon an earlier page of the same book is another significant paragraph, which I shall also quote because it throws light upon a manner of approach.

"Philip hated Watson, and yet he would have given anything to change places with him. The old feeling that he had had at school came back to him, and he tried to throw himself into the other's skin, imagining what life would be if he were Watson."

And finally, this time from "Ashenden":

> "Ashenden admired goodness, but was not outraged by wicked-ness. People sometimes thought him heartless because he was more often interested in others than attached to them, and even in the few to whom he was attached his eyes saw with equal clearness the merits and the defects. . . . He was able to pursue his study of the Caypors without prejudice and without passion."

Those remarks all refer to one who was a born novelist and dramatist of the non-heroic type; in fact to a realist. One cannot imagine Maugham writing a romance. Melodrama was possible to him; the flippant is often upon the tongues of his characters. But besides being vulgar, as Maugham says it is, the life known to all except those who dwell in literary selectness is apt—once it leaves the humdrum—to be slightly sensational. Melodrama is quite proper, therefore, in the work of a realistic writer. But romance calls for a different temperament, a love of coloured raiment and display. It also calls for a little glad self-deception. Now Maugham could not possibly deceive himself with any kind of gladness.

It so happened, as I have previously explained, that when he began to write there was a vogue for tales of mean streets. Gissing and George Moore were established writers, Barrie had given fancy to desperate poverty in the early pages of "Sentimental Tommy," Arthur Morrison, Israel Zangwill, Pett Ridge, and the Edwin Pugh of "Tony Drum" were in one way or another using the very poor as literary material. At work all day in St. Thomas's Hospital, and living in the South of London, Maugham had learnt as much about the life and speech and thoughts of the poor as anybody not born among them could do; and he experimented, after he had sold some short stories, with a book in this vein called "Liza of Lambeth." It took its place in the fashion, and was thought to be very stark; and although it is a rather lifeless book and not quite accurate in Cockney vocabulary and phrase its aim is truth and its seriousness perfect. However, Maugham did not intend to keep his talent in Lambeth, and he was not long in moving farther afield. He had his eyes upon the stage, and he was free to dramatize in fiction some aspects of the middle-class life in which he had been born. "Mrs. Craddock," for example, was the tale—it might first have been written in three acts—of an emotional woman of means who married a stupid farmer, cherished him, discovered his stupidity, and was in due time released from bondage by his exceedingly stupid death. Again the book was thought very bold (so that Maugham had difficulty in getting it published), and it really was interesting and original. But it helped to label its author, who was also, very shortly afterwards, the author of a gloomy play called "A Man of Honour," as a pessi-

mist, a cynic, and a teller of sordid tales. As such, though unpopular, he was admired by those who regard themselves
as the select few. "The highbrow in turn is duped by the disagreeable."

Maugham was perfectly ready to deal with disagreeable subjects,
and he always dealt with them when it pleased him to do so.
The disagreeable has slightly more tang than the agreeable. But his
true bent was for comedy. Having been serious because he
wanted to be serious, he became a determined writer of comedies for
the stage. Before he was thirty-five he had achieved his object. He
had three plays running at the same time in London theatres, all of
them flippant and amoral, all of them salted with witticisms which
readily occurred to him as he wrote; and he had completely removed
the stigma of seriousness, although not that of cynicism. "Ashenden," wrote Maugham, "had no illusions about himself and such
success in current letters as had come to him had left his head un-
turned. He distinguished acutely between fame and the notoriety
that rewards the author of a successful novel or a popular play;
and he was indifferent to this except in so far as it was attended
with tangible benefits." But the tangible benefits without doubt
enabled Maugham to fulfil a great ambition; they enabled him to
travel.

He travelled until old age. He must have gone very nearly all over
the world—to China, to Spain, to Burma, to the South Seas, to
Canada and the United States. And, true to his conceptions of the
novelist's art, he used his travels as material from which to draw
new and ever-varied tales, and he also enriched the literature of
travel with at least one very delightful book entitled "The Gentlemen in the Parlour." Wherever he went about the world, moreover,
he took his neat figure, his neat mind, his quick tongue and pen;
and if he had written nothing else but "The Painted Veil," which is
about China, or "The Moon and Sixpence" and "The Trembling of a
Leaf," which are about the South Seas (the former being about
Gauguin and his life in Tahiti), we should have known him as a
writer in a thousand who had seen curious and unforgettable things
with his own eyes.

Nevertheless, his most ambitious book is that long account of a
young man's life, from early childhood to marriage, which is called
"Of Human Bondage." Home life at Blackstable, school life at
Tercanbury (both names so easily decipherable), university life at
Heidelberg, art study in Paris, hospital training in the South of
London, hardships, love affairs—all these in chronological order
follow (with innumerable vignettes of character bearing all the
marks of verisimilitude) what must have been the outline of
Maugham's own experience. But it would not therefore be wise to

regard the book as a literal transcript of the author's life. No author, not even the most realistic, copies exactly.

"I am a little sensitive on the point," says Maugham in his preface to "First Person Singular", "since I have at one time or another been charged with portraying certain persons so exactly that it was impossible not to know them. I have been accused of bad taste. . . . I think indeed that most novelists, and surely the best, have worked from life. But though they have had in mind a particular person this is not to say that they have copied him nor that the character they have devised is to be taken for a portrait. In the first place they have seen him through their own temperament and if they are writers of originality this means that what they have seen is somewhat different from the fact. They have taken what they wanted of him. . . . Nothing is so unsafe as to put into a novel a person drawn line by line from life. His values are all wrong."

That is sufficient. "Of Human Bondage" is to be read as fiction, but fiction with so clear an air of truth as to be as absorbing as candid autobiography.

It cannot be denied that the autobiographical chronicle novel—"David Copperfield" is the great English prototype—had become a vogue by 1915, when "Of Human Bondage" was written. Modern readers were well acquainted with "Tono-Bungay," with "Clayhanger," with "Sinister Street" and many more which had impressed them in a greater or less degree. But "Of Human Bondage" differs from other chronicle novels in its peculiar simplicity and in the fact that Philip, its hero, is depicted without archness, defence, and unnecessary explanation. The temper of the book is neither busy nor benign nor romantic; it is as completely unsentimental, and as bold in its bare statements (I refer especially to the dialogue, which though that of a dramatist is courageously uncoloured) as a novel can be.

Setting aside for a moment all question of the quasi-autobiographical nature of "Of Human Bondage," and looking upon it solely as an example of realistic fiction, a comparison of the book's manner with that of George Moore's "A Modern Lover" is most interesting. In both books perfect simplicity of statement is aimed at. In both books a career is shown as crossed with love affairs. But whereas one reads "A Modern Lover" with reluctance, as if one were walking over a long stretch of sand with no goal in sight, one reads "Of Human Bondage" as if one ran effortlessly home upon a good road. Such lightness and sureness are excessively rare; few authors can leave well alone; they have not the nerve. In the two books the method is fundamentally the same—a narrative without comment, in which but for the most occasional contributory use of information outside the hero's knowledge all attention is concentrated upon the central figure;—but Maugham has mastered the art of writing both explicitly and suggestively, which Moore had not done when he wrote "A Modern Lover," and as Maugham said: "A natural effect can only be got by an artificial simplicity." Those who suppose that "Of Human Bondage" is a good book by chance, or by reason of the intrinsic interest of its material (considerable though it is), underrate self-critical and self-assured literary talent of a high order. Of all modern authors, Maugham is the man who most nearly says, hardly as it were opening his mouth, precisely what he means to say.

As to what he says, which does of course matter a great deal, I think it would be true to suggest that he was at his best with the personal and the concrete. For the dissemination or even the discussion of general ideas he has little inclination; in a play or a novel he would believe it literary and in fact laboriously clumsy. Nor did he as a rule wish to impress, as do those who parade learning and familiarity with current metaphysics. It is the object of the realist to decipher and record; never to display his own ingenuity.

Maugham's reading, which was wide, was practical where it was done for any purpose but that of pleasure. He was the least academic of men, and without iconoclasm the most independent in literary opinion. He regarded it as the novelist's business, and the playwright's business, to present a situation and drop the curtain. He was not a moralist, and not an apologist. He had coldness, wit, and malice. He at once saw what he looked for in a man or an affair (as a doctor might do), and abstracted it for his own purposes. And since he did not credit the perfectibility of the world or humankind, but found life continuously interesting (if he was bored, he moved on), he was the nearest thing to a true realist among those named in this chapter. While Moore was maliciously vain in his fundamental attitude, and Bennett magnanimous; while Galsworthy was full of pity, Maugham, who thought sympathy next door to condescension, seemed to bring to his contemplation of the world the spirit in which Philip contemplated the out-patients' room at St. Luke's Hospital:

"On the whole the impression was neither of tragedy nor of comedy. There was no describing it. It was manifold and various; there were tears and laughter, happiness and woe; it was tedious and interesting and indifferent; it was as you saw it; it was tumultuous and passionate; it was grave; it was sad and comic; it was trivial; it was simple and complex; joy was there and despair; the love of mothers for their children, and of men for women; lust trailed itself through the rooms with leaden feet, punishing the guilty and the innocent, helpless wives and wretched children; drink seized men and women and cost its inevitable price; death sighed in these rooms; and the beginning of life, filling some poor girl with terror and shame, was diagonosed there. There was neither good nor bad there. There were just facts. It was life."

To some, an inexplicable conclusion; but to the artist in black and white by no means displeasing.

Chapter Eight

THE CRITICAL THEATRE

GRANVILLE-BARKER, ALLAN MONKHOUSE, ST. JOHN ERVINE

i

"The advocate for a National Theatre can plead its mere utility, can show that it will do what no other theatre is likely to. But he had better take yet higher ground. He must plead for the drama as something more than casual entertainment, as an art worthy to rank with other fine arts, and as having its spiritual functions too."

H. Granville-Barker: A National Theatre.

IN writing earlier of Bernard Shaw, I gave a slight sketch of the rise of Scandinavian and Teutonic drama in England, and of the part played in that rise by Shaw, Archer, and others. And in speaking of George Moore's work I spoke of the journey he took to Dublin to lend a hand in the formation of what was called the Irish Literary Theatre. Those events occurred before the end of the nineteenth century. It was not until the early years of the twentieth century that the New Drama (as it was named) began to drift into common consciousness; and when it did so the chief organizer was Annie Elizabeth Fredericka Horniman.

Miss Horniman was the lady who supplied money for the production of "Arms and the Man" at the Avenue Theatre in 1894. Nearly ten years later she acquired the lease of the Abbey Theatre in Dublin, rebuilt the theatre, and gave the Irish National Theatre Society free use of it. From that time may be dated the true activity of Irish folk drama, to which W. B. Yeats, J. M. Synge, and Lady Gregory all contributed plays according to their gifts. It was the day of the great Irish literary revival, justly celebrated by Ernest Boyd, Moore, and many subsequent writers. It falls quite outside the scope of the present book.

In London in 1904 there was established at the Court Theatre that "congregation," as Shaw called it, which gave support to what was not so much a Repertory Season as a season of short runs, mostly of plays by Shaw. The business manager of the experiment was J. E. Vedrenne; the producer a young actor named Harley Granville-Barker. At first the Court was engaged in Shakespearean production, and Barker's first experiment was with "The Two Gentlemen of Verona"; but there were some matinées of "Candida", and from these developed the famous Vedrenne-Barker partnership. It

167

gave nearly a thousand performances of Shaw, Barker, St. John
Hankin, John Masefield, Euripides, Galsworthy, and other at that
time non-commercial dramatists. Then in 1907-8 Vedrenne and
Barker took the Savoy Theatre, which was in the centre of London,
and the partnership ceased.

In those same years of 1907-8 Annie Elizabeth Fredericka
Horniman took it into her head to reform Manchester; and she did
there what she had already done in Dublin. She acquired the Gaiety
Theatre, rebuilt it, and established a second Repertory Theatre, thus
giving a tremendous fillip to Lancashire dramatic writing, which
accordingly produced a "school" of its own. Manchester had previously been famed for its school of political economists (now, alas,
quite outmoded); and with Miss Horniman's help it became the
home of advanced or intellectual drama—the drama of ideas, as it
was called—as that appeared to dwellers in the Edwardian and early
Georgian period. The dramatists who made their mark at the
Gaiety Theatre, Manchester, included Stanley Houghton, Allan
Monkhouse, Charles McEvoy, J. Sackville Martin and Basil
Dean.

In 1910, a little less than three months before King George came
to the throne, Charles Frohman opened at the Duke of York's
Theatre in St. Martin's Lane, London, a repertory season which
lasted for seventeen weeks; and in the course of that season a play of
Pinero's was revived, and new plays, either long or short, by
George Meredith, Anthony Hope, Shaw, Galsworthy, Barrie, Barker
and a new dramatist of lower-middle class or suburban life named
Elizabeth Baker, were performed. The producers for the season were
Dion Boucicault, who ordinarily produced for Frohman, and
Granville-Barker.

In these different seasons may be glimpsed something of the
dramatic situation as it stood when King George came to the
throne. Outside them, Hubert Henry Davies and Somerset Maugham
both entertained lovers of comedy, and Rudolf Besier had already
scored a success with "Don"; St. John Hankin, a follower of Wilde
in what is called artificial comedy (but in Hankin's case comedy of
such slightness as to seem too pale for the commercial theatre), was
dead in 1909. I have written of Shaw, Barrie, and Galsworthy;
some of the others have not quite held their places in dramatic
history; others I shall mention again later. Nearly all of them differed
from such veterans as Pinero and Henry Arthur Jones by reason of
the fact that they sought their inspiration in the moral and domestic
problems of unremarkable parents and children, and tried to solve
those problems, or at least to present them, without extravagance.
Not the best, but the most typical, of such dramatists was Stanley
Houghton, and the title of his first long play was significant. It was

"The Younger Generation." The new note in the novel was realism; in the play, it was an extremely natural treatment of social philosophy.

In a moment I shall speak a little of the Manchester school, with particular reference to Houghton, McEvoy, and Allan Monkhouse; but for the present I shall stay in London, where we all thought—those of us who were growing up in that time—that we discerned the first glory of a new great dramatist. His name was Harley Granville-Barker; he was known to us as an actor in Shakespeare, Shaw and Euripides—he played with success such parts as John Tanner, Marchbanks, Dick Dudgeon, General Burgoyne, Lance in "The Two Gentlemen of Verona," and the henchman in "Hippolytus";—and he was the producer who first in England managed to persuade actors to play naturally as a group. All these facts about him aroused expectation; but it was known, too, that he was the focal point of a great remonstrance against the dramatic censorship, for a play of his, of the most decent and thoughtful kind, had been refused an essential licence. And that play, together with two others against which nothing had been alleged save that the public would not care to see them, was printed in a book with a new conversational kind of stage directions, so that all could read his work in comfort.

ii. Harley Granville-Barker

"PHILIP. . . Finery sits so well on children. And they strut and make love absurdly . . . even their quarelling is in all good faith and innocence. But I don't see why we men and women should not find all happiness . . . all beauty, too . . . in soberer purposes. . . . And I want an art and a culture that shan't be just a veneer on savagery."

H. Granville-Barker: The Madras House.

BARKER was born in London in 1877; and at some very early age determined to be an actor. What he had done before he went to the Court Theatre I do not know (he acted as early as 1895 in a play by Alfred Robbins called "Mixed Marriage"); but he made a good Lance in "The Two Gentlemen of Verona" when he was twenty-six, and there is no doubt that in spite of possessing a voice which lacked resonance he would have become a leading actor if he had wished solely to act. However, he had too much versatility to care for playing only one part in life. He wanted to produce plays (for there was something new and good to be done in that direction); and he wanted to write plays; and he wanted most eagerly to discipline and instruct the world. He was an intellectual. He made one of his young spokesmen say that he (the spokesman) had married his wife because she preferred Bach to Offenbach. Nor did Barker see that this was the way to achieve a sterile union. He was too much in earnest, then, to laugh at himself. How that last act of "The Madras House" worried him ever after!

His first play, written when he was only twenty-three, was "The Marrying of Ann Leete," which was about a young lady who married a gardener. It was written, quite clearly, by one who adored the work of George Meredith. It has a charming preciosity; a touch of Pierrot and Pierrette; melancholy and tender smiles, exquisite speeches. But it moves rapidly; nobody without great feeling for the stage could have written it. His second, "The Voysey Inheritance," was written four years later. It was not only in the new movement, but must be considered as having done much to stir the movement towards a natural drama. Fancy had gone; great sobriety had taken its place. An audience was asked to be, not amused, but deeply interested in a middle-class family faced with a crisis both moral and financial.

With the third play, "Waste," Barker invited attention to the fact that by English social convention any man prominent in affairs who is guilty of a disclosed sexual offence must pay for indiscretion with disgrace. He had in mind, no doubt, the cases of Parnell and Sir Charles Dilke, both of whom were ruined as the result of divorce proceedings. Nor did he stop at the theme and at the comment indicated in his title, but supplied our rulers with advice, gratis, upon two or three other social questions. At this time, speaking in public, he demanded great range for the drama. Not only in the matter of morals, but in the matter of form and content. He said that he would like to see a play which was in effect the dramatization of a Blue Book. That shows how far the serious drama had progressed in England under his care.

Still engrossed in sociology, he wrote for the Frohman repertory season a fourth play, "The Madras House," in which he presented many aspects of the woman question. He showed half a dozen melancholy spinsters in a family; he showed the young intellectual to whom I have referred and his lovely, intelligent, and possibly extravagant wife; he showed an elderly man whose view of women was oriental; a young woman who took an original and independent view of her own misbehaviour and its consequences; and the whole discussion (for the play was a discussion as well as a piece of dramatic entertainment) took place in relation to a colossal drapery stores known as the Madras House. This was the last of Barker's original and full-length plays to be produced. It was, socially, the most ambitious of them. It was for three-quarters of its length engrossing in the theatre; and it made one feel that when the author had grown to his full stature he would be fit to paint the whole of English life as no other modern dramatist could do. Alas, we were disappointed. Barker's later plays, although printed, were obscure, with scenes of beautiful subtlety but considerable difficulty, and they remained un-performed; he preferred, so far as stage production is concerned, to collaborate with his wife in translations of Martinez Sierra, the Quinteros, Schnitzler, Guitry, and Jules Romains.

He also retired from the production of other men's plays; and all the promise to which we attached so much importance in the early days of King George's reign remained unfulfilled. I do not disguise the fact that I think this was a disaster to the living theatre. Other men—including Shaw—thought and said the same thing when it happened, thereby angering Barker and putting valuable friendships in peril. But we must not forget that, outside creative work, Barker wrote much practical analysis of the working of a National Theatre (to the idea of which he was devoted) and some prefaces to the plays of Shakespeare as seen by a great dramatic producer and a wise and subtle and ingenious mind which have already affected the production of Shakespeare and will do so still more in the future.

But it was a mind bent upon expressing views. To Barker a fact was not so much a fact as an instance. He was more didactic than Galsworthy, because more hardily an intellectual. Where Gals-worthy said "Be good, be honourable, be just!" Barker said "Be right!" Adversely, one could say he was a purist, which means "a prig"; but adverseness is always an easy choice for the critic, and it is untrue that Barker was a prig. His plays are fuller of valuable and explicit human insights and knowledges than any other plays of their day. Nevertheless, they are also fuller of a determination to talk things out in the interests of civilization. As their author said, "Neither art nor literature, nor even religion, are always on the heights, nor need they be. But they need to have the heights in view." That was his standpoint. And so while his characters do and say things which are of a natural and amusing and stimulating kind, the things they say are always related to an extremely high and dis-satisfied view of life and culture commoner nowadays than it was when they were written and never wholly free from pragmatism.

The plays of Barker are at their best when they permit of free exchange between character and opinion, view and counter-view; then they are astonishingly full and alert and courageous. But they are at their weakest when the persons of the play attempt to be idealistically constructive without altogether committing their creator to the line they take; because every timidity of ridicule steps in and constrains the author to anticipatory defence. Impos-sible to say or let them say this or that, for it is open to the same kind of destructive logic or laughter (but from a different angle) which one has so effectively used upon others. Oh, dear! One must not be *too* serious! One must guard oneself against absurdity by being rather deprecating. . . . Then, indeed, the persons of the play begin to mention their sense of humour; and—how terrible!— those who become whimsical and speak of their sense of humour are much in the position of Simple Simon when he was asked to show his penny. Seriousness of aim, and a view of the heights, interfere very considerably with the creative act, which must be free, unscrupulous, and unconstrained if it is to escape the paralysis of the literary.

Barker's work does not quite escape that paralysis. It is as though he drank in Meredith with his mother's milk, turned actor and learnt all that there is to be known about stagecraft, and then discovered the Fabian Society, and was sterilized by it. His genius was free when he wrote "The Voysey Inheritance"; but in "Waste" and "The Madras House" it was struggling with two powerful rivals— his intellect and his ethical sense. The Fabian Society had supervened. After "The Madras House" he swung back to Meredith, or perhaps to Shakespeare; and his drama was again experimental. His talent was great; his personality charming and subtly dominating (in his younger days he aroused the superstition of those who came under his spell, and some of them thought him inspired by God); and if he did not do all that was expected of him in the regeneration of English drama, it was because he preferred to do something that interested him more.

iii. Allan Monkhouse

"I want to make it intimate and searching; I want to get at the truth."
Prologue to Men and Ghosts.

Barker did not create a school of dramatists. The Abbey Theatre did, and the Gaiety Theatre, Manchester, did. The great dramatist of the Dublin stage was Synge; but there have been many others since Synge who have pictured the life of the Irish peasant, from Lady Gregory to Lennox Robinson and Sean O'Casey; and the object of the Irish dramatists had been to create folk drama. With Manchester the object was to persuade theatre audiences first that the ordinary, the commonplace, the hitherto negligible had its dramatic aspects and second that a decided change was in progress in both manners and morals, for which something interesting and thoughtful might be said. Patrons of the Manchester theatre heard that unmarried young women might go their own wayward way, that parents were sometimes behind the times, that restlessness and revolt were as much in the air in twentieth-century Lancashire as they had been elsewhere in the eighties of the previous century, and that even clerks (particularly if they were clerks with literary ambitions) could be made to challenge the minds and hearts of those who saw them truthfully presented. The first play to be given by Miss Horniman in Manchester was about just such a clerk and his family, and it was called "David Ballard."

The author of "David Ballard" was Charles McEvoy, who never repeated the success he had with this play. "David Ballard," imperfect though it is, was an excellent example of what could be done with plain material. The central character was a young man whose family scorned him because he was a poet; but he won a prize of one hundred pounds for a poem in praise of Sunlight Soap, and this brought about his emancipation, incidentally also enabling Percy, a more admired brother, to repay money which he had borrowed from the till of his employers. It was the first realistic play of the lower-middle class to be performed on the English stage. Its theme was over-simple, but the play had life of its own and its dialogue was written by a man who had listened well and with both amusement and indignation to the talk of stupid people. If its scene was London, and not Manchester, that was because it was written before the Manchester school came into being. Its influence upon that school was considerable.

Another influence, and a notable one, was that of *The Manchester Guardian*, the newspaper which has unrivalled prestige wherever the English language is read. The *Guardian* was owned and edited by C. P. Scott; and its chief leader-writer, C. E. Montague, was at the same time its chief dramatic critic.

"When Lindsay wanted a new man on the staff he wrote to some bigwig at Oxford and asked for a list of the best young men about. Brilliant young double-firsts tumbled over one another to get on the Herald, but they had to be something better than double-firsts to stay there. Yes, the pace was hot. . . . It was one of the jocular traditions of the office—and not without some foundation—that George Meredith had been refused a job there. He wasn't quite good enough. So the young intellectuals would put it to heavy outsiders. They played at being prigs. Never was such a set of boys. They were boys even when they verged on middle age, and they would write like boys. It came of the inspiration of the great Secretan, who was an article of religion in the office, and of a religion unstaled."

For the *Herald* in that quotation from a book by Allan Monkhouse called "True Love," read the *Guardian*; for "Lindsay" read "C. P. Scott," and for "Secretan" read "C. E. Montague."

The entire staff of the *Guardian* was literary: that is to say, all those who wrote for the paper (it is much the same today) represented what may be described as a state of polished intellectual culture. They wrote with conscious grace; they read with assiduity; their intellectual and æsthetic aims were high and rarefied. And they supported the Gaiety Theatre. They all, or nearly all, wrote plays to fill its repertory; and when they did not write such plays they made a point of going to see what their comrades had written, and of criticizing it as they would have done if they had been still in the literary set at Oxford. They made a family, and a happy one. And the family had the feeling that its affairs were of supreme importance to modern literature. Such confidence, which alone allows a group to tolerate the work of other groups, is uncommon, and today in a distracted literary England is non-existent.

I have said that Stanley Houghton was the most typical of the Manchester dramatists; and there can be no doubt that his play, "Hindle Wakes," made more stir in the theatre than any other play originating in Manchester. Houghton had been a dramatic critic on the *Guardian*, though he was not an Oxonian; and if he had lived (he died in 1913 at the age of 32) he might have done much to influence the course of the modern drama. On the other hand there was in his work an element of triteness which causes me to doubt whether he was capable of great expansion. I prefer to say only that "Hindle Wakes," marking a decided advance upon "The Younger Generation," set an interesting example to dramatists of the new school.

Another dramatist whose work continued into old age deserves to be noted on account of his plays and of his admirable and too little read novels. His name was Allan Noble Monkhouse; and he was born in 1858. He was a Durham man, but he emigrated early to Manchester, where he entered the cotton trade and presently joined the staff of *The Manchester Guardian*. That was inevitable, for from the first he was a booklover and an enthusiast of the right kind for the *Guardian* office. And his greatest enthusiasm—again very proper in a member of the *Guardian* staff at that time—was for George Meredith. The hero of "Men and Ghosts" (Monkhouse was fond of the first person singular, and used it with ease), in describing his boyhood, remarks:

> "I remember how we chanced on Meredith long before he was the fashion. We read all that we could find, we tried to get books that were out of print and even wrote reproachful, insulting letters to publishers for not reprinting them. For years, while we disputed among ourselves whether he was the greatest of novelists or only one among the greatest, we never met anybody who had heard of him. Later, his poetry was to become a big influence and his *Joy of Earth* became a notable qualification of such fragmentary philosophy as I picked up. It is still one of the great books of the world to me."

Enthusiasm for Meredith, whom he later put second to Dickens among the great English novelists, persisted in Monkhouse to the end of his life; as did an absorbing love of Shakespeare. But in

himself he was a local author, familiar only with the life of Manchester and Disley, Cheshire (which figured in his novels as Darley),
and the world of his novels and plays is comparatively small. It was
certainly and unashamedly provincial. In "True Love" as in "Men
and Ghosts," "My Daughter Helen," and "Farewell, Manchester,"
the note of autobiography, restrained and ironic, gives intimate,
almost conversational character to reflective treatment of a small
assembly.

Having written one novel, "A Deliverance," before the end of
the nineteenth century, and a couple more—"Love in a Life" and
"Dying Fires"—before the accession of King George, Monkhouse
was soon drawn into the Gaiety Theatre. He contributed to its
repertory, indeed, the best known of all his plays, "Mary Broome"
(1911), which was at once recognized as an outstanding addition to
the new drama. He was not, subsequently, a dramatist alone, but his
novels were brief and superficially slight in theme (whatever their
implications), and at all times it was the talk of people, their communication by words of mood and temper, which held his attention.

"Mary Broome" was a play about a maidservant who had been
seduced by the son of her employers, an improvident and para-
doxical young literary man, and who, following a forced marriage
to the futility of which the young man drew attention, and the birth
and death of her baby, resolved to go to Canada in company with
another lover, a milkman. In the first act news of Mary's indecorum
reached Leonard's father through her misappropriation of a photograph of Leonard; in the last act she announced to her father- and
mother-in-law with calm and dignity that she had decided to for-
sake her gasbag of a husband for another. Calmness and dignity, in
fact, were the chief characteristics of Mary Broome; and it is difficult
to imagine so discreet a young woman yielding to passion or the
importunities of an egoist. But the author was more concerned with
the effect upon others of Mary's conduct than with the consistency
of Mary herself; and the point of "Mary Broome" to which I direct
attention is that the young and talkative seducer addressed his
parents in these terms:

> "LEONARD: You parents are in a middle stage. Once you'd just
> have been brutal to the girl. I don't mean you, but parents gener-
> ally. Presently we may have more sense. I'm a selfish brute but I've
> got some sense. But I'm powerless. (*To his father*): Haven't you any
> imagination? It's all very fine to make a scene here and put down your
> foot and coerce me into your beastly righteousness, but think of the
> years to come. Do you see us married? Do you see our married life?"

That was the voice of self-conscious thought in 1911. That was the
critical theatre. "You parents . . . I don't mean you, but parents

generally . . . I'm a selfish brute but I'm powerless . . . Your beastly righteousness." Monkhouse, it is true, gave the moral an ironic twist highly personal to himself by allowing Mary to take the initiative in parting; but the argument was against Puritanism and against responsibility, and it revealed the fact that the post-Shavian stage in England, however quietly, was at last moving towards living commentary upon current morals and manners.

It was a pity, I think, that in so moving the Manchester dramatists, schooled by the *Guardian*, paid such fastidious heed to the literary tone of their work. But there is more truth than the ironic author realizes in this wry report upon Manchester's reception of Geoffrey Arden's play "Alice Dean" (which can be taken to represent "Mary Broome"):

> "People went to see *Alice Dean*, and it had a certain vogue; as a local attempt it was not so bad, though it was understood that these *Herald* people take themselves too seriously, and constitute a sort of mutual admiration society. Besides, such plays as *Alice Dean*, clever as they are, miss the broad, human touch."

If the broad, human touch as conceived by sentimentalists is legitimately matter for ridicule, absence of breadth may leave plays decidedly thin. Max Beerbohm mentions in his essay on Ouida that "Art, in a writer, is not everything. Indeed, it implies a certain limitation. If a list of consciously artistic writers were drawn up, one would find that most of them were lacking in great force of intellect or emotion." What Max Beerbohm says of books is true of plays. One can take the line that if a play is very good indeed it will be unintelligible to a large number of persons; and this justifies play-producing societies, little theatres, and the like. But if one prides oneself upon appealing only to the elect public, one may verge upon the private or family joke; and banality is often achieved by work that seeks to be superior. True superiority, I am confident, has no need of the applause, carefully modulated, of the few. In the case of "Mary Broome" there is a constant self-destructive quizzicalness and under-emphasis which, if the dialogue were not so delicately poised, would stultify the dramatic idea.

Monkhouse's chief inspiration was literary. His books are rich in references to the Shakespearean tragedies and in quotations from the poetry of Meredith. When the people talk to one another, their talk mounts quickly to the quasi-Meredithian. One man in "Men and Ghosts," for example, who has seduced a girl, holds in his hand an unopened letter from this girl to another. He wishes to open it:

> "'You must not do it,' I said.
> "'Not gentlemanlike?' he sneered.

"The thing was too preposterous. One speaks a madman fair and Bill had a streak of insanity.

"'Let's argue the point,' he said; 'it'll pass the time. Just what we needed to forget our weariness.'

"It didn't admit of argument but I humoured him by asking him to state his case. I was beginning to feel safer; he really had alarmed me. 'My case,' he said, 'is simply an overwhelming curiosity.'

"'That's no case.'

"'I said "overwhelming."'

"'It doesn't overwhelm. You've got a will.'

"'The will sings small before passion.'

"'Curiosity isn't a passion.'

"'Then it's a disease. I'm mastered by a disease.'

"'This is a matter of conduct. In discussing it I think we must presuppose sanity.'

"'What's logic to a man on fire?'"

You notice that this is all very quick; thought is always quick in Monkhouse's characters, and they speak briefly and in phrase—not brokenly and as if they groped for words. All have a flair for language. Either they are speaking, or the author himself is browsing among implications, turning them gravely and ironically, sometimes analysing, as in this:

"Men like me, who are modest enough on the surface and quiet and introspective, have our secrecies of insolence and elation. We are too wary to brag and strut—and, indeed, we scorn such crudities—but we can realize attitude and spectator in ourselves; we can indulge secretly an aptitude for showing off."

Elsewhere, Monkhouse causes a hero to recall a friend's saying that "when you want a thing the best plan is to take the simplest means of getting it"; and he adds "obvious as this is, it is not realized by those who conduct their lives on a complicated system of denials." "A complicated system of denials": is not that a most illuminating phrase? Does it not conjure up a temperament? Applying it to the author, does not one flashingly comprehend his restraint? Is it not a complicated system of denials, rather than of affirmations, that gives his plays and novels their air of fineness, of withdrawal from rough and tumble, of reflective treatment of the supposititious? Full as the books and plays are, if one once loses the sense of quality they become abstract, as if they dealt with posed situations, and as if the various misconducts of the errant characters had no greater reality than hearsay. Have these girls really been seduced? Is not their seduction merely a necessary preliminary to discussion?

This method is better suited (so far as the reader is concerned) to comedy than tragedy; since the fear of being extravagant caused

Monkhouse to muffle tragedy, and deprecatingly see its smallness in a world where individuals are unimportant. Comedy, then, was his forte; and perhaps the best of his comedies is the play called "The Education of Mr. Surrage," produced at the Liverpool Repertory Theatre in 1912. It is the variation of a favourite theme of the author's—a middle-aged father with up-to-date children who introduce to the paternal home odd people from the unscrupulous world of the arts. Mr. Surrage learns through personal contact the charms and disadvantages of acquaintance with the amoral; and he accepts his education with gusto. Though saved from marriage with one who boded no good to his peace of mind, he feels that he is living and has previously been dead. When his daughter tells him he has been lucky to escape one relenting charmer, Mr. Surrage spiritedly remarks: "It seems to me that all depends on what I've escaped to." The scene proceeds:

> Rose: Forgive me, father, but it's an infatuation. Mrs. Staines—well, compared with many of the women I know——
> Surrage: Hah! Introduce me to them, then.
> Archie: Really, sir——
> Surrage: I'm opening out to new ideas.
> Rose: But, father, we have an ideal of you that——
> Surrage: Oh, hang the ideal!
> Rose: Those horrible people would corrupt you.
> Surrage: Not a bit of it. I may do them some good.
> Archie: Leave well alone, sir, leave well alone.
> Surrage: It isn't well. I've been bored to death. This week-end has been most exhilarating, and strangely interesting. We must have more of them.

The artists, the literary men, in Monkhouse's work were usually queer fish. Queer fish enchanted him; but only as abnormalities flung disconcertingly into a small, intelligent, less unconventional group of persons, old or young, to do the things which a local code of honour condemns. They had no scruples—from Leonard in "Mary Broome" to Marmaduke in "My Daughter Helen" and Paul Felice in the play to which he gave his name. They paraded their lack of moral sense. They enlisted the author's sympathy without quite conquering ourselves. And they are always presented as masters of that quick literary talk of which I have given examples, with relish, with success. Granted the author's "case," whether it be that of the young writer who goes against his will to the War and returns sick with horror to dodge the village band and a reception which he regards as indecent, or the parlourmaid who is so innocently refined though she is going to have a baby by the young master, the treatment is at all times full of charm, wit, wisdom, and a sense of those heights which Granville-Barker thinks the dramatist should never forget. If they failed to arouse popular enthusiasm it was because they were too "literary," and because the small, the fine, the delicate, while they have their delicious joys for those of like mind, do lack robustness, power, and the colour and movement of irresistible life.

iv. St. John Greer Ervine

"Too much attention is devoted to these squawkers in contemporary literature. They may be the victims of their environment, although I suspect them of plain self-indulgence, but a man is a poor creature who is victimized by any environment, and I am not prepared to make a hero of him. . . . I am, as my readers will have observed, a very humble-minded man, and am always willing to learn from my betters."

St. John Ervine, in "The Observer," July 22nd, 1934.

NOBODY could accuse my last typical dramatic writer of being too "literary," for if St. John Ervine has a fault it is that he was, in his journalistic writing, too bluff and manly to be endured by the fastidious. I doubt whether there is any other writer who aroused such repulsion in the delicate-minded. In the same way, I doubt whether there is any other writer whose real gifts have been so much blanketed by that specious breeziness which was his version of what Keats might have called the Shavian or egotistical sublime. I should have difficulty in convincing quite a number of people that Ervine was a serious and extraordinarily able novelist. And yet I am persuaded that this is true. I would give all his plays (and of course all his dramatic criticism and comment upon current affairs) for his two novels, "Mr. Martin's Man" and "A Wayward Man." I take pleasure in saying that if these two books had been translated from the Icelandic they would have given pleasure to all who regarded Ervine as a noisy and offensive blasphemer against elegance and the recherché.

But Ervine, born in 1883, came from Belfast. For some good reason he was in 1915 made manager of the Abbey Theatre, Dublin. Prior to that he had been a clerk in the London office of an insurance company, and a member of the Fabian Nursery, and a riotous reviewer for A. R. Orage's weekly review, *The New Age.* He went to the War in 1916, and lost a leg; he was for many years the chief dramatic writer on the London weekly newspaper, *The Observer*; an untiring lecturer, a jocular commentator, who trailed his coat and banged heads at sight, and—as if incidentally—was the author of several plays (two of them celebrated and successful in the United States, a third one of the most popular ever performed at the Haymarket Theatre, London), and of six novels so casually produced over a period of twenty years that they have hardly at all impressed the general critical mind.

If he had been content to stick to Ulster and the novel Ervine would have been recognized everywhere as "the Ulster novelist." Instead, he created turmoil and ferocity in two countries by his outspoken theatrical criticisms, attacked Wilde, wrote an immense biography of General Booth, and another, equally long, of Shaw, and kept to his own opinion of the young when fashion decreed that they should be extolled. As an original writer he is still grievously underrated.

Further, his one highly successful play in England, "The First Mrs. Fraser," is by no means the best of his dramatic works, in spite of the fact that it enjoyed much popularity on the Continent of Europe. His best play is "John Ferguson," which has an Ulster scene; and this tells the not uncommon story of a mortgaged farm, the brutality of the mortgagor, his rape of the mortgagee's daughter, and his murder by the mortgagee's son, followed by an inevitable sad parting between the amiable characters as one of them goes to render himself to justice. The influence of Synge upon Ervine in this play was as great as (and no greater than) the influence of Synge upon all other contributors to the Irish drama. There is a half-wit who spins the plot, and there are some poetical phrases, local idioms, and a general air of enduring poverty. But the play has its own life, it moves clearly, and it is written with power.

Some of the other plays, while they show skill and accomplishment, do not rise sufficiently above those qualities to impress themselves upon a reader. "The Ship," sincere though it is in an attempt to make tragedy of a young man's death in the sinking of a ship in which he had no mind to sail, lacks resilience; "Mary, Mary, Quite Contrary," which aims at lightness, misses brilliance and is a little heavy: "Jane Clegg," produced at the Gaiety Theatre, Manchester, in 1913, belongs to what I have called the Manchester school, deals with poor people, a humbugging commercial traveller who embezzles to get his mistress out of the country, and his wife who parts with a legacy to save him from disgrace and then parts from him to save herself from further contamination; and despite slick character sketches does not escape obviousness and repetition.

It was in the two novels, "Mrs. Martin's Man" and "The Wayward Man," that Ervine's talent reached its most natural expression. Both are narratives, the former the simple tale of a long-suffering woman shopkeeper in what I understand is Donaghadee, the latter the tale of a wandering son of just such another woman. Mrs. Martin, marrying a sailor, has two children by him, guesses that he is unfaithful to her with her own sister, and at last, when she is deserted (for her husband clears out for America with the least humane of motives), she opens a shop and deals successfully in hardware. When her husband returns home again his children are grown up, and the situation as it then stands between all the members of the family provides material for the tale. It is original, beautiful, and deeply interesting. "The Wayward Man," also highly original, has something of the same quality. In that book, however, interest settles upon a boy who runs away to sea and spends some time in America before he turns to Ireland and marries. Here, as in "Mrs. Martin's Man," there is nothing of the conventional novel, but a clear narrative of which the impression throughout is complete authenticity. I do not regard Ervine's other novels as equal to these two books; but these two books seem to me to be so excellent that I am prepared to rank their author very high indeed, on the strength of them, among modern writers.

It may be said that I have strayed from "the critical theatre," and that is quite true. So have Granville-Barker, Allan Monkhouse, and St. John Ervine. The critical theatre, to be quite truthful, had not and has not the seeds of eternal literary life in it. A critical attitude, and a self-conscious attitude, does not and cannot develop creative literature. We need criticism; but we need it as a corrective, not as an inspiration. That is why, bad and vulgar as popular literature may be, it has a vitality denied to the writings of those who know only too well the weakness of the instrument. Shaw could criticize and create; but Shaw was Shaw, an exuberant force who would always risk folly for the sake of fun. There is no other contributor to the critical theatre who has not paralysed himself or petered out through fear of his own judgment.

Chapter Nine

LITERARY MEN

E. V. LUCAS, EDWARD GARNETT, FORD MADOX HUEFFER,
MAX BEERBOHM, C. E. MONTAGUE, KATHERINE MANSFIELD
AND MIDDLETON MURRY

i

THE author of a now forgotten manual for young writers
stated that "there is scarcely any necessity to read as models
any writer farther back than Stevenson and Gissing"; and a
young friend of mine who told the English Literature Master of a
large school for boys that he had with pleasure been reading "Tom
Jones" received the reply: "Who or what is Tom Jones?" These
two comments are both highly significant of the critical change occurring in the first third of this century; for when King George came
to the throne nothing written after 1850 was in any sense "literature,"
and in 1910 progressive authors raged in vain against some academic
veterans whom they styled "mandarins." It was the mandarins, one
understood, who then fixed the limits of "literature," and dropped a
curtain between the great and good and the merely current.

If I am asked to name the mandarins, I cannot do so. I assume
that they were the more stuffy professors of English literature
throughout the British Isles. Generations familiar with Arthur
Quiller-Couch as a professor will hardly believe that his Cambridge
appointment caused at the time profound academic disquiet. He
had written novels. He was suspect. Fortunately he had read widely,
and he had a way with undergraduates. Hence his success. But I
doubt whether even Quiller-Couch ventured to advance the canon
by many years. Shall we say as far as 1894? Nowadays everything is
altered. The mandarins are all "modn."

There were several mandarinic personages at whom no brick-
bats were aimed by original writers. They were growing elderly,
and of course they grew more elderly and in the fullness of time
died; but they never really grew older. The men I have in mind
were George Saintsbury, Edmund Gosse, and William Robertson
Nicoll. To them might be added Thomas Seccombe, genial lecturer
and journalist and historian. All four were practising men of
letters. Saintsbury was generally understood to have read everything ever written; and when he wrote a History of the French
Novel he gave a great deal of space to Paul de Kock, a fact which in

any less professional writer would have been censured but which, in the case of Saintsbury, who was much loved, aroused delighted murmurs. He also contributed prefaces which are the best things of their kind to forty translated volumes of Balzac's novels. He was a slovenly and eccentric writer, but an interesting and humanely learned man.

Gosse—pilloried at the beginning of the twentieth century by Churton Collins for writing about eighteenth-century literature without taking the trouble to read the whole of it, and by Duncan Tovey for reprinting a corrupt text of Gray's letters while boasting that he had collated every word with the originals, pilloried in 1934 by Carter and Pollard for accepting as genuine several glaring modern literary forgeries, and in fact ridiculed or lambasted by almost all who have seriously tilled the ground he lightly scratched —contributed much to English knowledge of French and Scandinavian literature and wrote a book about his father which, when it was published in 1907, caused every scholarly sin to be forgiven him by the non-pedantic. To the end of his life he gossiped in print about books, and hobnobbed with writers, old and young. He had in his temperament both malice and vanity, and perhaps was a snob (which means that he preferred the literary *ton*, and liked to stand well with the fashion); but he had taste, a pen, and a tender feeling for letters.

Robertson Nicoll was a very different man from either of these. He edited the great English nonconformist newspaper *The British Weekly*, for which he wrote under more than one pseudonym, and his activities were without end. He was a little Scotsman with a sighing voice, weary eyes, and a straggling moustache, and he would often muse, stroking his chin with a wavery hand, preparing gentle retorts which stung more the longer they were recollected. He figures in Wells's "Boon" as Dr. Tomlinson Keyhole, from which name one may gather that he also was something of a gossip. In fact he knew all the literary gossip ever told (or not told), and forgot nothing. Nor did Nicoll deal exclusively in gossip; for his interest in gossip was but a section of his interest in all human affairs. He had a keen eye for authors. It was he who sighted Barrie from afar and arranged the book publication of "Auld Licht Idylls"; it was he who persuaded Heinemann to reconsider and eventually to publish Maugham's "Mrs. Craddock," hitherto rejected; it was he who knew at once which young novelist would move towards fame and fortune (although he was keen to detect a fault, and in answer to a question he quietly said after meeting Hugh Walpole: "How *coooold* he be ainy goood? He knows naaaathing about saix!"); and it was he whose first editorial mistake—the commissioning of a series of highly critical articles on Lloyd George

G

which he could not have published without alienating a powerful friend—killed him.

Since I have mentioned Nicoll, who among other professional activities was a publishers' reader on a very large, indeed colossal, scale, I think I should name here two men whose chief activity in the panorama of Georgian literature was of great but anonymous importance. They are E. V. Lucas and Edward Garnett. Everybody of course knows Lucas for his own writing—his humorously senti-mental novels, his essays short or long, his anthologies, and his editorship of the works of Lamb, for these gave him unique celeb-rity;—not so many are familiar with the plays of Garnett, or his book of satires, "Papa's War," or his Conrad-prefaced study of Turgenev. And yet Lucas and Garnett, as publishers' readers, did more to encourage the growth of modern literature than any other men of their day. It was their business to find quality almost before it was evident, and certainly before it was mature. They were well-nigh unerring in the perception of merit, and between them they recognized and supported more of those afterwards noted in the book world than any other men whatever. Such work needs insight of a high order, as well as disinterested activity; just as it needs courage to risk a decision upon one's own judgment, and to go on risking it after a thousand discouragements. One imagines Lucas and Garnett as never discouraged; they were in their work for half a century; they were no ordinary men.

ii. Edward Verrall Lucas

"On the surface he might be mistaken for a mere cricket enthusiast. Dig down, and you will come, with not too much difficulty, to the simple man of letters. Dig further, and, with somewhat more difficulty, you will come to an agreeably ironic critic of human foibles. Try to dig still further, and you will probably encounter rock."
Arnold Bennett: Books and Persons.

WELL, if you were to study the subject of anthologies you would without any doubt at all find that the best known of all modern anthologies is one called "The Open Road," published in 1899, and edited by E. V. Lucas. Lucas was born about 1866; and by 1899 he had mastered the greater part of English light literature. He loved walking, and he loved dogs; he had urbanity, ruthlessness of observation (as witness his unsurpassed account of a visit to Swin-burne and Watts-Dunton towards the end of Swinburne's life), and taste. In a deep voice, hardly moving his lips, and certainly using little gesticulation, he quietly and not expansively talked with the grim wit of a rich and implacable mind. What he said was worth hearing.

His essays were among the most agreeable of their age. So were his historical and topographical works; for he was a traveller in cities and picture galleries as well as among books and men, and he recorded his every journey with the same slightly bitter benignity, and a charm which was never merely honeyed. His novels, while based upon ingenious ideas, and full of whimsy and information, were deficient in the continuity arising from persistent imaginative travail. Lucas had a great appetite for the curious, the human, and the ridiculous. If he were offered a story, an incident, or an absurdity, his mind instantly shaped it with wit and form. He read a character with wisdom, and gravely turned it to fun. He versified a fancy, or concentrated in an anecdote or instance all that a vaguer mind might stagger for an hour to express. But his was the mind of a critic and a commentator; and the hideous sustained labour of the ambitious novelist was impossible to him.

It would have involved digging below that rock to which Arnold Bennett referred; it would have involved for Lucas the excavation of harshness and passion. This was so because he was not a writer to whom the levels are final depths, and if once he had been determined to go deep he would have gone deep. In his thoughts he had no superficiality; but his essays and fictions were written with his fancy and his playful mind, and it is only at times, as in the Swinburne sketch, that one glimpses a judgment to which the facile enthusiasms of his fellow-creatures are as the idle howlings of tomcats on urban rooftops.

He is recognized as the pre-eminent editor of Charles Lamb's works and biographer of Lamb. No edition approaches his in completeness and fullness of annotation. It is a monument to lifelong sympathy and devoted research. As for his personally unobtrusive work as a publishers' reader, it was second only in serious value to that of Edward Garnett.

iii. Edward Garnett

"'Come and dine with me, Truth,' begged Justice, and his stern eyes shone with the undying passion he ever cherished to make her his own. . . . 'Come with me, Truth! Your eyes are the loveliest thing to me in the wide universe,'"

Edward Garnett: Papa's War.

EDWARD GARNETT was less known to the public as a bookman than Lucas. His plays, one of which deals with Joan of Arc, were published in book form, and single performances may have been given of them; but the chief bulk of his published writing was in the form of criticism, and in the way of reports to publishers he was among the most prolific of men. He used, long ago, to write for an old weekly called *The Speaker*, which was merged in *The Nation* (now in turn merged in *The New Statesman*); and his articles forever drew attention to new work by English and Continental novelists who otherwise might have whistled for praise. As a very young reader for Fisher Unwin (he was born in 1868) he was the first to discern Conrad's future greatness in the book submitted in 1894. He was the friend and encourager of W. H. Hudson and John Galsworthy. To him we owe the abridgment of Doughty's "Arabia Deserta" and a valuable selection from Cunninghame Graham's work. His encouraging connection with struggling younger writers, Lawrence, H. E. Bates, and others, is well known. But hardly a man or woman writing novels of serious intention in the period covered by this book failed to receive from Garnett essential praise and critical support.

Nor is this all, for his wife, Constance Garnett, was the translator into English of Turgenev, Dostoevsky, Tchehov, and some of Tolstoy. She was not the first translator to bring single works by these four authors to the notice of English readers; but she was the first to make complete translations, and therefore the first to fix them for ever in English minds as individuals. One could not exaggerate the impression made upon young readers in 1912 by the appearance of "The Brothers Karamazov." Nor could one exaggerate the influence of that translation of the Tales of Tchehov by Constance Garnett which by the active effort of her husband began in 1916. The Turgenev was an older debt owed to the Garnetts, and I think it is true that for Edward Garnett Turgenev remained the ideal novelist. For the glorious but occasionally shoddy thrillingness of Dostoevsky he had no enthusiasm. He deprecatingly thought Dostoevsky "a sort of Russian Dickens". Nevertheless, there the Dostoevsky translation stands; and it is no part of my present task to distinguish between the rival virtues of Russian authors.

Opinions as to the positive merits of Constance Garnett's translations differ. I have been told by those who write and speak Russian that they are deficient in exactitude; having at one time made a careful comparison between Ralston's "Lisa," Constance Garnett's "A House of Gentlefolk," and Davis's "A Nest of Hereditary Legislators" (all of them versions of the same book by Turgenev), I believe the Garnett translations to be, so far as the general character of the work is concerned, as accurate and as fine as translations from so difficult a language as Russian can be, but slightly lacking—more particularly in the dialogue—in what I shall call exquisiteness of rendering. I have not compared her translations of Tolstoy with those of Aylmer Maude; and I think that Long's two volumes of Tchehov, published before Constance Garnett began her work, have occasional superiorities. Nobody, however, conferred so substantial a benefit, and one of such consistent faithfulness, upon English readers of Russian fiction as she.

If I were to demur to that standpoint as to fiction indicated by Edward Garnett's preference of Turgenev to Dostoevsky, I should say that he loved the tidy, the restrained, and the inexplicit. Formal nearness was more to him than exuberance, though the exuberant might be work of genius. He was incorrigibly serious, as a member of the intellectual Left must be; his taste was fine; and he was the only critic of quality and standing known to me who throughout his life made the novel as a form of art his particular theme and his particular care.

iv. Ford Madox Hueffer

I CALL him Ford Madox Hueffer because that is the name he bore in the days of *The English Review*. He later changed his name to Ford Madox Ford; and under that name continued to publish his oddly uneven work in considerable quantity and to give rise in the literary world to innumerable rumours. It was the word "taste" which introduced memory of him to my mind; for Hueffer is to me one of the enigmas of current literature. He had great talent, and much taste, to which he added considerable coarseness of spirit and a carelessness of statement which constantly spoil a reader's enjoyment of his work. He wrote remarkable poetry, some historical romances which just miss being extraordinary, many novels on modern themes and situations which surpass the reach of most living authors and achieve the coldness of the mortuary, criticism which for a paragraph here and there seems like revealed truth and drifts off into perversity, and memoirs of his own life and the lives of others which exult—perhaps defiantly—in his own unpleasantness.

He collaborated with Conrad, and taught him valuable lessons in the art of expressing himself in English. He was editor of the most interesting periodical of the pre-Georgian period I have described, *The English Review*, in which were published (besides that bizarre relic, a poem by Arnold Bennett) specimens of the work of almost all the established and arriving writers to 1908–11 (*The English Review* continued its work under another editor after the first glad Huefferian dawn), and in which living literature for the first time in English history was treated as quite important and quite exciting— much more important, and much more exciting than students of English literature could imagine, and even more exciting than the contests of politicians or sportsmen. Before he died he produced immense and highly original works on literary history. And of his novels such books as "The Fifth Queen", "The

Good Soldier" and "Some Do Not" should be familiar to every investigator of what has been written in this century. "The Critical Attitude" as to about one-third is a stimulating and valuable work. "The March of Literature," a monster survey intended, I fancy, as a best-seller for the American public, contains much that is original and suggestive. And yet the total effect created by Hueffer during his lifetime was less than the total effect created by men of insignificant talent. It is now increasing; his war novels promise to be regarded as classics; and it may be that while alive he missed acclaim through excessive versatility and some aversion for the hackwork of revision and proof-correction, which made him appear contemptuous of critical opinion

In person, Hueffer was a large, rather unwieldy fair man whose mouth, like Coleridge's, was always open, and whose speech recalled Carlyle's description of Coleridge's speech. He told lengthy and delightful stories with absorption and skill; he was a rich and stimulating talker, with a considerable sense of his audience; he improvised to admiration, and was lyrical at a moment's notice. But for me he remains both in himself and in his writings an unsolved puzzle. I must not forget to mention that he wrote, as a rule, with both eloquence and beauty.

v. Charles Edward Montague

"But Dick had fads. One was for a kind of writing; not the right kind; not saying what he had to say, and that's the end of it, but a plaguey, itchy fussing over some phrase, planing it down or bevelling it off, inlaying it with picked words of a queer far-fetched aptness, making it clang with whole pomps of proper names, that boomed into their places like drums and cymbals in symphonies, or twinkle and tingle, shot with ironies, or rise and fall like a voice that means more by the tone than the words."

C. E. Montague: A Hind Let Loose.

ONE of the men who was introduced to the notice of a different —not a wider—audience by The English Review was Charles Edward Montague, who wrote for it an essay upon "the wholesome theatre." But Montague was by no means new to the world in 1910, for he was born in 1867, and for some years had been that perpetual boy on the staff of The Manchester Guardian as to whom I used earlier a reference of Monkhouse's. He was chief leader-writer to the paper; and as long as he wrote leading articles leading articles were dishes for literary epicures. Such epicures, I think, had to lean more to Latin feasts than to those of a purer classicism; but they had a daily edification. They still receive similar feasts from other hands, especially when they read of cricket and music; but it was Montague who set the example and created the style. His delight being in the theatre, he also attended many a Manchester first night in the spirit in which genial spinsters attend weddings—from a love of a good institution, and the sight of happiness in others. "A man," says Tennyson, "imputes himself." If he be decent he readily thinks other people are decent." That was an article of the Montague faith. He loved the stage, and especially the stage of the Elizabethans, in which he was word-perfect.

In 1910 he wrote his first novel; and that, curiously enough, was about a leader-writer. But Fay, in "A Hind Let Loose," was no Montague; he was a comic character, a man who wrote one leading article for the Liberal newspaper in a city called Halland (which in its pride much resembles Manchester), and another for the Conservative rival newspaper in the same city. In his double rôle he scourged and counter-scourged himself nightly. However, he was found out; and both his employers discharged him, only to find that their own substitutional efforts were thought as dull as tracts by every reader. So both surreptitiously returned to the rascal and pleaded for his sole service in future, which (to both, for a consideration) he promised; while a third employer, another rival and a new one, was added to the first two, and Fay's earnings were much increased by the entire transaction. Great fun, literary fun, but fun of richness and spirit throughout, and the author's fluency never at a loss. No doubt, like Dick in the quotation, he polished; but the art of polishing is to give a finer glow, and this art Montague had mastered early. One reads "A Hind Let Loose" as if it were the easiest of improvizations, although the minor portraits are as finished as that of Fay himself. There is the Meredithian air of comedy; sometimes a Meredithian ellipsis; but when verisimilitude is needed it is unobtrusively supplied, and the book is not solely a farce.

Montague followed this with another—"The Morning's War" —perhaps a rewriting of something said earlier, and certainly less striking than "A Hind Let Loose"; and what he would normally have done next I do not know. But the First World War came, and in spite of the fact that he was forty-seven (he was said to be white-haired, but that sounds like a story), he boldly and enthusiastically enlisted as a private soldier. "The early volunteer in his blindness imagined that there was between all Englishmen then that oneness of faith, love, and courage."

> "Here were hundreds of thousands of quite commonplace persons rendered, by comradeship in an enthusiasm, self-denying, cheerful, unexacting, sanely exalted, substantially good. To get the more fit to be quickly used men would give up even the little darling vices which are nearest to many simple hearts. Men who had entertained an almost reasoned passion for whisky, men who in civil life had messed up careers for it and left all and followed it, would cut off their

whisky lest it should spoil their marching. Little white, prim clerks from Putney—men whose souls were saturated with the consciousness of class—would abdicate freely and wholeheartedly their sense of the wide, unplumbed estranging seas that ought to roar between themselves and Covent Garden porters. Many men who had never been dangerous rivals to St. Anthony kept an unwonted hold on themselves during months when hundreds of reputable women and girls round every camp seemed to have been suddenly smitten with a Bacchantic frenzy. Real, constitutional lazy fellows would buy little cram-books of drill out of their pay and sweat them up at night so as to get on the faster. Men warned for a guard next day would agree among themselves to get up an hour before the pre-dawn winter Reveille to practise among themselves the beautiful symbolic ritual of mounting guard in the hope of approaching the far-off, longed-for ideal of smartness, the passport to France. . . . How could they not have the illusion that the whole nation's sense of comradeship went as far as their own?"

Montague, one of these eager ones, was duly sent to the Front, and after a time it dawned upon those under whose command he was that this was no common soldier, and perhaps that he was less of a youth than he pretended. So they gave him some sort of rank, and he had then the task of showing distinguished literary visitors here and there (some of them must have been war correspondents, for Tomlinson was among those whose company he kept) about the battle zone. As he did this, he would say: "I think we can just cut across here; it saves a mile; the Germans have all got their heads down; it will be all right." And with that he would lead the way across the open, while the visitor (it was Wells who vividly described such a scene to me) scampered after with his heart in his boots.

But the mood of ecstacy in which Montague went to the War did not survive his experience of the War. As soon as the fighting was done, and he was home again, he began to write fragmentary articles for *The Manchester Guardian* about his experiences and his views of war; and these were so much his own that he was urged to make a book of such material, which he did. And it was called "Disenchantment", a proper title for such a work; the work itself expressing the feelings of all that part of a generation whose thought could expand to comprehensiveness.

"In their vices as well as their virtues the English preserve a distinguished moderation. They do not utterly shrink from jobbery, for example; they do from a job that is flagrant or gross. They give judgeships as prizes for party support, but not to the utterly briefless, the dullard who knows no more law than necessity. Building contractors, when in the course of their rise they become town councillors, do not give bribes right and left: their businesses thrive without that.

An Irishman running a Tammany in the States cannot thus hold himself in: the humorous side of corruption charms him too much; he wants to let the grand farce of roguery rip for all it is worth. But the English private's pet dictum, 'There's reason in everything,' rules the jobber, the profiteer, the shirker and placeman of Albion as firmly as it controls the imagination of her Wordsworths and the political idealism of her Cromwells and Pitts. Like her native cockroaches and bugs, whose moderate stature excites the admiration and envy of human dwellers among the corresponding fauna of the tropics, the caterpillars of her commonwealth preserve the golden mean."

That is bitter, as well as true and amusing and eloquent; but Montague's was the first pen to tell England what returning idealists thought of the land for whose continued freedom they had struggled with the horrors of war. As they did, he saw and felt and thought so deeply that his mind at last was sunk in a mood of restless melancholy. He was not disillusioned with life, but with the post-war world:

"Of course, life itself is all right. It never grows dull. All dullness is in the mind; it comes out thence and diffuses itself over everything round the dull person, and then he terms everything dull, and thinks himself the victim of the impact of dull things. In stupid rich people, in boys and girls deadeningly taught at dead-alive schools, in all disappointed weaklings and in declining nations, this loss of power to shed anything but dullness upon what one sees and hears is common enough. Second-rate academic people, Victorian official art, the French Second Empire drama, late Latin literature exhibit its ravages well. In healthy children, in men and women of high mental vitality, in places where any of the radio-activity of gifted teaching breaks out for a while, and in swiftly and worthily rising nations the mind is easily delighted and absorbed by almost any atom of ordinary experience and its relation to the rest. The wonder and beauty and humour of life go on just the same as ever whether Spain or Holland or Italy feel them or miss them."

And so, when Montague had written this book, and eased his mind of the thoughts which buzzed there, he settled down to do the work he had always wished to do. He left the *Guardian*; he went to live at Oxford, near his old University; he began another novel; he published a volume of short stories called "Fiery Particles". And then, unexpectedly, he died. The greater works he had planned remained unwritten. We are to content ourselves with what is already in print.

That these planned masterpieces would indeed have been great works I now think improbable. Excellent and amusing as "A Hind Let Loose" was, it was not the work of one who would trouble to learn the technique of novel-writing and write as freshly of men outside the world of the press. "The Morning's War" confirms that view. "Fiery Particles", though some of the stories are in their way magnificent, does not contradict it. Montague, in my opinion, was a brilliant writer rather than a creative writer. He had astonishing command of language, so that if he wrote an article or a review it was never a commonplace. His fiction was always full of the movement of life as well as the swiftness of his style. But he was not a young man; his models were of a former day; he was in love with literature. That is why I have included him in this chapter on literary men, and not in another chapter dealing with novelists of later date.

vi. Max Beerbohm

"Well! For my own part, I am a dilettante, a *petit maître*. I love best in literature delicate and elaborate ingenuities of form and style. But my preference does not keep me from paying due homage to Titanic force, and delighting, now and again, in its manifestation."

Max Beerbohm: More.

FROM this early confession it would be easy to conceive Max Beerbohm as a literary dandy; and so, in a sense, he was. He was always elegant. Born in 1872, he was just old enough to contribute to *The Yellow Book*. But he was still up at Oxford in 1893, and was incapable of ever growing old. Also, in spite of elegance, he had not the mental characteristics of a dilettante. He was sincere. He was wise. He had both wit and humour (a rare conjunction). He had style, taste, the power to sympathize while laughing, a penetrating critical gift; and in verbal interchange his attention was so quick that he took any reference (however remote) and responded to it as soon as it was made. But he would not sacrifice the topic to the *mot*. That means that he was a conversationalist, and not a talker. These traits are so rare in one person as to confer distinction. The man who is as witty as Max Beerbohm was usually wishes to shine alone; the man who is as kind often has no elegance; the man who is as critical had no enjoyment. I wonder nobody has ever thought Max Beerbohm dull.

All are familiar with his later portraits, those of the polished nobleman with heavy-lidded eyes and a moustache acute as a wren's tail, demure lips and an expression of debonair calm. The portraits do not lie; the man was superficially recognizable from them. He was as quiet and as sad as they make him appear. But no portrait quite suggests the natural sweetness of his manner, for which we must go to his printed writings. Here, for example, is a picture of himself in youth, appearing in the early pages of "Enoch Soames". Ostensibly it presents the reader to William Rothenstein; but there is more in the art of writing than the ostensible. Says Beerbohm:

"In the Summer Term of '93, a bolt from the blue flashed down on Oxford. It drove deep, it hurtlingly embedded itself in the soil. Dons and undergraduates stood around, rather pale, discussing nothing but it. Whence came it, this meteorite? From Paris? Its name? Will Rothenstein. Its aim? To do a series of twenty-four portraits in lithograph. These were to be published from the Bodley Head, London. The matter was urgent. Already the Warden of A, and the Master of B, and the Regius Professor of C, had meekly 'sat'. Dignified and doddering old men, who had never consented to sit to any one, could not withstand this dynamic little stranger. He did not sue: he invited; he did not invite: he commanded. He was twenty-one years old. He wore spectacles that flashed more than any other pair ever seen. He was a wit. He was brimful of ideas. He knew Whistler. He knew Edmond de Goncourt. He knew every one in Paris. He knew them all by heart. He was Paris in Oxford. It was whispered that, so soon as he had polished off his section of dons, he was going to include a few undergraduates. It was a proud day for me when I—I was included. I liked Rothenstein not less than I feared him; and there arose between us a friendship that has grown ever warmer, and been more and more valued by me, with every passing year.

"At the end of Term he settled in—or rather, metecritically into—London. It was to him I owed my first knowledge of that forever enchanting little world-in-itself, Chelsea, and my first acquaintance with Walter Sickert and other august elders who dwelt there. It was Rothenstein that took me to see, in Cambridge Street, Pimlico, a young man whose drawings were already famous among the few—Aubrey Beardsley, by name. With Rothenstein I paid my first visit to the Bodley Head. By him I was inducted into another haunt of intellect and daring, the domino room of the Café Royal.

"There, on that October evening—there, in that exuberant vista of gilding and crimson velvet set amidst all those opposing mirrors and upholding caryatids, with fumes of tobacco ever rising to the painted and pagan ceiling, and with the hum of presumably cynical conversation broken into so sharply now and again by the clatter of dominoes shuffled on marble tables, I drew a deep breath, and 'This indeed,' said I to myself, 'is life!'"

On a later page:

"I avoided Soames because he made me feel rather vulgar. John Lane had published, by this time, two little books of mine, and they had had a pleasant little success of esteem. I was a—slight but definite —'personality.' Frank Harris had engaged me to kick up my heels in

The Saturday Review, Alfred Harmsworth was letting me do likewise in *The Daily Mail*."

In such words does Beerbohm describe his entry to London and the glories of the æsthetic nineties; and in such words does he hint at the association with *The Saturday Review* which led to his regular weekly appearances in that paper as successor to Bernard Shaw in the criticism of plays. You would not gather from what he says that he ever contributed more than a few "middles" to *The Saturday Review*; in fact he was dramatic critic for twelve years; and it was with a feeling of consternation that readers learned of his abandonment of this appalling task just at the beginning of the Georgian era. He had always been a critic; a literary man. But in the end, I think, he regarded the English literary scene with less pleasure; for English literature had passed into a different mood from his own. The elegant had grown malicious and factious. His old loves were dead or dreary. He was in fact out of touch with the Georgian era.

If he had been less modest he could have affected this era profoundly, for there is a similarity between some aspects of our own day and some aspects of the day in which Max Beerbohm found life at the Café Royal. But he was so far a dilettante that he wrote only what it amused him to write, and solemner talents than his strut their little hour upon a stage he might have occupied. It is to his elegance that all refer, as if he were no more than a survival from a gracious period; and not to that deep laughter which is the source of his quality as a writer. How unjust this is to Beerbohm! From the early nonsensical essays (which are so wise, as well as so fastidiously written) to the incomparable parodies brought together in "A Christmas Garland," the extravagance of "Zuleika Dobson" (that delicious supplement to the novels of his adored Ouida), and the fantastic literary anecdotes to which he gave the title "Seven Men," he spent a lifetime laughing pointedly and without cruelty at the foibles of men. According to the analyses of humour prepared by the humourless, Max Beerbohm was impossible. He could never have existed. He laughed where he loved; and loved where he laughed; but he neither beamed nor sniggered. By the annotated laws of laughter, no man could behave so anomalously. The question arises whether there was ever a real Max Beerbohm or whether he invented himself as he invented Enoch Soames and extra-illustrated the books in his library, for his own secret entertainment.

vii. Katherine Mansfield and John Middleton Murry

"Oh God! Suddenly it sweeps over me again. We are writers! You are a poet and write stories. But how this knowledge makes me *ache* for us to be together."

Katherine Mansfield to J. M. M., June 3, 1918.

I SHOULD not attempt to excuse the abrupt transition from so bland a writer of belles-lettres as Max Beerbohm to a couple of such serious literati as Katherine Mansfield and Middleton Murry if it were not that, as Stevenson says,

"The world is so full of a number of things,
I'm sure we should all be as happy as kings."

I therefore draw attention to the fact that the world of 1910 onwards (the world, in truth, of King George) was quite as full of other people as it was of Max Beerbohm. One cannot explain such heterogeneousness; one can only record and marvel at the busy activity of men and women with pens in their hands.

It was towards the end of 1912 that I received one day an unexpected letter from a complete stranger. The writer said she had just reviewed a novel of mine for *The Westminster Gazette* (of which Naomi Royde-Smith was then, I think, literary editor), and that she thought the book so good that she wished to meet me. The letter was signed Katherine Mansfield. It came from an address in Chancery Lane, London; and I remember going one day to tea to a not very cheerful flat in a block of buildings there. At that time Katherine Mansfield and Middleton Murry must have been very young (both about twenty-four); and I found myself enchanted by a small, very slim, very dark girl who spoke in a carefully modulated murmur, hardly parting her lips, as if she hummed or intoned her words. She sat very still, smiling faintly, and explained in this low voice, with much sweetness, that she did not know quite what she should do in the future—with her life, she meant, for the alternatives of children, literature, and a career seemed all to be possible;—while she and Murry, who was then as gently ingratiating as he always was, otherwise spoke a good deal of French and Russian authors, particularly of Stendhal, for whom we all felt intense admiration. The beautiful idol-like quietness of Katherine Mansfield made a great impression upon me then, as it always did—she was one of the most enchanting young women I had ever met; and I could tell, from the fact that two or three other young writers then unknown to me were also present, that something like a young group was in process of formation. I found that the Murrys (they were not then married, but as they married later it will be more convenient to refer to them so when I speak of them together) were conducting a periodical called *Rhythm*—that word was less common in 1912 than it has since become, and I think the Murrys must have been early among English users of it as an æsthetic term;—and they were looking for allies who would diversify *Rhythm* with stories and essays of a non-commercial character.

Within a short time, at a well-attended dinner-party given at the "Cheshire Cheese," *Rhythm* was merged in a new and—in its conception—much grander journal called *The Blue Review*; and those who attended the dinner were told that *The Blue Review* was a serious attempt to give a lead to modern literature. It was announced that, following the example of similar French periodicals, it would have regular causeries dealing with various branches of current literature; and Gilbert Cannan was to write about the drama, Hugh Walpole about new novels, D. H. Lawrence about German literature, myself about something called "General Literature." We were all in high spirits.

The Blue Review did not last; there was a collapse in the Murrys' financial situation; and for a long time I did not hear of them. I doubt if I heard anything more until, after the War, in 1919, Murry was appointed to the editorship of *The Athenæum*. This was a very important appointment; for under his editorship *The Athenæum* (which had ceased during the War to be a paper dealing with the arts, and had become a miscellany) was restored to its place in letters, and published a truly astonishing number of articles and reviews and letters written by men and women who have since taken leading places in the literary world. Not only older men such as Santayana; but those of two younger generations, including Aldous Huxley, T. S. Eliot, Herbert Read, and the entire force of Bloomsbury; Bertrand Russell, Lytton and James Strachey, Clive Bell and Virginia Woolf. I am not sure that Murry found himself absolutely at ease in this gallimaufry; but he certainly coped with it to admiration until further financial considerations led to the discontinuance of *The Athenæum* as a separate paper.

Katherine Mansfield wrote for *The Athenæum*, until she was too ill to write any more, a weekly review of some outstanding novel (these reviews have been collected into a book); but she also began to publish her books of short sketches in the manner of Tchehov, which decidedly established her as an original writer of distinction. Murry, meanwhile, wrote a book on Dostoevsky, a novel entitled "Still Life," and had other literary activities. In January, 1923, Katherine Mansfield died. She had always been delicate, had suffered much from rheumatism, and in 1917 she caught a chill which led to tuberculosis. Many different residences and treatments were experimented with, unavailingly; and the two constant features of her pilgrimages were increasing illness. Many of her letters were subsequently published, some more volumes of tales, her journals; all with Murry's approval and under his supervision.

Having been long associated in the public mind with Katherine Mansfield and her work (as well, of course, as with his own writing), Murry then took the eye as an old friend and biographer of D. H.

Lawrence, and as the subject of attacks from more than one of those whose loyalty to Lawrence forced them into indignant malice towards everybody who can be supposed to have wronged him. Murry was lampooned in novels, he turned first Christian and then Christian Communist, and became one of the chief exponents of what is called psychological criticism, writing of Shakespeare, Keats, and Blake rather as Frank Harris wrote of Shakespeare in 1909, but with something less than Harris's fire. To myself, this kind of criticism is completely exasperating; it seems to me to be full of desperate assumptions, completely unreliable, the application of a false principle to the study of art. But it impresses all who in earlier days would have enjoyed bathing with God and Truth and the Categorical Imperative in metaphysics, mysticism, and other searches for the Absolute; and to debate it would take more time and space than I can afford. My present object is merely to show some of the stages in Murry's progress, and, as I believe, his influence upon the literary concentrations of the Georgian era. I dwell upon his work with *The Blue Review* and *The Athenæum* for historical reasons; because both these periodicals successfully assembled in common effort other writers more *creatively* important than Murry. With his curiously emotional relationship with Lawrence I have no concern; his taste in the matter of Katherine Mansfield's literary remains and the biography of Lawrence is not mine, but it is a detail in the record of the time; with his critical writings about classic authors it is not my duty to deal at length.

There is naturally no question of comparing the respective talents of Murry and Katherine Mansfield. They were husband and wife, and good friends to the last; their ideas were not recognizably similar, and with the later developments of Murry's mind it is possible that Katherine Mansfield would not have sympathized. As a writer, Katherine Mansfield was fastidious. As a person, she was incalculable. Until I read the biography written by Anthony Alpers, I was under the impression that she was simple, and trying hard to be something a little more grandiose.

This may still have been true; but it takes no account of hectic early experiences of which nobody, not even Murry, was aware until Alpers made them public. I therefore say no more at this point; but pass to her tales, which are her most important work. These contain very many delicacies of touch and suggestion, and beautiful felicities of style. She had a great eye for little things, for simplicities and tendernesses which touch and please the reader. It was not a robust talent, however; and it was overweighed by an impulsive admiration for the tales of Chekhov. He was her author. She found in him, as others have found, a really perfect artistic satisfaction. If I say Katherine Mansfield imitated Chekhov, I wish not to be misunderstood. By "imitation" I do not mean plagiarism, but a kind of aspiring, exulting study and comparison which led the writer—sometimes—in the search for similar perfection to expunge every sign of life and sinew from work in hand. Katherine Mansfield's tales, like Chekhov's, were records of mood and sensitiveness; smaller moods, less generalized sensitiveness than Chekhov's, but authentic. At times they had a trembling beauty very pleasing to taste and perception. At other times they were fragilities. Occasionally they were sentimental.

Chapter Ten

POETS BEFORE 1914

ROBERT BRIDGES, W. B. YEATS, WALTER DE LA MARE,
JOHN MASEFIELD, JAMES ELROY FLECKER,
J. C. SQUIRE AND THE GEORGIANS

i

I AM aware that any attempt on my part to discuss with an appearance of seriousness the progress of poetry in the Georgian era would be ridiculous. I have not the necessary knowledge; and the plan of this book causes me to divert into other chapters the discussion of at least two of the most important of modern poets—D. H. Lawrence and T. S. Eliot. But having given this fair warning I feel constrained to sketch something of the poetical history of the time and to dwell upon several outstanding figures whose most notable contributions to modern literature have been in the form of poetry.

At the accession of King George the Fifth the living writer who held highest place as a poet was unquestionably Hardy. "The Dynasts" had been completed only two years earlier, and it was almost unanimously considered to be the most majestic poetic creation of the age. Hardy's lyrics, too, brimming with the sense of mortality and decay, had their temporary glories, now very much assailed by modern poet-critics and as stoutly defended by poets and critics to whom, as Saintsbury said, "the single appetite for modernity is the basest of limitations." At a distance stood Rudyard Kipling, then at the ebb of poetic reputation but, by virtue of his genius, repulsing the efforts of his detractors and continuing to exist as a major figure in literature. From Ireland W. B. Yeats shed the misty splendours of fairyland and legend upon the people of this country. In England Robert Bridges, physician, grammarian, and poet, had in late middle age his profound admirers, although these were fewer than they later became. And, enjoying wide respect but a slightly suspect eminence, were Alice Meynell, William Watson, Sturge Moore, Laurence Binyon, and Gordon Bottomley. John Masefield and Walter de la Mare were recognized as exceptional talents (the former very widely, the latter by a number of people); W. H. Davies had established himself by his earliest poems and by his "Autobiography of a Super-Tramp." Otherwise, though new poets were springing up in little books which they published for themselves or in the ordinary way, without hope of gain (and it is quite a mistake to suppose that the writing of poetry was a war-time innovation), interest was concentrated upon the novel and the play. Poetry—always excepting the thrilling doggerel of "The Everlasting Mercy" and "The Widow on the Bye Street"—was not in fashion.

But poetry was being written by a number of men who were not at all interested at that time in writing plays or novels; and these men were drawn together by a common interest, as well as by the existence in Georgian England of a truly remarkable character. This remarkable character was apparently destined by Nature to be Private Secretary to innumerable Cabinet Ministers, and in his spare time to be one of the greatest encouragers of young poets that the world had seen. His name, Edward Marsh, though familiar to poets, to those who read poetry, to those attending first performances of plays in the West End of London, and indeed to the whole of London Society, was less well known out of town. He delighted Americans, as one of the few Englishmen to wear a monocle; his tall and easy form was an adornment to any row of stalls; and his sweet, fragile voice was like the cooing of doves. He translated to perfection—it is a terribly difficult task, only to be accomplished by one who had a mastery of ingenious English and could do more than piece together the words of a foreign tongue—the Fables of La Fontaine; but it is as a patron of poets, rather than as poet in right of his own performance, that he will continue to be known with gratitude, by posterity. He did more, from 1911 to 1922, to further the cause of modern poetry than any other man. He organized its reception. He was not only Private Secretary to Winston Churchill and J. H. Thomas; he was Private Secretary, nay, Accoucheur and Wet Nurse, to Euterpe in her most respectable modern rebirth.

It was Edward Marsh who, one day in 1911 or 1912, as the result of a talk with Rupert Brooke in which their enthusiasm had mounted as high as action, gathered together in his Chambers Wilfrid Wilson Gibson, John Drinkwater, Harold Monro, and Arundel del Re (the two last respectively editor and sub-editor of *The Poetry Review*); and planned with these men to publish a new kind of anthology—an anthology of poems drawn entirely from publications of 1911 and 1912. Not all poets were to be included in the anthology (some, in fact, in later volumes, were almost harshly excluded from it, so that they fled into the pages of "Wheels"); but only those who came within the scope of a clear plan. As the editor of "Georgian Poetry, 1911–1912" remarked in his prefatory note:

"It has no pretension to cover the whole field. Every reader will notice the absence of poets whose work would be a necessary ornament of any anthology not limited by a definite aim. Two years ago some of the writers represented had published nothing; and only a very few of the others were known except to the eagerest 'watchers of the skies'. Those few are here because within the chosen period their work seemed to have gained some accession of power."

We need not take the words of this preface with absolute literalness (for in the making of anthologies a great variety of considerations enters upon which it would be tactless to dwell); but at least the editor's aim was unmistakable. It was to strike a blow for young and eager poets who felt that in the solid publicity accorded to the novel and play their own art was treated as of too little account. The poets who were included in the first volume of "Georgian Poetry" are worth noting here. In alphabetical order, they were Lascelles Abercrombie, Gordon Bottomley, Rupert Brooke, Gilbert Chesterton, W. H. Davies, Walter de la Mare, John Drinkwater, James Elroy Flecker, W. W. Gibson, D. H. Lawrence, John Masefield, Harold Monro, T. Sturge Moore, Ronald Ross, Edmund Beale Sargant, James Stephens, and R. C. Trevelyan.

Such was the official birth of Georgian poetry. But it would be unjust to ignore the claims of the two most eminent poets who fell outside the range of the anthology projected by Edward Marsh and his friends; and I must therefore speak briefly of both Robert Bridges and W. B. Yeats. Having done that, I shall pause for a moment with Walter de la Mare and John Masefield, whose talents one may consider individual rather than Georgian; and then I shall return to Marsh's "Georgians," to find them augmented in numbers with the passing of years, and at the same time subtly changed. As early as the fourth volume, of 1918–19, Masefield had disappeared, and the editor was replying to criticism.

ii. Robert Bridges

"I will be what God made me, nor protest
Against the bent of genius in my time,
That science of my friends robs all the best,
While I love beauty, and was born to rhyme."
Robert Bridges.

IN his lifetime, Robert Bridges was described by a friend as being "somewhat shy, somewhat austere, fastidious, difficult." He was also a man of fortune and culture, educated at Eton and Oxford, at one time a physician, a scholar and experimentalist in technique, a grammarian and exponent of something called "Pure English," and finally a poet. I mentioned all his other qualifications because I believe them to be handicaps to the poet. I think they were handicaps to Bridges. There was in him an extraordinarily beautiful vein of pure poetry, the poetry of restrained love (which he called "dignified passion") and of natural description. But while this vein was a clear one it was not powerful; it was even rather restricted. And though one may take exquisite pleasure in reading the shorter poems of Bridges, and may be conscious that they are full packed with thought and sensitiveness, the impression left upon myself (I speak for no other) is that of a rational and well-bred man of fine culture, who never used a word without comprehending its niceties of meaning, sitting upon the head of a true poet. One's relishing delight in Bridges's poetry is less in something spontaneously created than in something beautifully and carefully wrought. This is the case in his natural descriptions as in his experiments in classical prosody:

> "Nor more of heavy hyacinth now may drink,
>   Nor spicy pink,
> Nor summer's rose, nor garnered lavender,
>   But the new lingering scents
> Of streakéd pea, and gillyflower, and stocks
> Of courtly purple and aromatic phlox,"

where one notices every word as an illustration of the poet's art, but cannot receive—as one can in Shakespeare's lovely assemblies of flowers—the sense of an impulsive communication. Bridges is a poet for students, not for those who read poetry alone for its music and its evocations; he is a poet for students, not for those who read poetry for its rapture or its metaphysical refinements.

As far as rapture is concerned, Bridges would have none of it. The word "joy" was much upon his pen; but as the name of an abstraction. It was his word, perhaps, for some temporary escape of his genius from tutelage; one feels, at least, no joy as one reads, no light-hearted and light-headed nonsensical delight in playfulness. An ethical joy, perhaps. Bridges refers to Keats's remark that he was ill at ease in the society of women because they did not answer to his preconception, and adds: "Certainly what appears to be the delineation of his conception often offends taste without raising the imagination, and it reveals a plainly impossible foundation for dignified passion, in the representation of which Keats failed." Now one sees perfectly well what Bridges means in this curious piece of prose; but I am bound to say that dignified passion seems to me, after some thought, to be a rather priggish ideal. Bridges is after what Colvin used to call Keats's "under-breeding"; and I am myself conscious of a slightly disagreeable exhalation from some of Keats's raptures. But whether such fastidiousness is not a mark of over-civilization I cannot be sure. One can be passionate, and one can be dignified; but is not dignified passion a little gentlemanly? A more humorous Bridges would not have used such a phrase; a Bridges who was all poet could not have supposed it a serious criticism of Keats.

Bridges was extremely well read in the poets, and he could imitate old models with remarkable fidelity. He was also, given much leisure, engrossed in the study of the craft of poetry. Here lies his chief influence upon the next generation of poets, who owe him a great deal (I forget whether they admit the debt). The old models did not satisfy him, and he sought for new. He wanted to experiment in prosody, and to this end he not only practised incessantly, but conned the practice of others and wrote down in book and pamphlet the results of his observations. Invaluable work, devoted and often illuminating, possible only to one who was both poet and scholar. His conclusion was that

> "when English poets will write verse governed honestly by natural speech stress, they will discover the laws (of prosody) for themselves, and will find open to them an infinite field of rhythm as yet untouched. There is nothing which may not be done in it, and it is perhaps not the least of its advantages that it makes excellence difficult."

You observe the disdain, almost the arrogance, of that last remark? It is the scholar who speaks.

As a mentor, therefore, as one who can be studied with advantage, both in his theory and his slightly differing practice, by the most modern of poets, Bridges occupied a unique position. He is both student and executant—of a difficult excellence. I am not seeking in any way to minimize his standing as an original genius; although I think the genius is less than is sometimes assumed by those always impressed by hauteur. Since Bridges was born in 1844, and published "The Testament of Beauty" when he was eighty-four years of age, it is unquestioned that he provides an invaluable link between the old and the new poetry. I only suggest that his importance is greater as a link than as an individual master. As for his own work, the imitations are admittedly so expert that in some cases they might deceive those who began by assuming their antiquity. His original work is always distinguished, and often full of fervour expressed with great dignity and beauty; when it deals with very simple things it is usually exquisite. But it is never unrestrained; it is always, in my wicked view, middle class, the product of genius overlaid by breeding, or rather by those conventions by which the exclusive separate themselves from the world. If Keats was "underbred," as they say, is there not a possibility that the contrary may be true of themselves? "Somewhat shy, somewhat austere, fastidious," said Bridges's friend. He added 'difficult,'' which means, not that Bridges was hard to understand, but that he was hard to please. Hence the character of his work. Hence the extent and peculiar effects of his influence, the whole of which we have still to realize.

iii. William Butler Yeats

> "to him, who ponders well,
> My rhymes more than their rhyming tell
> Of things discovered in the deep,
> Where only body's laid asleep."
> *W. B. Yeats: To Ireland in the Coming Times.*

By contrast with Bridges, in spite of all his more recent activities, Yeats was not so much austere as pure, and not so much difficult as lost in a dream. He was a singer. He was born twenty-one years later than Bridges in 1865, and the place of his birth was Sandymount, near Dublin. He came from two families of the Anglo-Irish, and his father was a Protestant who supported the cause of the Irish patriots. He himself was a patriot, a mystic, and a mythologist. He was also a teller of lovely tales. But above all he was a singer, and it is no surprise to us that he was writing verses when he was a boy at school. He was publishing them by the time he was twenty; and at twenty-one had his first book printed in Dublin, a dramatic poem called "Mosada" which has disappeared from his collected works and is never mentioned by anybody except biographers.

Later on, in the eighteen-nineties, Yeats was in London, the friend of Ernest Dowson, Lionel Johnson, and Arthur Symons; and then, as I have mentioned in an earlier chapter, he was associated with the founding of the Irish literary movement in Dublin. He wrote plays for the Irish theatre; he supported Synge when Synge was attacked by the Irish who resented "The Playboy of the Western World"; he took his part in political controversy; and all the time he gave his heart to the study of the folk-lore of his native land, and wrote ballads and lyrics about the past and present and future of Ireland which were meant, not to be printed and read, but to be spoken, to be sung. That last is the reason why one never quite reads Yeat's poetry in solemn silence, with a finger to the brow, watching his metrical ingenuities. Metrical ingenuities are there—Yeats, too, is a theorist, and must have his say when poetry is the topic,—but for the reader unversed in technical complexities they might as well be absent. All he knows is that the words have been written to be said or chanted, and he instinctively sings them to himself.

Some of these words appear to me not to mean very much; but the poet expressly warns us that if we ponder well they will reveal—but that was his earlier version, and the later one, which I have quoted at the head of the section, is less plain——

> "more than their rhyming tell
> Of the dim wisdoms old and deep
> That God gives unto man in sleep."

Some of them are no more than a sigh; some tell a simple tale, and others of a pious resolve; some recall the men Yeats has known——

> "We were the last romantics—chose for theme
> Traditional sanctity and loveliness;
> Whatever's written in what poets name
> The book of the people; whatever most can bless
> The mind of man or elevate a rhyme",—

and some go deeper yet into self-communion, upon the subject of emblems and souls, enemies, life, and the secrets of understanding. But though the subjects vary, the voice is ever the same, a singing voice, the voice of one who listens for faery horns and sometimes thinks that he hears them, or that if they are not the horns of faery they may almost equally well be the voice of the spirit or a message from the stars, so long as it is agreed that they come from another world than ours. To all these possibilities he would offer his mind, at once credulous and sceptical; for he was a man of logical imagination, and not of illogical dogma, and would submit his intellect to anything finer than intellect, so long as he might after investigation of its properties turn away to something else.

He changed often, from this attention—it is hardly more than that—to Magic, to Mysticism, to esoteric Buddhism, to Symbolism, to a view that the hope of Irish literature lay in the discovery of a new ballad style that should be "musical and full of colour," to a belief that there are only two ways before literature,

> "upward into ever-growing subtlety, with Verhaeren, with Mallarmé, with Maeterlinck, until at last, it may be, a new agreement among refined and studious men gives birth to a new passion, and what seems literature becomes religion; or downward, taking the soul with us until all is simplified and solidified again."

Like George Moore, he re-wrote his earlier work (sometimes not to its improvement) in a sort of impatience with it; and in defence of his rewriting he said:

> "The friends that have it I do wrong
> Whenever I remake a song,
> Should know what issue is at stake:
> It is myself that I remake."

But in one sense he changed nothing, either in his work or in himself; for all these attentions and remakings were but the turnings of a mind powerful enough and confident enough in its own power to go freely upon its own business, disregarding the flutter of other minds less cold or less curious. Such a mind as Yeats's, with its complete aversion from the material, has already had its influence, and it will be at the service of future poets when (if ever) Yeats's old dream comes true, of a time when

> "the renewal of belief, which is the great movement of our time, will more and more liberate the arts from 'their age' and from life, and leave them more and more free to lose themselves in beauty."

iv. Walter de la Mare

> The bitter past
> And the untasted future I mix up,
> Making the present a dream-figured bowl."
>
> *T. L. Beddoes: Meditation.*

W H. Davies said it was impossible to ask Walter de la Mare any questions about himself, because he was always asking questions of his own. This is true. De la Mare's mind was naturally an inquiring mind, altogether incapable of either egotism or inactivity. It went upon long journeys by itself, journeys that carried it far from land and into the borders of horror and death as well as into the sunnier paths of make-believe; and if one travels with it awhile one may pass from a smart dinner party into dankness and ghastly fear as readily as into the mind of a child. Even the mind of a child may prove to be occupied with perplexity at a funeral. The thought of disease and mortality, indeed, is one to which de la Mare's muse constantly returned, he might be playing with airy fancy, mockingly engaged with butterfly or Jenny Wren, and suddenly at the turn of a page the stairs vanished and he was running madly through some terror-haunted wood with unseen and uncanny monsters panting at his heels or corpse or coffin before his eyes. To people such as myself, who do not dream, these mysteries are disconcerting; but nothing disconcerted an author whose imagination launched itself into space and eternity as the merry spider chances all upon the waywardness of a gossamer strand.

Walter de la Mare was born at Charlton, in Kent, in 1873. When he began to write he first of all used the pseudonym of "Walter Ramal," but when there was no longer any object in disguise he threw aside this pseudonym, and has ever since been widely known and admired under his own name. It was by his "Songs of Childhood," published in 1902, that he attracted attention, and by a collection of "Poems," in 1906, that he established himself as a poet; but when he cared to do so he could enchant more than children with his tale of monkeys, "The Three Mulla-Mulgars," and frighten adults, as well, with his prose romances, "Henry Brocken" and "The Return." "The Return" is still placed high by lovers of the occult; higher yet, upon all hands, rests "Memoirs of a Midget," which was published in 1921, and which details the experiences of a lady Hop o' my Thumb among men and women who almost all give me the impression of having been raised from the dead.

> "Once died—and lived—a corse named Lazarus:
> Remember, then, to all men else than they
> Who will not blab, you have been three days dead—
> And, that far gone, even princes are forgot."

His poetry and his prose alike were the writing of a man who lived upon familiar terms with trolls and gnomes, toads and owls, as well as with fairies, ghosts, smart society women, and others of the creatures who used to be described by a former employer of mine as "bizair and outray." Such acquaintance is bound to influence a poet's inventions; and sure enough through much of de la Mare's work there passes the air of deserted houses, forgotten ghosts, and the chilling melancholy of tombs and dread. When he essayed prose fiction, as in the celebrated "Memoirs of a Midget," he filled his pages with lovely descriptions such as this:

> "And he told me, whether in time or space I know not, of a country whose people were of my stature and slenderness. This was a land, he said, walled in by enormous, ice-capped mountains couching the furnace of the rising sun, and yet set at the ocean's edge. Its sand-dunes ring like dulcimers in the heat. Its valleys of swift rivers were of a green so pale and vivid and so flower-encrusted that an English— even a Kentish—spring is but a coarse and rustic prettiness by comparison. Vine and orange and trees of outlandish names gave their fruits there; yet there also willows swept the winds, and palms spiked the blue with their fans, and the cactus flourished with the tamarisk. Geese, of dark green and snow, were on its inland waters, and a bird clocked the hours of the night, and the conformation of its stars would be strange to my eyes. And such was the lowliness and simplicity of this people's habitations that the most powerful sea-glass, turned upon and searching their secret haunts from a ship becalmed

on the ocean, would spy out nothing—nothing there, only world wilderness of snow-dazzling mountain-top and green valley, ravine, and condor, and what might just be Nature's small ingenuities— mounds and traceries. Yet within all was quiet loveliness, feet light as goldfinch's, silks fine as gossamer, voices as of a watery beading of silence. And their life being all happiness they have no name for their God."

But, having captured our imagination for this land, and for a thousand other beauties, he had no story better to tell than that of ugliness, suicide, and deformity. It is strange to me that one who trod with such charm every kind of pleasant land should be thus mocked by the charnel house and post-mortem decay. But since it was so, I must say that I would as soon have de la Mare's guidance through a graveyard as anybody's. He saw every beauty there—the long grass, the flowers, the memory of dead loveliness and sorrow;—and he had so strong a power of conjuration that spirits did indeed arise from behind the broken tombs and speak authentic tales of life beyond reach of our eyes. It may be that my objection to the themes of de la Mare is based upon a feeling that he does not quite explain the journeyings of his mind from this world to the next, and that his characters are like Strephon, in "Iolanthe," fairy only as far down as the waist, and for the same reason; but if that is so it still remains to be said that he was unsurpassed in his generation for the delicate expression of what he had to tell, whether of the contrasted songs of birds or the murder of a prince or of terror by night. His poetic imagination was strong, his lyric gift delightful.

v. John Masefield

JOHN MASEFIELD was born in Herefordshire and educated on the training ship *Conway*. He is said to have sailed before the mast and to have worked in a New York saloon. How long he spent in this kind of life I do not know; but it cannot have been a great while, for he was back in England, and working for *The Manchester Guardian*, early in the new century. When he was twenty-seven he published a book of "Salt-Water Ballads" (containing two of the poems by which he is known to every English person who ever attended performances of a choral society). In 1905 and 1907 he published books of short stories called "A Mainsail Haul" and "A Tarpaulin Muster"; in 1908 his first novel, "Captain Margaret"; and in 1909 (but it was produced a year earlier by Granville Barker) his play "The Tragedy of Nan." When, in 1911, he wrote the long ballad, "The Everlasting Mercy," he became generally famous.

Although attacked and parodied, he was the first Georgian Poet; for he did something which at that time no other young poet could do—he made the general public read what he had written.

Time has led to certain changes of taste; and Masefield was left far behind. He became Poet Laureate, which fact in itself (despite his predecessor) was enough to alienate opinion. He wrote successful novels; his book about the Gallipoli campaign was extremely popular; he was tempted to repeat the kind of ballad which first brought him attention; he wrote rather more copiously than a great poet should do; and so on. Also his convictions were large and humane. He was not a satirical pessimist, but a serious and—of old— a fluent romantic. His place in the Georgian panorama is very important indeed, historically. For, quite by himself, before Edward Marsh schemed with his fellow-enthusiasts to produce an anthology, he made new poetry a rage; and "The Everlasting Mercy" was the work that started all the excitement which had such important sequels.

It started excitement because upon its publication nobody could positively decide for all whether it was good or not. It was vehement, the language used by some of the persons depicted in it had all the air of being obscene (e.g., "you closhy put," which proved to be disappointingly mild), the revivalist fervour of the later pages was to some very moving, and in fact those who prided themselves upon their fastidiousness were compelled to read it in order the better to ridicule it. As to whether "The Everlasting Mercy" deserved the praise or the condemnation given to it, I can only say that it always seemed to me to be unworthy of either. Probably Masefield had long admired A. E. Housman's "A Shropshire Lad," which is partly written in what I suppose to be a sort of Salopian vernacular, and almost certainly he was influenced by it. Though himself, clearly, a most serious and delicate-minded man, he was familiar with the doings and sayings of a number of rough customers. His feeling and his pen were both facile; verse came easily and naturally to him; he wrote "The Everlasting Mercy," as J. M. Dent thought all books should be written, *con amore*. And it was read, declaimed, interrupted, and discussed with a sort of inflamed fever of controversy such as, in a case of poetry, I cannot in memory match.

There was room for one other experiment in the same type of writing; and "The Widow in the Bye Street" followed very quickly upon "The Everlasting Mercy." Some thought it better than its predecessor, and some thought it worse; but again all read it. When Masefield did not stop, but went on to "Dauber" and "The Daffodil Fields," he lost critical esteem, and for some years he published no more ballads. When he returned to the ballad with "Reynard the Fox" he once more caused excitement, this time almost universally pleasurable, and of his longer poems I presume this to be the favourite. In my opinion it is, although over-long, the best.

Earlier than "The Everlasting Mercy" in chronological order come the first two plays in which Masefield told simple and either horrible or pathetic tales of a kind long absent from the English stage. They were attempts to do for England what the Irish drama-tists were doing in Dublin. Although "The Campden Wonder" and "Nan" are both written in prose, it is (always allowing for the difference of tongue) poetic prose of the kind to which readers of Synge were accustomed. Here again one is aware of Masefield's facility of emotion, always provoked by the suffering of others. He felt very quickly indeed—in some respects as Galsworthy felt, and with the same delicacy—and he recorded his feeling with great earnestness. It was at first thought that his feeling was deep, and that "The Tragedy of Nan" was indeed a masterpiece; now opinion among moderate-minded critics has veered, and he is described even by those who are not bent upon discrediting the established as a sentimentalist. Well, I think "The Tragedy of Nan" has a slightly portentous title, and that the author did mistake seriousness for something else; but the emotion he felt, though rapid and super-ficial, was a genuine emotion, and his expression of it (in the plays) embarrasses us rather because Masefield lapsed into bathos through lack of warning humour than because he was less than earnestly in-tent upon his theme. If to this it is retorted that he was in some sense deceiving himself by his own emotion I have no answer to make. The plays do not affect me as tragedies; but I think they affected Masefield as tragedies. He yielded in them to the impulse of pity.

In his novels, apart from "The Street of Today," which is tedious and a part of "Multitude and Solitude," which is conventional, he worked upon a high uniform level. He began in this genre a little elaborately with "Captain Margaret," and it took him a good many years to conquer a too staccato and highly self-conscious brevity of sentence (the first "Captain Margeret" I ever had in my hand was a library copy, in which some previous reader had written upon the first page: "This reads like the attempt of a child of five to write a book"); but in the long list from "Lost Endeavour" on-ward he at all times wrote well, with beauty and feeling, and as he matured he gained in narrative ease. He could, as in "The Haw-bucks," abruptly hand the rest of his story to the reader's imagina-tion with the words, "She was the woman whom he married; but it had cost him some pain to find her." On the other hand, he did not in the novels fall into pity and solemnity, because he was en-grossed either in telling a tale or in painting a countryside or some vivid scene upon or across the sea. His power of fluent, rapid description was one of the greatest of his gifts, for that swift movement of feeling which I have mentioned carried him tumultuously into fight or fall, and only the ensuing mood endangered his integrity as an artist. He was a painter extremely sensitive to sounds, sights, and suffering; these led to a kind of inebriation of the imaginative faculty, so that he painted with a full brush. In sober mood he was a little pedestrian, and possibly a little lachrymose.

Masefield was the first Georgian poet to arouse excitement in more than a clique. Since that time, which was in 1911, he has been subjected to so much condemnation on the part of successive schools of poets that he is rather in the position of Nanki Poo in "The Mikado," when Ko-Ko explains that he is "as good as dead—practically he *is* dead." Nanki Poo, of course, is not at all dead, and in fact is upon the stage at the time. I mention this parallel, not in order to be offensive to Masefield, but because he so plainly illustrates a curious fact regarding literary reputation. A man, because his talent is exceptional, rises above his fellows. No merely advertised person can do this for more than a season. But the moment a genuine talent has established itself in any certainty of reputation, the fashion changes; a new crowd comes in (much as a new South American government comes in) and sweeps out, as far as it can do, all trace of the older fashion. Nothing is so bad as the older fashion has been.

But for some inscrutable reason fashion never quite succeeds in impressing itself upon that strange general taste which really consolidates reputation. Perhaps it is too partisan or perhaps it is too centralized—I cannot tell. I only know that certain unfashionable writers, writers who have never been celebrated by a clique or a spontaneous movement, do in course of time attain to a place in the firmament higher and more respectable than that claimed by faction for its own particular stars. And, in another and more immediately apposite degree, a writer condemned is a writer mysteriously beyond condemnation. The condemners themselves feel respect for him; they would not, indeed, in England, have attacked him if they had not respected him, or if they had not feared his predominance. They say he is dead; but they know he is very much alive, or they would not be speaking of him at all. This happened to Shaw, during the First World War; and we know what has happened to Shaw since the First World War. I do not say that Masefield, who of course, although critically decried, maintained to the end a distinguished public reputation, will equal Shaw in literary survival; but I am inclined to think his ballads have a vitality which the critics of an age more generous than ours will acknowledge with enthusiasm. Their faults of excess in such a case will be set down rightly as I believe, to the contrast between Masefield's shrinking delicacy of temperament and the roughness and squalor or brutality of scene which his experience or some motive of enforced courage leads him to depict. From the fact that he never moved freely and relishingly in that scene arose his tendency to italicize it. But the effort, however febrile it may sometimes appear to us, to portray something of the life and manners of men (and not the chewings of a bookish mind) was commendable, and had its place in the Georgian literary scene.

vi. James Elroy Flecker

"He preferred the exact word to the vague; he was always on his guard against the 'pot-shot' and the complaisant epithet which will fit in anywhere. With passionate deliberation he clarified and crystallized his thoughts and intensified his pictures."

J. C. Squire: Preface to Fletcher's Poems.

I SHALL permit myself the invidiousness of separating Flecker from the Georgians because, like others of whom I have spoken or shall speak, he had a distinctive and not a group talent. How great that talent was, I am unable to judge; I know only that to me he always seemed to be following his own will, his own theory of the place and purpose of poetry, and not a theory generally applicable to the work of his day or accepted by his fellow-poets. This he did as an original; and not for the sake of being different from others. He claimed to be a Parnassian, that is to say, a Classicist; but his vision was a romantic vision, and it was the Orient, even before he went to the East, which coloured every imagining from which the verse-making inspiration sprang.

He was born in London in 1884, the son of a schoolmaster; and he fulfilled the dream of many a London beggar by attending the Universities of both Oxford and Cambridge. He then entered the Consular service, and went as a representative of Great Britain to Constantinople, Smyrna, and Beirut. Unfortunately he contracted tuberculosis, and the last years of his life (full of ferocious work as they were) had to be spent in what proved to be fruitless journeys to different Swiss resorts in pursuit of a cure. He was at all times, from youth onwards, a joyous and indefatigable talker, was no dreamer but one who had a thousand opinions upon the proper government of the world and the education best suited to the production of wise men, and from excessive readiness as a boy to versify upon every subject he gradually developed into a poet who united great self-discipline with a well-considered exoticism.

This exoticism was instinctive, but it was greatly enriched by his stay in the East, where he saw and tasted all those marvels of colour and strangeness which had been his mental feast from boyhood. From the East came his poetic drama, "Hassan," which was produced in London after his death, with great success; from the East, too, came his most mature work, such as "The Golden Journey to Samarkand," in which the zest and freedom of his personality were in full play:

> "What shall we tell you? Tales, marvellous tales
>   Of ships and stars and isles where good men rest,
> Where nevermore the rose of sunset pales,
>   And winds and shadows fall towards the West."

It was not in his power to use his poetry as an instrument of criticism or for the portrayal of English urban life, for his aim was beauty alone; but he could and did make what he wrote both shapely and thrillingly full of himself. The brilliance of his skill with words does not always cover the limitations of his interest; the poetry is never excessive in its ambition; but what Flecker knew and felt he could tell in such a way that he sang it separately to every reader.

Such a combination of passion and coldness as he displays is very rare indeed in English poetry; less rare, perhaps, in those very Parnassians to whom he gave his praise, but rare in any language. And in the same way such a union of colour and directness is so uncommon that if there were no other gift it would distinguish Flecker's work from that of his contemporaries. They had their virtues, of greater passion than his or of greater coldness, but they had not Flecker's magic. Furthermore, the older he grew the more he became a master of his mind and his poetic instrument; so that in his case regret for the untimely loss of a talent is heightened by a sense of what he might have done if he had lived. He could either have contributed to our day an untroubled beauty which it lacks, or have lent strengthening aid to those "modns" who in reaction from sentiment and copiousness are threatened with drouth. For himself, addressing "A Poet a Thousand Years Hence," he begged modestly only to be read:

> "O Friend unseen, unborn, unknown,
>   Student of our sweet English tongue
> Read out my words at night, alone:
>   I was a poet, I was young."

vii. J. C. Squire and the Georgians

"There was a general feeling among the younger poets that modern English poetry was very good, and sadly neglected by readers."

Edward Marsh: Memoir of Rupert Brooke.

FIVE volumes altogether of "Georgian Poetry" appeared, the last of them covering the years 1920–1922, and in them one can trace (with a little help from the imagination and by sundry glances between the lines) what was the progress of poetry between 1911 and 1922 in England. First of all, the book arose from the common enthusiasm of Edward Marsh and Rupert Brooke. They took into their counsels other poets or enthusiasts. And so bold and ingenious a plan to make poetry readable and—what was more important and no doubt was fully recognized—*discussable* as a literary phenomenon had its immediate success. You can take the title in several ways, for it was a stroke of genius. "Georgian"—with King George barely, you might say, upon his throne, a whole literature was announced: What! is the age as active as all that? "Poetry"—what! have we, then, some poetry apart from Masefield and the old ones? "Georgian Poetry"—what a claim! It suggested that the poetry of the age differed from the poetry of all other ages. The claim was more modest than the title; the claim was merely to present in a single volume examples of work done by a few proper writers in the preceding two years. These writers were poets admired by Edward Marsh and his collaborators. But "Georgian"! Did not that indicate something rather more than the preferences of a group?

As long as the group could deal with the numbers of poets who had published books within recent memory the difficulty, although great, was not overwhelming. But Marsh and his friends had not imagined that the First World War was coming to stir every undergraduate who took a commission into publishing his verses. They had not foreseen that their bold title would be turned against them. They had planned a peace-time rallying point for an unfashionable art; in time of war they found themselves bombarded with every kind of poetic artillery. The alternatives were an obstinate restriction of entries to those writers for whose work the editor felt some personal sympathy, or such an enlargement of scope as would turn the two hundred pages of the first volume into an omnibus book in which everything was printed *en masse*. Quite obviously, the latter alternative was unacceptable.

But by this time the title "Georgian Poetry" had a prestige, and similarly there had arisen some poets who did not quite conform to Edward Marsh's extremely gentle but extremely firm notion

of what poetry was and what it should be. The attitude of these
poets was: "You call this book 'Georgian Poetry'; I am a Georgian;
therefore my poetry ought to be included in your book." When
told that his poetry could not be printed in our book, every such
rebel replied with heat that the title "Georgian Poetry" was a lie.
He charged Marsh with trying to establish a canon. Marsh had intended no such thing; nevertheless, since inclusion in his book gave
a writer cachet he was sensitive in the matter. Everybody was
sensitive. A consciousness of wrong pressed down upon the poets
of the hour. In his final volume, Edward Marsh cried:

> "When the fourth volume of this series was published three years
> ago, many of the critics who had up till then, as Horace Walpole
> said of God, been the dearest creatures in the world to me, took an-
> other turn. Not only did they very properly disapprove my choice of
> poems: they went on to write as if the Editor of *Georgian Poetry* were
> a kind of public functionary, like the President of the Royal Academy;
> and they asked—again, on this assumption, very properly—who was
> E. M. that he should bestow and withhold crowns and sceptres, and
> decide that this or that poet was or was not to count.
>
> "This, in the words of Pirate Smee, was *a kind of a compliment*, but
> it was also, to quote the same hero, *galling*; and I have wished for an
> opportunity of disowning the pretension which I found attributed to
> me of setting up as a pundit, or a pontiff, or of a Petronius Arbiter;
> for I have neither the sure taste, nor the exhaustive reading nor the
> ample leisure which would be necessary in any such rôle . . .
>
> "I may add one word bearing on my aim in selection. Much
> admired modern work seems to me, in its lack of inspiration and its
> disregard of form, like gravy imitating lava. Its upholders may re-
> tort that much of the work I prefer seems to them, in its lack of in-
> spiration and its comparative finish, like tapioca imitating pearls.
> Either view—possibly both—may be right. I will only say that with
> an occasional exception for some piece of rebelliousness or even
> levity which may have taken my fancy, I have tried to choose no verse
> but such as in Wordsworth's phrase:
>
> > The high and tender Muses shall accept
> > With gracious smile, deliberately pleased."

That was a very pleasant retort to the grumblers. But it did, of
course, label "Georgian Poetry" as a conservative anthology; and
it did justify the poets excluded from Paradise in regarding themselves as martyrs. In one sense it assisted in changing group convention from passive hostility to the work of other groups into the
aggressive fury of political faction. Every malcontent either started
a rival show or rallied to slay all who were sealed of the tribe of
Marsh.

Several of the chief contributors to "Georgian Poetry" have

H

been or will be dealt with in other chapters; but of the rest I must not fail to mention here Lascelles Abercrombie, Rupert Brooke, W. H. Davies, John Drinkwater, W. W. Gibson, Harold Monro, Ralph Hodgson, Francis Ledwidge, W. J. Turner, John Freeman, and J. C. Squire. Rupert Brooke had more to do, by accident, with the renaissance of poetry in war-time than any of the others. He had started, with Abercrombie, Gibson, and Drinkwater, a quarterly anthology of verse (to which only the four were contributors) named "New Numbers"; and when the First World War broke out the fourth and last issue of "New Numbers" contained sonnets written by Brooke which moved to ecstasy all who read them. Brooke was personally very popular. He was a handsome, gay boy, who was loved by all who knew him. He had been born in 1887, and had been educated at Rugby and Cambridge University. He had all the talent of a happy and charming boy, and that talent sang in his verses. It was not a powerful talent, and it is not likely to survive in the memory of later generations; but when Brooke died the shock to numbers of people who knew him was shared by thousands who had never seen him. The thought that poets were dying for their country caused many to wish to read what these and other young poets, also soldiers, had to say of the great sacrifice; and there was a tremendous consumption of new poetry, published at the time in quite innumerable little books. That it was partly a sentimental consumption I think is true; but the production and consumption were great enough to create the legend that poetry had been reborn in the War. At that time, it must be remembered, all pathetically bellicose men of letters were prophesying a grand and glorious revival of splendour in our literature as the result of the purification of war.

Of Brooke's collaborators (who were also contributors to "Georgian Poetry"), the one to make a familiar reputation with the general public was John Drinkwater, whose play "Abraham Lincoln" impressed two nations, and whose other works kept him prominently in the news for a considerable period. Drinkwater was born in 1882, and for some time was associated with the Birmingham Repertory Theatre, where he acted. He lectured a great deal and read his poetry to large audiences, and besides writing this poetry followed "Abraham Lincoln" with a number of chronicle plays upon the same lines and a number of bucolic comedies and other dramatic works. His poetry was always polished and musical, but unmarked by any force of thought or feeling; his plays were the work of one whose sense of the stage was invaluable to him, and "Abraham Lincoln" at least of the chronicle plays is a remarkable piece of construction which set a fashion and a high standard for such pieces.

Lascelles Abercrombie, born a year earlier than Drinkwater, in 1881, was by far the most distinguished of the quartette which founded "New Numbers." In 1910, with "Mary of the Bramble," he began publishing his own poems from a cottage in the country; and afterwards he gathered them into larger volumes until at last he was honoured, as only one other author has been in his lifetime, by having a collected edition included in the Oxford Series of English Poets. I do not personally find Abercrombie's poetry very interesting, although it has great dignity and beauty of phrase; and it is for this reason, and not from any hesitation as to his talent, that I refrain from commenting upon it. I have great admiration for his contributions to the study of æsthetics.

Finally, W. W. Gibson, a poet devoted to simple narrative, telling quiet stories without number, always with feeling and reticence, gave his sober naturalism to the publication. If Aberdrombie was stately and measured, Brooke like a jet of flame, and Drinkwater a contented murmur, Gibson had ever the homeliness of peat and heather. All brought these same qualities into "Georgian Poetry," and helped to give its earliest volumes their character.

W. H. Davies was there, too, with his sweet songs; and Ralph Hodgson contributed his famous poem, "The Bull"; while W. J. Turner, an Australian whose imagination had a strangeness which often afterwards startled the reading world as much as his musical criticism did (his musical criticism was of the downright order), gave variety to the third volume, in which he occupied first place. But the name which is of most significance in the present survey is that of John Collings Squire, to whom I have already referred; and it is of Squire that I shall now, in conclusion, speak.

J. C. Squire was born in Plymouth in 1884. He was educated at Blundell's School and Cambridge University, and towards the end of 1912, when *The New Statesman* was first projected as a weekly political and literary journal expounding Fabian ideas under the editorship of Clifford Sharp, Squire was its literary editor. He had at that time written a biography of William the Silent which has disappeared from the lists of his published works; and if one may accept the testimony of Arnold Bennett's Journal for 1913 it is to this effect: "Long hair, Jaegerishly dressed. But sound, competent, honest in argument." Those were early days for Squire.

He contributed to *The New Statesman* a causerie which he wrote over the pseudonym "Solomon Eagle," and thus established himself as a literary critic. His first reputation as a writer came from his excellent parodies, "Imaginary Speeches" and "Steps to Parnassus"; but in the same year that he published "Steps to Parnassus" (1913), he published also his book of serious poems, "The Three Hills," and thus challenged the world upon higher ground. Whether these books and his work for *The New Statesman* would in themselves have been enough to make his reputation I cannot say, but Squire had a drive and assertiveness which distinguished him from other men, and at one time his personal influence was so strong that by the end of the First World War he had unrivalled power in London critical journalism. During the War he acted as literary editor of *The New Statesman* (part of the time he was in charge of the paper) and literary editor of *Land and Water*, and after the War he founded *The London Mercury*, in which he continued his work as an active force in the literary world. He also was for a number of years book critic-in-chief to *The Observer*.

Poets of all kinds (excepting the revolutionaries) gathered about Squire during the War and when "Georgian Poetry" had ended its series. He generously befriended them, and gave them work and encouragement. On them, especially in their capacity as reviewers, was bestowed the name of "the Squirearchy," by which they were not at all irritated; and it was thought that they represented a rather too solid phalanx of critical opinion, so that they became unpopular with other scribes. The assumption of solidarity, however ill-founded, increased that tendency towards factionism which had been created by annoyance with "Georgian Poetry." Squire, accordingly, was a centre for attack. He was never the spearhead of a retaliatory movement.

I have already told how Middleton Murry returned to editorial work on *The Athenæum* after the War; and it will be seen that with Squire leading a devoted band of poet-critics, and Murry leading a somewhat disunited band of æsthetes, intellectuals, and novelists, there was at this time great variety of critical judgment. Some people would say that criticism was in the melting-pot. It certainly was in a state of uncertainty. On Squire's part, all criticism was moderate in tone; for Squire was in literature a conservative with a strong bias in favour of novelty. And while his love of the new laid him open to attack from die-hards, he was more generally considered as the typical contributor to "Georgian Poetry," whose influence was all in favour of traditional forms of verse. This made him unpopular with rebels, and rebels use severe methods in literary controversy. Accordingly Squire stands in most minds today as a spokesman for what may be called the Marsh dynasty; and he fittingly concludes this chapter. The First World War hastened changes in taste. It is with a changed taste that the later chapters of the present book will deal.

As to Squire's original work, it is eloquent and vigorous, but not especially unfamiliar in sentiment and diction. His most famous poem, "To a Bull-Dog," now that the occasion is long past, has the misfortune to seem tearful; but there is good work elsewhere, in

"The Lily of Malud," and in other poems such as "The Birds," where his strong feeling for Nature inspired an equally strong and very striking sincerity. That was his characteristic: he was boldly sincere (and lacking in finesse) in both writing and speaking. It was to his sincerity and to that determination of which I spoke earlier that Squire owed his war-time and post-First World War dominance of the London literary scene, especially in the department of poetry.

Chapter Eleven

THE NOVELISTS OF THE NEXT GENERATION

ROSE MACAULAY, SHEILA KAYE-SMITH, HENRY
HANDEL RICHARDSON, OLIVER ONIONS, J. D.
BERESFORD, COMPTON MACKENZIE, HUGH
WALPOLE, GILBERT CANNAN, FRANCIS BRETT
YOUNG, CONSTANCE HOLME, MARY WEBB

i

"The business of trying to present one's contemporaries in a fair light is embarrass-
ing. Writers like Hugh Walpole, J. D. Beresford, Gilbert Cannan, Francis Brett Young
Frank Swinnerton, W. L. George, myself, and several others had the same general idea
of our direction, but our approaches were so different that each was inclined to fancy
that his own road was the best road to our destination."

Compton Mackenzie: Literature in My Time.

BEFORE a deluge there are usually a few preliminary warning
drops of rain, the edge of the coming storm; and this is true in
the matter of books as well as in the matter of weather. Somewhere about the year 1870 those forces which are productive of
literary depressions gave a glance into the future. They said, in
effect that in a dozen years or so a storm of young novelists would
arise; and as such a storm without presage would be disconcerting
a few large spots of literary talent must immediately be released.
Within the next ten years, accordingly, several novelists were born
who had their own non-sentimental way of looking at life. I dare not
guess at the ages of the women; but among men Charles Marriott,
J. D. Beresford, and Oliver Onions were born before 1880. The
deluge began in 1883, and reached its height in 1884, and its climax
in 1885.

That does not mean, of course, that each previous decade had not
seen the due arrival of a sufficiency of individual talents; for at all
times, according to Dean Inge, this is a world where everyone is
wanted, but no one is wanted very much, which means that there are
always enough of each kind of people to go round. If I were merely
to name the excellent novelists who have entertained the reading
public since the beginning of the century I should arouse disquiet
in the minds of those who think the novel a useless form of letters.
Violet Hunt, for example, was writing "The Maiden's Progress" in
1894, and still impressed critical readers with her subtle and powerful
"Tales of the Uneasy" in 1911; the Countess von Arnim published
"Elizabeth and Her German Garden" in 1898, and, as the Countess

Russell, wrote her best book, "Vera," in 1921; Ethel Colburn Mayne contributed to *The Yellow Book*, wrote her biography of Byron in 1912, and in fiction surpassed her best quite late in life with "Gold Lace." All these were writers bringing exceptional qualities of insight and courage to the modern novel. One who similarly deserves more than a mere mention is Maurice Baring, whose tales and explorations of character range from the incredibly long to the minimum of brevity. He brought to all a fine intelligence, style, humour, and distinction. In the same way, Charles Marriott, who left off writing novels because the post-War period created for him a new and unfamiliar world, produced between 1901 and 1915 a series of critical tales in which moral and intellectual tendencies of the day were presented and examined scrupulously and in an original manner. Of Beresford and Onions I shall speak at greater length hereafter, because while older than the others they shared (Beresford especially) the interest aroused by the younger novelists of the post-Victorian age. But to the rest I make my apologies for seeming cavalier; a book of this kind has inevitable limits and omissions, and do what I may I am bound to show inexcusable ignorances.

All the immediately pre-Georgian writers whom I have named, and others whom I cannot even mention, differed from their major rivals in the respect that, whereas these majors sought to build or rebuild a complete material universe, they were psychological novelists, penetrating inward towards subtleties of mind and character, and holding the world, as Antonio did,

> "but as the world;
> A stage where every man must play a part."

None of them, I believe, had any acquaintance with the German and Austrian pathologists who afterwards effected such a change in the ideas of exploratory novelists. Violet Hunt and Ethel Colburn Mayne almost certainly learnt a great deal from the Jacobean method and were more or less content to feminize it; Charles Marriott, cautious, thoughtful, and curiously sympathetic to the misfits of polite intercourse, was chiefly interested in the individual as he affected society and was affected by society, and brought his own training in medicine, psychology, and art to bear upon "the revolt of youth" and similar themes modern in the nineteen hundreds; Maurice Baring, highly familiar with Russian literature and Russian discursive concern with the psyche, amused himself with people from his own witty and teasing standpoint, and all his life remained an unplaced and mockingly unplaceable personality of unlimited fertility, versatility, and distinction. All were men and women of talent and intelligence; for some reason they did not shock critical and popular minds into a state of chronic attention.

And as I have mentioned the Russians, let me here emphasize the fact that in the early years of King George's reign Russian art and Russian literature were the rage with all those sensitive people who may be expected to produce the more cultured varieties of fiction, painting, music and formative criticism. Arnold Bennett, at the height of his influence with such people, committed himself to the statement that all the great novelists of the world were Russian; one heard for the first time—or at any rate for the first time with appreciation—of Goncharov, Schedrine, Leskov, even of Chekhov (but members of the Stage Society in 1911 walked out in large numbers at the first performance of "The Cherry Orchard"), and others; the novels of Dostoevsky, of which, previously, only "Crime and Punishment" and "Poor Folk" had been familiarly known in England, were translated complete from 1912 onwards.

They were not the only Russian novels to be brought to the notice of the literate, for every London publisher by this time was aware of the demand for such necessaries of life; and by 1916 a complete translation of Chekhov's tales was begun. Nor were novels the sole influences upon our younger pens, for Anna Pavlova, of the Russian ballet, reached England in 1910, at once created a furore, and was the forerunner of the Diaghilev ballet with Nijinsky as the sensation of the period. What the coming of the ballet did by infection for letters in England I cannot explicitly say. It created an entirely new state of mind. Its rich décor, so bold and at times so bizarre; the triumph of its strangeness and its beauty (upon artists its beauty, upon æsthetes its strangeness—for I take æsthetes to be the apes of art); the unfamiliar rhythms of its musical contributions; all had, for non-cosmopolitan stay-at-homes, the glory of a new world. To an English public weary of English things and already longing for whatever was savage and untamed, the wildnesses of "Scheherazade" and "Tamar" were like firewater to the innocent native; to a less jaded English public which prided itself upon its refinement, the sentimental delicacies of "Carnaval" were as exquisite as Turkish delight. Lovers of the romantic had "Le Pavillon d'Armide"; and lovers of the modern, "L'Oiseau de Feu." Diaghilev, with his contempt for Gounod and Delibes as composers of ballet, appealed infallibly to all classes of rich, patronizing, and intelligent English people. No wonder the snobs at this time, adopting a Russian word, began to call themselves the "intelligentsia."

As for Dostoevsky's novels, they had power and subtlety, emotion and picturesqueness, altogether outside the range of any English novelist whatsoever. They were overwhelmingly long and communicative; the characters in them, diseased, mad, and vehement, were like nothing ever seriously created in English. They were like the nightmares of an epileptic to whom Dickensian, grotesques were as serious as an empty stomach. Amid cries of dismay from the apostles of the fine, the delicate, the sought, and the confined, Dostoevsky became the rage. He seemed then (he now seems less) to pour all the terrors of emotion into print and all the truth; he drew away veils from souls in conflict and agony and showed them as struggling with the very devil; his readers had all a sense that when they read about the Karamazovs and the Versilovs they indulged in spiritual debauch; if these readers were humanitarians with a leaning towards mystical Christianity they embraced Prince Myshkin with passionate yearning for just such humility as his; we heard upon all sides, from our own voices as well as from the voices of others, roars of ecstatic discovery. How pale Turgenev seemed! How material and common in grain our own realistic writers! How drab our life of restrained feelings! From Russia came release. Possibly a little incoherence? Come, come, come! "Life is real, and life is earnest!" To the serious, every Continental master is or should be sacred.

However, the enthusiasm for Dostoevsky and the ballet succeeded at least two other influences. I say nothing of Bergson, who was intellectually a power at this time, or of Eucken; my business is with the younger novelists. There was the influence of Samuel Butler, the publication of whose "Notebooks" in 1912 intensified growing interest in his one novel, "The Way of All Flesh"; and there was, in my view unquestionably, the practical influence upon such novelists as Wells and Bennett. And while Wells and Bennett were totally different writers, there was, as James discovered, this likeness between the two, that both were profoundly interested in the physical life about them—the active social and sociological life of their time. This interest James did not share, and he thought it inartistic. Wells was interested as a participant; Bennett as an observer. Both used, in their different ways, the autobiographical method which James so decried. Wells in "Tono-Bungay" spread the whole of his zest for the movement of life before the reader; Bennett slowly narrated in "Clayhanger" the growth and progress of one man through the environment which had been his own. Young novelists, coming to books (for of course they read them) which appealed so strongly to their natural self-interest, saw that autobiography, disguised or undisguised, held decided possibilities. They did not, as a rule, want a copy. They wanted only a convenient looseness of form; and as they too were as interested as could be in life, and wished to speak the truth about it as they saw it, the invitation offered by the method was irresistible. Dostoevsky was the king of all novelists; but Wells and Bennett were more English and less vehemently abject in disclosure, and therefore were simpler models.

The statements I have made above are general; not particular.
There were exceptions, and only Beresford, among the writers of the
younger generation, ever, as far as I am aware, deliberately studied
the Wellsian or the Bennettian novel in order to assimilate its scheme
and style. But these things were in the air. They were a part of the
spirit of the time. Other influences, the influence of Hardy, the
temporary influence of Romain Rolland (also, by the way, lengthily
autobiographical), the influence upon those who knew them of
German thought and German pathological research, were all
effective. Everything was heading, perhaps, for change; but to the
casual eye it seemed only to be moving in a steady channel towards
—I must take this opportunity of saying—an extension of the
realistic method to the middle class. It is to be noted that whereas,
of all the novelists and playwrights of the older generation, Galsworthy was the only one to have had a public school and Oxford or
Cambridge University education, several of the newer novelists
belonged to families in which intensive culture was familiar; and
for this reason, when they came to write of familiar life, they no
longer dealt with poor boys and girls as Wells and Bennett, Moore
and Gissing, Pett Ridge and Arthur Morrison, had done. The novel
had taken a step upward in the social grade; it was still to be realistic,
but it had become what my gardener calls "more classical."

ii. Rose Macaulay

I MUST except Rose Macaulay at once from any general statement
as to the influence of the Wellsian or Bennettian novel. I must,
in fact, except all the young women writers of that day; for their
interest in the doings of cits and groundlings was small and unfriendly. Either they wrote of the cultured and financially independent, or they embraced the rural, the raggle-taggle gipsy, the
home farm, the Fells, and the old family. How conservative of
them!

Possibly the fact that Rose Macaulay was the daughter of a professor (her father was G. C. Macaulay, a good scholar, and Lecturer
in English Literature at Cambridge University) accounted for
her detached attitude towards the human species; but whatever the
cause she always, apparently, terrified others by a sort of immunity
from weakness and great causticity of comment. I take these items
on trust from printed or spoken report: personally, I never noticed
the causticity or indeed any occasion for terror. To me, Rose
Macaulay always seemed one of the kindest and least affected of all
English literary women. She did, it is true, bring her mind to bear

upon the conversation, and she was a little brisk (as well as indistinct of speech, in the manner of some Cantabs of her generation); but that is all. She never displayed the greatest sin of English women writers—the desire to impress.

As I see it, the trouble about Rose Macaulay was that she always felt herself to be fully adult in a world of children. Not her own children, and not altogether nasty little brats, but children in whom, for their own good, she took an aunty interest and to whom she found it necessary, in print, to administer slightly repressive words of reason. She had a strong moral sense, much scepticism, a great dislike of those who are cruel, thoughtless, stupid, and selfish, and a feeling between pity and contempt for those who are innocently silly. And she did not restrain her wish to demonstrate the undesirability in a civilized community of the stupid and the silly. At the beginning of her life she thought she could lecture these faults of mankind out of existence. Later she hoped to ridicule them to death. Later still, in her best novels, "And No Man's Wit"; "The Towers of Trebizond," and "They Were Defeated," she showed that the power of ridicule was not the greatest gift she had. But she always felt mature and wise; and in her very first novel, "Abbots Verney" (1906), there was the strongest possible air of grown-upness and knowing better than others.

Rose Macaulay continued to publish novels—one of them, "The Lee Shore," winning a £1,000 prize competition—upon themes suggested by the trend of current thought; and for several years her books were intelligent, serious, critical, and illuminative of the minds of middle-class people of culture. But the War changed many things for this writer, and life, from being a *pis aller*, became something of a futility. Had she preserved the solemnity of her first youthful tales, she no doubt would have become a sort of Mrs. Humphry Ward (cultured, current, and for those of goodwill and breeding highly instructive); but she had a faculty denied to Mrs. Humphry Ward. It was the faculty of derision; and derision became tremendously the fashion among intelligent people immediately after the War. It was a way of shrugging one's shoulders and washing one's hands of the politicians and admitting wryly that life was "a poor business," while at the same time indicating that one knew of much better ways of managing mankind than any that had been tried. Accordingly, after the War (and she tried hard to suppress her pre-War novels), Rose Macaulay definitely gave herself to the composition of topical comedies. These faintly extravagant and ridiculing novels follow a formula. They collect a number of cranks and sillies and puzzled people, twist and turn them for our laughter, burlesque common vulgarities by quotation (as Henry Mencken burlesques them in "Americana") or by merciless ridicule, and are

uniformly crushing towards sentimentalists. One pictures these unfortunate characters—who of course are primed with every contemporary cliché—as dashing, full of enthusiasm, like dirty little
boys, into the clean, well-aired, slightly underheated house of a
female connection. They are too excited with their fancies to wipe
their shoes or their noses; and they run up to Rose Macaulay (in the
silly way of thoughtless children) to pour our their fatal nonsense.
"And the bull . . . the aeroplane. . . . Positivism . . . advertisement
. . . amazing. . . . Youth . . ."—these are their excitements, the things
they have just found. Rose Macaulay listens with a quiet smile, a
little remote. Finally she says, crisply: "Yes, very interesting. Now,
don't you think you'd better wash your hands and come to luncheon?"
Or "Yes, I know; but that was said quite a hundred years ago by
William Godwin." Or "You shouldn't say 'mephitic,' darling; you
mean 'dense,' don't you? Like yourself." I wonder she was not at
times haunted by the poor wretches whom she so unsparingly
made amusing in her books. Perhaps that fate did overtake her. She
had sympathy for none but the critically alert, those who stand aside
from the follies of man and laugh (not jeer) lest they should weep
with exasperation and shame. As her first heroine said—I can hear
Rose Macaulay using the words herself: "It always rather riles me
. . . to see people behaving in what strikes me—well, as a foolish
manner of behaving, you know." She was not really angry, not hot
with the passion of a zealot; only impatient with the noisy and self-
deceiving and easily fooled. She could not endure their idocy. But
for the bystanders who virtuously never make fools of themselves
she had a fellow-feeling, because (she said it of Rome, the heroine of
"Told by an Idiot");

> "Without opposition and without heat, she had refused to be
> made an active participant in the business, but had watched it from
> her seat in the stalls as a curious and entertaining show."

Curious and entertaining. You might have thought she would be
a realist? Not at all; for the duffers and cranks and cowards, taken
as a matter of course by realists, and as a matter for reverent treatment by defenders of all emasculates from the pressure of machinery
and convention, moved her but to laughter.

The laughter was without malice. It was the laughter of one quick
to notice absurdity and drily to record it. It was the laughter of one
impatient of vanity and muddle; one who, while up-to-date with
news of all intellectual and social movements, and busily aware of all
the latest freaks and follies, was incurably conservative; one who,
with much kindness and goodness and indeed much sweetness in her
temperament, had little pure imagination.

iii. Sheila Kaye-Smith

CLOSELY following upon Rose Macaulay in this new movement of novelists came Sheila Kaye-Smith, whose first novel, "The Tramping Methodist," was published in 1908. She was born at St. Leonards, a Sussex seaside resort, and her father was a doctor. She had an entirely different opinion of mankind from Rose Macaulay. She was more humane, or more pitiful, than her sister-novelist. She was not amused by follies, or exasperated by them, but seriously traced their rise and influence. On the whole, her vision of life was tragic. Let her but see a dull woman looking over a hedge, and where Rose Macaulay pictured a sentimental gossip who might amusingly take her newspaper-fed mind on to a desert island in company with a dozen other absurd creatures, Sheila Kaye-Smith at once quietly pictured that woman in her home, a little dumb, and possibly doomed (as she would be in a novel by Hardy or Eden Phillpotts) to frustrated passion or contented matrimony with a poacher. She was not sceptical, but devout, a Catholic. She cared less for the town than for the countryside, which she knew by heart. If set down in a village, she would at once weave a story about it which brought in several generations of squires, the doctor, perhaps a gipsy, some animals, the ploughing of the land, both love and silent pain, lush grass, starry nights, a convincing picture of rural England. But I do not think anybody in the story ever made a joke, or was the subject of a joke.

Taking the county of Sussex for her own ground (and in spite of Kipling, Belloc, and E. V. Lucas, Sussex had no official novelist), Sheila Kaye-Smith made Sussex, which to many of us is a holiday home and the name of an adored cricket team, as much a place of simple passion and pride as Devon or Dorset. She was influenced in theme and conception by the novels of Thomas Hardy and by Galsworthy's chronicle of the Forsyte family; but when she began writing novels a love of writing, and no literary influence, was the spur. The early books were slight, a young girl's dreams of romance in dingles and upon the Downs; but the later ones, as the author's touch grew more sure, show an increase in confidence and power, as well as in bulk and solidity. "Little England" and "Joanna Godden," the more ambitious "Tamarisk Town" and "The End of the House of Alard," and their companions, brought Sheila Kaye-Smith to a high place among her male and female professional contemporaries; and in one respect she was, I believe, superior to all the other equally industrious traditional novelists of about her own age.

That respect is an important one in the craft of fiction, although it is often under-valued by amateurs. Sheila Kaye-Smith's novels, which at first took a rather conventionally unconventional view of love, grew steadily in that substance which comes of care in building. They told sober and progressive stories, into which one was slowly inducted and in which one never—the point is two-edged, and yet I must make it—wholly lost oneself. And above all they were models of construction, with the quiet beginning, the natural development of interest, the clean drawing of character, the attainment of a serious warmth of emotion, and sometimes—for she had courage—the climax of death or disaster. Conscience was in them, and comment was absent from them. They were dramatic narratives, which stood of their own accord as excellent, honourable work.

iv. Henry Handel Richardson

In that same year of 1908 which saw the publication of Sheila Kaye-Smith's "The Tramping Methodist," another first novel appeared of which the history has been one of the strange records of our time. The book was called "Maurice Guest," and the author was described as Henry Handel Richardson. Nobody knew anything of Henry Handel Richardson, and "Maurice Guest," being published, was praised in the newspapers, sold out its first edition, was reprinted seven months later, and thereafter seemed to be at the end of its active life. Never was such an assumption more false. The book remained out of print; but its life continued very extraordinarily, for writers of all kinds passed the word to each other that this was something of a masterpiece, and "Maurice Guest" was a legend in the professional world. The author published another novel, "The Getting of Wisdom," in 1910, and this novel failed to repeat the mysterious success of "Maurice Guest," so that just as the public ignored Henry Handel Richardson the writers knew him only as the unidentified author of a single book. Between 1910 and 1914 it was a favourite sport of literary journalists to write articles naming outstanding young novelists, and to paw the young reputations by asking whether this one was better than that, or whether this one had increased his reputation by his latest book or slipped back a point in the busy race for distinction and the like. But Henry Handel Richardson was never, as far as I recall, included in the field. D. H. Lawrence, Compton Mackenzie, Hugh Walpole, Gilbert Cannan, W. L. George, J. D. Beresford, Sheila Kaye-Smith;—but no mention of the author of "Maurice Guest." And yet, just as Falkner's "The Nebuly Coat" and "The Lost Stradivarius" had their cult, so "Maurice Guest" quietly passed from hand to hand, and its name from tongue to tongue.

Seven years elapsed before Henry Handel Richardson began to publish a three-volume history of the life of an Australian doctor named Richard Mahony; and at length a new edition of "Maurice Guest" made its appearance with what must have been one of the earliest prefaces written by Hugh Walpole. It was politely greeted (in 1922), and thereafter its admirers had less difficulty in obtaining copies for their friends; but even yet its great qualities were insufficiently recognized. "Maurice Guest" is a very good novel indeed. It combines apparent literalness with subtlety, and passion with wisdom, in an altogether exceptional manner. For those interested in the technique of the novel, it shows as few other books do the possibility of combining narrative with Henry James's "blessed law of successive aspects," and the unromantic treatment of a romantic theme which yet leaves no tenderness and no conflict of mood and personality unrevealed. It is a book full of subtlety, as rich as living memory, as detached as a philosopher's mind. Although it moves slowly, it is never tedious; although, towards the end, the scenes turn upon a single note, it is never repetitive. Every scene takes us deeper and deeper into heart and nature. It might, we feel, be transcript; but no transcript could so surely keep to the essential.

The story, if I state it baldly, will seem obvious enough. It is that of a young Englishman who, against the wish of his mother, abandons schoolmastering in England for a period of pianoforte study in Leipzig. There, besides meeting other men, he makes the acquaintance of a kind and very shrewd young Englishwoman; and he falls in love with an Australian girl who is already the mistress of a young composer and amorist. The stages by which Maurice moves, first to acquaintance, then to friendship, and finally to tragic, torturing emotional relationship with this girl are described in detail, for they form the substance of the narrative, and they culminate in his suicide. But the book is no simple study of frustrate love; it has a profundity and searching analysis which deeply excites the reader who cares at all to understand ways of thought and feeling.

"The Fortunes of Richard Mahony," a trilogy which occupies over a thousand pages and covers two-thirds of a man's life in Australia, back in England, and again in Australia, has many of the same qualities which make "Maurice Guest" so remarkable. It has not the poignancy of the shorter book, for the reason that its action is diffused; and most of the book is less immediate, less urgent in mood than the concentrated interest of "Maurice Guest" compels. But this very fact allows one to see the outstanding virtue of Henry Handel Richardson as a novelist—steadiness of vision and sobriety of judgment allied to very exceptional imaginative power.

The method is so quiet that its merit, and in fact the essential imagi-
nativeness of the work, may be missed by those eager for display; a
little formal as to style, it has not the pace and brilliance of the best
very modern exhibitions of life. But the touch is unerring.

Critics of "Maurice Guest" all assumed that the book was the
work of a man. Whether men or women are the actors they are portrayed with equal assurance; and some of the scenes between the
male characters are among the most memorable. But Henry Handel
Richardson was a woman, the daughter of an Australian doctor,
and the wife of Professor J. G. Robertson, who for many years was
Professor of German Language and Literature at London University. During her life of authorship she was hardly at all known to the
world as a novelist; and this without doubt long retarded that
general acclaim which came to her in time to cause legitimate
delight.

v. Oliver Onions and J. D. Beresford

"But today writers and painters no longer speak from Sinai-clouds. Rather, from
the pavement-edge, packed closer than the vendors of penny-toys."

Oliver Onions: Little Devil Doubt.

I TURN now to two men who belong more directly than any of the
women I have named to the school which was modern in 1910.
The major works of both are in the key of Wells and Bennett.
"Little Devil Doubt," by Onions, and the Jacob Stahl trilogy of
Beresford are alike in the sense that both skim the lives of young
men who, with artistic impulses, have their misadventures in
business, and especially in the business of advertising. Drawing was
Onions's first love; and architecture Beresford's. Both knew from
experience what the insides of business offices are like. Both were
rueful as to what happens in business offices; and as to what happens
to young men whose ambition surpasses performance. There is in the
work of both this air of ruefulness; but with Onions it has an
accompaniment of joyless jocularity and with Beresford that of a
melancholy smile. Onions is harsh, Beresford sad.

It is somewhat the same with the two men as with their work;
for Onions has a grimness of demeanour which throws out a suggestion of force and resentment, whereas Beresford, who was
early crippled as the result of an unfortunate accident, regarded
the world with thoughtful sweetness but without vivacity. Both
were realists, in the sense that if they contemplated any scene or
circumstance they did it without sentimentality: their reactions to it,
though not identical, were in accord. Having seen the world of
pushing and unscrupulous men, they did not hide it from themselves

by any curtain of false emotion. There it is, they said: what are you going to do about it? Neither would fake an attitude. The strength of both lay rather in associative memory than in imagination.

Onions, a Yorkshireman, was once for a period in control of an Art Department in the Amalgamated Press (publishers of many magazines and weekly periodicals founded by Alfred Harmsworth, Lord Northcliffe), and his first book was published at the beginning of the century. It was a collection of chats in the manner of "The Dolly Dialogues," but it did not achieve the lightness of the original. He then wrote a number of short stories, many of them powerful and some of them dealing with uncanny themes, which he has collected into volume form as "Tales of a Far Riding," "Widdershins," and "Draw in Your Stool." But until the nineteen-forties, when he had a new flowering, and achieved a new reputation, with some remarkable historical tales, his chief books were the two semi-autobiographical studies of ambitious young men, "Little Devil Doubt" and "Good Boy Seldom," and the brief masterpiece of grimness, "In Accordance with the Evidence." This last, which he injudiciously followed with sequels called "The Debit Account" and "The Story of Louie," remains in its own genre unsurpassed.

It was begun as a short story; and it grew by the demands of its material to the length of a brief novel. It arose from the notion that a young student of shorthand, bent upon murdering a rival, might obtain from that rival, under pretence of speed-exercise and subsequent transcription, a confession of suicide. He would thus clear his own path, and escape detection. The ruse succeeds; the tale, being told in the first person singular, is an exercise in that harsh vigour for which Onions's character yields all the stuff. "In Accordance with the Evidence" is not a pretty book; the manner of it is even common and gritty, as such a theme demands that it should be; but it is like no other book, and it bears rereading after its dénouement has lost all surprise. It has, that is to say, a permanent quality.

The remaining realistic works of Onions lack momentum; one reads them with respect for their veracity, but one is conscious that the author is not a natural creator of illusion. He has no magic. And in the case of "Little Devil Doubt" and "Good Boy Seldom," both of which are very sincere books based upon experience, the biographical method has a serious defect. It has always, in the work of every writer who has essayed it, had this defect. A novelist using, with however much skill and finesse, the skeleton of his own life and memory, tends to leave his central figure of colourless nonentity, a something to which experiences occur. For himself, that central figure is filled in by substantial memory—by egotism; but for the reader the central figure, a name only, represents vacuum. He has traits, but no character. He may suffer; but he is not objectively present. That is a cause of loss of interest in the progress of the book; for unless every detail has importance of its own (which it has for the writer) the book ceases to hold attention. It is the same whether the book is a narrative or an introspective study of personality; for unless the author deliberately creates for his chief actor a personality larger than life, there is nothing upon which the reader can fix his eye or his imagination. "Little Devil Doubt" and "Good Boy Seldom" are iridescent to the author, because they are charged with the colours of living memory: to the reader, who unfortunately, however eager, has no comparable self-identification, they are dead because recognition of truth is an insufficient challenge to sympathy.

This criticism, in effect, could be levelled with almost as much force at the Jacob Stahl trilogy of Beresford, which has the advantage, however, that Beresford does make recognizable persons of those with whom Stahl is brought into contact. Whether these are men or women, they are seen—shall we say?—with greater malice than any of Onions's characters; with clearer incisiveness. Moreover, there is an attempt to create the personality of Jacob Stahl: the other people in the tales do react to such a man, and criticize him as if he were there. We come to believe that however lacking he may be in the positives of human nature, at least he is rich in negatives. But if you take away from "The Early History of Jacob Stahl," "A Candidate for Truth," and "The Invisible Event" the plain veracity with which they tell what happened to Jacob Stahl, I wonder how much is left for the imagination to dwell upon?

As if in response to that criticism, for he gave a truthful answer to any question one put to him, Beresford only once after the publication of "The Invisible Event" returned to the personal memoir. He probably saw its weakness as clearly as anybody could do. He experimented with other technical methods, and went so far as to tell a couple of mystery stories; but while his most vigorous novel is probably "The House in Demetrius Road" (also his greatest success, ruined by the outbreak of the First World War), his most characteristic books were those in which he sought to express in the form of fiction some of the philosophical conceptions of the modern world. He was always a reader of philosophy, was always interested in current ideas. His books tended more and more to present these ideas, and his reflections upon intellectual tendencies, in the form of stories. What Rose Macaulay did with mirth and ridicule, Beresford did meditatively and with greater respect for the thoughts of others. Where Rose Macaulay dismissed what her rather old-fashioned mind did not much relish, Beresford absorbed it all without for a moment changing his expression of resigned calm.

"What is happening in the world?" he asked; and by the world he meant the universal mind. And instead of answering, as Rose Macaulay might briskly do, "A lot of nonsense," he inclined his ear gravely, patiently for an answer.

He wanted to know whatever men thought. His thirst for such knowledge was unquenchable. That early book of his, "The Hamp-denshire Wonder," which some suppose to be the tale of a monster, is in reality a dream fantasy, the tale of a child who fulfilled Beres-ford's own ambition, to be as full of knowledge as the "Encyclo-pædia Britannica." Health and temperament and circumstance were against him in the personal quest for omniscience. A delicate boyhood, with its lasting effect upon his constitution, greatly de-layed his maturity. Failure in muscular energy accounted for the absence of all boisterousness from his work. Because of such delicacy, Beresford's early reading was desultory, and it was only after other ways of life had been tried that he became at last a writer and systematic reader. First he planned to be an architect; but, tiring of architecture, he wrote advertising copy. Novel-writing was, if not an after-thought, a slowly-developed aim, and it was not until he was nearly forty that he joined the ranks of those who were known in the 1910's as "the younger generation of novelists."

Even then, in 1911, when he was influenced by the vogue for which "The Way of All Flesh," "Tono-Bungay," and "Clay-hanger" had been original models, he was far from being one of the joyous amateurs. On the contrary, he had less profusion than mastery. His hand was firm; he was not adventurous; it was his own story that he candidly related. And the story? The man? Not without significance are the facts that he was at one time an expert chess-player and that his chief hobby was joinery. Architecture; chess; joinery; all of them crafts of form and adjustment and rule. Beres-ford wrote many books; and not one of those books was casual or untidy or tumultuous. All were written with precision and scrupu-lousness; all are reflective and without colour. If one cannot read them with excitement, one does at least read them with respect and deep admiration of the skill, the practised and finished craft of their opening, development, and resolution.

vi. Compton Mackenzie, Hugh Walpole, Gilbert Cannan

WHETHER he was stirred by the coming of a new King, or not, I cannot say: I have never asked him. But a young man decided in 1910 to change his employment. He thought that instead of reading books for another publisher he would start a publishing business of his own. For the purpose, he would use the very large sum of one thousand pounds which happened to be in his possession at the time. Within a few months he had acquired offices in the Adelphi, had arranged to publish one or two books by writers known to him, and had cast his eye expertly among the young authors of the day for those whom it would interest him to publish. He was resolved to confine his list to those whose work he personally admired. And first of all he wrote to a novelist whose book he had formerly recommended to his employer, only to be overruled by a higher power. He mentioned his earlier recommendation. The author responded that the admired book had since been declined by several other publishers, and that he would be delighted to accept the offer now made to him. His name was Compton Mackenzie; the book was "The Passionate Elopement"; and the publisher was Martin Secker.

Another young writer of novels happened also to be ready to consider a new publisher; and he too brought his work to the Adelphi, with the result that Gilbert Cannan's "Round the Corner" was added to Secker's list. And as Hugh Walpole at the same time published (with the same publisher) his fourth novel, "Fortitude," and Mackenzie followed "The Passionate Elopement" with "Carnival," the new firm made so definite an impression upon general attention that most people supposed a new school of novelists to have been founded. Mackenzie, Cannan, Walpole; they were not in the least like the three musketeers; but they stood together in the bold advertisements as if they were inseparable.

In Henry James's famous article on the novelists of his day, to the seniors Wells, Bennett, and Conrad, were added four juniors. They were Mackenzie, Cannan, Walpole, and ("toiling in the dusty rear") D. H. Lawrence. James did not mention Beresford, W. L. George, Sheila Kaye-Smith, E. M. Forster, or Oliver Onions. He highly praised Mackenzie, whom he had known as a child, was a little shy of Cannan, and while hedging on the books spoke of Walpole personally with warm affection and hope. Lawrence, of course, he could not stomach: it is clear that Lawrence must have affected James as anything wild, screeching, and unprofitable would have done. That is not the point at the moment (Lawrence will be spoken of in a later chapter): what I wish to establish is that once again these three novelists were linked together and, simultaneously, singled out as typical of their generation. Henry James had then great power to influence the minds of the fashionable minority.

Mackenzie was off to the best start. His first book had been very highly praised, and his second book, "Carnival," which had the title of a favourite sentimental ballet, took readers behind the scenes of the theatre, into young men's love affairs, and into the

West Country, which for some time previously had been a recognized venue for passion and tragedy. It had other qualities, which are those of the author; but these were the features which assured popular success. "Carnival" ran away with the English public; just as "Fortitude" did with the American public. Of the three, Cannan was the least generally read, but his work, too, was considered to have special distinction; and all the world knew that successors to Wells, Bennett, and Galsworthy had been found. It became a favourite pastime for critics to compile lists of young novelists destined to greatness. Gradually it was established that Mackenzie, Cannan, Walpole, Forster, Lawrence, and Beresford were the coming boys. Brett Young was heard of later (his first single-handed novel was not published until 1914); and W. L. George, although he wrote at least one interesting book, "The Making of an Englishman," did not quite fit into the galley. Of the Big Six four had been to either Oxford or Cambridge, and Beresford was a public school boy. Only Lawrence continued the tradition of Shaw, Wells, and Bennett in coming to literature by the direct route.

Now Mackenzie was related to half the theatrical families in England. The theatre was thus in his blood, a fact which should not be forgotten in any consideration of his work. His father was Edward Compton, a very celebrated player in old comedy and in costume drama; his mother was Virginia Bateman, member of an equally distinguished family of actors and actresses. It is no wonder that his first literary work should have been a play, and when he attempted the novel he made it a romantic tale of Bath in the days of its glory, when manners were manners and petticoats petticoats. He was born in West Hartlepool at the beginning of 1883, went to St. Paul's School, in London, and subsequently to Oxford. It was his ambition to be a poet, an ambition encouraged (it must be observed) by the atmosphere of Oxford, which developed in its undergraduates a taste for verse; and when he left the University Mackenzie retired to the West of England to cultivate a garden and the Muse.

Following the success of "The Passionate Elopement," he returned to London, and there, amid all the excitements of the Russian ballet, some work for the theatre, and much talk, for which he had a great gift, he wrote his second novel, "Carnival," a book about contemporary life. "Carnival" showed that Mackenzie was one of the few writers able to dramatize the Cockney scene. The Cockney passages in the book are among the best things of their kind in modern writing; for Mackenzie's strong humour and power of improvisation are at their freest. But the book also showed that when inspiration (and the Cockney scene) failed him he was inclined to relapse into romance, Cornishness, and a rather *fin-de-siècle* emotionalism. The end of "Carnival," accordingly, was in a different genre from the rest of the book.

It is upon the successor to "Carnival," which was called "Sinister Street," and a greatly admired appendage called "Guy and Pauline," that Mackenzie's fame long rested and perhaps still rests. "Sinister Street" is among the few novels of its period which are remembered. It is the picture of the development of a very precocious boy into a sophisticated young man of the nineteen-tens, and the picture is painted with a detail and wealth of reference unattempted by other authors of Mackenzie's experience. It illustrates most of its author's gifts, and all his faults. It is lavish, it contains rodomontade, it is literary, sentimental, and florid. But it has no timidities; it is large and confident; it is a picture of something more than a single life. It is the record of a departed generation. That it contains many passages in false taste I believe: it is so much the more true for that.

Mackenzie followed "Sinister Street" with "Guy and Pauline," always considered to be his best novel by those who are not troubled by its sentiment; and there seemed to be before him a long and unbroken career of romantic writing, fluent, beautiful, and picturesque. Of all the young writers of the time, he had the widest range—from fashion to the theatre, from common life among the London poor to life among the rural middle class, from poets to comedians, from highways to byways of human nature. Assuming the continuance of tradition, he could do anything he liked. But at this point the First European War broke out; and he was immediately involved in it. None of the writers of his generation so eagerly welcomed the path of glory.

He was attached to Ian Hamilton's staff, and went to the Dardanelles, as to which he has given a picture in "Gallipoli Memories" of his own natural courage and enjoyment of danger; later, he was Military Control Officer in Athens and Director of Intelligence elsewhere in Greece. At once he became legendary; tales were told of his exploits with spies and uniforms; he was in his element as a romantic leader and counter-plotter, fearless, adventurous, and extraordinarily receptive to all the delights of so romantic a life. The quickness of his mind, the power he had of establishing what is not so much friendship as a ruthless intimacy of understanding, his sense of the picturesque, all made him enjoy his work as a boy enjoys playing at pirates. For the duration of the First World War he had a whole international situation at his fingertips.

But this ended, and he resumed his writing of novels. In 1918 and 1919 he published the two halves of "The Adventures of Sylvia Scarlett," which he personally considered his best book. He followed this with a trilogy dealing with the life of a parson; and he also wrote very rapidly a number of less serious books which were widely read but which disappointed those who had expected from Mackenzie many additions to the serious literature of his country. He could still begin a book—as, for example, "The Seven Ages of Woman" —in a way to capture imagination and set it roving into adventurous distance; but he was for a time victimized by his own fluency, and the books were less good than one had hoped from their beginnings that they were going to be. Farce was always possible to him; no man alive had a greater readiness of comic invention, comic dialogue, general absurdity. "Poor Relations," "Rich Relatives," "The Old Men of the Sea" (an adventure book full of Stevensonian enjoyment of treasure, barratry, and combat) followed each other with rapidity. Charming evocations of the past, such as "Our Street" and "The Darkening Green," revived general appreciation of his great gifts. But it was not until he began to write in the vein of reminiscence that he achieved fully once again the status of the pre-War years. Here for the first time that delightful side of his talent, the gift of anecdote, mimicry, and narration which made him so admirable a conversationalist, was offered to the public in literary form.

I am particularly glad of the fact, for while it is easy for those who study such matters to imagine that "Sinister Street," "Guy and Pauline," "Carnival," and even the much later "Four Winds of Love" between them present a romanticized version of Mackenzie's own life, this version omits any record of the Mackenzie known to his friends. In the books, the young hero is from time to time neurotic, a prig, a verbose bore. Mackenzie was never one of these things. He had without doubt the most vivid personality of all the novelists of the generation young in 1910. He had also, in my opinion the greatest *talent* among these writers (observe the word italicized, and bear in mind its limitation). He must as a child have been very precocious; and he preserves an altogether exceptional memory of the events and surroundings of his life. But while memory plays an active part in a number both of his early and his late works, it is memory dramatized and newly charged with feeling. Mackenzie has dramatized childhood in "Our Street" and "The Darkening Green"; he dramatized the Cockney scene in "Carnival," and sophisticated youth in "Sinister Street," because it was his habit to dramatize everything in the world, from Compton Mackenzie to the last person he met in the street. Raconteur, mimic, and born improviser he has an actor's gift for making any scene in which he has taken part dramatically credible, and at the same time fantastically amusing. He is inexhaustible in puns, inventions, and memories.

In the long run, the author's personality and the accidents of his birth should not and do not affect a judgment of the value of his work; but as the present book is not exclusively a literary criticism I think it right to say that for all Mackenzie's friends his work is coloured by a sense of the irresistible personality from which it arises. If Mackenzie had never written a word he would be a character. There is something old and yet charmingly immature in his manner; a boyishness quite half composed of worldly wisdom. His juvenile demeanour, although never imperious, is lordly. His talk has never sunk to the floridness of his longer and more studied prose passages; it is high-spirited, droll, full of a sense of audience. He will in ten minutes give one an account of an episode in which he has taken part; and at the end of it one will have had— slightly caricatured—the deportment of everybody concerned in the episode.

That vividness of mimicry, of course, is absent from the printed word. One there has the inventiveness and the fun, but not the tone. Furthermore, I think Mackenzie gives so much of his talent first of all to sportive conversation and then to a recital of the plans he has made for future books that the novels themselves, when written, invariably seem to be less brilliant than the first sketches of them which one has heard rendered with such verve. This explains, I think, in part the discrepancy between different estimates of the importance of Mackenzie's work. To his friends, that work will always be charged with a thousand tones and expressions which strangers may miss. But at the same time there is this to be remembered: Mackenzie is not the only writer whose work is colder than his talk. And, since critics of books are to speak of them as books, it must I think be granted that Mackenzie's books suffer from two things. One of these things is a changed fashion; for Mackenzie belongs quite distinctly to his generation at Oxford, which adorned the poeticized phrase and a romanticized decadence. The other thing is his own conception of the novelist's obligation to entertain the reader.

Nobody who can take his nose out of æsthetics and ethics will doubt the right of the novelist to entertain readers. Indeed, the only pertinent question which one would be likely to hear from sagacious persons in response to such a claim is, "What readers?" We all try to entertain; but the person we try most eagerly to entertain is ourself. It is to ourself that we present each sentence we write; and if ourself is not pleased with it, we either push him upon one side or we rewrite the sentence. In Mackenzie's case, the self is at times indulgent. He has a very strong awareness of himself; he amuses himself. At his best, he is a good critic, because the range of his mind and sympathy is wide; but there are times when his taste betrays him, when an early tolerance of what he calls the *faux bon* supervenes. Then a flicker of what I should call false romanticism casts purple upon his writing and rose upon his picture. That is his chief fault as a serious writer. When he is in spirits, he has no superiors as a farcical raconteur; but for some reason, into which I have no time to probe, farce has still to be reckoned among the highest forms of literary art. If I were to add that his sense of the comic is too great to allow him passion or the depths of tragic imagination, I should go beyond knowledge: I therefore add only that Mackenzie has never quite, as a novelist, plumbed his talent to the depths.

There were some who thought in 1913 that a greater gift than Mackenzie's was in process of getting itself expressed. They found in Gilbert Cannan's "Round the Corner" the product of a less romantic mind more apt to give us in fiction something of the form and pressure of the time. Cannan was a young man from Manchester, who had been at Cambridge University, and who besides writing novel reviews for *The Manchester Guardian* had acted as dramatic critic for *The Star*. His dramatic criticism was scathing—as scathing, I believe, as anything written nowadays in criticism by our youngest intellectual bigots;—and his mind melancholy with regretful disdain of all elders whatsoever. He was a very tall and handsome young man, of whom one thought as Hamlet because he was so often lost in moody meditation, and because his expression, even when he smiled, was a sad one; but if statuesque he was not unfriendly, and he was a man of both talents and parts.

His first book, "Peter Homunculus," published in 1909, was by way of being a self-study; his second was a less interesting account of a disagreeable episode. The third, "Round the Corner" (that was where life was), had as its motto—or rather, as the first of its many mottoes, for it was studded with aphorisms—the words:

"On veut essayer de peindre à la postérité, non les actions d'un seul homme, mais l'esprit des hommes dans le siècle le plus éclairé qui fut jamais.—Siécle de Louis XIV."

And, true to his motto, Cannan proceeded to describe with much detail the lives and opinions of a father (he has unwillingly become a clergyman in his youth, because although promised a commission in the army he has had the commission filched from him by a younger brother), his children, and all those affiliated persons who go to make up a domestic and extra-domestic circle. "Round the Corner" was a good and opinionated novel; for it was not enough for Cannan that he should tell what happened to members of the family, and so he had many sententious things to say of life, marriage, freedom, and such-like matters. The book had vitality and humour, and it is as readable today as it was when it was published. But it was to be the best book Cannan ever wrote.

He wrote much after it, "Old Mole," "Young Earnest," "The

Stucco House," "Pink Roses," and others (a good dozen of them) before his lamentable illness; but of these only the novel called "Mendel," which told the story, or was Cannan's version of the story, of a young painter who was also Cannan's friend, was in any serious degree outstanding. Although opinions multiplied and verbosity increased, the talent remained stationary, and was covered at last with a kind of rank growth of words. He made no progress; while his rivals went their different ways to the War, he stayed in London or in a cottage in the country, and at last became so ill that his work had to be abandoned. But the talent had been real enough, as those who will read "Round the Corner" and "Mendel" can determine to this day.

Nor was its exercise confined to the novel; and at least one dramatic trifle—it is only a trifle in a single act—called "Everybody's Husband" is still played and is still charming to read. He had an ear for talk, although he was rather gravely monosyllabic himself, and it is one of the pleasures to be derived from "Round the Corner" that the talk is full-bodied; it is better than the disquisitions, and yet the disquisitions, until they became intolerable, were well enough in a grandiose way.

As for the third of this oddly-joined triumvirate, Hugh Walpole, like Cannan, was born in 1884, and like Cannan he published his first novel (which was called "The Wooden Horse") in 1909. Walpole was born in New Zealand, the son of an English clergyman who ultimately became Bishop of Edinburgh; and, again like Cannan, he went to Cambridge University. I do not know if the two were friends there; but I am sure that they had nothing at all in common. Where Cannan was unrelentingly severe towards his seniors, Walpole had no contempts. He was impulsive, generous, and immature. He had dallied with the idea of following his father's example and entering the Church, and the earnestness which was one of his traits, as well as his love of public speaking, testified to a natural bent for exhortation. If he had not been a writer he would have been a successful preacher; his lectures were always delivered with a spontaneity and energy of the most persuasive kind. But he did not feel, after some trial of his abilities, that he could properly remain in the Church; and with some brief experience of schoolmastering he determined that he wanted—as Henry James, nearly fifty years earlier, had wanted—to be "just literary."

When Walpole began to write novels he was deeply impressed by the work of Hawthorne and Henry James. Henry James was his friend, and to some extent his tutor; and there can be no doubt that for Walpole James's (and Hawthorne's) sense of the supernatural had a constant fascination. Although, as I have said, he was impulsive and generous and earnest, he was also very emotional and subject to nightmare terrors of the most extreme description. You can detect this, if you look for it, in his early work; for instance in "Mr. Perrin and Mr. Traill," where the writing has all the time a quiver of excitement. It dominates "The Portrait of a Man with Red Hair." It haunts other books, such as "The Green Mirror." Fear, merriment, cruelty: Walpole was not a simple character.

He was less simple than any other writer I have ever known. His cheerfulness and good nature, which were perfectly natural to him, his impulsive friendliness, his wish to establish sincere relationships with those whom he liked, were enmeshed with many reserves and distrusts, with shrewdness and good sense and another trait which I vaguely decipher as a power to shut his mind to unacceptable aspects of life. He was capable of great loyalty, ardent championship, candour; and at the same time bottomless suspicion, evasiveness, and deep trouble of spirit. He looked happy; his manner was always full of bonhomie; he could be—and was—teased; he laughed readily and plunged into a room with massive energy; he talked well and with humour as well as good humour; he was extremely likeable. If one had not known him, and had not known his work, one would have supposed him the most ingenuous soul in the world. The strange thing is that one would have been right, as well as profoundly wrong.

When he was young, Walpole thought the society of other writers the most delightful society of all. He wanted to write well, and he wanted to be liked. Accordingly, when his third novel, "Mr. Perrin and Mr. Traill," brought him to the notice of those watching for new talent, he was as happy as a young man could be. The book, that highly charged tale of schoolmasters who hate one another, was for a number of years Walpole's most admired novel. It remains one of his most interesting tales, although it is plainly immature. When, subsequently, he wrote "Fortitude," with its emphasis upon the need for courage in life, he had an even wider popularity than before; and while "The Duchess of Wrexe" had a less hearty welcome from some of his admirers it was well enough received to show that he had established his reputation.

Then the First World War came, and of course the literary life could not stand against such a storm of violence. Military service being impossible to him owing to shortness of sight, Walpole went to Russia on diplomatic business, and saw some service with a Red Cross unit on the Eastern Front. It was a wonderful experience for him, and, coupled with discovery of the Russian novelists, it powerfully affected his work. His next book, "The Dark Forest," was not only very much more generally successful than any of its predecessors (for all readers were then curious about Russia), but it was in every way more mature and more interesting than anything he had written. Parts of it were so good that they converted readers who had hitherto been sceptical of the author's talent, and it was with "The Dark Forest" that Walpole really took unquestioned place as a leader of the then younger generation. I should say that for the first time he was considered to be the best of the lot. His work was still in a literary sense derivative, but he had seen and felt strange, thrilling things, and a literary tea-party was no longer his ideal form of entertainment. His ambitions had expanded.

He remained in Russia, and was there all through the Revolution, writing "The Captives" while the whole bloody business was going on in Petrograd (refusing, indeed, to leave his work for the greater drama which was taking place); and after the War was over he travelled far and wide through the United States, where he was among the most popular of visiting Englishmen. Finally, having seen War and the New World, he settled down again to his literary task with an enthusiasm as rare as it is magnificent. He kept at that task, accepting a knighthood and becoming the "Uncle Hugh" of a slightly derisive younger generation; and when he died he was still busy, eager, sanguine, good-natured, secret, and in love with fame.

It is true that as his fame became greater his critical reputation was diminished. This is an inevitable consequence of fame, and the chillingly fastidious section of the critical public cannot endure to see an admired author taken to the arms of the mob. At the slightest hint of success it averts its head. Walpole suffered in England from the averted critical head.

It is possible that Walpole would in any case have been affected in literary reputation by the conflict between his desire to write well and his desire to be liked; but I think it is also true that his most famous single book, "The Cathedral," suffers from mechanical invention. I shall not dwell upon the obvious fact that Anthony Trollope had already created a complete church society in the Barsetshire novels, and that one of his leading characters was a powerful churchman named Dr. Grantly. What I have chiefly in mind is the fact that when a novelist conceives the idea of a book about any dominant personality who is brought low he is faced at once with certain plain possibilities of invention. That is, the personality, if he is in a profession, must suffer defeat in that profession; and he must also suffer defeat in his home. Otherwise the defeat is but partial; since many a man may be wounded in pride out of doors, and yet escape from complete destruction if, domestically, he is unharmed. If he is to be crushed in the home as well, he can only be affected by the loss of wife and children. Very well: the powerful Archdeacon of Polchester is given a wife and two children, one a girl, the other a boy (just as it happens in 'Poor Jenny is a-weeping"). The girl falls in love with a young man disapproved by the Archdeacon; the boy is sent down from his University, and runs away—you have guessed it—with a barmaid; the wife—have you not guessed that, too?—commits adultery. These events, singly, might have given the Archdeacon pause: all together, they have such an air of artificial contrivance that the reader is made uncomfortable. It is as though Walpole had naïvely taken the first suggestions offered by a mind overfamiliar with novelist ruses for the domestic discomfiture of the Archdeacon. Greater worldly experience would have started back from such an aggregation of simplicities. For the rest, scenic effects are splashed into the book; the drama is forced; the total impression of the tale is one, not of inevitability (which would have made it a tragedy), but of mechanism. The more sophisticated one is, the more one recoils from so little subtle a treatment of what might have been a suggestive and very powerful theme.

And yet "The Cathedral" is full of a quality which gave Walpole distinction among his fellow-novelists. It has a vivid and rapidly communicated scene; it is immediately readable; it attempts an ambitious subject and it carries that subject through with great address. The writing, though never better than brisk and nervous, is full of liveliness. The author does not waste time in dreary analysis; he goes straight to the dramatic and the informative. It would be easy to see from this one book—though it does his talent less than justice—that he was a natural novelist, and not one who had turned novelist in despair of doing something better. "The Old Ladies," where the scene is the same, but the plan less mechanical, is decidedly among his best books. Against the background of a cathedral city he occupied himself with the simple doings of pleasant people in that city, the good and the kind, the old and timid and gropingly super-stitious; and these are his proper concern. They brought out his sympathy for what was pleasant and true; they allowed his native ingenuousness full scope; and that delightful conversational style in which he told fairy stories for grown-ups did not swear with the grim or gruesome, the savage or the sublime.

In the last few years Walpole essayed his most ambitious task, the picture of a family through several generations and through several historical ages. None but an enthusiast could have ventured upon so tremendous a task. None but a tale-teller could have filled four large volumes with such a wealth of narrative, talk, life and death. To say that the Herries books fall short of complete success is not to arraign the design; for no novelist was ever more ambitious, and a glorious failure upon this large scale is in any event to be pre-ferred to a dozen safe little ventures in subtlety. The books show a really Gargantuan design. They attempt the business of heredity, the business of contemporary history (for portraits of historic persons are interpolated in the books, just as they were in Thackeray's "Esmond"), the business of entertainment, and a gigantic continuity. If the Herries books had been as good as only genius could have made them, they would have been monumental. If they are less than monumental, the heroism of the attempt remains.

vii. Francis Brett Young

"The green trees, when I saw them first through one of the gates, transported and ravished me; their sweetness and unusual beauty made my heart to leap and almost mad with ecstasy,—they were such strange and wonderful things. The skies were mine, and so were the sun and moon and stars,—and all the world was mine,—and I the only spectator and enjoyer of it."

Thomas Traherne.

FRANCIS BRETT YOUNG came too late to be included in the first onset of the "younger generation"; but he very quickly joined the band, and by 1914 had published not only a novel (written in collaboration with his brother Eric) called "Undergrowth," but a critical study of Robert Bridges. From the beginning of his literary career, therefore, Brett Young's name was associated with an intelligent interest in poetry; and if we remind ourselves of the history of Edwin Ingleby, written in 1919 as "The Young Physician," we shall remember how the little boy, Edwin, used to read Shenstone and Akenside and Prior and "nearly every volume of poetry that he could smuggle" from the school library. Edwin, without a doubt, in that respect was of the same temper as his creator; and his creator was a reader and writer of poetry for as long as he directed a pen.

Like Edwin, Francis Brett Young was born in the English Midlands, and while several of his novels, such as "Deep Sea" and "The Crescent Moon," "The Red Knight" and "Pilgrim's Rest," have a different setting (some of them foreign and romantic settings), those upon which his frame rests were markedly inspired by his love of the heart of England, Worcestershire and its neighbouring counties. It may in fact be true that Brett Young did not wholly find himself outside the Midland scene. His earliest works, though they included admirable studies of Midland life such as "The Iron Age," and though they were almost uniformly interesting work, suffered from a variousness of character which disturbed those who like to know what to expect of any author before they open his book. But he was known for ever as soon as he wrote:

"They crossed the drive and entered a grass alley within tall black hedges. The harsh odour of yews dropped, like a curtain, between them and the rose-garden on either side. Sometimes it seemed as if the curtains swayed and a ravishing gust blew through, so that Clare was conscious, without seeing, of masses of June roses breathing out sweetness under the heavy night. They passed quickly down the dark alley, Ralph with his long, free strides, Clare fluttering silently at his side. Where the yews ended stood a fountain of grey stone and a circular Palladian belvedere. The spray of the fountain rose in a starlit mist; its watery jets cracked in the air like whips; and when they reached it, everyone, of a common impulse, paused for a moment and turned to look backward down the long yew vista to the fantastic bulk and blazing windows of the castle."

Having been at school at Epsom, and at Birmingham University, Brett Young became a doctor, and for some years he practised in a small and very famous town in Devonshire. Travellers from the United States, after losing the Lizard light and a dim shadow upon the horizon which passes as soon as it has tantalized the eye, have often enough excitedly in the early morning darkness found their ship amid a fleet of small vessels; and it was at Brixham, from which these trawlers set out, that Brett Young acted as doctor. A glimpse of the place may be found in "Deep Sea." But his heart was never captured by that strange corner of England; he loved best his own richly inland scene. A great scene, by the way; the scene from which Shakespeare himself came four centuries ago. And, sure enough, although they will not find Shakespeare's greatness there, those who read the tales of Brett Young will find in them a peculiar Englishness born of the author's deep feeling for English poetry and an English countryside far from the sea.

He had a third love, not always to be found with the first of those I have named; and this is a love of music. That, too, is evidenced in his work. And, having lived for some years in Brixham, and then (as Mackenzie did, and both Norman Douglas and Lawrence) having spent some time in Capri, Brett Young settled in his most prosperous years of all in the countryside from which he sprang. He became an idol in county society; and from his home in Worcester he sent those long, slow, intimate studies of rural middle-class life which readers bereft of Galsworthy found so much to their taste. To him, rather than to any other writer, we owe the recent revival in amplitude in the novel; for "The Portrait of Clare," which was published in 1927, contains very nearly a thousand pages of polished, tender, and humane writing.

As compared with his immediate contemporaries, Brett Young has less humour and invention than Mackenzie and less sense of the dramatic macabre than Walpole. He is a more considered stylist than either. His writing is unfailingly mellow, graceful, and delicate. If he does not at any time give an air of sharp actuality to the life he describes, that is probably intentional, for strict realism is not his object. His object is rather to present in tranquillity, and with beauty, the life of his imagined lovers, his country squires, his schoolboys and nail-traders, his doctors and soldiers, so that they compose into a country painting, a long, leisurely panorama of England. Not for him the picture novel of Henry James, the novel of situation and the gropings of half-mystified brains after symbolic truth. Not for him the rapidities of Mackenzie or the vehemences of Lawrence or the winning zest of Walpole. His pace is slower; he passes along the lanes and through the fields, and so, eventually, reaches home in good order. At times he summons a little violence to his aid, and he is not afraid to marry his lovers and tell what happened afterwards; but when he does either of these things he does it with such measure and charm that his readers hardly know that their happiness has been threatened. In the full tide of his maturity he was one of the most generally popular novelists in England.

During the 1914–1918 War, Brett Young went to East Africa with British troops, and his book "Marching on Tanga" was the first thing he wrote which took him beyond enthusiastic reviews into the consciousness of the reading public; and it was to Africa that he returned for the rest of his life. He contributed to "Georgian Poetry"; and "The Portrait of Clare" gave him final standing among those who soon ceased to be the "younger generation" and became individuals known to all, and duly assailed as out of date.

viii. Constance Holme and Mary Webb

"When antique things are also country things, they are easier to write about, for there is a permanence, a continuity in country life which makes the lapse of centuries seem of little moment."

Mary Webb: Foreword to Precious Bane.

To conclude this chapter, I shall very briefly refer to two women novelists of real country life who belong to this generation, although they did not begin to publish novels until 1914 and 1917 respectively. They are Constance Holme and Mary Webb. Constance Holme was of Westmorland, and Mary Webb was of Shropshire. Constance Holme wrote eight novels of her own county, all marked by great sincerity and a natural purity of style which gave them value; Mary Webb, whose celebrity dated from a discovery by Stanley Baldwin, a Worcester man and Prime Minister at the time of his praise, wrote for several years without being widely appreciated. Her life began in 1881, and she was the eldest member of her small family, the children of a coach for the army and universities. She is now best known by a book, "Precious

HUGH WALPOLE

E . V . LUCAS

Bane," which tells in a local dialect what purports to be the self-story of a Shropshire girl; but her other work is not at all open to the charge of being pastiche, and is written upon a plane above that of the conventional novel.

The first thing one observes in these books, apart from the author's plain love of her native scene, is the exceptional flexibility of a poetic and beautiful style. But the style is only a reflection of the noble mind which it expresses; for Mary Webb lived and thought with a disinterested love of truth and eager seeking for ever deeper truth which filled her existence and gave it, even in poverty, clear purpose. She could command much humour of the countrified sort which one finds in those of Hardy's characters who are not gentle-folk; and could mock an old man or an old woman with readiness and without rancour. But she had great powers of sympathy, and a fierce hatred of cruelty and stupidity, so that her books are all charged with feeling and understanding of an uncommon order. It is the real country, we feel, that she brings quite livingly before us; and the people who dwell in it are of the soil. Their voices ring with truth; they are earnest, light-headed, stupid, or jovial, but always from nature. Though personally I feel discomfort at the dialect-narrative (there is a similarity between the manners of Girt Jan Ridd, in "Lorna Doone," and Prudence Sarn, in "Precious Bane"), which can never be quite flawless as a literary vehicle, I must confess that "Precious Bane" seems to me to be very rich, not only as a storehouse of country ways, but as a book about living creatures.

This woman had no happiness in city life; she loved hills and gardens. I saw her only once, when she made a little speech, composed and modest, about some subject which had been debated by others with a good deal of futility. She stood very straight, a slight figure with a serious face and rather protrusive eyes; and she spoke well and without nervousness. It was clear that she knew her mind, and would hold it in spite of any other opinion. That was the fact. She thought proudly and patiently, and as her writings show she was resolute to condemn or to support in accordance with her own belief and none other. As an instance of her assurance, and as an example of her writing, let the passage here quoted indicate what quality she had:

"Round the House of Dormer stood the forest, austerely aloof. The upper woods had never known the shuddering horror of the axe, the bitter and incurable destruction of the day when gnomes of ugly aspect are let loose with flashing weapons among the haughty sons and daughters of the gods, hacking and tearing at the steadfast forms of beauty, until beauty itself seems to have crashed earthwards.

J

Successive Darkes had threatened to fell the forest; but there was always plenty of wood from the reaping of the storms and from trees that fell from the rottenness of great age; so they had let it alone. The trees looked down upon time-shattered hulks of others in every stage of gentle decay. There were some mouldered trunks yet standing with a twig or two of green on them, especially among the yews, which must have weathered the winters of a thousand years. Others were of such antiquity that only a jagged point showed where once the leaf-shadows flickered on the wolf litters. Among these giants in their prime and in their dignified dissolution rose on all sides in supple grace the young trees and saplings. From the lissom creature that only needed the gradual massing of maturity to make its beauty perfect, down to the baby stem with two absurd, proudly waving leaves, all took part in that slow attainment of perfection through stages of beauty on which all Nature seems intent. They stood rank on rank, with rounded or pointed tops, their foliage sometimes heavy and solemn, as in the yew and the oak, sometimes fluffy as in the elm, or transparent and showing the sky through its traceries as in birch and larch. They seemed to peer at the house over one another's shoulders like people looking at something grotesque, not with blame or praise, but in a kind of disdainful indifference."

Chapter Twelve

THE WAR-TIME AFFLATUS, 1914–1918

CHARLOTTE MEW, ROBERT NICHOLS, WILFRED OWEN,
SIEGFRIED SASSOON, EDMUND BLUNDEN, ROBERT GRAVES,
THE SITWELLS

i

FOR the most part, this chapter will deal with the soldier-poets; but as I shall speak of Osbert Sitwell and his brother, and as it is usual for all writers (including members of the family) to speak of the Sitwells as though they were inseparable, I am going to conclude with Edith Sitwell. And as there was one woman poet whose work, first published in 1916, belongs to the First World War period (and to the future), I shall first speak of Charlotte Mew.

Before doing this, however, I wish to explain why I have grouped the other writers here. Robert Nichols comes first because his War experience was brief and quickly expressed; Wilfred Owen next because he was the most striking of all the poets killed in the War; Blunden, Robert Graves, and Sassoon as if they were three musketeers because all three wrote of their War experience in prose as well as in verse; the Sitwells last because while only Osbert had any practical contact with the War (he was in the Grenadier Guards from 1913 until 1919) they are a significant link between old and new poets. It was they who established the counter-blast to "Georgian Poetry" called "Wheels," and while they all turned triumphantly to prose they notably contributed to what is briefly called "this modernist stuff".

There was at the outbreak of the First World War a very rapid rush on the part of all sorts of young men to enlist in the Territorial Army, and as many of these young men had their education interrupted just at the time when they were naturally engaged in writing verses, the heightened emotion of those times led to a good deal of what was known as War-verse. Most of this was of no value at all. Some of it was as eager and burning as young hearts could make it. All found a ready market, because parents and friends wished for some record of their endangered boys, and—by some extension of sentiment—of the endangered boys of others. Several names detached themselves quite early from the rest—Julian Grenfell, Charles Sorley, Robert Nichols, Gilbert Frankau were among the earliest to tell in print what they felt or what they had seen and suffered—and they were duly read and celebrated. But then, after a time, the heroic note or the note of Kiplingesque onomatopœia favoured by Gilbert Frankau (Frankau, nevertheless, had something to describe, and he had great gifts of versification, as readers of "One of Us" did not need to be told) gave way to a note of quite another kind. War was not the splendour it was imagined by fever-struck home-stayers; it was an ugly dirty business. The poets began to tell us that. Later still, they let us farther yet into their hearts, to the bitter contempt for stupidity and incompetence which their War experience had awakened. Then we had, for the first time, a new personal poetry of the War; then was first sounded the cry of disillusion, of disenchantment, which in prose, more lengthily, less poignantly, we hear in the pages of C. E. Montague.

Disenchantment has been the cry of poets ever since that day; it is the cry of the youngest poets of all. although theirs, I sometimes think, is a factitious bitterness, arising less from individual than common inclination to declare the world not at all that sensitive hearts can desire. But the disenchantment of those earlier poets who fought in the War and who went into the fighting services with enthusiasm was by no means a convention: it was something true and original, the protest of men who, coming from peace and hope into a shambles, had had their beautiful dreams of life broken.

You will find in the poems of the women of War-time no comparable disenchantment; and yet their number can hardly have been less than that of the poems by young men of the same period. Little exercises in verse were as common to women as they were to men; the records of heightened mood, intuitions of pain, comments upon the exceptional scene, slight dramatic lyrics in which—it was the temper of war-time—they pretended to speak in the persons of harlots, dead men, and children puzzled by sorrow and brutality. Poetry seemed so easy, such a tender, delicate means of expressing a sense of darkened homes, darkened minds, darkened streets; and free verse was such a simple medium for light pens to use. One had but to take paper and break a slightly sentimental prose into unequal lengths; and lo! one was a part of the poetic impulse of the age.

ii. Charlotte Mew

"lend me, a little while, the key
That locks your heavy heart."
Charlotte Mew: The Pedlar.

HOWEVER, at least one of the women poets of the War years had something more than this casual emotion to set down; and she, a born poet, did not live long enough to bring her gift to its highest level. She was not well known outside a circle of poets, and I think she has still to be recognized as fully as she deserves. Thomas Hardy knew of her, and felt admiration for what she had written; there may have been others. To the best of my belief she published only two collections of what she had written, and since she died as obscurely (I speak in terms of public acquaintance) as she had lived she was overlooked.

Nevertheless the volume called "The Farmer's Bride" contains much that is of quite personal and unmistakable beauty. It has, of course, some callow verses which are timidly inquiring or in the fashionable mode of impersonation, but the effect of it as a whole is deeply moving. I should like to quote here, for example, in full, two long poems called "The Quiet House" and "The Forest Road," both of which achieve intense communication of feeling and reverie. I cannot do so, because of their length. The former, with its apparently inconclusive thoughts, by which a history is made plain to us, is the perplexity of a girl made manifest; the latter, a lover's dramatic apostrophe to a sleeping woman, I can only suggest by the use of a few lines:

"The forest road,
 The infinite straight road stretching away
 World without end: the breathless road between the walls
 Of the black listening trees: the hushed, grey road
 Beyond the window that you shut tonight
 Crying that you would look at it by day—
 There is a shadow there that sings and calls
 But not for you. Oh! hidden eyes that plead in sleep
 Against the lonely dark, if I could touch the fear
 And leave it kissed away on quiet lids—
 If I could hush these hands that are half-awake,
 Groping for me in sleep, I could go free.
 I wish that God would take them out of mine
 And fold them . . ."

"Madeleine in Church," another and at times acutely successful impersonation; the title poem, "The Farmer's Bride"; several pictures of children; and "Arracombe Wood," in dialect, all have their individual effect; but all are raised by their surroundings and the associations with what has been read before. In whatever she wrote, she was always guiltless of calculated gesture, which to me is in itself a mark of quality. Her aim was to communicate with scrupulous truth that vision which had come with strong feeling as the result of a personal impression of life.

iii. Robert Nichols

> ". . . despite these wars,
> My ship—though blindly blown,
> Long lost to sun or moon or stars——
> Still stands up alone."
>
> R. *Nichols: Thanksgiving.*

THE first of the poets to attempt onomatopœic renderings of the noises of battle were Gilbert Frankau and Robert Nichols. Both, in the first instance, were artillery officers, and both heard the guns in action with an enthusiastic sense of sound as well as the courage and splendour of those who took part in the warfare. Neither rendered, or sought to render, what to other and later soldier-poets was the dreary monotony of hopeless routine or the shocking waste of young life and young enthusiasm. For them the words of an Owen or a Sassoon lay in the distance: the immediate shock of conflict absorbed ears and minds. That was for the reason that they wrote in early days, and in heroic mood. Their vision of the War was still a vision of assault and counter-assault. Frankau, an extraordinarily skilled versifier, translated Kipling into modern terms; Nichols, all verve and excitement, pictured an attack as:

> "Something meets us.
>   Head down into the storm that greets us.
>   A wail.
>   Lights. Blurr.
>   Gone.
>   Oh, on. Lead. Lead. Hail.
>   Spatter. Whirr! Whirr!
>   *'Toward that patch of brown*;
>   *Directions left.'* Bullets stream.
>   Devouring thought crying in a dream.
>   Men, crumpled, going down . . ."

He knew, and celebrated, the sense of loss of friends; the horror of carnage. But he did not reach the stage of protest; perhaps he would never have reached it, so sanguine and thrilling was his temper. He was thus a War-poet of the second stage, the first being the purely patriotic or "this is for ever England" stage, and the third a stage signified by Sassoon's "But he did for them both by his plan of attack."

Like Wilfred Owen, Robert Malise Bowyer Nichols was born in 1893, and was educated at Winchester and Oxford. He had been a poet from boyhood, a poet in the vein of the immature Keats or the never quite continuously excellent Darley, familiar with fauns and dryads, and as ready as either Keats or Darley to write rapid melli-fluous verse about their pipings and sayings. I picture him in pre-University days as an eager youth whose imagination leapt high at a summer's day or a bosky grove, moods of joy and melancholy alter-nating, and his eyes in a fine frenzy rolling. It was at Oxford that he wrote fragments of a dozen ambitious poetic dramas or poetic romances, and, but for the First World War, he might have finished them at leisure and made his name as a romantic poet. He was not, I mean, a poet created by the excitement of the War; he had enough natural fire to warm his Muse without external aid. But he was a poet diverted by cataclysm from his impulsive vein. His vein, at that time, was:

> "Hark! a sound. Is it I sleep?
> Wake I? or do my senses keep
> Commune yet with thoughtful night
> And dream they feel, not see, the light
> That, with a chord as if a lyre
> Were upward swept by tongues of fire,
> Spreads in all-seeing majesty
> Over crag, dale, curvèd shore, and sea?"

During the inter-War period, with undermined health, Nichols made eloquent excursions into platform propaganda, the short story, the prose play, and lengthy poetic satire. Whatever he did, he did with such gusto that he seemed aflame with emotion; no man was ever more clearly a poet. Tall, eager, always in movement, talkative, exuberant, he flew at truth as if he would tear out its heart. But he had not the cruelty to harm a beetle, and for all his vehement assault the truth escaped again in the way it has done for as many centuries as scientists allow the world to have been peopled (I forget the latest number). Nichols was not discouraged.

He was a poet; not an intellectual. He said of English poetry that it is

> "a thing governed from within by its own necessities and not by rules of æsthetics imposed on it from without";

and this I take to be the true (as well as the romantic) definition of the unimportance of æsthetic theory in creative letters. But æsthetes will have nothing to do with such a definition, and Nichols towards the end of his life was mocked by his successors. He did not abandon poetry, but he ceased to challenge the stars. A copious letter-writer and talker, he became a champion of other poets, and was generous to the last towards his brethren, campaigning even for the payment to them of infinitesimal royalties on work included in anthologies. His campaign, like so much of his life, was a failure; but, again like so much of his life, it was unconsidered, impetuous, and most generously intended.

As a playwright, and he wrote, or began, several plays, including one on the Faust legend, he was still a poet, who dealt forcibly with great themes as did the minor Elizabethans or as they might do, in prose, if they lived nowadays. I like to see these plays as manifestations of a more recent Thomas Kyd (if that is the name of the man who wrote the better parts of "The Spanish Tragedy"); and none among modern writers could more exultingly than Nichols have relished the glorious retort of Hieronimo when he says:

> "In troth, my lord, it is a thing of nothing:
> The murder of a son, or so—
> A thing of nothing, my lord!"

The dramatic, the tremendous, the odd impress of guilty knowledge upon the souls of men, appealed strongly to Nichols's imagination. He would have been capable of any grandeur if something had not always inflated the grandeur; he might have written plays, in prose or poetry, in which spiritual problems were seriously tackled if only he had been able to discipline his own effervescence. He had the temperament for bold and lofty works, and perpetually promised a triumph of music and passion over the commonplace. But whether from fluency in excess of intellect or from a sort of opportunism that fell short of genius he did not fulfil his promise.

iv. Wilfred Owen

"I do not for a moment call myself a musician, nor do I suspect I ever shall be, but there! I love Music, with such *strength* that I have to conceal the passion, for fear it be thought weakness."

From a personal paper by Wilfred Owen.

WITH Wilfred Owen, we reach the height of what may be termed strictly War Poetry. In his work, which was first published posthumously under the editorship of Siegfried Sassoon, and which was finally collected and introduced by Edmund Blunden, there is no effort to render the delights of War, or the noises of guns and other instruments of death. We have, instead of impressionism, a peculiar reflective hatred of war from which hysteria is entirely absent; an attempt to give in poetry, not the "wukka-wukka" (as Hueffer) or "toc-toc-toc" (as Nichols) of the machine-guns, but the silent thoughts of men, the deadliness of trench warfare, the deep indignation of the soldier at civilian barbarism. Owen, who was posted to a unit of the regular Army, saw the whole First World War through; he was killed within a week of the Armistice. He was given the Military Cross for great bravery, and as an officer he represented the best type of unprofessional soldier.

He was born in 1893, and in 1910 he matriculated at London University. He went in 1913 to France, where for two years he acted as a tutor, returning to England in order to enlist as soon as his contract expired; and from that time onward he was almost constantly in physical danger and discomfort. His letters, frank and truthful, as well as humorous, show what horrors he had to endure; but they are full of courage. There was not in them, and there is not in any one of his poems, a slackening of courage. The horror of warfare which he expresses is reinforced by that fact.

He had, of course, written poetry before the War—some of it ingeniously experimental, as an example printed among his other poems clearly shows;—but it was the War which produced his rapid maturity. And even then it was during his stay in a War Hospital near Edinburgh, when Siegfried Sassoon was a fellow-patient, that he made the greatest progress. Sassoon was one of his poetic idols (for "The Old Huntsman" had been published, and Owen declared that nothing so good as the pictures of trench life in that book had ever been written), and Sassoon was a born mentor. He watched to the end of his long life over the talents of others, firm in criticism but ever kind in understanding, as no other man of his years could do. From Sassoon, therefore, Owen at once derived the best possible form of encouragement.

Encouragement was all he needed. His poetic instinct was so sure that he would sooner or later have discovered for himself all that could be taught. Since, however, time proved so brief, it is to Sassoon that we must give thanks for a friendship and influence which aided the production of Owen's best poems. If Owen had lived, he might have carried into the post-War period an even stronger power, as one infers from the magnificent fragment, "Strange Meeting." As it is, the poems that we have deal chiefly with war conditions and war reflections; and of all the men active at that time he is the one most accurately described as a poet of the War. How far we are from former picturesque renderings of sight and sound in the terrible stanzas of "Exposure", which begin:

"Our brains ache, in the merciless iced east winds that knive us . . .
Wearied we keep awake because the night is silent . . .
Low, drooping flares confuse our memory of the salient . . .
Worried by silence, sentries whisper, curious, nervous,
   But nothing happens.

Watching, we hear the mad gusts tugging on the wire,
Like twitching agonies of men among its brambles.
Northward, incessantly, the flickering gunnery rumbles,
Far off, like a dull rumour of some other war.
   What are we doing here?

The poignant misery of dawn begins to grow . . .
We only know war lasts, rain soaks, and clouds sag stormy.
Dawn massing in the east her melancholy army
Attacks once more in ranks on shivering ranks of grey,
   But nothing happens.

  .   .   .

Pale flakes with fingering stealth come feeling for our faces—
We cringe in holes, back on forgotten dreams, and stare, snow-dazed
Deep into grassier ditches. So we drowse, sun-dozed,
Littered with blossoms trickling where the blackbird fusses.
   Is it that we are dying?"

I have quoted this poem in order to show what is, as it seems to me, a point of progress between the mellifluous lyricism of pre-War days (and first consequent impressionisms of the War) and the righteous anger passionately felt and expressed in other moods by Owen or with characteristic irony by Sassoon. Such points hint only at a development which somebody more competent than myself should trace simply for the understanding of common people; for the disillusion of the War poets has been appropriated by a later generation as if that later generation, too, had suffered; whereas it has merely not been able to climb out of a bitter convention and remains self-righteous. Owen could not have remained a pessimist; he must have constituted himself a positive voice in a day of negations. One cannot read his poems without realizing his natural bravery. He had very exceptional talent, unusual skill and intelligence and enterprise in versification, the imaginative power to identify himself with other men and yet retain his own character unimpaired, and a breadth of sympathy unsurpassed by any of his contemporaries. For these qualities, in my opinion, he stands first among his peers.

v. Siegfried Sassoon, Edmund Blunden,
Robert Graves

I GROUP these three because they were friends, and wrote in prose some account of personal experience in the War. Sassoon was the eldest of them (he was born in 1886), and for myself the most outstanding. His War poetry first heroically expressed something other than patriotism and nervous excitement, and his own autobiographical volumes, first the "Memoirs of a Fox-Hunting Man" and "Memoirs of an Infantry Officer," and, later, the series of undisguised records of his own experience, are as excellent a record of character and feeling in pre-War and War years as any man of genius could have written. After the First World War Sassoon rigorously applied to himself, as a poet, the Malthusian doctrine which he untiringly pressed upon other creators, with the result that only a small quantity of poetry, tentative and reflective, has been printed; and even this he in some degree reserved for his friends by means of private publication.

Sassoon, asked to describe himself briefly, would hesitatingly have said: "I'm . . . er . . . ordinary sort of chap." He believed this. You could not persuade him that he was anything but a very simple fellow. Yet he had great pride—perhaps a pride in his simplicity, for of course he thought (as I do) that simplicity is better than sophistication. On the other hand Sassoon exaggerated his own simplicity; it is somehow confused in his head with austerity, and not wholly so, either. He was no metaphysician, and no debater. He tried to present himself in his autobiographies as an ordinary, shy, occasionally absent-minded cricketer and horselover who went to the War; who so hated it that he made up his mind to be killed—but was never hit; who after years of service was sent home ill; who resolved to make a public protest (which he did) against the continuance of so senseless a slaughter and horror; and—for the Army authorities were disconcerted by such behaviour on the part of one who had been rightly decorated for gallantry in the field, and hardly knew what to do with him—who outstripped his escort on the way to some institution which was a cross between prison and a sanatorium and arrived there first. His escort, by the way, was Robert Graves.

Well, whether you accept Sassoon's account of himself as a fair one or not (it is very sincere), there is one point upon which you must be clear. It is that nobody but Sassoon ever took him for an ordinary sort of chap. I doubt if anybody took him for anything but a poet. He had, for one thing, a handsome and noble head. He had, in his hesitating speech (I do not mean that he stammered, for he did not, but only that he was diffident of speech and with strangers often sat silent), a faculty for expressing wisdoms, fine taste, and eccentric ideas with considerable precision. I should say that he was not entirely incapable of enjoying other people's malice; but his own comments upon contemporaries were usually as kind as they were brief. They are not therefore saccharine. He had a true passion for music; a scrupulous honesty of mind which would not allow him to deceive himself—except about his ordinariness; a great capacity for emotion. On the whole, he might have been considered moody; but he was one of the most attractive men I ever met.

Sassoon, who on his mother's side was a Thornycroft, was educated at Marlborough and Cambridge. As the first volume of his autobiography shows, he lived much in the country as a boy, played cricket for the Sussex Martlets, rode to hounds, and read a good deal. Always solitary, he might not have made as many friends as he did if the War had not turned the current of his life; but since he was at Cambridge, and knew Robert Ross (a great friend to young poets and their like, and a charming man of letters), he was not completely a stranger in literary London when he began to publish his poetry. And here, for it was poetry of the War, we had that new note in which joyous sacrifice and amazed sense of noise and movement gave way to insistence upon—not only death and loss, which have long been commonplaces in poetry,—but the less inspiring aspects of modern warfare:

> ". . . drizzling daybreak that reveals
> Disconsolate men who stamp their sodden boots
> And turn dulled, sunken faces to the sky
> Haggard and hopeless."

And again:

> "I see them in foul dug-outs, gnawed by rats,
>   And in the ruined trenches, lashed with rain,
> Dreaming of things they did with balls and bats."

Elsewhere:

> "Crouched among thistle-tufts I've watched the glow
> Of a blurred orange sunset flare and fade;
> And I'm content. Tomorrow we must go
> To take some cursèd wood . . . O world God made!"

And finally:

> "The boys came back. Bands played and flags were flying,
>   And Yellow-Pressmen thronged the sunlit street
> To cheer the soldiers who'd refrained from dying,
>   And hear the music of returning feet,

'Of all the thrills and ardours War has brought,
This moment is the finest.' (So they thought.)

Snapping their bayonets on to charge the mob,
   Grim Fusiliers broke ranks with glint of steel.
At last the boys had found a cushy job.

.   .   .

   I heard the Yellow-Pressman grunt and squeal;
And with my trusty bombers turned and went
To clear those Junkers out of Parliament."

It was no wonder that when he resumed civilian life Sassoon
found himself a Liberal no longer, but a Socialist. He joined the staff
of George Lansbury's *Herald*, and became literary editor. He persuaded his friends to write the reviews for him, and a fine series of
candours invaded the *Herald*'s comments upon current literature.
These comments ran all over the world. They were carefree, original,
and slightly staggering. Many intelligent readers bought the paper
in which they appeared solely with the object of reading them. I do
not know if the publishers advertised in the columns of the *Herald*.
Possibly not. Publishers, like authors, prefer enthusiastic praise to
any other kind of comment. But Sassoon was taking the course indicated to him by that simplicity of mind which later was to give us
the masterpieces in prose by which he temporarily wiped out
memory of his poetry. That was as well, for he had been accused by
no less a person than Edmund Gosse of harping upon something
that was now over and better forgotten—the War. Sassoon could not
forget the War. If he had not harped upon the War he must have
been false to his faith. And, by so harping, he continued to attack
everybody who had been comfortably ready to sacrifice the young
in a late encounter, and by degrees (with the aid of others, similarly-
minded) he consolidated a general impression in the minds of youth
that anybody over forty years of age was inescapably a hypocrite
and a profiteer. I do not remember when the country first read the
words "My generation" as applied to a new and better race; but the
germ of that hostility to former generations can be found in the
Sassoon poem just quoted.

Of the now several books of autobiography I have only to say
that they are entirely free from affectation; they conjure up the
countryside of old peaceful days and the calms as well as the storms
and disgusts of War. They picture the author's days in saddle and
cricketing pads. They subtly communicate his affection, his modesty,
and that vagueness which all sensitive men feel within them while
the impression they make upon others is objectively concrete. They

are documents of our time. I see them as likely to be so regarded a century hence.

Edmund Blunden's "Undertones of War" is similarly remarkable as a sensitive man's description of encounter with a world altogether strange, for immersion in which every hour of his previous life had unfitted him. Blunden's war poems have less pungency than those of either Owen or Sassoon; the feeling in them is diffused; he was not a warrior, and War inspired his prose but not his best poetry. He had not the faculty which Owen and Sassoon shared for presenting ugly experience with imaginative force. The truth is that Blunden was always by nature a pastoral poet and a bookman. He loved old books. He would agree with that writer (at the moment I cannot recall his name) who said: "Whenever a new book comes out, I read an old one"; and while he read the new book also it was usually in his capacity as reviewer for *The Times Literary Supplement*. His dream would have been to dwell in a countryside peopled (besides the hinds and hodges and birds and beasts) with Lamb, Hazlitt, Leigh Hunt, and the men of their hour. Glorious prospect!

Imagine this reader and lover of nature being called from his books and cottage to deliver death to those whom he had no wish to harm! He no doubt wore his khaki with a difference. But while "Undertones of War," which is written in fine prose without ornament, is plainly the work of one who was not born for soldiering, it is equable in spirit. Blunden was never an indignant philosopher, nor a rebel, but a sweet-tempered poet reading a book by the roadside and noticing the hues and tenderness of the landscape. He gives us none of the bitterness of some of his peers. We read in his pages:

> "It was the weather when leaves begin to turn, and sing a little drily in the wind; when spiders apparently spend the night in making webs on fences; and when the distances dare assume the purple as the sunset dislimns. As far as battalion headquarters, one might notice these nocturnal effects. Beyond that point, the facts and probabilities of war obscured them . . . Recollection paints these autumn weeks in the Beaumont Hamel sector as a tranquil time, etc."

I do not say that disagreeables are ignored in Blunden's limpid pages; but they assuredly are not enforced with a curative purpose in view. They are used as contributory detail to a picture painted in sober and candid colours. That is because Blunden's true love was for the pastoral:

> "Along the baulk the grasses drenched in dews
> Soak through the morning gleaner's clumsy shoes,

And cloying cobwebs trammel their brown cheeks
While from the shouldering sun the dewfog reeks.
Now soon begun, on ground where yesterday
The rakers' warning-sheaf forbade their way,
Hard clucking dames in great white hoods make haste
To cram their lapbags with the barley waste,
Scrambling as if a thousand were but one."

As soon as we come to Robert Graves, we are conscious of a
difference of approach to the world. Sassoon, in his prose books,
is the quiet, meditative sort of chap with a love of a horse and a bat;
Blunden, dreaming of old authors and present contemplation, is
similarly at peace with a tranquil world, and the enemy of none. But
Graves—it is clear from his own account—is of a more active and
aggressive mental cast. He quarrels, not, as Sassoon, with gloom and
reluctance, but with zest. His verses are crisp. He says:

"I forced this quarrel; it was not
    So much disgust with all you did
As sudden doubt of whom and what
    My easy friendship hid;
    I carefully offended.
It would be best if you too broke
Acquaintance with a monstrous look.
    Rather than stay to temporize
    Or steal away with brimming eyes."

That is still another stage towards the modern temper, which is
impatient, imperious, little tolerant of other methods and other
sorrows. But Graves is far from being permanently angry; he has a
great singing, narrative, and creative gift, as his novels of Roman
emperors and the American War of Independence have shown. His
poems have often the simplicity of old ballads—they are not mimi-
cries:

"*Mother:* Alice, dear, what ails you,
        Dazed and white and shaken?
        Has the chill night numbed you?
        Is it fright you have taken?

                  .   .   .   .   .

        Soft and thick the snow lay,
        Stars danced in the sky.
        Not all the lambs of May-day
        Skip so bold and high.

> Your feet were dancing, Alice,
> Seemed to dance on air,
> You looked like a ghost or angel
> In the starlight there.
>
> Your eyes were frosted starlight,
> Your heart, fire and snow.
> Who was it said 'I love you'?
> *Alice:*   Mother, let me go!"

If you ask the reason for this difference between the three men, it is clearly perceptible. Sassoon and Blunden are English, Graves Irish. The Irish clearness of sight, impatience with what seems to be a soft slowness in the Anglo-Saxon (which slow softness, without doubt, is accompanied by inexplicable poetic riches) is again exemplified. Nor is this all; for Graves is not content, as Sassoon latterly was, with what he calls "lingual exercises" (some poems containing lovely lines and evocative pictures), but must carry experiment in verse to a pitch of almost obstinate obscurity as he searches for satisfying forms. He cannot endure the long pages of Dickens, but must arduously rewrite and condense "David Copperfield" until the echoes ring with Dickensian wails. He has told the tale of his own life from early years and roused conflict among all who remember those years in a different mood and different sense. He has written the story of John Milton's married life with consummate disrespect for greatness. And because of all these arrogant challenges to accepted views and canons the beauties of those earlier simplicities of diction have been obscured. Therefore I recall them here, and insist also that Graves's original talent is greater than his controversial prowess. He was a friend; he will remain for posterity in spite of every other assault upon his time a poet.

vi. The Sitwells

> "Let us prune the tree of language
>   Of its dead fruit.
>   Let us melt up the clichés
>   Into molten metal;
>   Fashion weapons that will scald and flay;
>   Let us curb this eternal humour,
>   And become witty."
>   *Osbert Sitwell: How Shall We Rise to Greet the Dawn?*

I T is unfair to each member of the Sitwell family to treat them as a trinity, for while when they began they might be confused one with another, all that is now changed. Edith retold fairy stories in glittering coloured rhyme and revived the eccentricities of old Bath

ure prose; Osbert, having taken to the novel, sailed to
ce as an autobiographer; and Sacheverell, though still faith-
poetry, has turned his attention to the Gothick in both archi-
e and music. But there has been in all these years something
rate in that insistence upon being not three, but one; and now
re inseparable in the public mind. I am not sure, either, that
is not something which may be regarded as a common Sit-
n base, and since I must try to define what that is I shall ask
rs to look again at the short quotation from Osbert's poem,
w Shall We Rise to Greet the Dawn?" They have all been wits.

n the beginning, they were three *enfants terribles*. Being excluded,
by their own act or by the repulsion of the editorial canon,
from "Georgian Poetry," they established a counterblast to which
they gave the name "Wheels"; and to this all three contributed
greatly, adding jovial and insulting annotations with which they
lambasted uncomplimentary reviewers. They engaged with reviewers upon every hand—though the reviewers were at times
hardly worth a word of reproof. They indulged in japes, such as
their successive entries in "Who's Who," advertisements in the
Personal columns of *The Times*, and so on. They satirized their
rivals, their so-called "enemies," in ribald poems, and sometimes
did the same for social ladies whose fault was only that they were
over-zealous in entertaining the latest lion in any art or craft. In this
way they drew attention to themselves, and caused warier folk to
shake heads at such mountebankery. The tactics obscured the
talent.

But the Sitwells did not mind. They were not poor young men,
struggling to find a public, but were children of rich parents, and
were very much in the fashionable world. They were more in the
fashionable world than any other writers. Osbert, with the profile
of a Roman emperor or a Hanoverian sovereign, with his cold eyes
and merciless tongue; Sacheverell, tall, more patently a young poet,
haughtier yet, and in early days unable to laugh without apparent
physical pain; Edith like a sibyl, beautiful and highly mysterious;
all three oddly kind and generous despite their diabolical skill in
ridicule, they held upon their resolute way. The talent was theirs.
It must be acknowledged. It must be acclaimed. Those who did not
acclaim it were traitors, who must die the death.

Now the talent of all three is admitted, but is not in all quarters
wholly approved. Osbert, who was always in such haste that he
could not give satire the final polish which made Pope a master of his
art, found a fitter, more generous, less cabined medium in the
record of his own past. His writing, in prose, has a most admirable
firmness and character; and if the characters in his novels are less
real than fantastically recognizable, that makes them only the more

amusing to all who are in the know (or wish they were). He amused himself in amusing others. Sacheverell, whose talent as a poet was always more delicious than his brother's, ruminated (with wit) upon architecture and the nature of man, turning from lovely fancies about cowslips and other wild and garden flowers to speculation which may be endless upon an endless theme. Edith, who collected her poems (thereby impressing as to quantity and quality, but none the less crying for some sparser selection in which nothing but the pure and variable gold shall remain), made her own anthology upon principles so original that hatred for Matthew Arnold seemed the only constant, and lent her wit to resuscitation of old and deadly figures of fun. And, between them, the three stand as one man for their chosen cause—the suppression of pulpy humour, and the exaltation of ruthlessness of thought and speech.

In this way they represent a turn of the hour. In a love for satire they were so early in the field that later comers (I am sure) will do them little justice unless they insist upon it. They were not alone in satire; but it was they who first revived a quasi-Augustan temper after the First World War, and first made scathingly merry with those over whom Siegfried Sassoon loosed his indignation. It was Osbert Sitwell who called his poem "War-Horses," and thus attacked aged fashionables who had been a little subdued in the War years:

> "How they come out
> —These Septuagenarian Butterflies—
> After resting
> For four years!
>
> Surely they are more spirited
> Than ever?
> Their enamelled wings
> Are rusty with waiting
> —Their eyelids
> Sag a little
> Like those of a bloodhound;
> But they swim gaily into the limelight."

Those were the days when old men and old women were publicly arraigned—not for the first time, for Shaw had set the example in those old nineties which he adorned—as humbugs with neither brains nor consciences, vampires and performers of blood-sacrifices. It was the new attitude.

Chapter Thirteen

BLOOMSBURY

BERTRAND RUSSELL, ROGER FRY AND CLIVE BELL,
LYTTON STRACHEY, VIRGINIA WOOLF

i

"They, the few,
The chosen, the peculiar."

M. R. Mitford: Rienzi.

BEFORE saying another word about books, I must explain to those who know no better that Central London is mapped for some forgotten reason into different quarters. Thus, Soho, which lies between Shaftesbury Avenue on the south and some not quite clearly defined point to the north of Oxford Street, is the home of a part of London's foreign population and is a centre for French and Italian restaurants; Belgravia is the old highly fashionable district west of the Green Park, Mayfair the extraordinarily aristocratic section north of Piccadilly and east of Hyde Park, and so on. And Bloomsbury, which I have made the title of this chapter lies to the north of New Oxford Street, between Tottenham Court Road upon the one side and Gray's Inn Road upon the other. It is the great quarter for squares and private hotels, straight plain Georgian houses (but Georgian in its eighteenth-century sense), publishers, and, residentially, a kind of bourgeois or æsthetic-bourgeois selectness. In it lie the British Museum and the great Foundling Hospital of Thomas Coram; and during and immediately after the First World War it became the spiritual, sometimes the actual, home of exiles from Cambridge University.

Other members of this fraternity, the so-called Intelligentsia, lived upon the farther side of Tottenham Court Road, and these were the artists and rebels; more still lived in Chelsea, down by the River Thames, where artists, poets, and mere frequenters of studios gave rise to more self-expository novels than any other class of people then living. Such younger æsthetes were not the real thing; they saw themselves as characters in a "modn" tale by Murger or a satirical novel by Aldous Huxley, and were of no account. The seat of intellectual *ton* lay in Bloomsbury. There, in the shadow of learning's home from home, Bloomsbury (as the embodiment of an assumption) felt strongly its intellectual superiority to the rest of British mankind. It represented culture. It was full of what Desmond MacCarthy called "alert, original men and women".

I must make two things clear. First that I write harshly of Bloomsbury from sheer malice. I have suffered no ill from Bloomsbury: whenever I have had any relation with its chief figures that relation has been mutually kind. My dislike of it (which I avow, although in writing of its leaders I shall try as usual to explain their incontestable excellences) is due entirely to what seems to me to be a conflict between its performance and its presumption. The second thing to be made clear is that—in consequence of my inability to share it—I believe the love of Bloomsbury on MacCarthy's part to be an aberration. He is a critic with whom I seldom agree (that can't be helped); but he is an intelligent man, an excellent and informative talker (given, perhaps, to monologue, but ever courteous to interrupters), and he reads poetry very well indeed. His essays are always urbane, and his knowledge of books and people far greater than my own.

The glory of Bloomsbury was not a modest glory, and for me modesty is the only true glory. It had no love for others; and for me a love of others, which was good enough for Shakespeare, is essential to the production of great literature. It claimed aristocracy. Criticism it regarded as *lèse-majesté*, and met it, or anticipated it, with personal insult—but that, perhaps, is a consequence of not being quite sure of its own superiority to criticism?

I presume that there was another side to the picture; and that Bloomsbury really imagined itself as suffering from the assaults of Philistia. I do not know why it should have done so. If the complaint was that ordinary people were too stupid to read the books of Bloomsbury, that seems to me a paradox, and Mahomet, you remember, went to the mountain. If nobody read my books, I should be sorry; but I should think it was because the books lacked interest. Bloomsbury, as to its own books, took a different view. Like an even later generation of dilettanti, it wanted to impress people into reading what it wrote, whether they liked it or not; that is, it wanted to be read from snobbery—a snobbery of culture;—and by writing above the heads of Tom, Dick, and Harry, to lead Tom, Dick, and Harry to higher things. In the same way, very stupid Englishmen shout in English at foreigners, and then say: "They're fools; they don't understand English." It is a kind of insularity—insulatedness—of mind, and rises from lack of familiar contact with other modes of thought and feeling than its own.

The odd thing about that is that Bloomsbury was politically Left, and only intellectually Royalist—royalist, you understand, to itself. It had a powerful wish to dominate the Labour Party by means of an aristicratic caucus, a kind of group dictatorship of brains, after, I suppose, the Russian model, in ignorance of the fact that the

English as a nation (apart from the unemployed) are practically a
petty bourgeoisie. Further, it alienated the very people it would have
impressed by its determined patronage of the arts and artists and a
tremendous parade of refinement. Ostentatious refinement, indeed,
was a part of its assertion of superiority; and I have so long believed
all ostentation to be vulgar that I am sure Bloomsbury, at heart,
was vulgar. It loved the eighteenth century—the wits, you know,—
and was fashionably coarse in its conversation. This you would
expect, if you had read Hazlitt's book of talks with Northcote;
for Hazlitt said (I have telescoped two passages):

> "As the common people sought for refinement as a *treat*, people
> in high life were fond of grossness as a relief to their over-strained
> affectation of gentility . . . Fashion is gentility running away from
> vulgarity, and afraid of being overtaken by it. It is a sign the two
> things are not very far asunder."

It dressed distinctively and—in the female part of it—did its hair as
Mrs. Gaskell used to do hers a hundred years ago, wearing long ear-
rings and in some way managing always to look sickly. When it
laughed, it grimaced desperately; for its laughter was painfully self-
conscious. It spoke with great affectation, introducing all the vowels
into so simple a word as "no." It was conversationally insincere,
what one would call "strained"; but although its tones were the
tones of wit I constantly hear far wittier talk at my Club, where
men think less of showing off than of contributing to the general
gaiety. It was very sensitive and sarcastic ("ahrony"); was full of
jealous contempts; was spiteful and resented being ignored, although
it went in a good deal for the wilful ignoring of others. And it had
the impudence to accuse all who did not support its pretensions to
superiority of either being fatuous or of selling the pass to the
enemy. The enemy was Democracy.

ii

"Cambridge is a world of subdued tones, of excessively subtle humours, of prim
conduct and free thinking; it fears the parent, but it has no fear of God; it offers amidst
surroundings that vary between dinginess and antiquarian charm the inflammation of
literature's purple draught."

H. G. *Wells: The New Machiavelli.*

So much for Bloomsbury as it was. It will have been noted that I
spoke of it as the home of exiles from Cambridge University;
and I should like to try and show, very briefly, how I think Bloomsbury came into being, and how during the First World War and

immediately after that War it found its opportunity for taking the town. If the account I have given of the progress of young warriors from idealistic patriotism to hatred of all civilians and old men is superficial, this will be equally superficial. The whole subject calls for much closer investigation than I can give it, and a more scholarly experience than mine. Nevertheless, if one could succeed in providing only a glimpse of groupings and directions it would be better than nothing at all. My account can always be corrected by those better informed; and I shall naturally speak only in the most general terms.

Earlier in the book I drew attention to the rise of what is not so much a convention of classicism as a convention of "classiness" in our modern authors. Until we reached the novelists of the "younger generation" very few of our subjects had been men and women educated at the older universities. They had been boys and girls who pushed themselves into notice as the result of character and talent, and not boys and girls whose education had lasted continuously from childhood until the twenty-third or twenty-fourth year of life, so that they reached London ignorant of practical affairs but primed with omniscience. This convention has been much increased of late years, and while the youngest critics are miniature pedagogues, the typical novelists are men of encyclopædic display.

I shall timidly venture a guess at the reason for this change. It is that authorship has become a specialized career for highly educated men. In the past, novelists were first of all printers, hack dramatists, or hack journalists, spinster ladies or Writers to the Signet; it was not until the Victorian day that they lived openly and creditably upon their royalties and could afford to be known socially as entertainers of the people. For a time then they glittered in the public eye, and were beloved. But when the Victorian heyday of novel-writing passed, and when other professions could absorb all the rising ambition, it was not smart to be a novelist. Sales were less remunerative; circulating libraries called the tune; competition with women was more intense than it had been. Young men of good birth or middle-class family went to the universities, and if a career was to be followed they entered Politics or the Law. There were great openings in Medicine or in the Banking or Shipping worlds; there was the Civil Service, Home and Indian, in which with constant expansion many plums could be gathered. And so on. Such university graduates as became novelists in those days slipped into novel-writing while they were briefless, or during holidays from banks, or because they found time hang heavy on their hands in some other respectable career. They never said in youth, as they did in the Georgian era of 1910–1935, that they were entering, not the Church or the Army, not Parliament or the Law, but the Novel.

But with the development of competitive examinations, the great growth of the scholarship system, and the overcrowding of the professions generally, it became increasingly difficult to find openings for young men of good birth and ordinary talent. Until the British Broadcasting Corporation expanded, there were offered to such men only the alternatives of Politics, the Bar, Schoolmastering, or Business. Now there is Literature as well. Hence the Pedagogishness. Talent and taste cannot be taught; but æsthetic rules can be taught, and if you call any æsthetic dogma a "principle" it can be used ever after as something indubitable and made a foundation for artistic practice.

When I was young, and the first burst of these University men with an inclination for novel-writing was upon the land, all young writers seemed to me to come from Oxford. I read manuscripts all day long, and they dealt with emotional adventures on the part of youths schooled in such matters upon the banks of the Cherwell. I heard a great deal about Aristotle, Keats, Matthew Arnold, and the Isis; nothing at all about the Backs, the Cam, or O.B. But most of those books remained unpublished; and among men of that generation only Compton Mackenzie made any serious mark upon the novel. On the other hand, Cambridge could boast Cannan, Walpole, and (not least) E. M. Forster. It was E. M. Forster who in 1910 received a colossal boost in *The Daily Mail* for "Howard's End," and was credibly reported in publishing circles as a sequel to have sold ten thousand copies. Cambridge had the advantage.

Since that time, and around and since the First World War, Cambridge University has supplied England with all the Intelligentsia it can do with. Among philosophers and scientific teachers, McTaggart, G. E. Moore, A. N. Whitehead, Lowes Dickinson, and Bertrand Russell make a formidable group. Roger Fry and Clive Bell had from 1913 onward a glorious æsthetic day; and in the later dazzling success of popularized astronomy Jeans and Eddington took every prize. There were novelists and poets innumerable, from Rupert Brooke to *les jeunes*. From the—to me, first-class—biographical works of F. A. Simpson and the charming caricatures of Lytton Strachey, we have all drawn our sense of the prowess of the age in this department of letters. And if I were to continue in detail I am sure everybody would suppose Cambridge the fount from which all learning and literary facility flow. Fortunately I shall be able to stop at this point; for I have said enough to show that Cambridge is a very much larger place than Bloomsbury ever was, and yet a place to which Bloomsbury owes both its best names and a certain devastatingness of mind little touched by the curious gift of imagination. Imagination I take to be the faculty by means of which one enters into the minds of others and is not surprised to find them full of good things. That is not the only power of imagination; but it is the one most interesting to myself. If he has any intellect at all, a Cambridge man can bring his intellect to bear upon a subject, and in so far as the subject can be put into mathematical or philosophical form he is capable of understanding it and possibly of illuminating it. But until he has brought out all his critical apparatus he is at a disadvantage and is highly suspicious of the subject, his interlocutor's knowledge of the subject, and the importance of the subject. Even then, he is impervious to outside suggestion. He knows best. It was a Cambridge don, I feel sure, who figured in Stanley Baldwin's story of the undergraduate and the don. The don said: "I met your sister last night"; the undergraduate said: "That was my mother; I have no sister." The don said: "I think, on reconsideration, you will find it was your sister."

iii

"L'inconvénient du règne de l'opinion, qui d'ailleurs procure *la liberté*, c'est qu'elle se mêle de ce dont elle n'a que faire; par exemple: la vie privée. De là la tristesse de l'Amérique et de l'Angleterre."

Stendhal: Le Rouge et le Noir.

I MUST now return to the moment of the outbreak of the First World War, because I wish to indicate what effect this outbreak had upon some sections of the civilian population, and particularly upon such writers as remained in civilian life. But before coming to the writers I want to speak of one or two things which seem pertinent to the assumption of the young poets that all civilians were morally responsible to the continuance and the horribleness of the First World War.

Never before in the history of modern England had the entire population been engaged in warfare. The Boer War, it is true, had produced a call for recruits; but it had been a very distant humiliation and it had been fought with the small British standing army against an enemy calculable in thousands. This European War was an immediate terror. The conditions were all new, frightful, and exceedingly disconcerting. The English are not a warlike people (their great generals, for the most part, have been Irishmen and Scotsmen); and they did not at first realize how much the War was going to interfere with the life of nearly everybody in the land. Taken aback by unexpected calamity, they looked about them—it was instinctive in a peace-loving people—for reassuring catchwords; and while some of the youngest and most ardent, and the least thoughtful of all, shouted in the way of mobs, the elders hung upon the words of statesmen—who solemnly declared that "we shall not sheathe the sword," and thereby I am sure created unconsciously a new test of sobriety—or prophet-journalists such as Horatio

Bottomley, or any other speakers or writers who could give them a verbal straw to clutch. Some genius at that moment seized upon a crucial aspect of the civilian problem. He said: "Business as usual."

That phrase was afterwards greatly condemned; but at the moment of utterance it was as excellent as the "Keep calm, ladies and gentlemen," of any theatre manager who soothes an audience in terror of fire. In effect, it said: "Don't rush madly to the exit; you'll only be in the way. Wait until you are told what to do." Casuists distorted it in a thousand ways, pretending that it was the cry of the profiteer, a smugness, an effort to ignore the War, and so on. They were wrong in doing this. The War brought many base things to the surface, horrible things; but I should include among these an intense and revolting self-righteousness upon the part of those who prided themselves upon being in a minority. "Business as usual" was only a phrase; but it was a phrase calculated to calm a population better employed then in going about its daily work than in yielding to hysteria. Misuse of the phrase grew; but by that time the country had settled down to the War, had forgotten some of its idealism, and was dealing in cliché.

This brings me to another point. It was made a cause of accusation against the elders that they said: "This is a young man's war." That, too, became a cliché. But then, contrary to E. M. Forster's view that Dickens's characters were unreal because they were embodied repetitions, the majority of English people express themselves by means of stereotyped phrases. They are not ready with eloquence. However deeply they feel, the words which issue from their lips are often enough stale old maxims which fastidious modern writers take elaborate pains to avoid. "This is a young man's war" meant, not, as the indignant have tried to prove, "we old men have made a war; thank God we haven't got to fight in it," but "I am ashamed of my own uselessness." It was an apology; that it became perfunctory, and was soon perverted by pacifists into "this is an old man's war," is true; but the first impulse was genuine.

However, opponents of the participation of Great Britain in any war whatever must fasten as they can upon phrase and bogey. It is thought that they are dishonest, that they are prigs, that they hate their native land, that they are such physical cowards that (taking advantage of personal immunity) they shout affronts from safe places. All these things are untrue. Some of them are prigs, some are physical cowards, some are dishonest; but most pacificists are either moral or intellectual pedants, and in most of them a love of England and belief in her superiority to all other lands whatever has attained a fantastic height. They really do believe that England leads the world; and that if England would but hang herself in olive branches and go forth unarmed all other peoples would be so impressed that they would follow suit and the millennium be attained. But they are not markedly courteous to opponents in their advocacy of this course, and might be not inaptly called Militant Pacificists.

When the First World War broke out, while poets and common men rushed at least to offer themselves as sacrifices to truth (or what they believed to be truth), many intellectuals who were fixed in their ways refused to recognize it as a fact. They had supposed war to be an anachronism; they had proved conclusively that it would not pay; and they said they would by no means endorse the action of any government which allowed the country to be dragged into any conflict. To heated (but stereotyped) inquiries as to what they would do if their sisters were being raped, and did they want to be ruled by Germans, etc., they returned various answers. They thought they were standing firm for principle; but perhaps they were only incapable of departing from theory.

Moreover, there were other elements in their argument. Nearly all intellectuals of that day were or had been old-fashioned Liberals, and to old-fashioned Liberals Czarist Russia had long been the Great Peril to Peace. They considered France as militarist and intransigent. They had German educational memories, or German social connections; and one at least of them, Arthur Ponsonby, had written and published a pamphlet called "Democracy and the Control of Foreign Affairs" (1912) in which the definitely anti-German trend of British foreign policy was arraigned and condemned. In so far, therefore, as there was any political leaning on the part of these Liberals it was in the direction of Germany. But they were not "pro-German," as was hastily said by the idiotic; their real interest was not in Germany but in the rectitude of their own country.

Now a zeal for rectitude can be very obstinate. It can be humourless. It can be a bigotry. For as you remember Macaulay says:

> "The doctrine which from the very first origin of religious dissensions, has been held by all bigots of all sects, when condensed into a few words, and stripped of rhetorical disguise is simply this: I am in the right, and you are in the wrong. When you are the stronger you ought to tolerate me; for it is your duty to tolerate truth. But when I am the stronger, I shall persecute you; for it is my duty to persecute error."

These men, being in a minority, felt themselves wronged. Some of them insisted, in the spirit of martyrdom or the spirit of obstinate consistency, upon saying things on behalf of truth which to the government of the day, heavy with responsibility for winning the War, seemed unhelpful. One or two of them were sent to prison.

Their disciples, who also refused to acknowledge the War, and who were of military age, suffered a great deal—I am not denying that the stupidest and most unimaginative people in the country, being narrow patriots in a funk, were terribly active in persecution, —and, when conscription was introduced into England, were forced into the ranks of what were called "Conscientious Objectors." Conscientious Objectors were supposed to be men who had a religious aversion from the idea of taking life; these more intellectual objectors were opposed to participation in any war because they thought war a stupid barbarism and because they saw no reason why they should be compelled to fight against their wills. Some of them were merely opinionated young men; others were men of such high principles that they would have died rather than sacrifice them. All, by their comfortably "indispensable" critics in the Jingo press, were labelled "pasty-faces."

Among those who went to prison for his opinions was Bertrand Russell, who on the outbreak of the War was a lecturer at Trinity College, Cambridge (of which college he was a scholar); and possibly the most distinguished of all the Intellectual Objectors was Lytton Strachey. There were many others who similarly objected, and where they were men known in good society they were sometimes lucky enough to be found what was called "Alternative" service, which left them at large and with time to follow normal pursuits. Others were less fortunate. Most of those whose names were known in the literary world, and who did not serve in France or the East, remained alive, and augmented the number of their publications. But they, too, like the young officers represented by Owen and Sassoon, detested the turn things had taken. They had come into conflict with Authority, with Patriotism at its crassest; and, having by their action in resisting military service revealed obstinacy and moral courage, they decidedly had moved in opinion towards something like political anarchy. A kind of moral anarchy had already been brought into existence by other circumstances; and this was quickly rationalized. The way was being opened for that inter-war world of fruitless intolerance which found literary expression in the highly theorized work of the Intelligentsia of all countries.

iv. Bertrand Russell

"Even if the open windows of science at first make us shiver after the cosy indoor warmth of traditional humanizing myths, in the end the fresh air brings vigour, and the great spaces have a splendour of their own."

Bertrand Russell: What I Believe.

I HAVE no business to write about Bertrand Russell—even as a writer: I am quite incompetent to discuss mathematics—while I ignore his great mathematical collaborator, Whitehead; and yet I shall do so for the reason that Russell is known to me and Whitehead is not (I speak in two senses), and for the further reason that Russell has far more directly influenced the England of his time than Whitehead has done.

Bertrand Russell belongs to one of the oldest aristocratic families in England, which I learn has been traced back as far as the god Thor. His grandfather, the first Earl Russell, was third son of the sixth Duke of Bedford, and Bertrand Russell himself, although he does not use the title in connection with his work, is the third Earl. He was born in 1872. In person he is not very tall, is thin, has a good deal of grey hair, a long clean-shaven upper lip and receding chin, and in conversation wears at all times a pleasant smile which is neither dry nor indulgent but which has in it the elements of both dryness and indulgence. His eyes, which one immediately notices, are luminous and amused. They are very intelligent eyes, bright and clear: I think they may be blue, but if not blue they are a particularly lively grey. His voice has no volume; it is slightly donnish, a buzzing tone vocalized chiefly between the tip of the tongue and the front teeth (I seem to hear him saying "Yiss, yiss" without opening his mouth at all). He lectures well and interestingly but without zest; I presume in the way that men lecture at our older universities, rather conversationally. Several of his books consist of reprinted lectures. In talk he is considerate and friendly, does not laugh much (according to my recollection), but pays heed to what is said and is amused by it.

Russell is a mathematician, a sceptic, and a Socialist. He believes in the utmost freedom for every human being (and for some years ran a school for children who were supposed to do whatever they pleased); and at the time I now discuss he demanded, or I understood him to demand, that the will of the individual should be subordinated to the good of the community. Later still, of course, he has emerged a grand champion of the individual, with all the greater power because, philosophically, he is aware of all the arguments for the omnipotent State. His belief is that "the good life is one inspired by love and guided by knowledge," but when he defines love he is constrained to do so by means of the chilly word "benevolence," which in turn he defines as "an indissoluble combination of the two elements, delight and well-wishing." Ecstasy is rather outside his sympathy. In the same way, his definition of knowledge was at one time "scientific knowledge and knowledge of particular facts." Wisdom, which lies less in a knowledge of facts than in a true interpretation of them, is unprovable, and therefore at this time interested him less. Art, which is a mystery, was for him, but a department of metaphysics. His universe was a material universe; his ideal world at that time represented for me a tyranny of the reason.

These remarks must all be modified in the light of Russell's later and as I think profounder teaching, which has been in favour of a more coloured kindness than "benevolence," and certainly of a more humane attitude to the individual. But I think I have not seriously misrepresented the view he took at the time of the First World War. And I think I am still right in saying, as I did in the first edition of "The Georgian Literary Scene," that when presented with a moral question Russell judges it, as far as I can tell, with as much prejudice as you or I would show. He has a great dislike of parents, schoolmasters, policemen, and judges—all of whom represent for him embodiments of authority. He hates the English Public School system, on the ground (among others, perhaps) that it encourages Public School boys to imagine themselves better than other boys. I feel bound here to say that the men in England who now attack the Public School system show no sign of humility; their line seems rather to be that they are as much superior to ordinary Public School boys as ordinary Public School boys are superior to the rest of mankind. Perhaps this arrogance does not strike themselves: it is evident to others. In Russell's case there has been a contempt for the herd. Whether he knew of old that the herd was made up of individuals I cannot say: I suspect that, being a logician and mathematician, he regarded the herd as a dehumanized extension of the individual, and represented it in his mind by an algebraical sign. He changed. He saw what totalitarianism can do, and he did not like what he saw.

His importance to his age, and incidentally to this portion of my book, lies in the fact that he gave a lead to the "modns." He resisted the First World War upon intellectual grounds; he wanted to try the method of non-resistance to aggression, which he thought would disorganize the Kaiser's Germans. That showed that he was no realist; and that he was less psychologist than logician. But he was courageous, and those who thought him a crank and a danger to his country respected his courage. They put him in prison—a sure sign of respect. But his opinions could not be put in prison; and those men whom he had taught shared them. They, too, as I have related, opposed themselves to the government in an emergency; they, too, made their claim to be above the State's command. Several of them put into excellent literary form a protest against compulsion of any kind. In so doing, they were conscious of going against the spirit of their countrymen; and became in a sense philosophic rebels, justifying rebellion upon logical grounds. They began more and more eagerly to consider the different forms of ideal government which had been suggested in the course of history by Plato, More, Hobbes, Morris, and Wells. They looked abroad, to the Continent of Europe; where, since the First World War, many forms of government have been tried. Democracy as England knew it, which was in effect government by the illiterate herd, would no longer answer. It gave no scope to superior brains.

What alternatives were there to Democracy? The Russian revolution gave one answer; but Bertrand Russell did not feel satisfied with what he saw in Russia in 1920, and he said so. Bolshevism was too much like government by the herd to suit what I must repeat is essentially an aristocratic temper. The common good was still his aim; but it was a common good reached through such liberty for the individual that every individual was an aristocrat. No authority ought to impose an arbitrary will upon men; all men should work for the good life by following their own untrammelled desires. Somehow their desires, fulfilled, would provide happiness for all. The lines, limitlessly extended, never cross, because they are all straight, and all aspiring. Not England, where freedom is destroyed by the Christian doctrine of rewards and punishments; not Russia, where things, although different, are hardly any better; not China (though he visited China, and like other visiting English philosophers was impressed by the possibilities of pure philosophy); not hysterical America—but Utopia is the ideal. In Utopia alone, where men are automata, things will be better, more logical, freer from the horrors of man-made authority.

There speaks the thoroughly dissatisfied man; the man who, in common with so many of the intellectual Left, is out of harmony with his fellow-creatures and curiously distorts their good nature, their selfishness, their absorbingly interesting manifestations of virtue and cruelty, and their unruliness, into a malignant system by which Bertrand Russell is oppressed and to which he opposes an uncompromising resistance. Russell can give you his analysis of social ills and his plan for a new and better world with the utmost clearness. His extensions are all accurately calculated, his arguments all well expressed. He is entirely convincing. If you want proof, he offers proof. If you are prejudiced, he confirms prejudice. He seems to win you not by heady eloquence, but by sober facts, facts, facts. If those facts are your type of facts, he is incontrovertible; for his argument from the facts is the argument of a considerable logician.

But for some people, such as myself, to whom logic is the enemy of truth, Russell is an unconvincing pleader. I think I know why it is so in my own case. It is because, sympathizing with so many of his views and assumptions, I find him entirely unreal in his pictures of life. They do not correspond to anything familiar in my own experience. He speaks, it is true, of men and women—but not of men and women as I have ever known them—as strange persecuting brutes, judges, policemen, schoolmasters, parents; all oppressors. These people, I say to myself, have never been anything but kind to me; the men and women—and then suddenly I realize that when Bertrand Russell says "men and women" he is not in fact talking about men and women at all. He is thinking of them, not as souls, or as Brown, Jones, Swinnerton, or Horatio Bottomley, but as x and y, j and k. He does not know them, and cannot think of them, as anything else. He is incapable of knowing men and women. They are no more to him than tables and chairs; much less—until they put him in prison for what they regard as irrelevance—than the quantum theory.

When once you have realized that about Bertrand Russell, you have encountered his paralysing limitation as a social philosopher. His training in logic and mathematics has given him a wonderful intellectual instrument, but he can only think upon straight lines. For him, knowledge is knowledge of demonstrable facts. In a world full of unreason he can only deal with phenomena by treating them as forces. To him the word "magistrate" is the power to punish; "good" the fulfilment of a positive desire; "love" a combination of delight and well-wishing; of the abstract or the mystic he has no conception, for the impulsive and irrational no formula and no patience. The suggestion that a man may know everything and understand nothing would be meaningless to him. In that respect he is typical of the modern temper, dominated by a sense of the law of science and economics, proud of its intellect and its formulæ, but out of touch with men and women. Men and women, indeed, unless they are represented, for statistical purposes, as figures or letters, mean as much as that "Man Power" upon which strategists used to lecture during the First World War (rather less in the more mobile Second World War), which is as much as to say that they are counters. To such counters, hypothetical as they are, hypothetically ideal freedom may be easily granted. One can picture a world of counters and rules, highly satisfying to scientists. But it is not the world as it exists today; and when the desires of real men conflict with Bertrand Russell's desires these men become in his view a mob, and their common view a tyranny to which anarchy is the only possible response. This is the aristocratic attitude; and can be held today only by those who favour dictatorship and those who are doctrinaires. Russell, politically, is a doctrinaire. The fact that he is also a very brilliant writer and philosopher helped him to spread doctrinaire views throughout that small section of "alert, original men and women" to whom imagination was a lost faculty.

v. Roger Fry and Clive Bell

"Every company is differently circumstanced and has its peculiar cant and jargon; which may give occasion to wit and mirth within that circle, but would seem flat and insipid in any other."

Chesterfield: Letters to His Son.

WHEN we take a step forward to the æsthetic views of Blooms-bury we are in a different country from that inhabited by Bertrand Russell. We are not concerned with facts, but emotions, and not concerned with general emotions, but with something which Fry and Bell seem both inclined to specify as a particular emotion, the æsthetic. The history of æsthetics must remain outside our purview; but it is necessary to remark upon the fact that late in the nineteenth century certain artists revolted against what had previously been considered unbreakable rules in representa-tional art. Whistler and his colleagues, who became known as Impressionists, claimed to be "pure" artists, in the sense that they wanted not to go on painting in accordance with common knowledge of the nature of objects, but to present something else, the artist's unspoilt and unsophisticated vision of appearance. Put crudely, this claim was to the effect "I *know* a table has four legs; but to me it looks like a shiny pool in the midst of shadow, and that is how I shall represent it. Stand away, close your eyes, peer, and see if you don't find something new—eh?" They were in revolt against literalism. The fact that their revolt was but a stage in the progress of art need not concern us here.

What concerns us is that when once Whistler and his fellow-workers had established Impressionism those who followed them carried the ideas of Impressionism farther and farther until they managed altogether to substitute design for representation, and to paint pictures which were not so much accomplished portraits of recognizable objects as (superficially) blobs of colour com-municating inexplicable emotion to the beholder. The English public knew nothing, or very little, about the new movement among painters; for it occurred in France. But in 1911, a year after King George came to the throne, there was a sensation in London. An exhibition was held of paintings by some men who

D. H. LAWRENCE

JAMES JOYCE

were called "Post-Impressionists." Screams and catcalls filled the air; one hastened to observe the newest horrors and decry them; or—either with sincerity or in the pursuit of taste—one reverently prostrated oneself before a tremendous innovation in the æsthetic ideas of the age.

Post-Impressionism had its sensation, and then, instead of passing away, it stayed. This is an important fact. To Bloomsbury, all æsthetically "first-class" stuff, from Impressionism to the stream of consciousness and existentialism, has arrived by way of Paris; and this was a crucial moment for Bloomsbury. The man who by chance had been responsible for the gathering of those pictures which made the fuss was Roger Fry.

Now Roger Fry was all his life a painter and a critic of art. He was more than that; he was a truly creative intelligence. Born in 1866, he had taken a science degree at Cambridge, and had then turned his mind to the study of painting, which he followed in Paris after leaving King's College. Being, as I presume, of independent means, he was always free to follow his own bent; and being, unquestionably, a man of altogether exceptional taste and sincerity, he never collated his writings in order to make quite sure that each was strictly consistent with all the others. The consequence is that he really progressed with the years. He was one of the few men who learnt wisdom by experience. That is a sure sign of greatness. Not an absolutely first-class painter, he during the whole of his life interested himself in, and was never obsessed by, æsthetic theory, and his influence in that department of speculation upon men born in the eighties was of great and ever-increasing virtue.

He himself dated some part of his development from a reading of Tolstoy's "What is Art?" that powerful, sometimes profound, and absurd and self-confuting book, in which a moralist, after pointing out that art is a means of communicating the emotions, then established to his own satisfaction that the only proper purpose of art is the promotion of good deeds. Tolstoy's theory would set a lively tract above the greatest paintings, symphonies, and plays and novels ever written. Naturally Fry was much too subtle a person to be deceived by any such assumption; and so he took what was valuable in Tolstoy's essay and proceeded to the creation of his own æsthetic.

He was not the only man to be doing this round about the turn of the century. Croce, the Italian philosopher, who was born in the same year as Fry, elaborately divides the mind of man into two faculties, the imaginative and the rational, the first taking the form of æsthetic activity, the second of philosophy, and builds upon this a tremendous structure. Less ambitious than Croce, whom he much admired, Arthur Clutton-Brock, who must have been another contemporary, and a friend of Fry's, did not as far as I know systematize his æsthetic theory, but applied exceptional sensitiveness to the study of individual paintings and individual books. All three were active at the same time; and of the three Fry published least. When he said anything he said it modestly and briefly and with great persuasiveness. You can find most of his opinions charmingly and beautifully expressed in a single volume of essays called "Vision and Design."

Fry, at the coming of Post-Impressionism as a cult, was not prepared to write a book crystallizing its theories. But his friend Clive Bell was prepared and did in fact write a story which in its day was one of the most striking of all expanded pamphlets on an artistic theme. It was Bell's "Art" which provided a rallying point for all who in 1914 were for the new as against the old. It was a tremendously amusing book for anybody; really witty, really brilliant; quite different in tone and lack of charity from Fry's writings. Fry quietly and gravely sets out his idea, first that "Morality appreciates emotion by the standard of resultant action. Art appreciates emotion in and for itself," and second that:

> "I think we are all agreed that we mean by significant form something other than agreeable arrangements of form, harmonious patterns, and the like. We feel that a work which possesses it is the outcome of an endeavour to express an idea rather than to create a pleasing object. Personally, at least, I always feel that it implies the effort on the part of the artist to bend to our emotional understanding by means of his passionate conviction some intractable material which is alien to our spirit."

But Bell, using that same term, "significant form," was by no means as tentative. He had not only the business of defending an idea, but the enjoyable task of demolishing a million popular pictures. He leapt to it (as Mrs. Benson said Robert Hugh Benson leapt towards the Roman Catholic faith) "as a lover to his mistress." Not content with demolishing pictures, he scattered through his pages a little general literary knowledge, vivacious statements about himself as a student of music and archæology, about the Gothic, about Renaissance millionaires (they "could be vulgar and brutal, but they were great gentlemen"), and many other things. The effect now is much less impressive than it was in 1914, but Bell was younger then, and the critical world was less nobly aloof from poor mortals than its present demand for "the best only" can allow. He was a bright portent.

He was born in 1881, so that he must have been thirty-three when "Art" was published. In the book he first discussed the nature of art, then its relations with religion, history, and ethics, then its history, and finally Post-Impressionism as theory, practice and influence. But the important part of his work was precisely his attempt to define what it is in any work of art which establishes its claim to be art. He said:

> "Either all works of visual art have some common quality, or when we speak of 'works of art' we gibber. Everyone speaks of 'art,' making a mental classification by which he distinguishes the class 'works of art' from all other classes. What is the quality common and peculiar to all members of this class? Whatever it be, no doubt it is often found in company with other qualities; but they are adventitious —it is essential. There must be some one quality without which a work of art cannot exist; possessing which, in the least degree, no work is altogether worthless. What is this quality? What quality is shared by all objects that provoke our æsthetic emotions? What quality is common to Sta. Sophia and the windows at Chartres, Mexican sculpture, a Persian bowl, Chinese carpets, Giotto's frescoes at Padua, and the masterpieces of Poussin, Piero della Francesca, and Cézanne? Only one answer is possible—significant form. In each, lines and colours combined in a particular way, certain forms and relations of forms stir our æsthetic emotions. These relations and combinations of lines and colours, these æsthetically moving forms, I call 'Significant Form'; and 'Significant Form' is the one quality common to all works of visual art.'

The quality, the assertiveness, and the seriousness of Clive Bell are all indicated in that extract. You see the admirable and urgent talker who had hit upon a hypothesis completely satisfying to himself, and who had but to look about the world for illustrations of a theory to find them. Bell was much more of a dogmatist than Fry. He was compelled for the sake of his theory to restrict significant form to works of visual art; although it might be competent to a sceptic to say: "If this one quality is shared by buildings and pictures and carpets, surely it ought to be found in works of literature?" Bell would have agreed at once to that. But when he left pictures he was forced to change the terms of his theory and to allow dissentients to substitute "reality" or "rhythm" as explanatory words. Now I am not an æsthete; but I cannot help thinking that all these words are a substitute for what Barrie's Admirable Crichton called a 'Je ne sais quoi." We know that we receive some positive and delightful impression from what we style a work of art, and that a book which draws easy tears is a bad book; but while something in us demands that whatever we respond to emotionally (æsthetically) shall not be inane the word "form" has so often to change its significance that it threatens to be meaningless. That is, it is only an x, an unknown quantity; and whether we call it significant form or rhythm or reality we are meaning the same thing but have not yet found a completely satisfying definition. To me, the magic word is "originality," by which I do not indicate (as a bright young Cambridge student once supposed) the works of Rider Haggard, but the works of Shakespeare, the music of Mozart, or the paintings of Vermeer, all of which are shot through and through by the creative genius from which they have sprung. That is, I believe the emotion which we feel at contact with any work of art is the result of a personal communication made to us by the creator of that work: if no emotion is engendered, the artist has no communication to make to us, although he may be said perfectly to chatter to others.

I ought not to have embarked upon this naïf dissertation: it is a proof of Bell's stimulative quality. He wrote as a debater, clearly, emphatically; and if he had provoked no retorts he would have felt, I am sure, that his speech had not been a success. I do not mean, I must explain, that he was anything but ardent in his advocacy.

Clive Bell himself I should describe as a bubbler. He bubbled with high spirits and laughter. He was very pale, and his hair was once rather tawny. He slightly resembled Winston Churchill as a younger man. He had great vivacity of manner, and a nervous laugh was always trying to run away with him. He was extremely pleasant in conversation; but in written controversy had some of the traits of a Bloomsbury retaliator. His ripostes to critics, for example, in *The Athenæum*, for which he wrote under Murry's editorship, make painful reading, especially when he is in the wrong. But he was a man of lively mind, genuinely sensitive to the beautiful; and "Art" is both a milestone in æsthetic theory and a work of entertainment deserving well of the shrinkers from the dreary.

vi. Lytton Strachey

"What then is the charm, the irresistible charm, of Walpole's writings? It consists, we think, in the art of amusing without exciting. He never convinces the reason or fills the imagination, or touches the heart; but he keeps the mind of the reader constantly attentive and constantly entertained. . . . If we were to adopt the classification, not a very accurate classification, which Akenside has given of the pleasures of the imagination, we should say that with the Sublime and Beautiful Walpole had nothing to do, but that the third province, the Odd, was his peculiar domain."

Macaulay on Horace Walpole.

WHEN "Eminent Victorians" was first published, Lytton Strachey was known, outside Cambridge literary circles, only as the author of a much more than good little primer on French literature in the "Home University Library." The primer still holds its place as the best work of its kind, and perhaps the best book to be written by its author. But "Eminent Victorians" was so important in its novelty, its malice, and its vivid caricature of four celebrated figures —Dr. Arnold, Cardinal Manning, General Gordon, and Florence Nightingale—that it caused a furore.

Strachey was an extraordinary figure. As anybody may see from Henry Lamb's brilliant portrait in the National Portrait Gallery, he was fairly tall, but his excessive thinness, almost emaciation, caused him to appear endless. He had a rather bulbous nose, the spectacles of a British Museum bookworm, a large and straggly dark brown beard (with a curious rufous tinge); no voice at all. He drooped if he stood upright, and sagged if he sat down. He seemed entirely without vitality; and most people would have mistaken him for an elderly professor of languages who was trying to remember some grammatical rule which he had forgotten all about. Sad merriment was in his eye, and about him a perpetual air of sickness and debility.

Sick and sorry he may have been; but he had a sportive mind. If one could have seen behind that disguising beard, one might possibly have found that he was smiling. Certainly he was amused by anybody dead; he may have been amused by one yet alive. He had the power to read an official biography (that was what he had done in the case of his first four subjects), think about it, and produce what was not so much a portrait as a vivid impression. He knew how to exaggerate a trait and give it an air of nature, how to contrast one man with another, how to select that slightly ridiculous aspect which is in each one of us, and, by pressing gently upon our elbows, how to draw attention to a comic stranger just as that stranger was about to pass. He was always in time to snap the ridiculous.

But he did not confine himself to the ridiculous. It was said, when he began to collect material for his book on Queen Victoria, that he had an unsurpassed comic character for extended lampoon; but as the months passed, and Strachey found out more and more about the queen who was to be his subject, he found laughter fade before a growing respect, admiration, affection. That is the note of his "Queen Victoria," amused and respectful malice. He found her a queen after all, a real person surrounded by Teutonic artists, governesses, husbands, and uncles. At the others he laughed very continuously; but for Queen Victoria he developed something of a love.

When Strachey had finished writing about Queen Victoria he could not make up his mind what he would write about next. His favourite reading (easy reading, I think) was among the memoirs of the eighteenth century, Horace Walpole's chief among them, and the first half of the nineteenth century; and here he found material for admirable brief sketches. But a large subject, one fit to follow that of a queen, did not suggest itself. He played for some time with the notion that he could write a new biography of Charles Darwin; but that notion came to nothing. At last—I know not upon what impulse—he carried his mind back to another queen, and one who had been as great in her day as Victoria, perhaps yet greater than Victoria. Why he should have chosen Elizabeth, queen of a time of which his knowledge was—by comparison with the eighteenth century—so small, can only be told by somebody who knew him. But the book he wrote, successful though it was in the matter of popular reception, was in the larger sense a failure. It has few friends.

It was the last long book he was to attempt, and for the rest of his life he dwelt again upon familiar themes, such as Voltaire, of whom he made such a hero in his "Landmarks in French Literature." I presume that his strength was ebbing, and that he could no longer venture upon ambitious work; if, indeed, it was not apparent to him that the short sketch was peculiarly his *métier*.

It was his *métier* because he had an admirable gift for the picturesque, a quick rather than a powerful mind, and a habit, not unlike the romantic novelist's habit, of dramatizing every scene he described. He could browse through a book of memoirs and then sketch the writer of those memoirs; a lightning sketch such as one used to see executed in music-halls by clever artists with charcoal and colossal sheets of paper. Instantly recognizable, nose, hat, strut, haw-haw, and baggy trousers or sharp-pointed collar. When Strachey's first drawings were made, the contrast between Manning and Newman was just such as a dexterous artist would choose—light and dark, the world and the spirit, vigour and weakness. When his last elaborate drawing, of the Elizabethan era, was attempted, the contrasts in a rapid narrative were necessarily so numerous that they had to be more and more heightened, and in the end "Elizabeth and Essex" is more like costume drama than history. No wonder Virginia Woolf, in a list of half a dozen approved Georgian novelists, included Strachey. Though he had not the power to invent stories, he loved effects, and he could get them.

Some of the best of his effects were obtained in the short and excellent "Landmarks in French Literature." There he was completely master of the material he wished to use. He could explain and defend Racine against English distaste for the neo-classic, could rejoice in the badinage of Marivaux and the brilliance of Diderot, and could to perfection picture dramatically the life and person of Voltaire, for whom he had great laughing admiration. Indeed, the eighteenth-century world of wits and poets and letter-writers was his natural element. He knew it, so to speak, at first hand, in all those letters of Walpole and Madame de Sévigné, the Marquise du Deffand, Madame de Grafigny, Madame d'Epinay, and the rest; in the Memoirs of Saint-Simon, the "Confessions" of Rousseau, and a hundred more. He knew it at second hand in the "Causeries du Lundi" of Sainte-Beuve and that string of French inquirers to whom we owe such curious and interesting glimpses into the manners of a past age. To a man of education and some leisure, a taste for wit and a love of oddity, this whole literature of the personal is an

inexhaustible store of delight; and that was what it proved to Strachey. Though he wrote more ambitiously, he never, I think, wrote so much from his own enthusiasm as he did in "Landmarks in French Literature."

Sainte-Beuve, I shall continue to believe, was the prime literary inspiration of Strachey's life. That does not mean that he copied Sainte-Beuve. He brought to such memoirs as he wrote his own characteristic manner of approach. But his inspiration was from the French. The inspiration of Bloomsbury was always from the French. Roger Fry and Clive Bell owed much to their study in Paris; Strachey to his reading in French memoirs; Virginia Woolf to encouraging acquaintance, at least, with Proust's endless master-piece of psychologizing and memory; T. S. Eliot to his reading in French poets who for the most part are unintelligible to English readers. And in Strachey's case, particularly, the brevity and illuminatingness of Sainte-Beuve's portraits was a clear call to parallel but of course dissimilar work. He had wit and malice enough to point every likeness; he had a clear, if not profound, sense of character; a pen free and vivid. To these obvious literary gifts he brought the temperament of a physically feeble person who could not endure the boisterousness of aggressive men and therefore sat aside and ridiculed it.

He was on the side of the weak, those who could not fight for themselves. He shrank from the loud and efficient, the smug and successful. He did not like them, and could not crush them; but he could think of all sorts of amusing things to say which would discredit them. He disliked the force of Cardinal Manning and Arnold of Rugby; he felt that Florence Nightingale was something of a busybody, one of these go-getters; he resented the industry of the Prince Consort, the solemnity of those Germans who came to the English Court and held their sway. They were all serious, and although he did not altogether mean to misrepresent them he saw them as butts and allowed his eye to choose only those facts—even if other facts contradicted those of his choice—which helped his ridicule. This reaction from the inconvenient resulted from per-sonal inability to cope with a world apparently (I mean, in his eyes) given over to the strong and vulgar. He had not the ecstasies of the eremite; but he had something of the spirit that drives a man to sit alone in a cave for the sake of spiritual peace. Unlike the eremite, he had a very curious, rather donnish, interest in the human species, and if men were dead he could laugh at them with a good deal of satisfaction. Quite half the pleasure snobs obtain from Strachey is due to the fact that he amuses them at the expense of others. Others, it may be said, with virtues of character which are out of reach of the smartly insincere.

His deficiences arise, possibly, from a lack of intellectual intercourse with men of different breeding and culture from himself. He did not care for such men. All his work was taken from books, and not from nen. He was a bookworm and a talker with bookworms, a male bluestocking. When he left off laughing and tried seriously to sympathize he became slightly sentimental, and fell into a falsity indicated either by tremendously careful, cat-stepping use of language or a kind of writing sacred to romantic novelists. Therefore he preferred to keep his subjects ar arm's length; and so by holding them up—how small they grow when so held!—exhibited them very prettily to our eyes. Homunculae to a man!

He did this with great skill. He did not pretend that he had created his characters out of nothing, or out of a deep research into archives, but, with an appearance of honesty which F. A. Simpson much damaged in two powerful articles published by "The Cambridge Review" and "The Spectator," he gave us the material from which he has drawn information. His idol was Horace Walpole, and his ideal life was that led by eighteenth-century ladies and gentlemen who had little to do but gather together and produce their well-rehearsed wit. He could picture the Regency, for that was a sophisticated era in some respects not unlike our own, and almost voluptuously documented with authentic letters and diaries. But the multitude and splendour of the Elizabethan age were inexplicable by any rules learnt at Cambridge; the Victorians were altogether too solemn in their virtues; and of what happened in everyday homes he knew, and wished to know, nothing at all.

vii

THE Stracheyan method had its imitators. Clever writers observed his success in puppetry and his use of the discovery that all sorts of things happened at the same moment in time; and having noticed both these facts they jumped into Stracheyan biography as wasps jump into jars of beer. Their sense of chronology was poor, and there came a time when they said recklessly that certain things had happened simultaneously which in fact had been separated by many years, and were rightly exposed as quacks. That whole simultaneous action business was a trick, and Strachey had used it as much as it could be used. It was a facile way of stippling in background or chiaroscuro. Furthermore, the debunking biography became a craze. Writers set out, with none of Strachey's skill, to make game of famous men. They took their man, called him throughout "Mr." or by some Christian name which struck them as ludicrous, and in showing off their own cleverness took all the character out of him. Great men were butchered to make a smart suburban holiday. It is a great injustice to Strachey to associate him with such deplorable guying. His success, however, was so great that it was an encouragement to others.

It was an encouragement, possibly yo Philip Guedalla, who lived no nearer Bloomsbury than Bayswater and no nearer to quizzing Cambridge than romantic Oxford. He began as poet, parodist, and historian; attacking reputation with a serious educational book on "The Partition of Europe" between 1715 and 1915. But he was very ambitious; and in the intervals of standing for Parliament in the interests of a moribund Party, he proceeded to biography. At first he was content with quite brief essays; but he grew bolder, and with an able, laborious and over-jewelled gift for portraiture carried on the method of slightly ribald biography until he reached the Duke of Wellington. Now the Duke of Wellington was, without doubt, a great character. The memoirs of Greville, Croker, and Creevey, to name only three of the most famous men who make their day gossip again for our benefit, constantly provide delicious examples of the Duke's speech; his dealings with a lady who tried to frighten him are celebrated. One might have expected Guedalla to take the easy course of making him a figure of fun. To his credit he preferred to write an official and well-documented book which was far better than anything else he had attempted. It was both a portrait of a great man and an historical account of a great soldier's campaigns abroad and at home. I cannot say that it is wholly free from that straining after wit which was Guedalla's weakness; for it is not. Guedalla was a deliberate inventor of *bons mots*. He seemed to produce them by an elaborate process, to polish and repeat them, but never quite to achieve the necessary triumph of wit, apparent spontaneity. Thus he did injustice to his real talent, which was for work.

An honourable exception to the fancy biographical school is F. A. Simpson, whose two volumes dealing with the life of Napoleon III are among the best books of historical biography to be published in our day. The first of them, written when the author was only five-and-twenty, is "The Rise of Louis Napoleon"; the second "Louis Napoleon and the Recovery of France." Although a Fellow and Lecturer of Trinity College, Cambridge, F. A. Simpson belongs neither to Bloomsbury nor Bayswater; his exposure of Strachey's less than perfect honesty in dealing with authorities was that of a fastidious scholar; and I mention him here because otherwise I could pay no tribute to an exceptional gift.

viii. Women

"The women are splendid."

War-time Saying.

Now in my earlier remarks on the subject of 1914–18 war-time influences, I said nothing about one of these, and this one among the most important of all. It was not because I had forgotten it, but because I thought I would wait until I reached this part of the chapter. And the influence is that of the so-called emancipation of women. Prior to the First World War, while women had for nearly a hundred years been making a steady advance (with the aid of the more just-minded men) towards something approaching political equality with men, they had not absolutely succeeded in attaining their object. In the election years of 1906 and 1910, and of course in the years between those years and after them, the Suffrage movement had gained ground and had been making itself a nuisance in a number of ways to the more obstinate among males. It had the support, I think I may say, of at least two kinds of men—those who cared for justice and those who hoped, as Bernard Shaw hoped, that if women were given the vote, and allowed to do some reasonable work, they would cease to be obsessed by the notion of love, and would become sensible. But it had no support from all who believed that women were a mystical cross between angels and drudges.

At last, in or around 1910, women really did take the most violent steps to attract notice to what they believed to be their importance in the world of men. They began to break windows, and burn letter-boxes, and cause other rumpuses. They were told that they did themselves no good by these violences, since men could always be more violent than women; and many women were also greatly distressed by the violences and disowned them as unwise and harmful exhibitions. But what always happens in England is that when men are sufficiently worried they yield; this is because they have a passion for peace, which is sometimes called a love of justice and sometimes the British Genius for Compromise, but which, as many women know, is nothing but a hatred of fuss. "Anything for a quiet life" is the English motto; that is why there are so many Scots and Irish leaders in our land. And I think that probably the Suffragettes would in any case have won the day. They did not succeed in winning the day, because the First World War came, and the whole surface of life was convulsed.

I shall no doubt be contradicted for saying it, but I have always believed that the majority of women enjoy war. That is, they have an insatiable relish for sensation. Not the finest women, not the most intelligent women, but women in mass. Also, our two great wars have given all English women an overwhelming sense of emancipation from everything the Victorians insisted that they should be and do. They no longer stay at home, waiting for children or spinsterhood. They go out and meet life with the utmost daring.

In almost every human activity they have shown that with equal opportunities they can do as good a job as men; and it was customary during the First World War, when this truth became apparent, for every newspaper in England at least once a day to print upon its own account or as a quotation from some political leader the words: "The women are splendid." They then earned, and were given, the vote for which they had long been agitating.

But the vote was only a symbol; what women wanted was much more than a say in the election of Parliamentary candidates. At first they wanted a new standard of chastity for men; they wanted equality in the matter of divorce (that a husband should be divorceable on grounds of misconduct alone, whereas previously a wife had had to prove either desertion or cruelty); they wanted equality of pay; and many other things. Over a long term of years more and more women had been receiving a scholastic education in advance of anything they had known in the greater part of the nineteenth century, and all these educated women were in conflict with what seemed to them to be the vested interests of men in the Professions. The women who demanded Rights, for the most part, were educated women. The others, the lorry-drivers and the tram-conductors, were happy-go-lucky enough, and only took the chances that offered; but the educated women were in this position, that without a change in the status of women they were doomed to waste their education upon domestic life or futile drudgery as subordinates. Something could be said, they thought, for Oriental notions of the hareem; but nothing could be said for the incessant humiliation of the educated women who had nothing to do.

In the First World War, women naturally brought their education to a better market. In literature, with which I am concerned (for these remarks have been but a brief explanation), the War-time gave a great opportunity to educated women. The male writers left to function in England were those too old for military service, those who were physically unfit, and the intellectual objectors. And as the weary months went by, more and more women presented the country with books of one sort and another. Of course there had always been women-writers; but these women-writers were different. They were women-conscious; and because of this their influence upon the kind of books written and read was all-important. Moreover, they and the intellectual objectors had usually been intensively educated. This, too, was new. Literature in England during and since the First World War has thus been largely produced by educated persons; and even novelists have been less concerned with portraying the simplicities of young love and the strangeness of circumstance than with exhibiting their own fastidiousness, scathingness, and erudition. Chief among the women of the age, and, since every class must have a rallying point much vaunted by enthusiastic cheer-leaders, idol of them all, was Virginia Woolf. It is with Virginia Woolf that I now end my chapter on Bloomsbury.

ix. Virginia Woolf

"It always happened that when I awoke like this, and my mind struggled in an unsuccessful attempt to discover where I was, everything would be moving round me through the darkness: things, places, years. My body . . . would make an effort to construe the form which its tiredness took as an orientation of its various members, so as to induce from that where the wall lay and the furniture stood, to piece together and to give a name to the house in which it must be living. Its memory, the composite memory of its ribs, knees, and shoulder-blades offered it a whole series of rooms in which it had at one time or another slept; while the unseen walls kept changing, adapting themselves to the shape of each successive room that it remembered, whirling madly through the darkness."

Proust: Swann's Way: translated by C. K. Scott-Moncrieff.

IT was Clive Bell who said "great writers, like Dostoevsky, Joseph Conrad, and Virginia Woolf"; and I now wonder whether Bell would entirely hold by his words. Dostoevsky and Conrad, although still as good as ever they were, are démodé, and few Bloomsbury-ish men would like to link their names with that of any newer idol. But I quote the phrase because as far as I know it was the first public claim ever aggressively made on behalf of Virginia Woolf. The fact that Clive Bell was Virginia Woolf's brother-in-law gave it a fine domestic loyalty, but must not be taken as indicating bias. Bell was courageous. Where many men are timid in making claims on behalf of their friends or on behalf of any writers at all, he braved ridicule as he braved challenge. The time had come, he felt, to speak up. "Great writers, like Dostoevsky, Joseph Conrad, and Virginia Woolf," he said. Virginia Woolf then had published only one novel, "The Voyage Out."

She continued, apart from her immediate circle, to be nothing more than a faintly recognized name until "Jacob's Room" in 1922 and "Mrs. Dalloway" in 1925 attracted more general attention; but it was in 1929, when she published her feminist tract, "A Room of One's Own," that she enjoyed real celebrity for the first time. Having long had the support of Bloomsbury, which was very propagandist, she now had the support of all educated women, to whom she had given a bible.

Virginia Woolf was the daughter of Sir Leslie Stephen, who edited the "Dictionary of National Biography" and wrote many essays of varying interest and accuracy upon the writers and philosophers of his country, especially those of the eighteenth century, in whom he took great interest. Stephen was a mountaineer, and the friend of George Meredith and others of the literary men of his day; and his daughter was thus from her earliest years familiar with a bookish atmosphere. She married in 1912 Leonard Woolf, a Cambridge man who had for some years previously been in the Ceylon Civil Service, and in 1915 she published her first novel.

It was a novel unremarkable for incident, but was full of conversation, and—for this way of writing continued to grow upon the author—it was full of a sense that when speaking or when thinking people were not exclusively occupied with a single subject. They said and thought one thing; but they also thought, and did not say, another. Their thoughts were apparently inconsecutive: it has never been quite possible for any person to identify that liaison between thought and thought which is too rapid to be caught in action. Still, however, both "The Voyage Out" and "Night and Day," which in 1919 followed it, were recognizably attempts to spin from the author's preoccupations coherent and continuous narratives. With "Jacob's Room" there was a change, and with two later books, "Mrs. Dalloway" and "To the Lighthouse," narrative gave place to what must be considered Virginia Woolf's distinctive contributions to the modern English novel. These were curious weavings of impression and memory, the comings and goings of whimsical thoughts and fancies, sometimes from the moment, sometimes from yesterday, sometimes from long ago. Distastes for other individuals arose as if they were blown suddenly by a gust of wind; associations spread and narrowed, speculations jumped from nowhere, phrases came and went. A constant twitter of words and notions dominated these books. They specialized in disconnectedness.

To minds used to the solid four-square of traditional English fiction, the building up of a practicable *milieu*, the history of a family, or a pair of families, the plain long formal description of faces, clothes, and circumstances, these novels by Virginia Woolf had one of two appearances. Either they were eccentric and wrongheaded, or they were wonderful novelties, works of genius. Virginia Woolf herself tried to assist readers by publishing, first of all as an article in *The Nation* and then as a pamphlet, an essay challenging something said previously as to the nature of the novel by Arnold Bennett. Bennett had described as a fault in (I think unspecified) Georgian novelists excessive interest in details at the expense of characterization; and in his downright way had said "the foundation of good fiction is a character-creating, and nothing more." Henry James, as I have shown earlier, would hardly have contradicted him. But Virginia Woolf represented a different school. She was forced to defend her own practice; and in the factious manner of Bloomsbury could not answer Bennett without counter-attack. She therefore charged him with being quite antediluvian, and accused his work, and that of Wells and Galsworthy, of being "already a little chill." She maintained that the Georgian novelists were pursuing essential character, a will-o'-the-wisp, simply, for truth's sake, showing the reaction of a human being to its surroundings. Thereby, it appeared, they were doing something really exciting, which distinguished them from their forerunners. Her list of Georgian novelists, published later, contained the names of James Joyce, E. M. Forster, Lytton Strachey, D. H. Lawrence, and T. S. Eliot; that is to say, three novelists, one biographer, and a poet. These men (to whom must be added herself) were re-creating the English novel.

It was a most ingenious claim. As to Lytton Strachey I think it is unproven and unprovable, for his characters were made up, not of essentials, but of seizable lineaments; as to the other writers I have still to speak, and shall do so in the next chapter. But the claim is very important in considering the work of Virginia Woolf herself, because in that work more than in the work of any of the writers she named, excepting T. S. Eliot, the tottering pursuit of the will-o'-the-wisp continued to the last. Objective reality had little importance; her interest was almost solely in the subjective. But not in what Aldous Huxley says is the only thing he cares about, the *Psyche*; rather in the flutterings of mood and fancy. She took a person and showed us the jumping of thought that went on all the time in that person's consciousness. Having done this, she passed to another person. And since she introduced us to several persons, who all jumped in the same way, it is fair to assume that she had in her own mind some clear conception of these persons as separate individualities and believed herself to be successfully rendering them as individuals. That is not my impression of them. Nor has the quiver and shake of their thoughts, for me, any deeper revelation than that of a kind of mental sickness, the sort of jumble that people have in their heads when they are going under or emerging from an anæsthetic. At such times, I agree, they are not very distinctly themselves. I should make this assertion of vagueness regarding "Mrs. Dalloway," "To the Lighthouse," and "The Waves." Of these books I should say, also, that they are extremely well-written, and full of ingenuities, the last-named full of beauty. "Orlando," also, which is similarly very ingenious, is exceedingly interesting as narrative, and is easily comprehensible, but as far as I know does not pretend to be a novel. It is a calculatedly original work (but calculated originality is for me a contradiction in terms).

Some readers of Virginia Woolf apparently obtained a satisfaction from her work which they did not find elsewhere. For me, this work seems very clever, very ingenious, but creatively unimportant. It was done—as so much modern un-creative writing is done—with the superficial wits; there was nothing in it for those who did not pride themselves upon intellectual superiority to the herd. There was nothing in it which was not offered to current middle-class culture, the culture in which—post-Freud, post-Jung, and so on—all our younger minds were preoccupied by self-analysis. With the cleverness of young minds, they recognized in Virginia Woolf's characters leaps and mental states familiar to themselves, and in that sense, making allowance for the difference of class, did no more than poor people do when they read novelettes.

What Arnold Bennett meant, I feel sure, in charging Georgian writers with ignoring the first essential of novel-writing, the creation of character, was that in the novels he had in mind (let us say that one of them was a book by Virginia Woolf), there was no person seen and presented, as they say, in the round. In a book about Mrs. Brown, there was, for the reader, no Mrs. Brown. Virginia Woolf replied in her pamphlet that in life itself there never was a Mrs. Brown, only a "Mrs. Brownness," the essential something which to Mrs. Brown was all that Mrs. Brown knew when she went about her day's life. She claimed to be presenting not Mrs. Brown, but Mrs. Brownness. But in order to discover the Mrs. Brownness Virginia Woolf was forced to write solely of ruminative or introspective persons, and when she had carried her exploration to the four minds in "The Waves" she had reached as far as that particular method would take her. There were four poetic somethings; but they all thought alike. The explanation was that Virginia Woolf was an impressionist; a catcher at memory of her own mental vagaries; not a creator. She was aware, too, of many of the latest scientific facts and theories about human beings, but she was unable to imagine, to create, a human being who was not exactly like herself. "I can't imagine what goes on behind faces," she said. This meant that she was forced to turn inward. Too sensitive, too intelligent, too playful and wayward in mind to have the emotional depth of an imaginative person, she was as much at fault as the realist, in thinking that if she chased every detail she would reveal truth. Jane Austen was wiser.

And since I have mentioned Jane Austen, I must again refer to the charming book, "A Room of One's Own," which is a mingling of feminism with reverie and invention. In this book Virginia Woolf traced, as well as the available material would allow her to do, the history of the education of women. Saying nothing of the Pastons, she looked through English literature and letters for news of the way in which through the centuries women learned to write and then, in time, came to write books and plays. She said nothing of several people who would possibly have been unhelpful to her examination, such as Maria Edgeworth, Mrs. Inchbald, Mrs. Gaskell, and Mrs. Trollope; but came to the conclusion that until a woman had a private income of five hundred pounds a year and a room of her own of which she could lock the door she could not hope to be free to write good books—or do anything else. For the writing of good books, says Virginia Woolf, needs leisure, and no woman in the past had had any life of her own, neither liberty nor opportunity to do what she would best do.

With the argument of this piece I have no concern, for I am not here discussing feminism (I only object specifically to the statement that no genius ever came from the working class, because even if genius is confined by Virginia Woolf to literature there is always D. H. Lawrence, who never had a room of his own); but with the assumption that fiction is only to be written by educated women I must deal because it has a larger application. It was the view of Virginia Woolf, and those who thought as she did, that no literary work done by any but highly educated persons of their own kind of culture can or should be interesting. This was educational snobbery, which in Bloomsbury succeeded the social snobbery of pre-Georgian days.

Chapter Fourteen

POST-FREUD

MAY SINCLAIR, DOROTHY RICHARDSON, REBECCA WEST,
E. M. FORSTER, D. H. LAWRENCE, JAMES JOYCE

i

"In our modern mythology, Custom, Circumstance, and Heredity are the three Fates that weave the web of human life."

May Sinclair: Audrey Craven (1897).

A WORD as to the title of this chapter. It is a convenient term by which I indicate certain novelists who interested themselves inquiringly or with the vehemence of genius in abnormal psychology, in psycho-pathology. I do not mean that they were all necessarily Freudians; but all were aware of a certain progress in medical theory and were affected by this knowledge in writing about their fellow-creatures. In the case of May Sinclair it may be said that the chief interest of her work lay in its gradual adaptation to successive modern psychological conceptions. In 1897, when she published "Audrey Craven," she was content to picture a silly woman who made a fool of herself; but as soon as she could do so she went father than that into a sort of psychological realism, and took interesting steps in the novel for which she has not received full credit.

If one compares a psychological novel by Henry James, whom we took as the starting point of the present book, with a psychological novel written in the Georgian period (following the stages represented by Violet Hunt, Jessie Leckie Herbertson, Ethel Colburn Mayne, May Sinclair, Rebecca West, Virginia Woolf, and her successors—but the same trip might be made through the works of American writers with even greater interest), the differences in assumption will be found almost startling. For one thing, the gentle discreetness of James has disappeared; its place has been taken by outspoken declaration and a much more professional vocabulary. For another, and as an accompaniment to the vocabulary, explanations of personal vagary have ceased to be romantic and have become medical. An eccentric woman who in James's eyes (or at any rate in a novel by James) was incalculable, material for endless and to the author fascinating speculation, was given a series of symptoms which could be checked by any quasi-pathologist. If she suffered from hallucination or hysteria, our novelists could tell us all we needed to know about the explicatory repressions and complexes which were at the root of her trouble. If they refrained from using these very words, it was in mercy, and because they were novelists still, who preferred to suggest rather than diagnose. But it is clear that the psychological novel became a more formidable affair than it was; and, as Grape-Nuts packets used to say, "there is a reason."

The reason can be expressed quite simply. After King George V ascended the throne English novelists became more book-learned. They no longer groped by the light of their own incandescence, but had the aid of handbooks, experts, and considerable quantities of statistics. I do not know what Henry James would have thought of Havelock Ellis's "Studies in the Psychology of Sex": I do know that the six volumes of that magnum opus are not in general circulation in England, and that if one bought a copy one was thereafter pursued for a time with offers of Beautiful Art Books relating to the Female Form Divine which one's specialist bookseller also had in stock. But to all modern psychological novelists Havelock Ellis's books, once familiar, are out of date. They were the first extensive studies of phenomena which are now freely discussed; but when King George V became king they were not freely discussed. In those days the perfect limit of comprehensive psychological knowledge was contained in an extraordinary book by a young German suicide named Otto Weininger. This book was called "Sex and Character."

The Germans and Austrians long led the field in the study of mental processes. They still lead the field. While American students, and in a lesser degree French students, made considerable investigations in psychology, the English did not do so. Only in or around the year 1910 did innocents of the kind known to myself—young men able to read the weekly reviews of that time—first learn, still through Havelock Ellis, of the existence of Sigmund Freud; and only in 1913 did we discover that his great book, "The Interpretation of Dreams," translated by Brill, was available for consumption. Brill's translation was of the third German edition. We had hitherto passed very little beyond those three Fates which May Sinclair declared in 1897 were the dominating myths of modernity—Custom, Circumstance, and Heredity. We now learned of the Conscious, the Preconscious, and the Unconscious. We learned of Psychic Censorship and Repressions; the Ego, the Super-Ego, and the Id. We learned, in effect, the language of Psycho-Analysis, now a jargon.

Really to understand what Freud and his fellow-analysts teach one should be an unremitting student of psycho-analysis. I am not such a student, and I cannot pretend to give a reliable account of this very fascinating and suggestive branch of investigation. I am still in the simple stages, where the picture of our normal conscious

life as but a small part of our full mental life is a sufficiently delightful concept to provoke meditation. But psycho-analysis as taught
by Freud, Jung, and their successors is very much more than that.
It is a great system of pessimistic philosophy. From Frued's first
definition of a dominating human urge, which he calls the "libido,"
as the sexual instinct, through a point at which it became a general
principle of "pleasure," to later definition by Jung which gave it
kinship with our old friends the Life Force and the Élan Vital,
psycho-analysis has grown into a very intricate affair which no
amateur can criticize. All the average person learns—when he does
not see red, and with wild cries of "Filth! Obscenity!" fall into a
fever of denunciation—is that the child is a sensual being who
gratifies simple impulses until, as the result of discipline or awareness
that certain acts are unpopular, he forcibly represses them. The
average person learns that these repressions seriously influence the
after-life of each child, and sometimes produce mental disease. He is
told how the conscious life of an individual is affected by these
early influences (and even by ante-natal influences and racial influences), and how there is a constant activity of mind and instinct
of which we become aware for the most part in dreams or with the
aid of the psycho-analyst.

What more the average person learns depends upon himself.
The divisions and definitions of psycho-analysis are almost innumerable. Whether we hear of the child's response to its parents
or its own Ego, Super-Ego, or Id, or whether we plunge into
symbolism or a species of fatalism, we shall discover unlimited
possibilities in this extraordinary revelation of the mind. No wonder
Freud has influenced modern thought to an incalculable extent.
Merely to have given us that highly imaginative picture of the Unconscious perpetually struggling and intriguing—particularly by the
agency of dreams—to get through the jealous guard of the Preconscious into the Conscious would have assured him of a place
among the magicians. Though he left physiological causes almost
entirely out of account, and though he was for that reason much
criticised by physiologists, he built up an entire system to explain
human behaviour. He was an artist who was at the same time an
unshockable scientist, and whatever may be the defects of his system
it has a fundamental simplicity which has violently impressed the
world.

Of his fellow-analysts, Jung and Alder, who have had a lesser
but considerable influence, something must be said. I know nothing
of Adler, excepting that he is a practical physician who has added
more than one suggestive theory to the body of psycho-analysis,
including one which he calls the "impulse of aggression" or com-
pensatory fortification of the weakest aspect in ourselves; but by

Jung I was at first quite confounded. Whether the original writing was turgid or the translation was at fault, I cannot tell. I now think Jung was a very great man indeed; but I doubt whether Freud was completely master of his own theories.

It would be too severe upon my first subjects—for I must now return to the Georgian Literary Scene—excellent though they are in their respective ways, to confront them with the whole theory and practice of psycho-analysis. Though they must have been affected, as all modern writers have been, by some knowledge of Freudian theory, they were none of them avowed experts in that theory, and I would rather deal with them as novelists and experimenters in techniques. It was necessary at the beginning of the chapter to tell why I had used the title Post-Freud; and the application of that title to the three later writers will be more explicit. E. M. Forster, to take the first of these writers, dealt more than once with morbid psychology; D. H. Lawrence discovered for himself, independently of Freud and as it proves without kindliness to Freud, a theory of the Unconscious; and James Joyce, whether he was ever a Freudian or not, belonged "definitely" (that is still a popular word) to a Europe aware of inhibition as a vice.

May Sinclair, Dorothy Richardson, and Rebecca West were all typical writers, each of her own generation and each perfectly alive to the movement of ideas as they affected that generation. I shall now speak of the three, and before doing so ought to say that the conjunction of their names does not indicate a grouping by sex or a wish to identify one with either or both of the others.

ii. May Sinclair, Dorothy Richardson, Rebecca West

THE eldest of these ladies was very prolific, and not all of her work was in one key or upon one level of quality. She had her early manner, in which she wrote about not very agreeable people who married or failed to marry, and who did not rise above a well-described mediocrity. In 1904 she had her first success with a very long and leisurely novel about a young bookseller's assistant or librarian who was also a poet, and this novel was called "The Divine Fire." It is hard now to recover the powerful impression created by this book, so much has fashion in the novel changed; but I remember how at the time of its publication the most intelligent and sophisticated man known to me shook his head over May Sinclair's knowledge of what a man felt like when he was drunk. My friend said, gravely: "She knows too much." This comment, being authentic, seems to me unerringly to call up past standards and indicate something of what

May Sinclair helped to do for the novel. If in 1904 a woman was bold who portrayed drunkenness in a tale, she is a portent.

May Sinclair was to go farther still. She was to be the first, I think, who wrote of the Brontë sisters from a psychological point of view, and she did this, not only in a book about them, but in a novel, "The Three Sisters," which may have been suggested by reflection upon their story as it was seen by a modern woman. Her method here was less ample than it had been in "The Divine Fire"; it was more excitedly emotional. But in 1922 she wrote a book called "The Life and Death of Harriet Frean" which was a genuine advance in a particular form of impressionistic realism then first attracting notice. This short novel, which told the story of a woman from childhood until her death under anæsthetic, was significant. It skimmed the cream, as it were, of a life; there were no redundancies, no comments, only such selected details as contributed to our calm knowledge of the way things happened to one ordinary woman. For that reason, its brief simplicity, "The Life and Death of Harriet Frean" is worthy of remembrance. It is very nearly medical.

May Sinclair, besides writing a philosophic "Defence of Idealism," experimented further in later studies of male characters, and one of her earlier books, "Tasker Jevons," a rather severe portrait of a successful author who may have been a combination of two of her male contemporaries, unkindly seen, had its virtues; but none of these books has quite the effectiveness of "Harriet Frean," and it was on account of that book that she took her place among moderns.

It is possible that she derived some inspiration in writing it from a curious work of which ten volumes were published (as "chapter volumes") under the general title "Pilgrimage." This work was a biography of one Miriam; and in the history of modern novels it has a place entirely its own. The author, Dorothy Richardson, invented a new kind of impression in literature. She did not dodge, as Virginia Woolf did, among the past and present moods and memories of her heroine, but with extremely dexterous selectiveness managed to tell a continuous life-story as if it were in progress under our eyes. But so exact and indeed endless is her recollection that instead of compressing the life of Miriam into 184 pages, as May Sinclair compressed that of Harriet Frean, she made every few weeks or months of it fill three hundred pages and could seemingly have gone on for ever.

This was a feat. Still more of a feat is the fact that Dorothy Richardson managed to persuade the reader that she could not possibly have been any more succinct. There was no haste in the ten volumes, but there was no padding either. They were all full to the brim of what seemed like actual history. That is just the doubt that assails my mind in contemplating "Pilgrimage": I find it excellent as impressionism—tones, looks, turns of speech all as they might, as they *must*, have been. But if I am asked whether I consider such impressionism anything more than a marvellous feat of memory, of reproduction, I must answer that somewhere between volume one and volume ten there comes a moment in which one wishes that Miriam had died young, or that she had moved through life at a less even and ample pace. The whole question of "importance" in fiction seems to arise.

I know well that this is a view not held by at least one critic for whom I have a respect, who has celebrated Dorothy Richardson's book in unmeasured language, saying that "in all the literary work of our time none retains so high, so rare, so curious a value"; but there are limits to the curiosity of man, and for me "Pilgrimage" passes beyond them. One is overwhelmed by the multitude of little things which Miriam noticed in the course of her journey through life. They do not compose into a picture, but are like the collections of a lifetime, a boxful of scraps of old silk and stuff such as hoarding women gather and leave behind at death. That Miriam guessed a good deal at secrets half—or quarter—revealed by demeanour shows that she was not without inquisitiveness and even a rather harsh and ruthless judgment of other people, and so a picture of Miriam herself grows steadily, volume by volume. But how far deliberate is that portrait? Is it not there, inferentially, as it were, by the accident of accumulated indications? How far is the character *created*?

You see in Miriam what may be regarded as the first adumbration of Virginia Woolf's idea of character as no more than a series of reactions to *milieu*. She does not impose herself upon life, but suffers its impress and its humiliations. She does not act; she resents and records. She does this without apology or explanation from Dorothy Richardson, and so far is "presented" as she would be by an artist of importance. On the other hand, no attempt is made to extract significance from her experience; and so the work is as little comprehensive as a tape-machine. At one time it was usual to call the method of Dorothy Richardson "the stream of life"; and I freely grant its interestingness as technical experiment. Its value in the art of fiction I find it less easy to admit. Curious, novel, for a time attractive, it seems to me in the end to be a little pointless.

Pointlessness is the last thing one would urge against the youngest of these three women writers—Rebecca West. Rebecca West always brought to everything her own restless *élan*. She must have been quite a child when she arrived in London journalism as a contributor to that feminist review, *The Freewoman*, and when she was hardly out of her teens she was already an alert commentator upon the claims of women and the serious disadvantages under which they carried on their work in the world. From the first she was an ardent suffragist, as quick and eager on behalf of her sex as any woman has ever been, and with a pen as full of fire. But she became widely known to the literary community, not by her views on the suffrage, but, with reason, by her reviews of novels for *The New Statesman*. I doubt whether any such brilliant reviews of novels were ever seen before; they certainly have not been seen since; for when Rebecca West left *The New Statesman* her peculiar combination of wit and justice could not be replaced. Those who read novel reviews are thankful if they find either wit or justice in them, and the difficulty of writing any form of criticism which is sensitive to the aims of authors and at the same time inexorable in appraisal of their performance is extreme. This difficulty, commonly evaded by means of impudence or disingenuousness, Rebecca West mastered. She amused, she stung; but she held fast to her own standard of quality, and was just.

Her place in the present chapter depends, it is clear, not upon such novel reviews, however good, and hardly at all upon the long, intelligent study of a woman contained in "The Judge," which is her most ambitious performance, but upon the very brief anecdote of amnesia called "The Return of the Soldier." This book is as simple as its theme—the return home of a shell-shocked soldier who has forgotten all the years intervening between his first love and his disablement. The appearance of his first love as a tired and ill-dressed woman, and her cure of his ailment by the exhibition of garments once worn by a dead child, is definitely inspired (as to the novel) by knowledge of modern psychological methods. Technically the book holds no novelty. It has few characters, and the device is used of the all-comprehending onlooker who is upon intimate terms with the protagonists; there are two women and one man (the onlooker being also a woman). What is novel is the fictional use of a treatment of amnesia which war-time experience showed to be reliable. The vignettes of husband and wife, and a cheerful doctor who resembled a famous contemporary writer, are all effective, and the study of the old love is full of emphatic sympathy.

It is customary to express wonderment at Rebecca West's omission to write many more novels. The explanation is that her intelligence was always critical. She always wrote and re-wrote, very scrupulously being much interested in the world about her, in the cause of women, in politics, in sociology, and bringing her mind to consideration of all these forces with a disinterestedness which belongs rightly and properly to the critic. Her really outstanding literary work is a superb survey of Yugoslavia, "Black Lamb and Grey Falcon." She was not driven to fiction by either an over-

mastering impulse to tell what she imagined or by a similar impulse
to right wrongs by means of impassioned appeal to the emotions.
In each case, her novel was written because a particular idea presented itself to her mind rather than to her imagination: in one case
the cure of amnesia, in another the possibility of the judgment of one
person by another, in a third the psychology of a strange woman.
And the author of these tales, although we may suppose memory to
have gone into the pictures of Glasgow and London which appear in
"The Judge," was very much the detached spectator of every action
recorded in the book. Such detachment is a critical detachment; and
the union of the creative with the critical faculty, when one or other
is exceptional, is very uncommon. Coleridge had it in a supreme
degree (he was one of the few great critics and great poets); Henry
James had subtlety in both his fiction and his criticism; but as a rule
if a man or a woman has too keen a critical sense it will react un-
favourably upon his or her creative work. Such work will become
arid, or, in the effort for emotion, it will tend to be sentimental. In
each case the cause will be the same; the mind's interfering control of
the imagination. Freud, illustrating this point, quotes the following
remarkable letter from Schiller to a friend who complained of his
lack of creative power:

> "The reason for your complaint," says Schiller, "lies, it seems
> to me, in the constraint which your intellect imposes upon your
> imagination. . . . Apparently it is not good—and indeed it hinders
> the creative work of the mind—if the intellect examine too closely the
> ideas already pouring in, as it were, at the gates. Regarded in isolation,
> an idea may be quite insignificant, and venturesome in the extreme,
> but it may acquire importance from an idea which follows it; perhaps,
> in a certain collocation with other ideas, which may seem equally
> absurd, it may be capable of furnishing a very serviceable link. The
> intellect cannot judge all these ideas unless it can retain them until it
> has considered them in connection with these other ideas. In the case
> of a creative mind, it seems to me, the intellect has withdrawn its
> watchers from the gates, and the ideas rush in pell-mell, and only then
> does it review and inspect the multitude. You worthy critics, or what-
> ever you may call yourselves, are ashamed or afraid of the momentary
> and passing madness which is found in all real creators, the longer or
> shorter duration of which distinguishes the thinking artist from the
> dreamer. Hence your complaints of unfruitfulness, for you reject
> too soon and discriminate too severely."

iii. Edward Morgan Forster

"And a third man he says in a sort of drooping regretful voice, 'Yes—oh dear yes—the novel tells a story' . . . And the third is myself. Yes—oh dear yes—the novel tells a story."

E. M. Forster: Aspects of the Novel.

ONE of my earliest recollections is of my Scottish grandfather, who was vocally indefatigable, singing:

"My name's Edward Morgan; I live in Llanelly:
Of a truth I was born in the sweetest of vales."

I do not know whether E. M. Forster descended from this Edward Morgan (his father was Edward Morgan Llewellyn Forster); but the possibility offers some explanation of his subtle and complex nature. A Welshman, a lover of the Classics, an intellectual, a Fellow of King's College, Cambridge, a novelist, a critic. But above all a moralist. Perhaps he did not himself realize that he was a moralist; but this I shall explain.

In person, Forster was in early days very pale (he reminded me in several respects of André Gide; for both shared a similar ivorine pallor, a similar grave sincerity of manner, a similar rather implacable courtesy), and with a peculiarly modest bearing. One accepted his perfect integrity, calm, sympathy; but was aware of a little remoteness, too. He was the most intelligent of all the novelists of the 1880–90 generation.

This enabled him to play with all his themes, and interpenetrate them with a kind of piercing light of the spirit. But it was also a disadvantage, for his books, however incandescent, hold little warmth. They do not embrace the whole of life; they are more like luminous demonstrations of cause and effect. They arise from deliberately realized ideas, and not from imaginative conceptions. But nevertheless they are full of fluctuating imagination which comes and goes from scene to scene, from paragraph to paragraph. He could be exquisitely malicious in sketching the spinster of foreign boarding-houses; very scathing at the expense of a male busybody or at strange discomfitures: those are the things which amuse us in his work. They were never his chief concern, which was with something valued above all else—Nature, Honesty, the need for mutual comprehension, the Good Life. He perpetually tried to personify this; never, I think, with complete success, but always thoughtfully and with a range of reference beyond the understanding of simple readers.

At the risk of having it thought that Cambridge is an obsession of mine (whereas I regard it only as a curiously insistent and very important phenomenon in modern letters), I should wish to make an observation. It is this. At its lowest, the esteem in which Cambridge is held may be a snobbish esteem: "Charlie's up at Cambridge"—oh, *Cambridge*; that means money, position, a career, such friends for after-life, etc. Oxford, would be just as impressive: none of the other Universities has such social *cachet*. That is the least interesting aspect. At its most persistent in the modern literary world, the pride of the Cambridge man is in a form of intellectual culture. I do not question the culture, and pride in it—with its contempt for all who have not shared its influence—is almost equalled by the comparable pride of the Oxford man who speaks of "the best thought." But there is a third pride, a much higher pride, that in spiritual culture; and it is this pride in Cambridge that should be associated with Forster. It is illustrated at intervals in all his work; it perfectly shouts in his comment on an aspiring Cockney clerk in "Howard's End," of whom Forster says: "Perhaps the keenest happiness he had ever known was during a railway journey to Cambridge, where a decent-mannered undergraduate had spoken to him."

I am not ridiculing that remark, although I think it shows alarming frigidity of the imagination. The point I wish to make is that to Forster his experience at Cambridge is the most wonderful thing that ever happened to him. At Cambridge he came greatly under the influence of a man of exceptionally fine temper and gift for teaching—Goldsworthy Lowes Dickinson. Dickinson, the ideal don, whose biography Forster has written, is to ordinary readers known chiefly by his little manual, "The Greek View of Life," which, though less than his best book, illustrates particularly his humane attitude of helpfulness towards unscholarly people. In this book he summarizes, very persuasively, the Greek attitudes to Religion, Art, the State, the Individual; and while it may be true that to scholars the work contains some jejune material and perhaps some sentimentality, its appeal to the uneducated is very strong. Dickinson is known otherwise to students as the author of certain dialogues on the nature of Good and the varieties of political philosophy, in which a love of discussion for its own sake is joined to a very earnest wish to ascertain by means of contrasts and definitions whether there is any common basis upon which thoughtful minds can build a more helpful philosophy of life. These dialogues, for those who relish points of view, are easy and delightful. They show a sense of character, and a willingness to preserve not only differences of opinion but the natural origins in personality of such differences. Though interested in abstract ideas, Dickinson was not therefore debarred from complete humane sympathy with men of many types. It was a beautiful mind, and a beautiful character, as these dialogues demonstrate. But his best work is contained in two books, one a fantasy suggested by Mozart's opera, "The Magic Flute," the other a survey of European pre-war diplomacy entitled "The European Anarchy." In these books the same beauty of mind and character is revealed; fastidious yet sympathetic, anxious yet tolerant; earnest yet playful. In the dialogues, no traps, such as we find in Plato; in the very simple "Greek View of Life" a loving wish to explain without condescension; in "The Magic Flute" a charming venture into the empyrean; and in "The European Anarchy" clear sight and honourable adoration of truth brought to the most controversial branch of history and analysis.

The power of such a man, who was Forster's friend as well as his teacher, is unquestionable. It is supported by much testimony, including Forster's own. And it must have helped, with those actual debates at Cambridge which Dickinson loved and in which, at the beginning of the century, Forster joined, to give clarity to a mind already possessed of unusual resource. Forster owed much to Cambridge, and this he acknowledged by his assurance that a Cockney clerk had his happiest moments as the result of being spoken to by a decent-mannered undergraduate. In himself he managed, it seems to me, to be more intelligent than his contemporaries without sinking to their fatal aridity.

His novels, excluding shorter works, are five in number. Two of them are brilliant exercises in comedy, two lengthy and to me not altogether intelligible or admirable serious studies of middle-class people in various moral pickles, and one subtle, very patient, brilliant analysis of the Anglo-Indian problem. I use the word "brilliant" with a sense of responsibility; for I can think of no term which better describes the peculiar quality of radiant intelligence which the three books share. All five books are written in a style at first markedly formal and later still decidedly cool, distinguished by wit and new-minted phrase. All five, in the matter of invention, are fantastic.

The fantasticality is an advantage in the extravagant "Where Angels Fear to Tread" and "A Room with a View," a disadvantage in "The Longest Journey" and "Howard's End," and a bewilderment in "A Passage to India." This I shall hope to show. "Where Angels Fear to Tread" is about a shiftless widow of means who marries a cheap Italian, has a baby, and dies. Her brother-in-law, an amusing prig, is sent with his sister to a small Italian town to demand the baby for its English relations, and there is great comedy in the ambassadorial interviews with the baby's father. Finally the baby is stolen, is accidentally jolted from the thief's arms in the darkness to death in a ditch; there is a shocking night fight between the prig and the father; and the expedition, routed, comes to an end with, on the part of a contributory young woman, the confession of her hidden and horrified love for the cheap Italian. In some respects this is the most successful of all Forster's books; for the protagonists are vividly rendered, the talk full of verve, the zestful invention upon a uniform plane, and the total effect unmarred by contradiction or obscurity. It is brimming with laughter.

The book which followed "Where Angels Fear to Tread" has no such relishable zest. It is a long tale about a cripple of some private means who becomes under-master at a country school. He marries a girl bereaved by death of her first, instinctive lover. This girl at first mothers the cripple and encourages his literary experiments in paganism; and at last, because she is conventional, malignantly binds and seeks to crush him into a conventional shape. Her character changes, always for the worse, as the book proceeds, and for every malignance she shows to her husband Forster repays her tenfold by what becomes quite persecutionary arraignment. Now the cripple has an irresponsible half-brother (illegitimate); and this brother, an incalculable and savage bore for whom the author has a mystical veneration, is always breaking into the book as a curious symbolic figure. He upsets the conventionals; he arouses in the cripple an emotional sense of duty and distaste; he and his case both evoke from an obstinate young philosopher harangues of the utmost severity; but while one feels that he represents for Forster some truth, some reality of importance, he never succeeds in being for the reader anything but a tiresome oaf who would be better dead. Because of him, the story is involved with argument and symbolism, and the fantastic invention which has been in place in brilliant farce such as "Where Angels Fear to Tread" is in "The Longest Journey," where it is perfectly sober, a cause of tedium and unconvincingness. The author, it seems, has at this period become attached to some "Back to Nature" concept whereby his cripple is saddled with terrible responsibilities for the sins of the mothers; and he has also developed what might nowadays be called a Conventionality-Complex. Conventionality is a horror to him. It is the enemy of Truth, Purity, and Romance. It is the unforgivable sin. It is to him what the Church was to Voltaire. In face of it he loses all command of his judgment. Instead of seeking truth below conventionality, and trying to understand why convention has such power, he can do nothing but vehemently expose it, caricature it, exaggerate it altogether beyond its natural proportions, punish it, and exalt its opposite, which he calls Honesty.

That same passion for the irrational—which seems odd and never entirely clear-headed in a man as civilized as Forster—is the driving force in "A Room with a View." In this third novel, with something of the farcical brilliance of "Where Angels Fear to Tread," we are introduced to a party at a Florentine *pension*, whose manners and timidities and snobbishnesses are all mimicked without mercy. But, to our horror, we find in the *pension* a truth-telling eccentric who, if he had been in a novel by Galsworthy, would long ago have been ridiculed to death by the intelligentsia; and we hear the rather worse than not-quite-veritable pipes of Pan. Our young heroine is kissed by a young man named George. After the fashion of heroines, she nevertheless engages herself to another, quite unsuitable, young man; and it takes coincidence and other fantastic works to break the engagement and land her in the properly unconventional arms. In particular we are shown that as she could play Beethoven's less popular pieces she has some core of superiority to common young women; and as for the men, they all return to nature by stripping and taking a bathe in a muddy pool. A rather Meredithian scene, this; but the book as a whole, though often delicious in phase and sature, will not, in its composition, bear looking into. If we were to peer, we should see that just as Meredith's novels owe nearly all to their treatment (and little but ill to their mechanism), so this book is no more than a novelette with a sentimental invocation of faunishness and eccentricity and momentary nudism to carry the graver message about Truth which the author has in his heart. Convention is still the enemy; despite the fact that Unconventionality thus applauded is but an inversion of the hideous foe. I doubt if a naturally unconventional person is ever conscious of the vileness of convention. He is more like the little girl who was told the story of the Golden Calf. She remarked, thoughtfully: "And God was angry?" "Terribly angry." "Hn. Funny. Of course, anybody else would only have laughed."

In many of its details and assumptions "Howard's End" is much the most mature and richly diversified book Forster wrote. If I say that it is a puzzling book, that is because I think that here, above all, Forster's invention is entirely arbitrary. I am not, as I hope it has been made clear in earlier chapters, a stickler for neatness in the novel; to me each book is to be judged accordingly as its author's aim (as I understand it) has been a worthy aim and well executed. What is called "richness" has its artistic value no less than scrupulous observance of the unities and other pseudo-classical technical devices. I do not ask of a book that it should be pellucid. In a sense, also, I realize that probability, as the French historian said, "is not a scientific notion; there was a King of Siam who refused to believe in the existence of ice." But over "Howard's End" I am in a quandary. I only believe it here and there.

In this book there are two half-German orphan sisters named

Schlegel and their brother. The brother may be eliminated; he is but an adjunct. There are also a family called Wilcox, father, mother, two sons and a daughter; the children for the time being may be set aside, excepting that the younger son and one of the two Schlegel sisters, Helen, for a few moments at the beginning of the book are engaged to be married. The sole point of the engagement is to show that Helen is amorously impulsive. And there are a young un-educated Cockney clerk and his wife (at first his mistress). It is this uneducated Cockney clerk, as you may recall, whose happiest hour has been given him by a decent-mannered undergraduate; and he and his wife, so far as the intrigue is concerned, are the dominating characters in the novel. They are not the chief char-acters; but their actions precipitate the moral crises of the book.

What am I to do with two persons, in a class well known to me, who, though they are apparently seriously offered as portraits, never say or do a single thing which I find credible? Is it I who am so besotted with the realistic method that I cannot appreciate essential truth? Or are these two incredibles indeed taken seriously by the author as persons? Or are they symbols? Or merely in-struments in his plot? Let me tell you what happens, and then let me explain what troubles me.

At the beginning of the book occurs the abortive engagement. It is quite an impossible engagement, and is broken off the morning after. It is also beautifully handled by Forster, who in the treatment of the whole episode shows himself to be a distinguished novelist; nothing in that respect could be finer. But shortly afterwards the sisters go to a classical concert at Queen's Hall, where they sit next to the uneducated Cockney clerk—there to *improve* himself. One of the sisters accidentally takes his umbrella; the other, when he suspiciously and accusingly announces the abstraction, first gives him her card and then takes him home to recover what proves to be a tattered relic. Subsequently the Wilcox family, hitherto resident in the country, at a house called Howard's End, rent a flat immedi-ately opposite the home of the sisters, and, as Helen (the emotional) has gone to Germany, and her quondam fiancé to Nigeria, Margaret the elder Schlegel, makes friends with Mrs. Wilcox, the mother. From this friendship springs the curious fact that upon her death shortly afterwards Mrs. Wilcox leaves a note asking that Howard's End shall be given to Margaret. Since the note is unsigned, and has no legal significance, the Wilcox family ignores the wish. However, Mr. Wilcox, the widower, presently falls soberly in love with Margaret, proposes to her, and (quite appropriately and explicably) is accepted. The two marry.

Meanwhile, however, the sisters have had further encounters with the uneducated Cockney clerk and his wife. Both turn up rather oddly at the Schlegels' home; the wife because her husband has mysteriously absented himself, the husband to explain that, having heard the call of the wild, he has been for a week-end walk. He quotes poetry; the Schlegel sisters patronize him, learn that he is a clerk in an insurance company, and, as Mr. Wilcox tells them that this particular insurance company is unsound, advise the clerk to find another job. The clerk finds another job—in a bank!—but is dismissed from it for incompetence; also his insurance company is proved to be sound. He and his wife are therefore brought by Helen, the emotional, to a country house from which Mr. Wilcox's daughter has just been married. Helen Schlegel is beside herself with panic fury, and insists that Mr. Wilcox shall find the clerk work in his own business. Unfortunately the clerk's wife has been Mr. Wilcox's mistress in a former incarnation, and as she is drunk she accosts him familiarly, arouses disturbance, and brings about an estrangement between the Schlegel sisters. Helen, having tried to give part of her fortune to the clerk, who declines it, goes abroad; Margaret is married to Mr. Wilcox, and goes down to Howard's End, where she finds that an insane woman has unpacked all her belongings, and Helen's belongings, in a house which for some time has been unoccupied. Time passes. Then, very mysteriously, Helen turns up again, shunning her family, and is only trapped in Howard's End—hunting up her books—by strategy. She is eight months gone with child; and it appears that this is the result of another emotional moment in which the Cockney clerk has been involved. When Mr. Wilcox's elder son, who is not the one who has been engaged to Helen, attacks the Cockney a bookcase falls over; the clerk dies, the son gets three years for manslaughter. Thereafter nothing remains but to gather together the fragments, and the sisters share Helen's trial—"the supreme agony of motherhood, which is even yet not a matter of common knowledge."

Forster must not be blamed for my shortcomings as a summarizer, and I do not ask that the story as told by me shall be regarded as the story told by him. All I ask is that we should quietly discuss the question whether the inconsecutiveness of this story is precisely the inconsecutiveness of life. In so far as Margaret and Mr. Wilcox are concerned, I think it is. There seems to me no incongruity at all in their relation, which is entirely reasonable, though not untouched by emotion. In the same way Helen's performances could I think have been made credible; although as the book stands they are to me not credible. She fluctuates between hardness and emotionalism (not an uncommon mixture), and is only convincing because both her passionate scenes occur "off" stage, when probability as well as pruriency demands that they should be witnessed in order that they should be understood. We are presented with the after-facts only: no wonder we are surprised. As for the uneducated Cockney clerk and his wife, I am an uneducated Cockney, and I have been a clerk. I was never learned enough to be employed in a bank; but my knowledge of clerks is very extensive. I have never met one who would be overwhelmed by decent behaviour on the part of an undergraduate, or one to whom such decent behaviour would seem less than his due. A consciousness of condescension would seem rather to belong to the undergraduate. How can I possibly believe in a being so uncouth, when I am told that he springs from a class which I know to be above all others decent, well-behaved, and self-respecting?

This is far from being an idle point as to Forster's portrayal of life. Here is another instance. In "The Longest Journey" the irrational half-brother arrives one night, drunk, at the cripple's home. His sister-in-law wearily notes his condition and states it; the cripple greets him cordially, but receives no answer, because the visitor has become insensible. And a third sober conventionalist exclaims on the spot: "Good gracious me! My advice is, that we all go to bed." I do not know precisely what *can* be said when a relation tumbles into the house drunk quite late at night; but I am absolutely positive that nobody says: "Good gracious me! My advice is, that we all go to bed." All might wish to say it, hoping that the disfigurement would disappear by morning; but such complete washing of the hands at the first moment of contemplation is inconceivable to me. After all, the speaker was a busybody, strong in the sense of conventional duty.

Well, I shall be told that Forster was not a realistic novelist, which is true; and that brings me to "A Passage to India," which is the most coherent of his later novels, sacrificing no brilliance as a result of that coherence. This is a picture of Anglo-Indian relations, drawn with much sympathy and beautifully presented. But the book turns upon something that happened in a cave. A young woman believes herself to have been assaulted in this cave by a Moslem doctor, and brings a charge against him which might have ruined his life. He is clearly innocent, and the young woman, when in the witness-box, retracts her charge. We are not told what did happen, whether the young woman had a hallucination or whether she was in fact assaulted by a guide. We should like to know. Forster will not tell us. In his quiet way he sighs: "Yes—oh dear yes—the novel tells a story." He is interested in expressing by means of fiction—it could be done as well by no other means—what he feels to be the truth about the British in India, and the Indian reaction to British rule. For him the story, such as it is, is but a vehicle for the ideas. As a result of this, "A Passage to India" is less interesting as a novel than as a presentation, a crystallization, of Forster's thoughts and emotions after two long exploratory visits to the East. He does not like British rule; it is in the hands of Conventionalists. However, he has some doubts as to the consequences of its abandonment. In this conclusion, having been a Liberal, he becomes a philosopher, and leaves everything where he found it.

"Yes—oh dear yes—the novel tells a story." In his study called "Aspects of the Novel" Forster imagines the problem of whether a novel should tell a story being posed to three persons. The first doubtfully admits that perhaps a novel *should* tell a story; the second bluffly demands a story; the third, who, Forster says, is himself, very unwillingly agrees that the novel does in fact tell a story; he wishes it did not. He would so much rather it concerned itself with melody or perception of the truth. I should like to discuss this question at length, but that would take time and space. Having, however, been turned from the story-less novel by much experience of the story-less novel as written by others, I am inclined to think that the novel which tells a story is a much purer form of art than the novel which regards story as factitious. Unfortunately there are fewer artists than teachers; and as between the explicit and the implicit, explicit will always seem to persons of culture more immediately important than anything in which the object is not stated. That is by the way. I only introduce the point now for two reasons: one, that it illustrates the attitude of many very intelligent and respectable writers of the present day; the other, that it illuminates the nature of Forster's talent as well as the greatness of his gifts.

By some fatality, which we have all noticed, we bring, perhaps responsively, to any author of exacting mind a similar exactingness of demand. Forster is an instance of such exactingness in an author. I consider his work full of faults—faults of exaggeration, inventive perfunctoriness, property babies, tiresome insistence upon the virtues of irrationality and unpreparedness, and so on. I think it deficient in emotion, though strangely complaisant towards emotionalism. For a man who preaches the need of kindness he seems to me to show very little kindness towards those men and women in his books who suffer from the deadly illness of conventionality; in early books his detachment sometimes, even to unconventional characters, is detached to the verge of distaste; in all his work (but he regards it as a fortune, not a virtue) there is a half-reluctant hint: Some of us were at King's; the rest, oh dear yes, not. But in spite of these accidents, which many will think falsely charged and many others unnecessarily mentioned, he is as far above the generality of novelists as, in another respect, he is above the generality of the intelligentsia. He has not only exceptional brains; he has exceptional honesty. He is not only deft and perceptive; he is

L

original. While, when he is serious, he is sometimes, to me, displeasing, harsh, excited, he has a glorious sense of comedy in which over and over again everything rises as by the most delightful legerdemain into glittering, many-coloured absurdity. In the case of Margaret Schlegel, in "Howard's End," where his sympathy is never at fault, he achieves great subtlety of understanding and communication. In "A Passage to India" one believes that he has truly penetrated some of the disguises and evasions of the oriental mind. In all his novels he adroitly suggests *milieu*, mental attitude, conversational skill, and the difficulties of social and personal adjustment as no other novelist of his time could do with comparable brilliance. There may be life, movement, rich laughter, eccentricity, accident, or gloom in his books, all of them presented with the greatest possible economy and precision. And there will be something else too.

That something is the ethical preoccupation of the author. "Ought," "ought not." We have our responsibilities. We guard and are cautious, when we should be unprepared. We are hypocrites and liars, when we should at all costs tell the truth and do what is right; live freely and in harmony with Nature. Tyranny is abhorrent to him; both tyranny and sham. He will show a pleasant girl slipping from candour into conventionality, to a lie or obedience to a lie; but always there is somebody across whose face (though it be his own) a warning shadow of disappointment passes at that moment, and, if she is a good girl, she recovers her self-respect, and plays some lesser-known Beethoven and so scrambles back to—not safety, but truth, sincerity, awareness of the best, pursuit of the unconventional. Just how positive a faith that is, we may doubt; it is at least a faith which is very fit for those who do not manage the world's affairs, and so modest a man as Forster obviously did not wish in any way to urge human beings beyond their capacity. For that reason, while we may not share his particular enthusiasms, we can all value his integrity, and can delight in the fact that it only occasionally obscures his imaginative gift.

iv. David Herbert Lawrence

> "God, that I have no choice!
> That my own fulfilment is up against me
> Timelessly!
> The burden of self-accomplishment!
> The charge of fulfilment!"
>
> *D. H. Lawrence: Humiliation.*

YOUNGER than Forster, and younger than the talented young novelists of the 1883–4 generation—Mackenzie, Cannan, Walpole, Brett Young—D. H. Lawrence stands out from them all.

He stands out in the first place by his genius; but he occupies more accidentally and less enviably a place of his own in contemporary literature. If we here glance back to the beginning of the Georgian era, and recall what Henry James thought of him, it will amuse us to find that phrase—toiling "in the dusty rear"—as the first comment of age to seal him an original; and he was an original, or "sport" in several unfortunate respects as well as in the all-important one of genius. He was, for example, one of the few writers ever to be threatened with prosecution for obscenity; one of the few painters to have the exhibition of their works closed by police order and the works themselves taken in charge; one of the few poets to have a packet of poems stopped in transit through the English post. He might well claim to have been the victim of persecution; he might well feel hatred and misery at thought of his country and its laws; he might well feel himself a rebel with nowhere to rest his head. Since his death he has had an equally strange fate in being made the subject of biographies and counter-biographies and replies to counter-biographies, and books and books of memoirs, letters, selections, collections, and every kind of analysis. His life, both private and secret, has been published abroad, first by himself either in the disguise of the novel or the passionate candours of poetry, and then by his friends and enemies and those who have axes to grind and those who hope to gain a little publicity for themselves from his posthumous fame. His work and his personality have evoked such emotion that any breath of adverse comment upon one of them or both has been met with fury from one class, while every word of praise has aroused in another class such shocked and repulsive surprise that protests have passed into paroxysms of the most alarming kind. His effect upon the young has been great; his effect upon the old has often enough been that of nausea. It is difficult to foresee his future; it is even more difficult in such an atmosphere calmly to assess his genius.

For one thing, much of the fuss about Lawrence has been of a purely temporary order. It was bound to be so. Psycho-analysis has been a new hobby for thousands of people, and Lawrence is a writer who lends himself—only too readily—to psycho-analysis. He asks for it; demands it. His work was full of autobiography; his poems can be made plainly to tell the story of a life as Shakespeare's Sonnets have only been made to do by force; his illustration of the Œdipus Complex is terribly timely; the accounts of him which have been published have all dealt in matters of which, concerning nearly every other writer, nothing, or very little, is known. His private life has been turned inside out, not because he was a genius but because he is ready material for such disclosure. There he is: the man, the author; compare this with that, his own words.

Was he sexually impotent, was he mad, was he a good friend, an ungrateful biter of the hand that fed him? Are his works obscene or fiercely moral?—It has been a really extraordinary situation. If ever man was made for moment, it was Lawrence. But must one accept the verdicts of the moment? Is there something yet more true to be said of him? Are not these disciples by way of being ghouls or unconscious misrepresenters of the man? Was he, as they say, a great man; or was he a weakling? Some of them, while saying he was a great man, depict him as a weakling. He himself said that, as compared with the people who wrote about him, "nice, well-behaved dogs," he was a giraffe; and the Lawrence who wrote letters to his friends bears no resemblance at all to the Lawrence who has been described by others.

He was born in Eastwood, Nottinghamshire, on September 11th, 1885, the fourth child of a coal-miner. He was what is known as a "mother's boy," and was his mother's pet, companion, and confidant. When he was thirteen, he won a scholarship to Nottingham High School, and later went to Nottingham University College to obtain a teaching certificate. He was a teacher for several years; but after the publication of his first novel, "The White Peacock," in 1911 (it was advertised in 1910) he abandoned teaching and gave himself wholly to writing. The beginning of his literary career was marked by the active interest of two men, Ford Madox Hueffer, who published some poems in *The English Review*, and Edward Garnett, who told him to submit "The White Peacock" to Heinemann, the London publisher, and in other ways gave him encouragement of the most valuable kind. For a long time Garnett was his chief contact with the book world; later he disappears altogether from among Lawrence's correspondents. Then Lawrence made the acquaintance of Middleton Murry and Katherine Mansfield, and contributed to their journal, *Rhythm*, and embraced them with a full heart of friendship, while at the same time he steadily increased his half-friendships with others who were either producing what was thought to be advanced literature or cultivating the society of the artists and *littérateurs* of the day. His feelings for Murry were more emotional than they seem to have been for any other man; but having thought of him as a John the Baptist he came to regard him as a Judas, so that although the friendship lasted long, and flared up again, it was in the end a failure and a cause of pain and disillusion. Having spent his boyhood among Midland workers, Lawrence became through Murry and Garnett and Edward Marsh (another early enthusiast) the associate of the cultivated few in London, bringing to that association a whole body of experience quite alien to the experience of his companions. He was thus from the outset a critical stranger in middle-class æsthetic society.

Middleton Murry, in his curious, rather powerful, and dis-
tressingly emotional story of Lawrence's character called "Son of
Woman," delves far into the Œdipus Complex for his explanation
of Lawrence, and I think convincingly attributes to the relation
subsisting between Lawrence and his mother a share in that conflict
to which in poems and novels he again and again returned. Aldous
Huxley, always fastidiously repelled by the profuse (and therefore
by Murry's literary manner and the mind which it expresses), will
have nothing to do with any such notion, and truly remarks that
Lawrence would have been Lawrence if his mother had died when
he was a child. The two views are compatible. We are all agreed (I
mean, in this case, Murry, Huxley, and myself) that Lawrence was a
genius, and that his genius would have found expression: what is
still possible, nevertheless, is that the note of horror pervading all
those passages from his writings which Murry quotes might have
been mitigated if as a boy he had not lived so constantly in his
mother's company. Huxley has had no personal experience of the
nearness with which poor people live together, and of the steamy
mother-son intimacy, almost identification, which such a life can
produce. It is indicated well enough in Lawrence's autobiographical
"Sons and Lovers," where the relationship is underlined but not,
as yet, mystically analysed into those terms which Lawrence was
later forced to repeat *ad nauseam* owing to the poverty of the English
language.

"Paul would be built like his mother, slightly and rather small.
His fair hair went reddish, and then dark brown; his eyes were grey.
He was a pale, quiet child, with eyes that seemed to listen, and with a
full, dropping underlip.

"As a rule he seemed old for his years. He was so conscious of
what other people felt, particularly his mother. When she fretted he
understood, and could have no peace. His soul seemed always attentive to her. . . .

". . . When she was quiet, so, she looked brave and rich with
life, but as if she had been done out of her rights. It hurt the boy
keenly, this feeling about her that she had never had her life's fulfilment: and his own incapacity to make up to her hurt him inside with
a sense of impotence, yet made him patiently dogged inside. It was his
childish aim.

.   .   .   .

"Paul was now fourteen, and was looking for work. He was a
rather small and rather finely-made boy, with dark brown hair and light
blue eyes. His face . . . was extraordinarily mobile. Usually he looked
as if he saw things, was full of life, and warm; then his smile, like
his mother's, came suddenly and was very lovable; and then, when
there was any clog in his soul's quick running, his face went stupid

and ugly. He was the sort of boy that becomes a clown and a lout as soon as he is not understood, or feels himself held cheap; and, again, is adorable at the first touch of warmth."

These quotations (they are telescoped here, but are from two early chapters of "Sons and Lovers") give us the close relationship of mother and son, and they explain Lawrence's character better than much elaborate exposition can do. He was sensitive as few men are sensitive; sensitive, clever, an artist; "so conscious of what other people felt, particularly his mother." (I mean, by "clever," mentally agile.) In those days his only ambition was to "earn his thirty or thirty-five shillings a week somewhere near home, and then, when his father died, have a cottage with his mother, paint and go out as he liked, and live happy ever after." But in "Fantasia of the Unconscious," if Murry is to be believed, Lawrence has himself in mind when he speaks of a woman "seeking, seeking the fulfilment in the deep passional self, . . . seeking whom she may devour."

"And usually, she turns to her child. Here she provokes what she wants. Here, in her own son who belongs to her, she seems to find the last perfect response for which she is craving. He is a medium to her, she provokes from him her own answer. So she throws herself into a last great love for her son, a final and fatal devotion, that which would have been the richness and strength of her husband and is poison to her boy."

Since Lawrence is an exceedingly personal writer, and since he spent the greater part of his literary life in explaining the relations between himself and his mother, his wife, and two other women whom he knew in youth, I incline to Murry's view. It is only important in an account of Lawrence's life; and I shall not again refer to it.

He was twenty-five when his first novel was written, and this was published in 1911, when it was widely assumed that any author who used initials instead of a Christian name and who wrote as emotionally as Lawrence did of a hero named Cyril must be a woman. In "Sons and Lovers," which was published in 1913, he told with tremendous force and sincerity the story of his life as it had been up to his mother's death. In the following year, after his wife had been divorced by her first husband, he was married; and in August the First World War broke out. The War, to Lawrence, was a merely horrible stupidity. He refused to have any part in it, believing that each man's responsibility was to himself and not to his fellows, and that at bottom the War was waged by England no less than by other countries on behalf of property, trade, and empire.

He was already desperately agitated when, in 1915, his new novel, "The Rainbow," was attacked as filth and the publishers ordered to withdraw it from circulation and destroy the remaining stock.

Lawrence then wrote another novel, "Women in Love," and for this he failed for another five years to find a publisher. According to my recollection of the time, hesitation on the part of publishers to make themselves responsible for this book was due less to fear of prosecution on grounds of indecency than to another fear altogether. This I must explain. In his simplicity, Lawrence put real people into his books. He put himself over and over and over again; his mother, his wife, the two other women many times; his acquaintances as he needed them. If he was there, naked but splendid, why should they object to a lesser splendour? And there was a portrait in "Women in Love" as to which it was believed that proceedings for libel would be taken if the book were published. I suppose that nobody objects to a favourable portrait: Lawrence's were usually unfavourable. He would meet somebody, take a liking or a disliking, see very intensely whatever he liked or disliked, meditate upon the person, see more and more and more, and then, at white heat, would put that person into a story. The story would often be quite invented; only the person vividly portrayed as if by forked lightning. The consequences were painful. At least one person began proceedings against a Lawrence novel, and had to be soothed by a present from the publisher. Many others were wounded and unsoothed. For those in whose company Lawrence had been uncomfortable (though they had intended nothing but kindness) punishment was exemplary and inexorable.

What with his horror of war, the humiliation he felt at successive medical examinations by the Army authorities (for he was by no means a conscientious objector, and would have fought for any cause of the spirit which he approved), the persecution which he suffered through the suspicions of neighbours in Cornwall, who believed his German wife to be a spy, the prosecution of "The Rainbow," the publishers' dread of "Women in Love," and the desperate poverty in which—even with the aid of gifts and loans of money from those who could ill afford to lose what they had—the Lawrences lived, this period must have been enough to send so extraordinarily sensitive a man insane. I believe he did feel the bitterest hatred of England and the English—not the people, but the whole organization of the life of the people. When he wished to leave the country, although he had no longer any fear of being forced to serve in the Army (he was obviously unfit for military training), he was refused a passport. He could not go until after the War, in 1919, and from that time to the end of his life, though he paid at least three brief visits, he could not again bear to live in England.

He lived in Italy, Sicily, Germany, Sardinia, Ceylon, Australia, the United States, Mexico, in Italy again, and in the South of France. He travelled extensively and almost incessantly, looking for some part of the world which had not been—in Lawrence's view—demoralized by civilization. He wrote a great deal. He must have been among the most prolific of all modern English writers. Wherever he went he took a readiness to be delighted with what he saw, an enthusiasm, an eagerness; but it always failed him, so that he was forced to haste away to farther and farther places of exile in order that he might set down some account of the horror he had just escaped. He was in this way the first of the moderns, for the materialism of contemporary life was too much for him; and he sought horrified escape from it. But he was greater than any other of the moderns, because he brought to life an extraordinary sweetness of nature, a belief in the virtue of self-knowledge which in his case and in no other known to me was passionate, a peculiarly simple and original genius which no accumulation of dross can conceal, and a power which I believe nobody will deny of attaching to himself as admirers the most diverse body of people that can be imagined. I have not met anybody who knew Lawrence who did not love him.

Perhaps I have been lucky; for it is clear that Lawrence felt himself to be a very lonely man. Nor do I think he always showed good judgment in the choice of those whose company he must have endured. He was largely cut off from the class from which he had come: literary people and amateurs of literature were his only friends. Common literary interests, in my view, provide a false basis for true friendship; and I believe Lawrence knew it. He did not want literary friends. Unfortunately, admirers were necessary to him; in particular, women admirers. He was in this difficulty, that he had exceptional intellectual powers, and yet detested intellectualism. Though he quarrelled with many of the tenets of Christianity, and developed a kind of jealousy of Christ, he was more nearly a Christian mystic than anything else. Therefore he had no patience with the Scientific obsession of so many intellectuals. He could be friendly with Bertrand Russell, but he was forced to tell Russell that a synopsis of some lectures which they were to give together was "pernicious," and while the acquaintance continued it was seen by both parties to be an impossible alliance. He astonishingly maintained friendship with Middleton Murry (astonishingly, I mean, in view of their constant breaks), with whom he at one time seems to have felt himself so much a sort of soul-mate that only Murry can do justice to the relationship. But what he needed above all, and what he never found, even in Catherine Carswell, whom he liked and respected, was the perfection of understanding which could only have been given by a man of his own origins who, like himself, had genius. He was a giraffe among other animals (not only dogs, as he thought), and had a giraffe's high head as well as a giraffe's shyness and disconcerting speed. Has a giraffe any retaliatory weapon? Lawrence had one.

What, actually, were his qualities and his defects? One has to make up one's own mind, I feel sure, as to these; for if one reads what those who knew Lawrence say one finds a hundred contradictions—Murry, Catherine Carswell, Huxley, David Garnett, all say different things about him. As a man, it seems that he would never be rude to anybody when face to face. He could destroy such a person in a tale; but he could not be impolite. This seems to me to be a remarkable trait in one so fearless in condemnation. Then, as one sees his letters thrown together, one realizes that he *was* affected by the wish to placate or maintain the friendship of some for whom he felt qualified regard. One catches piercing criticisms of friends as well as of books; much kindness to individuals coupled with scathing comments upon groups. Was there a cowardice in him? For he greatly disliked compromise: "I do like plain outspokenness." He would say very harsh things about his fellow-novelists, especially his seniors; but was oddly anxious to know what they thought of *him*. What did James, Bennett, Forster, and others, think of "The Rainbow"? He did not care; and yet what *did* they think? All writers should admire him; and if they did not do homage they were no good. They were no good, anyway. He could not stand James Joyce; Mackenzie ("the dashing Monty"), who was very kind to Lawrence and had a share in bringing about a resumption of his novel-writing, though "I get on with" him, was "a fool not to know (in 1914) that times are too serious to bother about his *Sinister Street* frippery"; even Aldous Huxley, praised in a letter on "Point Counter Point," suffers later from a cool belittlement: "No, I don't like his books: even if I admire a sort of desperate courage of repulsion and repudiation in them. But again, I feel only half a man writes the books—a sort of precocious adolescent."

The explanation lies in Lawrence's feeling that he is an original genius, and the others for the most part fakes or imitators of the dead. He believes that in their hearts all other writers hate him and deny him. That faith in Lawrence is what his intense admirers experience. They are not critical; they *believe*. It is an extraordinary circumstance, and it prevents one who did not know him from criticizing the novels of Lawrence by any except special standards. He was a prophet. His novels, so full of lifeless passages, dull dialogue which when it is not urgently expressive of his own beliefs is no more than echo, and terribly monotonous use of words such as "dark" and "obscene," are charged with spiritual intimations. His beautifully simple "Fantasia of the Unconscious" (which should be read by all who still suppose him to be a wallower) is a gospel. Even "Lady Chatterley's Lover," which he says is symbolic, although it reads to the uninstructed as the merest pornography, is a passionate plea for purity. To write of such a man as one would do of one of his contemporaries, and to say that his novels are "good" or "not so good," is to go away from faith into blasphemy, and not to appraise with admired discriminating-ness. How impossible, then, to speak of the work apart from the man!

Murry says that Lawrence was never an artist; Huxley says he was an artist above all. They are using the word in different senses. What Murry means is that Lawrence had none of the Jacobean picture technique and subordination of the part of the whole; Huxley, that Lawrence is describable by no other word than "artist." I agree with both. To Lawrence a novel was not a work of art, but a new reading of life, an exhortation, a picture of soul-states. He wrote novels as poems, by a sort of spontaneous imaginative energy; and while he re-wrote some of them more than once it was never with the object of reducing them to lozenge-shape, only with that of giving more emphatic form to his arugment. I do not think he would ever have produced a book to please the technicians; nor do I think he shows a real talent for the creation of character, as distinguished from the creation of mood and passion or the repro-duction of idiosyncrasies. Such creation of character for its own sake would have seemed to him artificial, a playing with serious things, an abdication of moral purpose. I don't agree with the view; but the point thus made against the "artistic" novel is much more than an arguable one: it is crucial. I cannot argue it here, though I suggest an answer to Lawrence's claim for his own method may be found in work written in imitation of Lawrence. Bereft of his passion, and composed by young men and women who have never felt a stronger emotion than dislike, it is both tedious and ludicrous, a peppering of the commonplace with lurid verbs, adverbs, and adjectives. Lawrence's books were apocalyptic visions: unless one has such visions, a tamer and finer technique is quite a virtue.

Just how excellent Lawrence's visions were, time will show. They were produced by the impact upon an original genius of modern conditions and a particular crisis in the world's affairs, and the kind of society to which Lawrence was condemned. That the momentary vision itself was vehement is undeniable. No author has ever pictured a scene with comparable passion. One cannot read such chapters as the "Water Party," "Mino," and "Crème de Menthe" in "Women in Love" without realizing that the author is a great writer. But the books as wholes are lacking in momentum;

intrinsically, apart from minors and superficial traits in the principals, all the characters are the same. All are torturers and self-torturers, absorbed in the foulnesses of hatred and disgust. At times, especially in such books as "The Rainbow" and "Women in Love," Lawrence seems to be obsessed by the passion of gloating, malignant cruelty; and his people have thick, ugly darknesses of soul which cause them to become, not humans, but pagan and terrible creatures. His language in describing them is equally extravagant. The dictionary does not contain adjectives enough for him, and he falls back upon "obscene" for all purposes. He returns again and again to the emotion of hatred, until the hatred his characters feel moves us no more than does the indifference of our neighbours. With every strong word to describe strong feeling, he produces a loss of value in the word and the emotion. That he felt this hatred himself, and that he attributed it to others (unless he found them, as I am sure he found the intellectuals, bloodless and false), I do not doubt. That such vehemence is a true sign of strength it is hard for one temperamentally indisposed to vehemence to admit. I do not accept the Lawrentian psychology; if I were to pretend to do so I should stultify my own experience, and as Lawrence said once: "Excuse me if I want to get out of the train." He came from a poor, opinionated, and outspoken section of the community; and he entered a half-rich, opinionated, and intensely reserved section of the community. He had to do this, for nowhere else could he find intellectual companionship; but he was never at home in it, as a hundred malicious portraits in his books testify. When he offered his soul, these people looked down their noses. No wonder he hated them. But they were not all the people, even in England.

Another fact is that, remaining poor, and having in fact no wish to have that agglomeration of goods and responsibilities which we call a home, he lived nomadically, and always very much alone and at close quarters with his wife. His relations with her were an absorbing topic for thought. When he was not in her company, he was turning over in his mind what had happened between them, what she felt and thought—it was so different from what he thought and felt—how uncomfortable she was, how bent upon her own will, her own self, and so on. He had much time in which to think, really to brood; and out of his intensities of feeling and thought he drew poems and generalizations and novels (or rather, scenes in novels) which were of a kind never previously attempted in English. There is a nakedness of honesty, as well as a fierceness of emotion, in his writing for which the reserved English were unprepared. Only those who in some degree shared his independence of mind were able to appreciate them; the curious were another matter, and at once collected him and his writings for their own diversion. Lawrence knew that: the knowledge explains some of his exasperation, his hatred for the admirers who were so necessary to him. He sometimes hesitated about publication. But his simplicity was so great that he did not, for any consequences to himself, fear the results of disclosure. He returned over and over again to the same theme, with its inevitable variations; mother, wife, self:

> "ultimately, she is all beyond me,
> She is all not-me, ultimately.
> It is that that one comes to.
> A curious agony, and a relief. . . .
> When she has put her hand on my secret, darkest sources, the darkest
>   outgoings,
> When it has struck home to her, like a death, 'this is *him*!'
> She has no part in it, no part whatever,
> It is the terrible *other* . . ."

>> "What should I do if you were gone again
>>   So soon?
>> What should I look for?
>> Where should I go?
>> What should I be, I myself,
>> 'I'?
>> What would it mean, this
>> 'I'?"

The need for sincerity, for sincere explanation, for the dispelling of all non-comprehension, was ever urgent with him: "I do like plain outspokenness." And his wife the only person in the world with whom he could thus speak plain and true:

> "How quaveringly I depend on you, to keep me alive,
>   Like a flame on a wick.

> Suppose you didn't want me! I should sink down
>   Like a light that has no sustenance."

Is it any wonder that his work, though thought ranges wide, is at its best so intense and in general so monotonous? It was all from within; given coherence and meaning by its relation to his own life. I think the growth of appreciation for Lawrence's genius has come very much from an increase in knowledge of Lawrence himself. That seems to be so in Catherine Carswell's case, although she always admired him; I myself, having read his Letters, which, like the "Fantasia of the Unconscious," are the work of a man supremely sane and sure, have realized better than ever before Lawrence's strong personal charm and clearness of thought. Many others

must be in the same position. For his hatred and his flights and
eager affections and disillusionments, his insistence upon John
Thomas and Lady Jane, his mysticism and revivalistic summons to
abandon the sense of sin, we may have fluctuating sympathy (in my
case, none for hatred, pity for such magnificent ingenuousness as to
intellectual friends, distaste for mysticism, but entire support for
the abandonment of the sense of sin, which I have fortunately
escaped); but for his genius warm admiration and for his character
new esteem are the inevitable result of any dispassionate inquiry.
I have said that I think "Lady Chatterley's Lover" is pornography: it was not intended as such, and there is no harm in its
common little story or the silly use of common terms for copulation
and the generative organs; but so far as it finds readers at all it will
be on account of its aphrodisiac character. I do not think "The Rainbow" pornography, but a great bad book, full of wonderful beauties
and truths, beside which every other novel of its immediate age
seems timid, neat, and at least upon the verge of banality, if not over
the verge.

Lawrence's appeal is really to the heart, and not to the head.
For this reason "precocious adolescents" and unimaginative elders,
desperately chewing the husks of physical science, cultivated and
misunderstood him as a demi-god. They have continued to misunderstand, but ceased to cultivate him, since a newer fashion arose.
Meanwhile, since they could no longer believe in salvation or the
divine adequacy of Jesus Christ, and since they had to have faith in
something or else fall into abject despair, they clutched at Lawrence
as a new Messiah, and were as emotional about him as their own
frigidity allowed. It was not as a writer that they valued him; but as a
teacher: "Verily, verily, I say unto you . . ." They searched his
work for meanings. "Very gnomic," as Mr. Barbecue-Smith would
say.

There was something pathetic and grotesque about all this, for
so many of Lawrence's disciples were men and women whom he
would have run thousands of miles to avoid—from whom he did
run thousands of miles, only to find that, like God, they were everywhere. That is to say, the people who arouse distaste in such as myself
roused furious horror in Lawrence. They were Lawrentians. They
chattered about "otherness" and "darkness"; they were serious
about sex, and worried about it, finding Lawrence an advanced and
esoteric Marie Stopes; they assumed Lawrence's arrogance, which
did not fit them; and they were consciously "free" and at the same
time self-analytical, which was as near as they could get to the
Lawrentian insistence upon candour. But they had no true connection with the Lawrentian idea. His cry was for innocence, for
purity ("unless ye become as little children"), for a clear distinction

between the sexes; theirs was for a different sophistication, a psychologized faith from which they could get what Americans call a "kick" no longer obtainable from Christianity. Either sophisticates or cranks were Lawrence's followers; genuine Lawrentians are to be found only among those to whom much of Lawrence's work is a tortured nightmare, a writhing, sweating struggle to express personal truths and give them by the use of mystical terms a general application. The reputation of this author has declined since his death. As men and women have learned more about their own minds, his remarkable pioneer work has fallen in importance; as the history of mankind has pursued its course his beliefs have been either absorbed or rejected, and even now, in the midst of a new aridity of culture and "first-class"-ness, no longer obtain loyalties. He was a product of his day, a portent, a noble-minded man of strong personality, a begetter of faith, a sort of latter-day Carlyle rather than a latter-day Blake, as he has been called. In a hundred years or less he may, I think, be found a little fervid. He will be seen as a poet, an impressionist; not as a rival to Christ, and not as a great expert in the *psyche*. Let there be no mistake, however; in a hundred years he will probably still be on the literary map, while most of his contemporaries will have sunk without trace from every record of the Georgian age.

v. James Joyce

"My God, what a clumsy *olla putrida* James Joyce is! Nothing but old fags and cabbage-stumps of quotations from the Bible and the rest, stewed in the juice of deliberate, journalistic dirty-mindedness—what old and hard-worked staleness, masquerading as the all-new!"

D. H. *Lawrence to M. and A. Huxley.*

IF Lawrence was unsophisticated, Joyce was the reverse. One can trace his steady progress in sophistication from the close realistic studies contained in "Dubliners," impressions mostly of squalid life in a city, through the quickened reminiscence of "Portrait of the Artist as a Young Man," to the extended and often very brilliant display of "Ulysses" and the incomprehensible musical and linguistic splendours of "Finnegan's Wake." Only hard-headed Irish poets and cosmopolitan Jews are as sophisticated as he, or could have written anything in such an idiom as that of "Ulysses," or its culminating obscurity, "Finnegan's Wake." They are the men, journalists, *entrepreneurs*, and the like, who take a professionally knowing view of everything that goes on in the world, turning like lightning from one subject to another, and summing each in an expert phrase which is like a password and which still leaves the soft world rolling unconsciously through eternity.

They know the argot of every language, the drinks and bywords of every nation, the "shop" of every profession, the sewage of every mind. They are without reverence, hard as stone, proud of their knowingness and exhibitionary of it, but at heart wearied to death because they are without illusions. They automatically and professionally notice and remember for ever headlines and solecisms in newspapers, the clichés of barmaids, slips made by common, genteel, and ridiculous persons, smells, lingerie, betrayals of vulgarity, scandals about well-known persons, and the *faux pas* of ingénues. It is their business to notice and to know these things. It is a part of the professional training. At will, these men can run all their observations together in a never-ending patter of expert talk. Their note is a hard, bright cleverness, a knowingness regarding the baser aspects of humanity; but for the good and the pure, since they believe in neither, they can feel nothing but contempt.

Joyce had some of the traits of the sophisticated journalistic or *entrepreneur*. Being an Irishman, he was poet, musician, fanatic, and master of an inexhaustible pen. His knowledge of the life of back streets, of saloons, the lewd thoughts of maidens, the doings at Catholic seminaries in Ireland, of foul old men, and a thousand other disagreeable matters was extensive and peculiar. He could rise to dithyrambic heights; the base was known to him without mercy. He could lay his hand upon its heart and feel the very beat of it. He could imaginatively enter it and be of it, so that the reader of what he wrote felt this to be at that moment the whole of life. And as he progressed in sophistication he also progressed in his own quite special technique, which became more and more a mass of punning, allusive, erudite legerdemain, incomprehensible to all except those who pride themselves upon their Irishness of birth or understanding. He carried a kind of literary post-impressionism farther than any man had previously done—farther than any other writer except Gertrude Stein, who was much his inferior. Sometimes he wrote in a series of jotted shorthand notes; sometimes as if he overheard and recorded a dialogue between strangers; sometimes in wild fantasy; sometimes in a jumble of disconnected thoughts. The jumble is his mainstay in some of the best passages in "Ulysses."

"Might manage a sketch. By Mr. and Mrs. L. M. Bloom. Invent a story for some proverb which? Time I used to try jotting down on my cuff what she said dressing. Dislike dressing together. Nicked myself shaving. Biting her nether lip, hooking the placket of her skirt. Timing her. 9.15. Did Roberts pay you yet? 9.20. What had Greta Conroy on? 9.23. What possessed me to buy this comb? 9.24. I'm swelled after that cabbage. A speck of dust on the patent leather of her boot.

"Rubbing smartly in turn each welt against her stocking calf.

Morning after the bazaar dance when May's band played Ponchielli's dance of the hours. Explain that morning hours, noon, then evening coming on, then night hours. Washing her teeth. That was the first night. Her head dancing. Her fansticks clicking. Is that Boyland well off? He has money. Why? I noticed he had a good smell off his breath dancing. No use humming then. Allude to it. Strange kind of music that last night. The mirror was in shadow. She rubbed her handglass briskly on her woollen vest against her full wagging bub. Peering into it. Lines in her eyes. It wouldn't pan out somehow.

"Evening hours, girls in grey gauze. Night hours than black with daggers and eyemasks. Poetical ides pink, then golden, then grey, then black. Still true to life also. Day, then the night."

Now to a quick mind, self-observant, ready to catch notes and take them, to sight contradictions in mood and response, and to explore memory, the concoction of such a jumble is not difficult. The method is familiar enough in scraps of impressionist fiction. What gave Joyce's jumble its peculiar merit was his wit and the frequent malicious precision of his exposure, which went deeper into soliloquy than the work of any other writer. He had an extraordinary ear for words (he was a singer, and well understood the art of phrasing and enunciation), and an intricate mind of which the sensitiveness jumped out like flame to kindle significant associations. He had a strong taste for Irish slang and idiom (that was a chief obstacle to understanding for those who had not the Irish voice and vocabulary), a memory abnormally long and exact, and a range of reading to which Stephen Dedalus's mother once objected, as she did to his "queer mind." He had not, I think, a truly creative imagination, but abnormal cleverness, in which he took a virtuoso's delight. Those words of Lawrence's which I have quoted put the matter over-strongly. Though they are so amusing, they represent the puritan's point of view. But they have a penetration natural to Lawrence's literary criticism. Lawrence, though it was his way to see the defects of other authors, rather than their qualities, made no mistake in the nature of the defects, and in a phrase summed up what most of us would take pages to express, even if, at the end of them, we reached the same conclusion.

Joyce was born in Dublin in 1882, and was educated at Catholic colleges and the Royal University, Dublin. He lived for most of his manhood in various Continental cities, Vienna, Trieste, Zurich, and Paris, giving lessons in the English language, translating, and it is possible, though of this I am not sure, doing some journalistic work. In person he was fairly tall, some five feet nine and a half, but so slim that he seemed taller. He was dark, his hair dark brown, his beard a lighter brown; and his eyes, with which he had great trouble all his life, almost to the point of complete blindness, were blue.

His manner was quiet and his tongue, when moved by arrogance, deadly; he would sometimes, to please a host, spend an entire evening at the piano, singing and playing old Irish airs in a beautiful tenor voice; but at other times was wholly silent, though never *farouche*. And he worked slowly and with absorbed deliberation; for those odd phrases, which seem to us to be such rapid shorthand, often took long to compose, so packed were they with meanings, over-meanings, under-meanings, hints to the learned, cheek, and the subtleties of every language he knew.

These merits, however, are the merits of virtuosity. Joyce's work has quite other merits. Nobody ever presented the thoughts of a vulgar woman such as Mrs. Bloom with such terrible convincingness. They have the air of being complete and unerring. In a lesser degree, the thoughts of a cheap girl, earlier in the book, a girl who leans back and shows her knickers for the sake of exciting a stranger, have amusing and edifying precision. There is a wild scene of great length and orgiastic obscenity which shows Joyce to have been a master of extravagant invention. It is also packed with brilliant mimicry; mimicry and impersonation. If mimicry and impersonation made great literature, "Ulysses" would be a great book. It is, I think, a great Irish performance, which in a hundred years' time will have for connoisseurs of literature an interest comparable to that of "Euphues."

Chapter Fifteen

AN INTER-WAR SYMPTOM

EDGAR WALLACE AND OTHERS

i

"The art of self-tormenting is an ancient one, with a long and honourable literary tradition. Man, not satisfied with the mental confusion and unhappiness to be derived from contemplating the cruelties of life and the riddle of the universe, delights to occupy his leisure moments with puzzles and bugaboos."
    Dorothy L. Sayers: Preface to Great Short Stories of Detection, Mystery and Horror.

WHILE the idealisms and disillusions of the First World War charged the newer poetry with a mixture of horror and flippancy, and while psycho-analysis and metaphysics drew a number of novelists into abnormal paths, and pacificism into the considered defence of weakness, other influences affected public taste and produced a demand for entirely different ingenuities. There was, in the years immediately following the War, an intense desire for easy reading. That the easy reading should have been subtilized and sophisticated, until what was easy became complicated and difficult, was but a sign of the times: the first call, and the first effort, were both simple enough.

Those learned in the matter have demonstrated that tales of crime and detection were written by early scribes. They track them to the Apocrypha, in the tale of Susanna and the Elders, and to Herodotus. The most simple-minded of them demonstrate that Voltaire, in "Zadig," had the whole matter of logical deduction from clues at his command. But whether in fact he was anticipated by the ancients or by Voltaire, it is quite clear that Edgar Allan Poe invented for himself the formula later so successfully used by Conan Doyle; and that most subsequent stories devoted to the detection of crime have been variants or avoidances of the Poe-Doyle method. Interest in the crime itself gives place in such stories to interest in the conduct of those who investigate the crime, or rather (since that loose definition would apply equally well to Gaboriau) to interest in the acute reasoning by which these investigators convert otherwise insignificant pointers into conclusive proofs of guilt or innocence. That the reasoning, for the greater part of the tale, is as mysterious as the crime itself matters nothing. When Sherlock Holmes found the wax vesta at the scene of John Straker's death, the Inspector, annoyed, exclaimed: "I cannot think how I came to overlook it"; to which Holmes rejoined: "It was invisible, buried in the mud. I only saw it because I was looking for it." And again, in the same story, a favourite with lovers of Holmes ("Silver Blaze"), when the Inspector says to Holmes: "Is there any other point to which you would wish to draw my attention?" Holmes answers: "To the curious incident of the dog in the night-time." "The dog did nothing in the night-time." "That was the curious incident."

Just how much these early tales by Conan Doyle owed to the fact that Sherlock Holmes was a character will never be known. He was so great a character that he trembled upon the borders of farce—never over them, of course: I speak as a Fan. His vanity, his eccentricities, his nettling rebukes to Watson, all made him, much to his creator's annoyance (for Doyle thought he had better books, more sober, laboured books, to his credit than the Holmes tales), a character in the full tradition of the Victorian novelists. He stands for all time as a warning to those who think the way to produce immortal literature is to take oneself very seriously.

Imitators perhaps invented better mysteries for their detectives to unravel, as indeed it was their duty to do; but none of them invented a Sherlock Holmes. But what Doyle had done caused a rush of imitations. Most of them are forgotten, or would be forgotten if the inter-war spiritual drouth had not already produced for detective stories (as for other writings) a host of Dryasdusts, scholars, and (ghastly, deadening accompaniments to the capture of literature by the uncreative) fixed canons. Because of these scholars certain phosphorescent corpses of old mystery have been propped up, post-mortemed, and bottled and labelled for ever. And because of these scholars, a definite view has been adopted regarding what does or does not make one kind of book superior to another kind of book. The detective mystery story has been given a certificate of quality; the story which has a long tradition, the story in which crime plays its part as a leading interest, and in which criminals are shown in action, is reduced to the ranks. As E. M. Wrong says, "The crime story has on the whole been a failure as compared with the tale of detection. . . . In fact the tale of crime is best seen from the detective's angle."

I wonder if Wrong is right? I wonder whether this canon does not merely represent the cultivated point of view? If one has been elaborately educated, so that one's brains must be given some problem to chew, any naïveté will seem jejune, and one will despise very readily whatever does not supply this necessary fuel. But I think it is fallacious to assume that a highly cultivated mind is a truly critical mind. The cultivated mind brings to a consideration of art a system of laws and principles acquired with pains and perhaps with devotion. But the application of acquired principles to particular books and kinds of books is as arbitrary as the purely instinctive judgment of the less cultivated. I personally prefer the detective story to the story of crime. But the modern worship of ratiocination may be a fault.

The crime story has not failed to interest others. Scholars have given many years to the study of Dickens's incomplete "Mystery of Edwin Drood," begun when the Master, in Gissing's terrible words, "casting about him for a new story, saw murder at the end of every vista." Oliver Onions's short novel, "In Accordance with the Evidence," is more important to its readers than many detective stories, although the commission of an undiscovered crime is its central interest. The adventurous histories of John Buchan and others of his type may be as engrossing, and certainly as imaginative, as the majority of detective stories. Dostoevsky's "Crime and Punishment" is without doubt a greater book than Gaboriau's "Crime of Orcival." It may be that the mind which requires a problem is not necessarily superior to the gullible mind, but only one that prefers pencil-and-paper games to pure sport.

The gullible bought or otherwise acquired in the year 1905 38,000 copies of a short, vigorous, and highly sensational novel about the conscientious removal of a wicked Cabinet Minister. The book was called "The Four Just Men," and the public read "The Four Just Men" for much the same reason as that which had led them to read "The Woman in White," "The Mystery of a Hansom Cab," "Called Back," "Lady Audley's Secret," and "Lost Sir Massingberd." It told a thrilling story, in which time, troubles, and tedium were annihilated. The author's name was unfamiliar to readers of novels, and it remained so, apart from this one book, for a space. But later, after the First World War ended, news began to creep about of this book and that by a single writer, and it was found that he had produced a number of such books; and then, as the demand for them grew, more and more books came tumbling out with his name on the title-page, so that one name was known to all who read books, from Pall Mall to Penzance and from Chester to Chicago, and Berlin to Budapest and Buenos Aires.

In England, formerly, two men had held the throne of popularity with masses of their fellow-countrymen. One was Nat Gould, whose racing novels were said to have sold two million copies; the other was Charles Garvice, whose novelettes, contributed as serial stories to a women's paper, and republished by himself, swept the land. We had had startling successes, such as those of Hall Caine and Marie Corelli, and latterly Ethel M. Dell and Florence Barclay. We had had our conjunctions of quality and popularity, such as Wells. But there had not previously been quite such universal reading of a single author as occurred in the case of Edgar Wallace in the years immediately following the First World War.

ii. Edgar Wallace

"I shall be broke again and rich again; but broke or rich, I shall, if the Lord keeps me in good health, be grateful and happy for every new experience, for every novel aspect which the slow-moving circle of life presents to me. I have made many big friends and provoked a few little enmities, which will clear up some day. And I am here! Newspaper-boy, cabin-boy, soldier, journalist, writer—what next? Whatever it is, I'll bet it is interesting."

Edgar Wallace: People.

EDGAR WALLACE, born in 1875, was the son of an actress who abandoned him; and at the age of nine days he was adopted by a Billingsgate fish porter. When he was very small, much against the wish and without the knowledge of his adoptive mother, he began to sell newspapers at a pitch near Ludgate Circus at the bottom of Fleet Street. He then took a number of jobs in factories, which he did not keep, had a single voyage at sea, and joined the Army. While in the Army he wrote a comic song which was bought by Arthur Roberts, and composed a number of doggerel verses; and when his regiment was sent to South Africa he formed by degrees so persistent a journalistic connection that he got into trouble with superior officers, was persuaded to buy his discharge, and set up in Cape Town as a journalist. When the Boer War began he acted as correspondent, at first for Reuters, and then, through an accident, directly for London newspapers; and he was the first to transmit to England news that Peace was signed. When he eventually left South Africa for home he acted as reporter for *The Daily Mail*, was for a brief time editor of the London *Evening News*, and as a special correspondent for a year or two knocked about all over Europe.

While all this was happening to Wallace he published several books of verses—most of them admittedly written in imitation of Kipling, who was his idol. And in 1905, as I have said, he wrote and personally published from a room in Temple Chambers "The Four Just Men," upon which he lost money. He also published at least one other book, the author of which was a Durham schoolmaster named Ian Hay Beith. But publishing and the writing of stories were both unremunerative; and as that was the time of E. D. Morel's denunciation of atrocities on the Belgian Congo Wallace returned to Africa to investigate matters on behalf of *The Daily Mail*. His experiences on the Congo gave him a new theme; and although the literary world did not realize the fact until long afterwards he began his first successful fiction-writing with a series of stories which had the Congo as a background. "Sanders of the River," "People of the River," "Bosambo of the River" were all in this vein. He now had at his command first-hand experience of the life of London's respectable poor (with sidelights on those less respectable which arose from the police-bashing habits of his step-brothers), Army life, War, South African life and politics, Journalism, the Congo; he had taught himself with a good deal of labour how to write with a fair semblance of grammatical accuracy; he was adventurous; and when the First World War came, as he was too old for military service, he wrote from home, for *The Birmingham Daily Post*, articles commenting on the progress of operations, and a number of very popular short stories for an American magazine about a Scottish mechanic and airman known as "Tam o' the Scouts." After the War he settled to the writing of sensational stories, serials, detective mysteries, and the like; and then indeed his success verged upon the incredible.

The time was propitious, because men and women were crying for distraction from the misery, disgust, and boredom which the War and the Peace had produced. Most people were weary; they were in no mood as yet to adore those later loves, erudition and ingenuity; they wanted a writer who could tell a story, and whose invention was equal to the task of keeping them agog for three hundred pages. Smack, crash, bang: "For a second only the old man stared spellbound, and then his pistol jerked up and he fired twice." Wallace was their man. He says in his really excellent autobiography, "People," speaking of an earlier time:

"I had learnt the habit of early rising and early working, and always I worked at top speed."

He worked at top speed. He could deliver the goods. More; his invention was inexhaustible, and he could and did—without the smallest help from a "ghost"—supply with gusto what everybody was waiting for. In that period, and for that period, he became the best-known writer in the world.

Edgar Wallace's appearance is known to all through many photographs in which his long cigarette-holder always protrudes from a pair of thin lips set in a mask-like white face. A plump face, the flesh about the eyes slightly swollen and the eyes themselves cold and steady; the face of a card-player of perfect nerve. He was a man of good size, but not above middle height. His head was clear; he was modest but self-assured, a good public speaker, a fluent talker and tale-teller. He knew what he knew, and never went outside that knowledge in his talk and writing. It is a remarkable fact that the success of his tales owed nothing whatever to salaciousness or suggestiveness, and that his conversation was entirely free from any of the prevailing coarseness to be found in more intellectually ambitious circles. He drank little, if at all, except a great deal of tea. He worked and gambled, worked and gambled, from morning to night. He was typical of the respectable poor of England; and was only unlike them in the fact that he had a highly remunerative talent, of which he made full use to the last days of his life.

It is true that the most successful novels he wrote were of a disconnectedly sensational kind, and that he never was an artist or a polished *littérateur*. It is also true that some of his books are bad books, and that the best of them do not bear re-reading. But the qualities which were in the man are in the books. He knew the criminal world better than most of his rivals; he knew the racing world (but apparently not the horses, for he was a poor tipster) to the extent that he could make it an effective background for fiction and drama. And his aim was the continuous excitement and entertainment of his readers, in which aim he was successful. As an ever-afterwards-quoted reviewer once said: "It is impossible not to be thrilled by Edgar Wallace." There were times—now past—when nobody but Edgar Wallace could supply just that unsuggestive, plain diet of crime that a world in lassitude needed as tonic or anodyne. Wallace was superlatively honest. He did not bother about readers who might prefer Flaubert (and of course, being a wise man, he did not decry Flaubert); but followed his own bent and did his work as a craftsman. He was distinctly a figure in the Georgian literary scene.

iii. Dorothy L. Sayers

"The mental features discoursed of as the analytical are, in themselves, but little susceptible of analysis. We appreciate them only in their effects. We know of them, among other things, that they are always to their possessor, when inordinately possessed, a source of the liveliest enjoyment. As the strong man exults in his physical ability, delighting in such exercises as call his muscles into action, so glories the analyst in that moral activity which *disentangles*. He derives pleasure from even the most trivial occupations bringing his talent into play."

E. A. Poe: The Murders in the Rue Morgue.

THE inevitable invidiousness of such a book as this leads me to omit reference to many excellent writers of tales of crime and tales of the detection of crime. If I were seriously to attempt an exhaustive study of each school of writers in every genre my task would be unending, and each chapter in this book would be a book in itself. So just as I have taken Edgar Wallace as something more than himself, as in fact the archetype of his kind of writer, I shall skip all sorts of interesting composers of detective novels— from E. C. Bentley and A. E. W. Mason to Agatha Christie and Margery Allingham, and from Ronald Knox to Crofts and the Coles, for the sake of reaching one who represents the farthest point yet reached in the development of detective stories towards complete

sophistication. It is my personal view that the three best long detective stories written in English are "The Hound of the Basker-
villes," "The House of the Arrow," and "Trent's Last Case," and
there can be no doubt that Agatha Christie is the queen of the craft,
with Josephine Tey and Ngaio Marsh in attendance. Nevertheless, I
shall refer boldly to Dorothy Sayers.

The contrast between Edgar Wallace and Miss Sayers is as the
contrast between a walk in Chicago and an inquest at Oxford. In the
first one is still alive, but apprehensive; in the second apprehension
is past but one has become extremely interesting only as a specimen.
The coroner talks a good deal, from A to Z.

It is not surprising that Dorothy Sayers should be erudite; for
she graduated at Oxford University round about the end of the First
World War period. In those days she was less sophisticated than she
became; and after beginning cheerfully enough in 1916 with a
diminutive collection of poems called "Op. I" she became graver
two years later with a second volume entitled "Catholic Tales and
Christian Songs." These little prepared their readers for a later em-
barkation into a sea of crime. And yet within half a dozen years
"Whose Body?" revealed an addition to the ranks of those who ask
such disagreeable questions and proceed to deliver the answers at
length.

From the first, Dorothy Sayers insisted upon being humorously
informative. She had that inconvenient readiness of comment which
flows from a mind lively and in good order. She knew a great
many things which ordinarily would not find a place in the tale of
crime and its detection; she had a number of opinions, also, which
no respect for the wooden tradition of Dick Donovan and his peers
led her to repress. From her mental encyclopædia, accordingly,
came richly spiced thoughts and views; and all were stirred into the
mystery, or mysteries, until one really felt as if Aldous Huxley himself had taken to lethal weapons. Dorothy Sayers decorated the
corpse with jovial detail; she then produced quite a dozen persons
whom, as it is shown with Socratic cunning, one must suspect of
committing the crime. These persons were all exceedingly tortuous
in character and movement upon essential days; and they had
peculiar occupations or hobbies which needed to be explored and
dilated upon. She was a mistress of complications, a perfect fisher-
woman of red herrings; and complications and herrings are of
Brobdingnagian size and detail. When, as sometimes happened,
Lord Peter Wimsey viewed the body and illustrated his love of in-
cunabula, wines, and haberdashery, everything assumed so facetious
and fantastic a turn that from being a light diversion the detective
mystery novel became what has been described to me as "deep."
It became, that is, very intricate, and for adult intellects only.

This is because the scholastic or scholarly mind is never content with the simple. For Dorothy Sayers, the plots of Doyle were thin; she knew all about Aristotle and his unities and E. M. Forster and his dislike of "story." And as she found the Aristotelian unities well observable in the modern detective story it is clear that in spite of her admission that the detective story may never hope to rise to the extremist heights of art she could approve as well as write tales in which form is of more significance than emotion. On the subject of the detective story she was a scholar *facile princeps*. Her preface to the collection she first made of "Great Short Stories of Detection, Mystery, and Horror" is the best and most authoritative survey of the whole ground yet written. And her novels became increasingly and impressively the work of a scholar to whom every formula and every possible deviation from formula was already a sentence in single syllables. Could one who had passed the sixth standard be content with child's play?

If I dwell for a moment longer, as I fear I must, upon the weakness of too much scholarship in the arts, it is because I think scholarship is nowadays excessively valued as a necessary preliminary to creative writing. Much as I admire Dorothy Sayers, it is my suspicion that she led the detective story into dust. She wrote with distinction; she invented with ingenuity. But in the same way that modern composers consciously and deliberately serve out music representing the acme of musical scholarship and little else, she, it seems to me (like equally accomplished workers in other literary fields), by her very virtuosity began to kill the thing she loved.

Chapter Sixteen

INTER-WAR PESSIMISM

ALDOUS HUXLEY, NOEL COWARD, RICHARD ALDINGTON,
WYNDHAM LEWIS

i

I HAVE shown in previous chapters how, during the First World War, the imaginations of the young poets soured as the result of their experience, and how the intellectual protesters against the futility of war gradually came to have a voice in the popular ear, and how, when men and women at home were severely tried, they escaped as they could by means of a different kind of violence from that of which they had been reading for four years in their newspapers. I must now mention certain writers whose literary reputation was almost wholly inter-War, and whose work was a direct outcome of the mood of dissatisfaction, even despair, by which honest and thoughtful young people were seized as they saw the consequences of four years of slaughter.

I have chosen four writers who represent different and highly significant aspects of the inter-War literary movement. They did not escape other literary influences, of course; but they took views of life which were not apparent in the generation young in 1914. The young of 1914, however false their expectation may have been, could contemplate a stable future. Nevertheless, Lawrence was young in 1914; Joyce was young in 1914; and Gilbert Cannan, who, more than any other of his immediate contemporaries, had what might be called an inter-War mind, was young in 1914. You could not print, in those days, what you can print now; but you could say the same things in a different way. You could not speak in crude words of Homosexuality and Lesbianism, the Œdipus Complex or casual fornication; but you were not prevented from the portrayal of abnormal people, and if there had to be greater discretion in language I am not sure that some feeble little books which have seemed bold by their use of vulgar words did after all a tremendous deal for literature. I say nothing of that new freedom between the sexes of which we used to read in the newspapers; that was only a further stage in self-consciousness.

But as I have used the word "self-consciousness" it is time that I should explain in what way the inter-War writers differed from the pre-First World War writers. It was in one of its more noteworthy aspects by painfully increased self-consciousness. We were all so self-conscious that some were paralysed in their animal spirits and some carried Narcissism to a point at which it became an extravagance. Half our writers were defending themselves against disapproval of their abnormality; and half were making self-conscious fun of the self-consciousness of others (or of their abnormality). Nearly all were showing-off.

They felt that the world was a revolting place, and a hopeless place. They wanted to do as Omar Khayyám wanted to do so long ago, shatter it to bits and remould it nearer to the heart's desire. They were nearly all politicians. Some of them thought writers had no business to sit down and write simply of irrational human beings; that they ought to struggle for something, no matter what, even if it be only Peace or War, a new currency or sterilization of the unfit. Others that writers should mercilessly criticize and condemn the old, or the young, orthodox or unorthodox economics, or graft or political intrigue. And if there were some whose ways, moral or immoral, did not please the majority, so that they were said to be diseased or criminal, they felt themselves to be personally involved in all condemnations of the age, and they, too, rose up into defensive polemics and assertion. "I'm right, and you're wrong." "Punish, persecute, destroy." "Why shouldn't we be abnormal, if we want to? Instead of bullying us, you should realize that we're *different*. Not only different, but *better*." As in the international sphere, so in the literary there were everywhere hostility, pretensions, threats, fear, and misery. The air was full of spiteful criticism and bad words.

With some justification, but not the justification of art. Some said (following the lead of the Soviet government) that there can be no art which is not propagandist. They said we must choose to be either for Communism or for Fascism; never above party, never for disinterested truth. Others, contemplating our frantic anthill, knowing that the universe is finite and moving unrescuably towards its end, knowing that every phenomenon is reducible to statistics and scientific laws, seeing around them only the disheartening manifestations of corruption, a furious paroxysm of nullity, were appalled by realization of the littleness of man. They were the idealists, bereft of hope. Man was no more man; only a bundle of atoms, strutting, mouthing, functioning, one of so many thousand millions of his kind, an insect with no God to guide, no heaven to promise. Nothing was of any importance; what we were we had been for ages and should be until the earth ceased to be able to support life. There was no virtue in us.

There were quacks and egotists, the former with nostrums and the latter with grievances. "I haven't had a fair deal from Society.

Damn Society!" "Everybody's mad; but I'm sane." "Look out! The bogeys will get you!" "Ladies and gentlemen, if you will only buy this little pill, it will transport you to better trade or better morals or better art. But if you don't buy it, you're doomed." "We're all doomed; everybody's against me, and always has been, and always will be. They don't like my face; they're brutes, cads, bitches . . ." Lawrence thought there was too much tolerance in the world; he wanted to destroy tolerance, because he believed that it was softness and the enemy of light. But he justifiably complained of intolerance towards himself; intolerance rising to persecution. His successors, who had not Lawrence's genius, complained before anything had happened to them, and were so intolerant of each other that the literary world was full of faction. It was a kind of hysteria, perhaps. Just as Captain Hook made his dying speech when he had an opportunity, in case the moment of death should give him no opening for it, they retorted upon persecutors who really had been quite innocently wondering what they would have for dinner that day and had no other mischief in mind at all.

No wonder the pessimists, looking upon this scene, and deafened by the row, the tub-thumping and the squeals, were depressed. They shuddered again at one more illustration of the increasing vulgarity of life; they criticized yet more stringently. They were used to hypocrisy and stupidity in the mass of people (of whom they knew little, and wanted to know nothing at all); but to find noise and rottenness even in men who were supposedly of some intellect was a fresh horror to them, and one they could ill endure. They could only endure it if they had a power seldom found in company with pessimism or with intellectual prowess—the power of tumultuous laughter. And with that laughter they could ridicule as they groaned. Said Elizabeth Bennet, in "Pride and Prejudice": "I hope I never ridicule what is wise and good. Follies and nonsense, whims and inconsistencies, do divert me, I own, and I laugh at them whenever I can." Apart from the fact that he had grave doubts as to whether there are such things as wisdom and goodness, Aldous Huxley could echo Elizabeth's words. He was the one considerable intellectual of his generation who had a great heart and a great humour, who was as fastidious as a maiden aunt, as bawdy as a highbrow, and as unaffected in his amusement as a common man.

ii. Aldous Leonard Huxley

"He handed Burlap the drawing. It was in ink touched with coloured washes, extraordinarily brilliant and lively. Curving in a magnificently sweeping S, a grotesque procession of monsters marched diagonally down and across the paper. Dinosaurs, pterodactyls, titanotheriums, ichthyosauruses walked, swam, or flew at the tail of the procession; the van was composed of human monsters, huge-headed creatures, without limbs or bodies, creeping slug-like on vaguely slimy extensions of chin and neck. The faces were mostly those of eminent contemporaries."

Aldous Huxley: Point Counter Point.

LIKE other celebrated and less celebrated writers of the day, Huxley, who was born in 1894, published poetry as his first step towards self-expression. He was a contributor to "Wheels," the Sitwell rival to "Georgian Poetry," published a book of verses of his own, "The Burning Wheel" in 1916, and in 1917 was one of the editors of an annual called "Oxford Poetry." Unlike some of the others, he in spite of everything else remained a poet. He became a poet in revolt against the planned scientific world of the future; and accordingly was read and condemned as the author of a book about bottled babies and other abominations. Such condemnation was not new; it helped Huxley to a wider public than that enjoyed by any other writer of similar intellectual preoccupation, but it was regrettable.

Aldous Huxley was the grandson of Thomas Henry Huxley (to whom, according to H. G. Wells, who was T. H. Huxley's pupil, he had a facial resemblance), and on his mother's side was of the family of Thomas Arnold, the famous headmaster of Rugby. Schoolmasters, scientists, poets, and novelists (Mrs. Humphry Ward was Huxley's aunt) were among the notable assembly of his relations; if one were to picture them as fairy godfathers and godmothers, gathered about his bed in 1894, one could trace in his character a benevolent gift from each. He set out thereafter upon a road full of distinguished fingerposts, all pointing to fame by way of the intellect and the pen. It must have been a blessing, but a doubtful blessing, to have such famous relations; pleasant to think "my aunt" or "my grandfather," difficult, nevertheless, to ignore a certain imperiousness in the fingerposts.

However, although it is true that few great poets have been more assailed of late than Matthew Arnold, Huxley was not to be envied or commiserated with over his heredity. He is more properly to be discussed on account of his own performance. And first of all, I must say for those who are interested in such things (I have been encouraged all through this book to add notes on personal appearance and traits by reading that such details would be invaluable to writers of biographies for the *D.N.B.*) that he was the tallest

English author known to me. He was so tall (and thin, so that he seemed to stretch to infinity) that when, long ago, he lived in Hampstead, ribald little boys in that neighbourhood used to call out to him: "Cole up there, guv'nor?" Naturally this great height gave some of those who encountered him the impression that he lived remote from the world, wrapped in distant hauteur. That was not the case. Expecting conscious superiority in him, casual observers recorded an excessively lofty manner; whereas the truth is that Huxley conversed easily, and was full of gleeful high spirits. He used long words, because he thought in long words; and not because he was aware that they were long words. The words he used most often in conversation (or at least in narrative) were "fantastic" and "incredible." They were appropriate words; for the narratives, made credible by his skill, were more fantastic than anything he wrote, and they were also true. He had a happy knack of meeting odd people and seeing odd sights; and while this does not mean that he was himself odd it does mean that he was prepared for every oddity.

As a boy, Huxley suffered greatly in the matter of his eyesight, which it was feared that he would altogether lose. He spent many days alone, in a dark room, unable to read, unable to see: the introspective results of that time are plainly to be found in the nervous gravity—he did not like the word "morbidity"—of his work. But the fear passed; though it would never be normal, his sight was saved, and he enjoyed it to the last. He was able to go to Oxford. At Oxford he published some poems, as I have said; and when he came down he found work on *The Athenæum*, under Middleton Murry's editorship. Over the name "Autolycus" he contributed a regular essay to *The Athenæum* (a number of these essays are to be found in the volume entitled "On the Margin"), and subsequently he collected several stories in a volume, called "Limbo," which provided an auspicious opening to his literary career.

After "Limbo" was published Huxley used to speak of a "Peacockian novel" which he was writing, and I mention this fact, otherwise nowhere noted, because it is so interesting to realize that his impulse towards fiction came from a scholar-satirist, Thomas Love Peacock, rather than from a novelist. Huxley was never a novelist in the ordinary sense: always a scholar-satirist. He could tell a story when he wished to do so (it was usually a short story); but he was a man who used the fiction form as a vehicle for his ideas, and not a man who wrote novels because he must do so or remain sterile.

In the early days of his fame, when the "modns" were all scientific intellectuals, this caused him to be what is called a fashionable

writer; but Huxley never commanded the suffrages of Bloomsbury, because his ideas were not quite those of Bloomsbury, and
because, to the disgust of the exclusives, he became a popular
and very widely read publicist. His interests were multifarious. He
was the only man I ever heard of (my informant was his brother,
Julian, so I assume the story to be well-founded) who, on setting
out to go round the world, caused a special packing-case to be
made for his "Encyclopædia Britannica." He was likewise the only
man who, with the "Encyclopædia Britannica" ever to hand, took
an even greater interest in the world of flesh and blood. Though
a bookworm, he was a human being: the combination is rare.

First of all in "Limbo," but more markedly in his first, or
Peacockian novel, "Crome Yellow," he gave evidence of those
remarkable high spirits which made him laugh wholeheartedly at
the prigs, smugs, and snobs of the æsthetic world. The novel
seemed to be full of portraits, all full of jovial irony; and I think
it must have been the portraits which first roused a doubt of Huxley
in the minds of really first-rate people. He dared to laugh at first-
rate people:

>   "'What are you reading?' She looked at the book. 'Rather second-
> rate, isn't it?' The tone in which Mary pronounced the word 'second-
> rate' implied an almost infinite denigration. She was accustomed in
> London to associate only with first-rate people who liked first-rate
> things, and she knew that there were very, very few first-rate things in
> the world, and that these were mostly French."

That was War, you know. Because if one laughs at first-rate people,
and at the same time shows that one may not retaliatively be called
illiterate, one is at once an enemy. However, Huxley did not care.
He went on laughing at first-rate people and succeeded in making
them what they never sought to make themselves—amusing.
Laughter at every affectation, indeed, for a long time was his lighter
strain.

But in that same book "Crome Yellow" (a very slight book by
comparison with some that he wrote afterwards, though a delight-
fully amusing one), Huxley announced the major problem of all his
work:

>   "One entered the world, Denis pursued, having ready-made ideas
> about everything. One had a philosophy and tried to make life fit into
> it. One should have lived first and then made one's philosophy to fit
> life. . . . Life, facts, things were horribly complicated; ideas, even the
> most difficult of them, deceptively simple In the world of ideas
> everything was clear; in life all was obscure, embroiled. Was it sur-
> prising that one was miserable, horribly unhappy?"

You see there the reverse of the academic adherence to "principles," i.e., rules made by dons and rigidly applied in advance of practical knowledge. Huxley, although almost boastfully an intellectual, was not an academic intellectual. He was ready, able, and even eager to learn by experience. For this reason his books provided a most interesting library of modern ideas. I take it that he arrived in town from the University, as Denis did, full of system; and found, as Denis and many others have done, that the system which looks so secure in cloistered calm does not quite deal with the urgent immensities that follow. That is, a tutor's room has its simplicity; but there are more things in heaven and earth than are dreamt of—or at least are demonstrable—in any system of philosophy. Huxley, coming to London, and going among other, older men, found his ideas not completely satisfying. When, a little later, he became a hard-working practical journalist, and began to discover how men and women behaved, and how work was done, although he remained, as he was bound to remain, a very cultured man in the academic sense, he learned a thousand and one things which had not been in the University curriculum.

There were some things he could not learn, but could only glimpse. He was born in the middle, not quite perfectly leisured class, and not, as Lawrence was, in the class of what Gissing used to call "the ignobly poor." It was accordingly impossible for him to get out of the class in which he was born. He could see the ridiculousnesses and affectations of the æsthetic sets, and the ugly little round of their squirrel-cage life; but he could not help feeling that fastidious recoil from lower classes which is a part of the middle-class breeding. Very few people of that breeding can make the journey into another type of mind; and Huxley could not make that journey. In the same way, the ignobly poor, to which Lawrence in childhood belonged, are never at ease in newer surroundings, Lawrence never did justice to those of different breeding from his own. You see the contrast in the scornful but not quite vivid descriptions of flannel-trousered intellectuals in "Lady Chatterley's Lover" and the account of squalors and fashions, given at first hand, which Huxley supplied in "Point Counter Point." But Lawrence and Huxley could be, and were, friends towards the end of Lawrence's life; and there is no doubt in my mind that in spite of his "Encyclopædia Britannica" Huxley was better able than any other man of his generation to take a comprehensive view of society. He had book-learning and some practical acquaintance with men's actions; if only he could perfectly have synthesized the two kinds of knowledge he would have achieved the highest of which he was capable.

He did not achieve the synthesis; for some time before the

outbreak of the Second World War he began to despair altogether of human nature, adopted that peculiar form of "escapism" which makes men long for remote islands and monastic communities, and became an expositor of mysticism. It may be inferred (a) that he lost touch with reality or (b) that he reached a higher altitude of spiritual knowledge than most men can bear.

When he first began to write, and I was his constant reader, I was delighted and amused by his wit and the fun which he innocently (and yet naughtily) levelled at the vulnerable prigs of the arts. I then felt that in his sincere search for truth by way of further and further disillusion, still confining himself to the æsthetic and intellectual few, he had come to the end of his power to range more widely or to believe in anything at all. He seemed without hope, and therefore without philosophy, without anything but horror at the futility of all things; and obviously drying up. Even the brilliance of "Point Counter Point" did not reassure me, for that book only did with more mature elaborateness what he had done before. It might have been written, as Lawrence said it was written, by a "precocious adolescent." An adolescent peculiarly aware of his own adolescence, it is true; and therefore an adolescent for whom there was still high hope.

"'The essence of the new way of looking is multiplicity,' says Philip, in 'Point Counter Point.' 'Multiplicity of eyes and multiplicity of aspects seen. For instance, one person interprets events in terms of bishops; another in terms of the price of flannel camisoles; another, like that young lady from Gulmerg, . . . thinks of it in terms of good times. And then there's the biologist, the chemist, the physicist, the historian. Each sees, professionally, a different layer of reality. What I want to do is to look with all those eyes at once. With religious eyes, scientific eyes, economic eyes, *homme moyen sensuel* eyes . . . !"

.   .   .   .   .

"But the heart, the heart . . . The heart was Burlap's speciality. 'You'll never write a good book,' he had said oracularly, 'unless you write from the heart.' It was true; Philip knew it. . . . It was so easy for him to be almost anybody, theoretically and with his intelligence. He had such a power of assimilation, that he was often in danger of being unable to distinguish the assimilator from the assimilated, of not knowing among the multiplicity of his rôles who was the actor. . . . He had been a cynic and also a mystic, a humanitarian and also a contemptuous misanthrope; he had tried to live the life of detached and stoical reason and another time he had aspired to the unreasonableness of natural and uncivilized existence."

M

You must not take that as a self-portrait; but the first quotation represents Huxley's own ideal; and the admissions in the second quotation show how searching and critical Huxley's mind was concerning his own work and the workings of his own mind. He was a modern in a good sense; the sense indicated in the remark attributed to Socrates that "an unexamined life is not worth living." The difficulty is that with so much examination one hardly expects to find that flow of the imagination from which the best novels have come.

But Huxley realized, I think, that he had reached a dead end; that the intelligentsia had amused for the last time, and that they were in such a state that to deal with them longer would be a cruelty and a boredom. He went right away from his pictures of Chelsea bedrooms and drawing-rooms, and leapt into the future of the scientists. The emotion which had been gathering in him as he realized with his imagination what such a world would mean to real men and women gave him new power. In "Brave New World" he wrote a book which, whatever may be its ultimate place in literature, was once again a step in advance of the general consciousness of Huxley's time. It was the work of a poet.

The book was that of a man who had the courage and imagination to envisage the Utopia of scientists in the full horror of being. All those accepted visions of a hygienic and sterilized future, from which emotion, poetry, and beauty are eliminated, were synthesized in "Brave New World." Everything was mechanical. Everything planned, bottled, dehumanized, and frightful. And Huxley, of all living writers, was the only man who could have illustrated with such address the consequences of the scientists' dream. The result is a picture from which one recoils with loathing, even as the author, in painting it, must have done.

The defect of this book, as of all Huxley's writing, is that it was negative. He first lived in the small world of the æsthetes, and found it damnable. Every shoddy pretence in it, every silly and ugly piece of sophisticated futility, aroused his dislike and contempt. From ridicule he passed to deliberate exposure. From the views of life which that world stood for he dissented with energy. But he could offer instead of those views only his own disgust of the people who accepted them. If he went to the Cinema, he saw films which caused him loathing; the people crowded into the Cinema were reekingly cloddish and foul, mind and body; their conceptions were stupid, and their self-deceptions beastly. If he read books, they were wretched and full of base ideas. If he travelled, he found —always with a sort of jovial gusto—that the new human beings he met were morons and cretins similar to those he had left at home. If he looked into politics, he found them corrupt; into

morals, he found them libidinous and sanctimonious; into spiritual-
ism, he found it nothing but telepathy; into the animal kingdom, he
found it sniffing and raising its legs and blindly procreating without a
thought for the *psyche*. And it was the same with the scientific
Utopia; for that, too, was the imagining of men in whom spirit
burns feebly and the rationalizing impulse thrusts with busybody
strength.

The interesting point about Huxley is that with all his encyclopædic knowledge, his scepticism, his far-ranging thought and
imagination, he came at last to utter only the mystic's cry for the
old simple earth, the old simplicities of relation, motherhood,
mother-tended babies, and the unsullied countryside. It is as if,
having scornfully ridden far beyond the army of Chestertons and
Bellocs, he had mysteriously caught up again with them and joined
the staff of these two stout generals. The picture which the mind
conjures up of Huxley between his two seniors is as amusingly
fantastic as anything in the work of the three. It is quite incredible.
Nevertheless, something has gone wrong, it seems to me, with the
Huxleyan campaign.

That is an exaggeration. Huxley is not a Chestertonian or a
Bellocian. He is not really for the natural man who had that wonderful imaginary heyday in Merrie England. He stands for intellect
in a world of scientists and hedonists. He believes as strongly as any
Bloomsbury æsthete that Demos is a devil which threatens culture.
Whatever happened, he would always be on the side of the fastidious.
But you see what difficulties arise when, being an intellectual, one
courageously ceases to be a pedant. It is impossible for Huxley or
anybody else with generosity of mind and humour to be solely an
intellectual; it is equally impossible for a man pledged in his being
to a reverence for culture to be a democrat. One can imagine him
crying:

"The time is out of joint: O cursèd spite,
    That ever I was born to set it right."

That he was born, not to set right the dreadful time in which we
live, but by a process of successive loathings to reach some positive
philosophy, I believe. He would shrink from promulgating a
positive philosophy, perhaps; for all his reachings out to truth are
tentative, lacking in self-confidence, in the modern manner, and
in his original work have been largely expressed in the questionings
of his sceptical heroes; but he has the integrity to attain and to hold a
view of life which shall be satisfying to more than himself.

ii. Noel Coward

"The fact that this *is* an age of scientific enlightenment does not yet appear to have penetrated into the minds of those placed by fate and birth and circumstances on pedestals of authority, from which it is their duty to decide what is, and what is not, conducive to corruption of the public morals."

Noel Coward, in a Preface.

HAVING been born in 1899, Noel Coward probably heard the songs of the Boer War period as he lay in his cradle. "Dolly Grey," "The Soldiers of the Queen," "Bluebell," those haunting tunes of which he made such tear-drawing use in "Cavalcade," must have nourished the young heart as infant food fattened the young body. He was hardly out of the cradle when he appeared upon the stage (that was in 1910); and had hardly appeared upon the stage before he became a dramatic author. I seem to remember walking up St. Martin's Lane when I was not so very old myself, and observing that Winifred Emery, a celebrated actress of those days, was appearing at the New Theatre in a play by a marvellous boy named Noel Coward. But perhaps I am wrong. Certainly there was a play called "The Young Idea," and certainly something in the nature of a play called "Woman and Whisky" in which our author was concerned was produced in 1919, when Coward had not attained his twentieth birthday. He was precocious enough, full of the theatre from boyhood.

He wrote and he acted. Later, when he entered into association with C. B. Cochran, he wrote the text of a revue, wrote the lyrics for it, and wrote the music too. I am not sure that he did not produce. He could have produced. He was always a good producer and a finished actor. His music is endlessly played by innumerable popular orchestras. His plays were once booed (Coward facing the boos with every appearance of dignity), as well as billed, in the Cinemas of England, as the greatest living dramatist. He was inaccurately reported as marooned upon a desert island; plays of his were banned by the Censor in England; he wrote prefaces (and they were printed) in italics. Knowing all the smart people, he yet neither drank nor stayed up late with them. He was popular wherever he went; and might at any time have been mobbed by those outrageous harpies who molest actors and actresses at stage doors in London. His plays are denied wit by the superior critics, and yet in their way they are wittier than most other smart plays excepting those by Frederick Lonsdale.

It would appear that exception has been taken to some of Coward's work on the ground that it directly encourages immorality. That is very strange. His plays are among the most moral plays ever written. Unfortunately all sorts of very odd people insist upon going to the theatre; and while, if these same people read a book, they may complain to the library about it, and have it put under the counter for those who ask for it, or even bring about a wide demand for that same book at the bookshops, if they go to the theatre (or if they stay away from the theatre) and make complaints about the morality of a play, they can rarely do it anything but harm. One can read a banned book on the sly; but one may jib at the idea of being seen at an immoral play. Unless one is an intellectual rebel; but then the support of intellectual rebels makes little difference to the box office. The theatre is a target for all those moral busybodies who like to denounce the stream of filth poured forth by the novelists and playwrights of the earth. However, not all Coward's plays have been banned, even when they showed young ladies drunk or young men hysterical; and it may be that he exaggerated the sufferings he endured at the instance of Mrs. Grundy and her official cousins. He has been one of the most successful playwrights of modern times, and he has had much applause.

Why should he be banned? The answer is, according to Coward, that the Middle Classes impose the weight of their "massed illiteracy" upon the theatre. He says: "I do resent very deeply, on my own behalf and on the behalf of those young writers who are sincerely attempting to mirror contemporary life honestly and truthfully . . . that this weight of bourgeois ignorance and false sentimentality should not only be allowed to force those in authority to crush down rising talent for the sole reason that its outlook doesn't quite conform with the moral traditions of twenty-five years ago, but that it should be encouraged in every possible way by the Press."

One can tell from this protest that Coward, though a writer supposedly frivolous, has a serious purpose. It is his object to mirror contemporary life. Not all contemporary life, but sections of it. And the part he has mirrored most amusingly is a part given to promiscuity, drunkenness, drugging, and domestic fisticuffs. There can be no question that there is such a part; the part which lives always upon the verge of emotional crises, which either earns money by painting or writing or does not earn money at all and has a great deal of time upon its hands. If it is competent for a dramatist to bore us for three acts with the tale of two young men who miss a boat or a bank cashier who goes on the loose with his bank's cash, then it is quite legitimate for Coward to tell us with great verve about some of the equally boring people who have affairs and quarrel, who get tipsy, who leave their wearisome spouses for lovers, or who divorce each other and re-marry, only to feel the old sentiment when they meet by chance at an hotel.

The trouble is that Coward's plays about neurotics do not quite satisfy us that neuroticism is a compulsive theme; or that Coward has seen it more than superficially. The plays are written with a delightful sense of the theatre, and are adorned with chit-chat which is insulting, irreverent, cheeky, and full of surprise. They are less good when the author is serious, for then he gropes a little in the profundities, and long theatrical experience serves him ill. Therefore, until he found a perfect medium for his talent in later shows of lower middle-class life or dramatic anecdotes of scrupulous lovers, his lighter plays, or the lighter moments in his less frivolous plays, were the best things he wrote. I must mention here, also, two brilliant short stories published in a collection called "To Step Aside." There is no mistaking the success of such plays as "Private Lives" and "Blithe Spirit," where Coward's spirits are at their highest throughout and his sense of stage tableau irresistible. Some of the other plays, the ones which may not be produced in London (I do not know why they may not be produced, and Coward's complaint is legitimate enough), are less amusing. He is quick rather than wise; when the characters are shallow, and he knows they are shallow, he is master of them, and has lovely fun; when he over-estimates their significance the audience misses the fun.

That is the problem with Coward. If he may laugh, he has such a light touch that we must laugh, too. Whenever the people talk nonsense—the significant use of the word "yours' in "Private Lives", by which we are made at once to know that although they are now married to others the protagonists still feel intimately proprietary towards each other; the young man in "Home Chat" who arrives at a moment of crisis, finds he has not said "How d'ye do" until it is too late to do so; and so on—the author's glee shoots high. But when he expounds Life and Freedom our hearts sink. "Design for Living," for instance, has an interesting theme, but is in fact about people who are not made interesting. Coward wishes to establish the theory that if people are Bohemian they ought to be Bohemian, and do as they like, without being blamed for their Bohemianism. He causes one young woman to have two lovers and then a husband, from whom the lovers at last jointly remove the young woman for what apparently will be a perpetual interchangeable spree. That play is not particularly bad in moral, and parts of it are very well written; but as a piece of mirroring it is restricted. I doubt if Coward, though he pictures one kind of life with great honesty, is justified in believing it to be of social or æsthetic importance.

His quality lies in his fun. He has great sense of the stage, and can picture to admiration the comic and emotional effects of pyjamas, fights, the mischievous ghosts of dead wives, hotel balconies by night with bands playing his own music. His sense of dramatic surprise, shown in "Cavalcade" as well as in his character pieces is extraordinary. These three excellences have made him a much-admired and I think a loved dramatist. His wit, though not of the most subtle and distinguished kind, is fresh and amusing; his characters "toss the ball lightly to one another," and rarely drop it. Having tossed the ball, they have done all that in the theatre can be expected of them; and for my part I always wish them to go on tossing with the same lightness throughout the evening.

iv. Richard Aldington

"The great English middle-class mass, that dreadful squat pillar of the nation, will only tolerate art and literature that are fifty years out of date, eviscerated, detesticulated, bowdlerized, humbuggered, slip-slopped, subject to their Anglicized Jehovah . . . So, look out, my friend. Hasten to adopt the slimy mask of British humbug and British fear of life, or expect to be smashed."

R. *Aldington: Death of a Hero.*

LONG, long ago, before the War, Richard Aldington was an Imagist poet. He said that "the poetry of the nineteenth century —from Shelley right down through Tennyson and Swinburne and Arnold and all the rest to Francis Thompson—is turgid and boresome and sloppy and wordy to an almost incredible extent. . . . In the poetry of those days there was very little of the clear precise writing with which the young poets of today are in love; there was nothing hard or marble-like about it." That was said in 1914.

He was also, in those days, a somewhat iconoclastic critic, writing as one may see thinly disguised in "Death of a Hero" for, among other papers, *The New Age*. It must have been a very difficult time for him, because he had no popular wares; only none too accommodating literary criticism, and poems for which he had difficulty in finding a publisher. He lived at Hampstead or in the country, and translated from the Greek of Meleager and Anyte of Tegea. As late as 1916 he was busy with the work of introducing lesser-known Greek and Latin writers to those unfamiliar with the dead languages. The series of small booklets or leaflets called "The Poets' Translations" owed much to his enthusiasm, and it was admirable pioneer work. Unfortunately for us, its publication ceased during the First World War. Aldington, instead, published his Collected Verse, and he took to writing long novels in the post-First World War manner.

It is as a novelist that he appears in this chapter, for although he took to destructive biography of T. E. Lawrence and others he was ever inter-War pessimist. He tried to laugh off his pessimism; but (like that of Jack Point) "his laughter had an echo that is grim," and he made a hollow job of it. The world and that frightful British middle class which was likewise Noel Coward's bugbear, were too much for him. He was indignant with both. Being by temperament serious, he covered his seriousness with a crust of merriment. In print the crust wore off.

I explain this fact to myself by thinking that Aldington was not really a humorist at all, but one who unfortunately, when he was holding forth with grandeur, heard the sound of his own voice, and so could not continue with his address. He "laughed it off," as they say. His indignation over the bourgeoisie had the same right-eousness as bourgeois indignation over backsliding, and a similar irrelevance. Having embraced, for some reason unknown to me, a contrary view of life from that of the ultra-respectable, he saw all who were not happy in their environment as victims of mass cruelty, individually defensible upon moral grounds. This, I need hardly point out, is the attitude of sentimentality. "You brute! Leave the poor child alone! What if the dog did bite you? A great strong creature like you, to attack somebody or something smaller——"

Accordingly nobody can be surprised if I say I think Aldington, as a novelist, was a sentimentalist. I think Coward, as a serious dramatist, was a sentimentalist. They had this much in common, that they were driven by their sympathy for the misfits into a general arraignment of all who were wise or lucky enough to make successes of their lives upon normal lines. It was a simple view of life. Far too simple, and too emotional, to be a profound one. Aldington could not see a spinster as anything but one thwarted by a damnable society of prudes, or a Victorian married woman as anything but the victim of her husband's lust; Coward could not see a tempera-mental harlot as a harlot, but—how the familiar euphemism rises to the lips!—as an "unfortunate," and must defend her as one who, whatever the world might say, was as God made her. His sympathy was always for a pretty woman or an "unconventional" egoist. It was the prudish view inside out, and not a new morality.

Both Coward and Aldington hit back at the blind force of the bourgeoisie, which they personified, the one as Mrs. Grundy, the other as Dora. Both had kind hearts; Aldington, clearly, a very affectionate nature. Neither envisaged a world beyond the little world he knew; neither made any attempt to comprehend the bourgeois point of view, which is the view of organized society defending its organization, before condemning it. No, no; respect-ability was wrong; as Dr. Stockmann said in "An Enemy of the People": "The compact Liberal Majority is *always* wrong." That is not a new idea; it is as old, you see, as Ibsen. Even older; as old as the hills.

Now it does not, or should not, affect the critic that this rather than another moral attitude is adopted by any author. But a feeling that indignation is too easy and too obvious to be quite intellectually sincere must arise in him. Aldous Huxley was as little satisfied as Aldington or Coward with the inter-War world; but he began with the mental capacity to distinguish good from pseudo-good and unco' guid; and when he satirized he was not morally indignant over smugness, but æsthetically revolted by whatever is ugly and useless in the life of mankind. It was his taste that was offended; not his facile moral judgment. Both Coward and Aldington reacted emotionally to the problem of conduct. They unconsciously distorted an echo of the bourgeoisie. Where the respectables said, with Mr. Growser of Toytown, "Disgraceful! It ought not to be allowed!' and, self-righteously, "Thank God I at least am above such vice or such weakness or such stupidity!" they retorted, with equal feeling: "Why shouldn't she? Poor thing! It's *natural* to her to misbehave; or it's *unnatural* that she should be made to behave as you think she ought to!" Coward, although indignant, said this with perfect discreetness, and decorated and obvious with buoyant laughter; Aldington, more serious, more "modn," naïvely used words for which his publishers substituted asterisks. In that respect Coward was more adult than Aldington.

Coward, when in the mood, is capable of pure fun which forces delighted laughter from a *reader* of his plays, as well as from an audience in the theatre; Aldington, keeping up persistent laughter of his own, cannot think of anything funny to say, even about T. S. Eliot. He raps out a few oaths and extravagances; he is ribald at the expense of æsthetes and gossips and sophisticates; but his performance is that of a boy who remembers what bewilderment these people have caused him, and not that of one who laughs with detachment at the pretentiousness and ill-nature he scorns. The gospel of Lawrence, that one should not be tolerant of the intolerable, but should Crush the Infamy, played havoc with the native gentleness of a mind never too speedy or light-witted. He did not mean to be rude; but was nervously exaggerative and his hand was often as heavy as a brick. The dazzle of satire, or irony (I can never distinguish between them in modern writing) was too much for him, and he struggled to translate bewildered pain into a frolicsome comment from the heights of worldly wisdom. Thackeray did the same thing with more successful archness. Aldington's satire, unsweetened and unsalted by strong humour, remains too often as rudimentary as the back answers of an adolescent.

When he is willing to be serious, as he is in the scenes of "Death of a Hero" which picture war experience, this author fully demonstrates his quality, which is considerable. As these scenes show, and as his poems and such passages in other novels as slip past his earnest jocularity show, he had great capacity for emotion. Though the style is often slap-dash, as if he wrote headlong, he had a power to picture events and surroundings as if he felt them. If not subtle he was honest and impatient of humbug. He bustled the bourgeois, and did not sneer at them. Having naturally great sensitiveness and (I infer, for I never met him) great shyness, he did not therefore sit coldly in a corner and devise witticisms at the expense of other comers, but blurted out what was in his mind, stumbled, laughed uproariously, and then finding that nobody else laughed, condemned them all roundly for being such fish-hearted and sanctimonious prigs. "That dreadful squat pillar," he said. "Look out, my friend. Hasten to adopt the slimy mask of British humbug and British fear of life, or expect to be smashed!"

v. Percy Wyndham Lewis

"'I am a pessimist, Hobson. But I'm a new sort of pessimist. I think I am the sort that will please! I am the Panurgic-pessimist, drunken with the laughing gas of the abyss.'"

Percy Wyndham Lewis: Tarr.

BEFORE I deal with Wyndham Lewis, the author of "Tarr" and other works of fiction, I must detach him from all possible confusion with his namesake, D. B. Wyndham-Lewis, the humorist and Catholic biographer. They were not the same person. D. B. made many jokes about popular novelists and lived in the great world from which humorists draw their inspiration; Percy was constantly at war with the smaller fry of the æsthetic world and wrote, he said, from the standpoint of genius. He was also an original and very striking draughtsman; but his drawings have no place in the present book, much as they would adorn it, and must now pass from our notice. It is with the written word that we are concerned.

Wyndham Lewis began writing character sketches long before the First World War, brief and vivid ironic studies: those are his *forte*. If one could pick them out from among the verbiage of his longer books and bring them together in series they would reveal better than anything else could do the strength and liveliness of his talent. Just before the War began he was at work upon an ambitious novel of which all sorts of people heard and of which several people had glimpses; but the War arrived, Lewis was ill, and it was July 1918 before "Tarr" was published by a firm (calling itself after the name of a short-lived periodical) known as The Egoist, Ltd. The same firm first published in England Joyce's "Portrait of the Artist as a Young Man." "Tarr" had its great admirers, mostly among young artists and writers from Chelsea and the Café Royal, who were personally acquainted with the author; but outside these it made little stir, and the larger public never heard of it. The larger public never hears of anything until it has a united push behind it, and Lewis always missed the united push, for a reason which I shall give in a moment.

"Tarr" remained an only visible child for some time. Then, on the wings of the newer modernism, Lewis shook a little shower of works upon the public, from "Time and Western Man" to the first part of "The Childermass," at last publishing "The Apes of God" under his own supervision, and a number of smaller pamphlets, polemics, and diatribes attacking individuals, abuses, political theories, and venality. All these works were written with the utmost freedom and ebullience of style, and were either greatly and properly admired as invective or shunned as tiresome vehemence or set aside as incomprehensible nonsense. They were mostly in the nature of denunciations, in the expression of which the author excelled; and while, following Joyce, he frequently abstained from the use of punctuation he was never designedly gnomic, and as a rule becomes incomprehensible only when one misses the point through ignorance of the people he is lambasting.

The people themselves, no doubt, understood only too well who was portrayed and what was intended. Some of them, in obscure sheets or in counterblasts, hit back. Most of them ignored what was said of them. That was their best offensive weapon; for if Lewis was unanswered he had to pass on to another subject, which is distinctly hard on one who must fight or sink into gloomy inaction. I think he had a genuine grievance against those best able to appreciate his great gifts, in the fact that too often, perhaps offended, perhaps ungenerous, they for personal reasons cold-shouldered him and his writings.

They did not like him. He was not of the right colour or the right tone. The standpoint of genius is apt to make a man egotistical and aggressive, and Lewis was egotistical and aggressive. He was afraid that if he were otherwise he would be overlooked. Yet Lewis, like every other author, needed praise, lashings of praise. He hungered and thirsted for it. Because he saw all sorts of men scratching each other's backs and rolling each other's logs, he shouted in holy horror at the spectacle. However, he was so much concerned with himself that it never occurred to him to hand the same gross flattery to any friend; and so he remained a lonely figure in the little Café Royal, Chelsea, and Quartier Latin nests of pseudo-artists. Having in himself the coterie temperament, he could not cordially snuggle up to anybody else, and so was forced to do his own scratching. If one took away from Lewis the consciousness of being a genius, he became a forlorn figure, and a very pathetic one.

I have not the heart to attack any man's belief in his own genius. If so modest and at the same time so comparatively prosperous a writer as myself has his anguishes and humiliations, such as no man who has never written a book can understand, one who had constantly to be his own blazoner, who faced the coldness of those he would tickle to fury or enthusiasm, and who remained outside the (financially essential) sympathy of the library public, needed support from within if he was to endure life at all. Besides, I am not sure that Lewis was wrong about himself. If egotism and ebullience, a multitudinous vocabulary and a capacity for the grotesque which (among moderns) only Joyce surpasses, are enough to make a man a genius, he was one. He certainly had extraordinary talent. He had a furiously energetic brain, full of fire and odd knowledges and scraps of profundity which bob among the general gas; sometimes he could quite brilliantly execute a scene in a book or tear the inside out of a man in polemic. But he must all the time, so tiresomely, melodramatize everything, enlarge it to the proportions of sensational intrigue or monstrous perversion, proclaim a betrayal or a disaster, and denounce all who are not of his party. Since that party consisted of Lewis alone, he was never done with mares' nests and dirty linen.

Furthermore, he was too much concerned in his fiction—e.g. "Tarr" and "The Apes of God"—with the silly little tribe of unimportant artists and writers, the unpublished, the barely publishable, the half-known, the eccentric, the homosexual, and the dilettantish. He could bowl them over like ninepins, a fearful slaughter; but he had to pretend, as another famous fighter did, that they were more dangerous as opponents than in fact they were:

> "'Look there,' said this knight, 'friend Sancho Panza, where thirty or more monstrous giants present themselves, all of whom I mean to engage in battle and slay, and with whose spoils we shall begin to make our fortunes; for this is righteous warfare, and it is God's good service to sweep so evil a breed from off the face of the earth.'
>
> "'What giants?' said Sancho Panza.
>
> "'Those thou seest there,' answered his master, 'with the long arms, and some have them well-nigh two leagues long.'
>
> "'Look, your worship,' said Sancho; 'what we see there are not giants but windmills, and what seem to be their arms are the sails that turned by the wind make the millstone go.'
>
> "'It is easy to see,' replied Don Quixote, 'that thou art not used to this business of adventures; those are giants; and if thou art afraid, away with thee out of this and betake thyself to prayer while I engage them in fierce and unequal combat.'"

The windmills with which Lewis so furiously engaged for a good part of his time were unimportant windmills. He was mistaken in thinking that he was attacking essentials. What with the small life he led among pettifogging artistic sets and in his own company, and his apparent admiration for Joyce as an artist; what with his sense of genius and genius denied and that nervous excitability which caused him to reach for a pen as soon as he saw or heard of something he did not like, he was forever producing work which irritated without angering, and which amused without producing the admiration which was its due. He had a manner of glorious flamboyance; sometimes rhetorical, sometimes pretentious, sometimes magnificent. He had a gift for uproarious farce and another gift for superbly savage irony. With such gifts he should have been sure of the applause of all who know how rare are any gifts at all in the realm of modern literature.

It was not the case. He had admirers; but unless they said the right word every time, he treated them as other windmills. It was necessary to praise him very hard indeed to have a chance of his endorsement. And the truth, which must be told, however disagreeable it may be to all of us, is that Lewis's matter was often commonplace. Some of it had been dead for a long time; much of it was, without foundation; most of it, stripped of the enchanting heat and fun of the author's vituperation, was nothing but Café Royal chit-chat and back-chat, unworthy of such gorgeous apparel. The standpoint of genius as an excuse for irresponsible polemic is justifiable. I think Lewis had literary genius. But what he wrote about seems to me to be very nearly worthless.

vi

So much for the inter-War pessimists. With the exception of Aldous Huxley, they all found life rather too difficult for them, and as that was a common illness they impressed some of the similarly sick as fearless critics of whatever, being established, must be wrong. Their importance in such a survey as this lies in the fact that they did in some measure speak for their bewildered and indignant fellows, and were very much of their age. None of them, I think, had any considered plan for the ultimate improvement of the world; each was content to remark with warmth upon the inconveniences which have come under his own notice.

But while it may be true—it probably is true—that the majority of people are very stupid, these writers, arraigning stupidity without pity for the stupid, did but invert the conventionality they detested. To wish to be safely like everybody else is one convention; to wish to be markedly different from everybody else is an alternative convention. In either case the aim is self-justificatory.

Chapter Seventeen

SOME LATER NOVELISTS

DAVID GARNETT, P. G. WODEHOUSE,
J. B. PRIESTLEY, A. P. HERBERT

"He will be the most popular artist who gives that view with which the world in general sympathize. A merely professional reputation is not very extensive, nor will it last long."

W. Hazlitt: Conversations with Northcote.

i

A
s I approach the end of my long task, which was undertaken so lightly, and which is now somewhat of a nightmare, I am filled with consternation. I do not wish to go back upon what I said in my original preface and beg forgiveness from readers: Pardon me, as Mrs. Cluppins said, I would scorn the haction. But I do deeply feel the fact that I must have omitted from my panorama the figures of many excellent men and women writers now living. To have included all would have been impossible; and I have chosen to speak of those whom I regard as most typical. Nor has it seemed to me to be good policy to run hastily through a list of omissions, handing a few words of comment to each, although I might have done this. The truth is that there are always large numbers of talented writers who shine among their contemporaries, and if all those who adorned the quarter-century which I have called the Georgian Age had been included (as they deserve) my book would have been endless. Moreover, many younger writers, active in 1935, had then still to reach their maturity. They will figure in later and better books written by others than myself. I purposely confined my record to men and women whose reputations were well established at the time I wrote.

Now I have never wished to suggest that interesting writers are only those whose work appealed to small and select audiences. I do not take the view that a popular book is necessarily bad; on the contrary, if a book is a failure it is because it has some intrinsic defect—generally deficiency of interest. Those who disagree with me in this will feel for me some of the slight distaste I feel for them. We shall both survive the distaste, which I regard as decidedly a point in my favour. And, having said so much, I think fit, as Oliver Cromwell used to say, to speak for a chapter upon one novelist who has not quite come within the scope of any of my earlier chapters and three novelists who have been quite uncompromisingly popular. If I can suggest a reason for their popularity, or for the popularity of any one of them, I shall do so. But first let me speak of a writer whose originality has been both emphasized and cloaked by his use (I have no doubt a quite natural use) of a style which seems to be compounded from equal parts of Defoe and Jonathan Swift, and whose ingenious maiden effort in fiction was hailed by one critic as being "as æsthetically important as a carved coconut." I mean David Garnett.

ii. David Garnett

DAVID GARNETT's forbears were distinguished. His great-grandfather, Richard Garnett, became Assistant-Keeper of Printed Books in the British Museum and helped to found the Philological Society. His grandfather, Richard Garnett the second, was the author of scholarly, ironic, and fantastic tales collected into one volume as "The Twilight of the Gods," and besides being an able literary historian also became Keeper of Printed Books in the British Museum. His father and mother were Edward and Constance Garnett, to whom I have already paid tribute. And David Garnett himself, who as a boy was a devoted student of nature, and whose first work was a manual on the management of a kitchen garden, became a bookseller and publisher as well as author of "Lady into Fox" and its successors.

There are some who see in David Garnett's work no more than a stylistic exercise; but I do not agree. He uses, it is true, an elaborately simple style which at times echoes "Robinson Crusoe" or "Gulliver's Travels," and which suggests that he is deeply influenced by a reading of eighteenth-century authors. If there were nothing in the books but their manner of writing, as some say, these books would be less than important. But the demureness of such a book as "Lady into Fox" (which is much superior to its successor, "A Man in the Zoo," despite the fact that "A Man in the Zoo" has moments of great excellence) is proper to the theme, which is nothing less than the sudden transformation of a young and loving wife into a real female fox, her life thenceforward with her husband, her desertion of the husband for a vulpine mate, and the final tragedy in which both husband and lady are killed by hounds. I said "demureness," and that implies a criticism, for it is quite true that Garnett did not really believe that a lady had been changed into a fox and that she had gone on as he related, and he was telling her story with a false gravity which amused himself and his friends less because they believed what he wrote than because they thought it very ingenious of him to write in that way. On the other hand, while I personally do not believe that the lady changed into a fox (though many ladies are said after marriage to be perfect vixens, which some people imagined was Garnett's meaning), I am astonished and delighted by the art with which Garnett tells the extremely beautiful story of what happens after the mishap. There is in my mind no doubt that "Lady into Fox" was virtuosity, the result of a twist of queer humourless humour; but it is exquisitely told, and has its far deeper virtues of imagination and feeling.

After that book was written and published Garnett extended his range; but he has never yet been ambitious enough, or mentally supple enough, to shake himself free of the shackles of style. All his books, so quietly and slowly told, are cramped, or they end before they have developed their full growth, or they make a demand upon credence by being odd to no apparent purpose. They are like engravings upon very small surfaces (I do not mean the Lord's Prayer upon a threepenny piece, but rather that they are intaglio). They do not quite achieve artistic importance. One must be something of a virtuoso oneself to relish their performance. The effect is one of costiveness rather than one of restrained power; as if he found it difficult to obtain a theme, and then difficult to give more than half-paralysed development to that theme. This is true even of such a book, striking though it is, and very peculiar and interesting (was it inspired by T. F. Powys?), as "The Sailor's Return."

And yet what a hand Garnett has for a picture of wild life or the countryside, where in a few words he can give the reader a true experience. With how much taste does he refrain from every brutality in "Lady into Fox," while he indicates the progress of the lady's first transformation through her interest in the dove, and her new rough habit of eating, to the moment when she allows her mate to be seen. How lovely is the monotone of this passage from "The Sailor's Return" describing the journey of Targett and his Tulip into Dorset village of Maiden Newbarrow:

"They started early in the morning and had gone some miles when the sun rose. Their way lay along bye-roads which led through rolling country towards the sea. The sun shone, the grass sparkled with dew, in the hedges there were bushes of faintly blushing dogrose in full blossom. Tulip, perched high above the chestnut carthorse in the shafts, began singing. Presently she fell silent and the seaman began a loud and rolling chanty. There was no one on the road that morning to hear them singing, or to watch them pass by.

"Goldfinches flew out of the hedges, yellow-hammers sped from bush to bush in front of them. A cuckoo late in changing his tune mocked as he flew from tree to tree. They passed through two villages and stopped in each of them long enough for the carter to get a can of beer and drink it.

"At midday they entered a green valley which led through the downs to the sea. The road was enclosed by stone walls and bordered by occasional ash trees. A mile further on the walls fell away and at the ends of the fields gates barred their progress.

"Both Tulip and the sailor were silent as they drew round a corner into view of a small village.

"There was an open green with high and mighty sycamores, and underneath them scattered groups of thatched cottages, with white walls.

"Geese, grazing by the roadside, lifted their heads and walked away at their approach. A little boy who had been playing knuckle-bones stood up and stared while they passed.

"They turned the corner and saw 'The Sailor's Return' before them . . .'"

How extraordinarily fine, too, is the description of the situation of those stranded aviators in "The Grasshoppers Come." How intently we turn the pages, devout and eager—and find that the book has stopped! Testimony enough to Garnett's power to interest; testimony to the ingenuity of his invention. But is not our disappointment a confession that we miss a significance which, though expected, though promised, though dangled before us, is not there?

iii. P. G. Wodehouse

"'For some little time I have been endeavouring to instruct you in the principles of pure English. My efforts seem to have been wasted.'

"The policeman blushed.

"'I beg your pardon, Mr. Beamish. One keeps slipping into it. It's the effect of mixing with the boys—with my colleagues—at the station-house. They are very lax in their speech.'"

P. G. Wodehouse: The Small Bachelor.

IT is many years since P. G. Wodehouse began to instruct the world in the principles of what is not so much pure English as the language of pure nonsense. He and the world were both lads, "he and self having been at private school, Eton and Oxford together," as Bertie Wooster would say. Not perhaps quite Eton and Oxford, but at least private school, and in Wodehouse's case Dulwich College. And at the very beginning of time, when boys were boys and boys would be boys, there was published under the editorship of one R. S. Warren Bell a monthly magazine for such boys which was called *The Captain*. It was a good magazine, and there was nothing pious in it about prayers and such disagreeables, but stories and articles fit to be read by the self-respecting of tender years. I do not know when there first appeared in this magazine something very unusual indeed; but I do know that about the beginning of the twentieth century somebody called Psmith fled like a meteor through the pages of *The Captain*.

Psmith? you say; how is that spelt? I must refer you to P. G. Wodehouse. For Psmith was one of his earliest attempts at world instruction in pure English; and it must be said at once that the readers of *The Captain* were so entranced by their lessons that they went without the common necessaries of life in order to satisfy this greater need. They saved their pennies, and denied themselves extra food (such as I see the present degenerate race of schoolboys munching from paper bags) in order to buy this wonder-filled magazine and learn more of a language new and irresistible to them.

As Wodehouse was born in 1881, and as he took England in hand with a first book, "The Pothunters," published in 1902, it is fair to assume that he was slightly precocious; but you would never suppose from the fair, bland, highly innocent appearance which he presented in the nineteen-thirties that he had been born longer ago than 1904, or that there was behind that ingenuous façade a unique capacity for verbal gymnastic. As Bertie Wooster would say, again illuminatingly:

"I don't know that you would call me an irascible man. I rather think not. Ask them about me at the Drones, and they will probably tell you that Bertram Wooster, wind and weather permitting, is as a general rule suavity itself."

Wodehouse (Pelham Grenville), suavity itself, was at the age of fifty-odd less like a humorous author than any man I have ever met. He was not funereal, and he was not laboriously funny. He did not tell comic anecdotes until the dawn rose or look as if his poor heart never rejoiced. On the contrary, he was quiet, orderly, and benign. He was like a young English sportsman, a good friend and a sympathetic listener. You could have told him your troubles. You could have pictured him streaking for the corner flag with an oval ball under his arm, or making what an erudite young woman once described to me as "a crisp cut to leg." You could have imagined him driving an automobile or pushing a garden-roller, and doing all these things with good temper. But you would never have imagined him educating the world, as he did, in a new lingo. Not only that part of the world which was England and America, but that part which was Europe and Asia; although what the Asiatics, reading his work, as they must have done, in Chinese, can gather of that magnificent vocabulary of new words I do not know. He was a world benefactor (without, as Bertrand Russell would say, "any feeling of superiority such as is sometimes associated with the word") until the Second World War put him in something of a quandary and raised difficulties for us all.

The activity of Wodehouse was always indescribable, and provided him with a constant inspiration for his comic works. For he entered the theatre young as a librettist and did other odd jobs about the stage, as any reader of "Jill the Reckless" will perfectly understand. He has written about a hundred books of one sort or another. He wrote, either with help or without any help, plays which so impressed one actor that he announced the taking of a theatre for the sole purpose of producing Wodehouse plays. And he has been a cause of happiness—of laughing happiness—to uncountable readers of all classes.

His admirers are sometimes poor people and sometimes rich people; they are people with brains and people without brains and people with just a few brains. I remember having my meals in a French hotel spoiled by the sniggering of a lonely man who read a book at lunch and dinner and went without most of his food because he forgot it in the delights of "Bill the Conqueror." At the height of his own fame Arnold Bennett abruptly and candidly said to me: "I . . . saw *The Strand Magazine*; the cover. . . . There was a tablet: 'Short Stories by Arnold Benn——, Eden Phillpotts, de Vere Stacpoole—a lot of them. But, across the top, a red streamer: 'NEW STORY BY P. G. WODEHOUSE' . . . I thought . . . 'This has to be looked into.' I read it. He had every right to it. I laffed like anything. It was terrific!" Thinking then for a moment, he pursed up his lips, and added: "He's awfully able. Far . . . abler than any of these highbrows." Nor was Arnold Bennett alone in his view. Lord Oxford, leaving Paisley after the election defeat which ended his Parliamentary life, and suffering bitterly from the knowledge of all that was involved, sat in the train for London, was momentarily a cause for great anxiety on the part of his daughter, and then produced from his bag the latest Wodehouse and lived again.

The long books of Wodehouse are less satisfactory than his short stories, where the effects are instant and unquestionable. In the long stories the reader may find attention wandering; reason (and not cheerfulness) may keep breaking in; actions may appear to have some fortuitousness; that significant form to which Clive Bell attached such importance may vanish under scrutiny and the whole book turn out to be a series of episodes. But significance of any kind is not Wodehouse's object, any more than the portrayal of a shadow of the real world is his object. The world in which his characters move and exchange speech is a world of his spontaneous creation, a fantastic world resembling the scene of an irrational dream. It is a gravely consistent world, like that of a drunken man; all the people who live in it are ready to play the game so concisely invented by Wodehouse. They will black their faces or run amok or scramble upon all fours, will change their minds or their whiskers, will fly from their sweethearts or take charge of wild-living dipsomaniacs without serious qualm. But they will not change their terse manner of conversation (sometimes, as in Jeeves's case, it is orotund), their use of the exclusive Wodehouse vocabulary, the Wodehouse idiom, the Wodehouse lunatic lightness of wit and mood. And as they perform all their antics with the same charming viceless simplicity which is a feature of the Wodehouse world, they never soil nonsense with vulgarity. For this reason, if for a time we tire of them, and set down the book in which their adventures are un-rolled in the candid Wodehouse fashion, we always resume their acquaintance with the same delight in the familiar breezy greeting. They advance upon us, removing the lid with as much courtly grace as they can muster and crying: "Hullo-ullo-ullo"; and we, similarly responding: "Hullo-ullo-ullo" (though we should use that greeting with no other creatures ever invented), grab the old hand warmly and park ourselves for a happy hour. Who among us, that are not curmudgeons, could resist such pleasantness and pleasantry as this author offers?

iv. J. B. Priestley

"'I nivver knew there were so many folk wandering about. Once you've fairly set off, you come on 'em all over t'place.'"

J. B. Priestley: *The Good Companions.*

Back in the 'thirties a young woman was arrested in one of the great Australian cities, and spent the night in gaol. In the morning the magistrate, fining her ten shillings, remarked that she had committed no crime to warrant her arrest, but that she had brought punishment upon herself by "her unfortunate Yorkshire manner."

This was a most extraordinary remark, but one which I have often remembered since I read it in the newspapers; for it is quite true that Yorkshire people are among the unsolved problems of the British Isles. For one thing, they live a life of their own; their huge county is large enough to hold and employ all but those of a definitely exploratory inclination; and their local patriotism, accordingly, is very strong. They have, as indeed have all the northerners, large manufacturing cities and therefore large urban populations, closely packed, much preoccupied by the claims of local industry, and with manners differing from the manners of all Southrons. When they come south to London and the southern coasts for holidays, or to live, they move among southerners as strangers; and in their fear of being thought simple and overawed they give the impression of being aggressive, conceited, and provincial. But they are naturally much less self-satisfied than they seem, for while they are often conceited that is because they have been tigers up north, and because in a strange city, amid strange people who ignore them, all the impulse to justify their existence rises up into hard boastfulness.

Now you will have guessed that I had some object in speaking about Yorkshire in this place; and you were right. I was thinking of J. B. Priestley, whose best work in fiction has been the presentment of Yorkshire types. There have been other Yorkshire novelists, as for example Halliwell Sutcliffe, Oliver Onions, and Storm Jameson; but of all these Priestley has made the biggest stir in the world, and has been most attacked. He has been attacked, in chief, because he was a Yorkshireman; only secondarily because in 1929 he had the greatest single success that any novelist in England had had for many years.

He was born in Bradford in the year 1894, and is the son of a schoolmaster. He was educated at Cambridge University. Before he began to write novels he was a reviewer and essayist; and when he first wrote a novel all the critics said that it was the novel of an essayist, just as when he first wrote a play all the critics said that it was the play of a novelist. But the critics, although they attacked this play of Priestley's, gave one the impression (which perhaps they did not intend) that it was really an interesting piece of work; and as far as I am concerned the play, "Dangerous Corner," aroused an interest in Priestley which I had not felt as the result of reading several of his essays and his novel "Angel Pavement."

The novel with which Priestley made his reputation was, as the world knows, "The Good Companions," the long and ingenious narrative of the adventures of several people who, setting out from different parts of England, were brought together by accident and formed a concert party. That book, rapturously received by nearly all who read it, was in my opinion a great blow struck on behalf of the normal and the large scale in fiction. It was a work showing exceptional talent, boldness, and self-confidence. It succeeded because it was original, very varied, and very entertaining. It was full of natural homeliness, and readers felt that they could like the people in its pages, whom they recognized as being very similar in nature to themselves. Those who did not care for the book did not wish to recognize themselves in persons so commonplace;

but that was because in their daily lives they were all pretending not to be commonplace.

The opening of "The Good Companions," which recalled the work of Arnold Bennett, although it was freer and more copious than Bennett, was full of invitation, especially to those who had any familiarity with scenes similar to those depicted. It was all true, and well and clearly visualized. The conversation was very natural; easy and amusing. In its way it was as good as any conversation of a realistic character that modern times have seen. Everything was recognizable. But Priestley did not make the mistake of writing, as he might have done, a merely realistic novel. He was in pursuit of something else—something which I regard as important—the creation of a large-scale roving tale such as we had not seen (apart from "The Pickwick Papers") since the eighteenth century. He had his conception, and he had the confidence to aim at its fulfilment.

I think there is no doubt that the first part of "The Good Companions," besides being admirable in its own way, was an excellent beginning to any tale of length. I think that what followed was equally well handled; all true, copious, interesting; but that while Priestley tried to give variety by means of differences in scene and character and class he was unable to bring to each difference that subtle difference of method which would have made "The Good Companions" continuously interesting to those who have read a great deal of fiction with some exactitude. I do not think the positive interest flagged, or the quality of the work declined; but only that one could have too much of a good thing.

When similar faults are found, as I believe they are found, in "Angel Pavement" and its successors (I do not speak here of Priestley's later polemical novels), the limits of a technique seem to be indicated. In "Angel Pavement" there was again a gathering of characters, none of whom was profoundly seen, but all of whom were suggested excellently by means of some one or two traits and habits of speech and thought; and there was a more deliberately told story. But whether it is that there was less novelty in the plan of the book, or whether the copiousness which helped one to relish the opening of "The Good Companions" was a fault, a fault of improvisation, "Angel Pavement" was not, in my judgment, a satisfactory book. It was not greatly different in tone from the novels of Pett Ridge, an excellent and very shrewd writer who, however, lacked just that distinction which would have made him important.

However, the adverse press criticisms of Priestley's play, "Dangerous Corner," suggested that in this play he had done something exceptional; and it is in fact the work of a first-class dramatist, the most variously able in the modern British theatre. "Dangerous

Corner," which turns inside out half a dozen apparently happy and agreeable people, has such force that it completely dominates the mind. If upon after-consideration it becomes less striking, that may be because one realizes how "arranged" the disclosures have been in their progress to climax, and because we have been harshly taken to the sight of ugly things which remain in the end merely ugly.

"Dangerous Corner" is savagely devoted to the task of stripping a conventional party of its pleasant appearance. Something similar was begun by Barrie in "Shall We Join the Ladies?" and something subtler was done by the same author in "Dear Brutus." But "Dangerous Corner," which has no finesse, is uncompromising, and has great power, which from the point of view taken throughout the present book (the work as indication of the author's talent) is an important quality.

The play opens with the conclusion of a drama on the Radio; four women listening to a pistol-shot which ends a wireless "tragedy." The tragedy has been about a husband who has wanted to hear the truth, has found it unbearable, and has shot himself. The women discuss the desirability of knowing the truth, and one of them refers to the others as forming, two of them with their husbands, a cosy little group. She then, with seeming innocence, refers to a man, known to them all, who has shot himself about a year previously, and thus precipitates an extraordinary series of revelations as to the past doings and secret emotions of all those pleasant and apparently contented people. Martin, it seems, has been found dead; it has been assumed that as a cheque for five hundred pounds to which nobody had any right has been cashed he must have stolen it and for some inexplicable reason lost his head and shot himself. But that is not at all what has happened. The original word of inquiry leads to talk, explanation begets disclosure, disclosure leads to challenge, confession after confession is forced; and what has seemed to be a simple, if remarkable, matter is shown to have been, and still to be, an imbroglio. Finally, when not a shred of ugliness remains decently covered, the play returns magically to its first moments, and the secrets are again hidden and the relationships between these pleasant people are as they were at our first encounter. What we have seen is the truth; but the truth as known only to ourselves.

This play was only the first of a long succession of plays by the same author, some of which have failed but the best of which have been good enough, on the stage and in print, to provoke emotion, thought, and wide and vigorous discussion. They have almost all shown power, great skill, humour, and, above all, dramatic purpose. While, therefore, I do not regard Priestley (in spite of the fact that he can produce scenes and descriptions worthy in their richness of

Dickens himself) as a traditional novelist of the highest order, I insist that he is the most interesting of all modern English dramatists, and a credit both to Yorkshire and our much abused country.

v. Alan Patrick Herbert

A. P. HERBERT was born in 1890, was educated at Winchester and Oxford, and became not only a Member of Parliament but President of the Black Lion Skittles Club. He served in Gallipoli and in France during the First World War, was called to the Bar, joined the staff of *Punch*, has written comic opera, revue, much light verse, a novel about divorce, a thriller, a novel about a hero who was shot for cowardice, and "The Water Gipsies," the tale of a young woman who lived on a river hulk and had as strange a series of adventures as any man might dream of. He sails a barge, assails the licensing laws, has done more than any other man to get the River Thames used once more as a thoroughfare, and is a thorn in the side of every proletarian humbug in England. Being a humorist, he is deadly serious. Sometimes he is so serious that his humour is lost and buried. He speaks a great deal in public, and makes his audiences laugh tumultuously.

Now one advantage of having certain definite ideas about life is that you know where you are with yourself; and Herbert knows where he is. But one disadvantage is that you may be considered a crank. I once heard a man whom I revered say: "Oh, I'm tired of Herbert." But that was because Herbert had said again something that this delightful friend of mine had heard so often, with irritation, that he felt he would sooner be dead than hear it again. Whether he would ever have been converted by Herbert I do not know; but he is now dead, and nothing further can be done for him. It is also true that Herbert sometimes has the air of repeating himself.

Furthermore, he might say, as a lady once said to my mother: "I'm so *miscellaneous*." The lady did not mean what she said (I think she meant "impulsive," or possibly "scatterbrained"); but if Herbert were to be asked what, as a writer and publicist, he called himself he could say what she said and mean it, and be accurate. I am not, indeed, sure how I ought to describe him, whether as a Reformer or a Conservative, a Humorist or a Bargee. He is all these things, a champion Skittles player, a believer in the working man's beer, a defender of the Middle Class, and a satirist of all that Intellectuals consider irreproachable. I am told by an expert that his light verse is not completely excellent in technique; and I am convinced that he suffers from what is for me the defect of moral indignation. But his

novel "The Secret Battle" is the best fictional account of the First
World War on two Fronts that I have ever read, and "The Water
Gipsies," although it has defects of construction, is a delectable
panorama or peepshow of London life, combining all Herbert's
views of that life with his own delightful kind of nonsense.

"The Water Gipsies" centres around a London girl of the not
quite perfectly educated class, who reads a spicy Sunday newspaper,
sits as a model, has the most disagreeable honeymoon in fiction, takes
a journey upon a barge, and takes a plunge into London Society.
She has a series of remarkable adventures, which include something resembling a murder, before she settles down to what one
supposes will be a permanent happiness. "The Water Gipsies,"
in fact, is a fairy tale; written for fun with great seriousness. It is
the epitome of Herbert's talent.

How great that talent is, his miscellaneousness at times tends
to hide. When a man is conducting ferocious attacks upon the
administration of English Law in the form of mock Leading Cases,
and writing the ridiculous letters of a gushing young lady of the
Smart Set, piling up the horrors of the English Divorce Law so
that they quite overpower the poor wretches who wish decently
to break their matrimonial bonds, translating the text of an Offenbach operetta which he has not been allowed to read, and speaking
upon all sorts of subjects, from drink to politics, he leads a really
busy life. He may possibly fail always to reproduce his best form.
Also, he may lose sight of his true gift in his zeal for propaganda.

There is in his first novel, "The Secret Battle," no hint of
humour; merely the wit arising from his keen eye for the contradictions of the moment. It is a serious and deliberate work in
which the effects of warfare are illustrated. The narrator describes
the war-life of an ardent boy in his own regiment—his self-dis-
trust, his bravery in very difficult circumstances, his extraordinary
courage in face of acute danger, his illness and return from Gallipoli
to England, his resumption of military life in France, continued
daring, a wound, return to duty, loss of nerve, and disastrous end.
That is all. The book is written in an easy conversational style
which does not conceal the author's gift for narrative; and it
presents a case. It pictures the scene in Gallipoli as no other novel
has done, very simply and effectively:

> "In the Spring nights it was very cold, and men shivered in their
> single blanket under the unimaginable stars; but very early the sun came
> up, and by five o'clock all the camp were singing; and there were three
> hours of fresh coolness when it was very good to wash in a canvas
> bucket, and smoke in the sun before the torrid time came on; and
> again at seven, when the sun sat perched on the great rock of Samo-

thrace, and Imbros was set in a fleecy marvel of pink and saffron clouds, there were two hours of pure physical content; but these, I think, were more nearly perfect than the morning because they succeeded the irritable fevers of the day. Then the crickets in the branches sang less tediously, and the flies melted away, and all over the Peninsula the wood fires began to twinkle in the dusk, as the men cooked over a few sticks the little delicacies which were preserved for this hour of respite. When we had done we sat under our olive tree in the clear twilight, and watched the last aeroplanes sail home to Rabbit Islands, and talked and argued till the glow-worms glimmering in the scrub, and up the hill the long roll of the Turks' rapid fire, told us that darkness was at hand, and the chill dew sent us into our crannies to sleep."

No man who could so quietly create that picture could be anything but a good writer. No man who could so sensitively tell the story of the boy Harry could be anything but a good novelist. But Herbert has not been content to be a good novelist. Nor has he ever been content, as Wodehouse has, to make fun alone. Having as ready a power as James Stephens to make an aura of enchantment about a Cockney girl, he can show her surviving every vulgarity of surrounding and remaining a Cockney girl; but all through "The Water Gipsies," with its happy descriptions of the Derby and barge life, he is watching for the chance to interpret in his own sense all that happens. He wants to change the hearts of men by defending Liberty and condemning both Libertines and Labour Leaders. He has so much wisdom in his nature—that sagacity which is superior to all the knowledge of facts admired by Bertrand Russell, that he excessively dislikes seeing his possession shared by so few. Confronted by complacent folly and pretentiousness, by the solemn egotism of other reformers and the puritanism of those who want to manage the poor, he brings cold fury to his ridicule of their absurdity. Such a man cannot be only a novelist; and since he cannot be only a novelist I doubt whether he will ever write a first-class novel. A first-class entertainment, yes; he has done it.

vi. Conclusion

THAT brings to an end all I shall say about the novelists of normality. I have not concealed my opinion that such novelists are as talented as those other writers who have greater intellectual impressiveness. That is because I believe that to be creative one must have imagination, a faculty which is starved when the intellect (and especially the scientific capacity) is over-cultivated. To all the four novelists presented in this chapter, a human being is first of all a human being, a creature of instincts, habits, and actions peculiar to himself. He is not simply a type, and not simply a pathological case or a Brownness. These novelists, who are novelists because they are interested in simple phenomena and wish to tell stories about such phenomena, might be described as extroverts (as distinguished from the introverts who preen themselves before our eyes); and since they present us with a world of objective reality, I think their claim to importance is high. To deny them merit is not, as some people imagine, to show great judgment; it is to show insensibility. Exclusiveness is the worst form of provincialism.

Chapter Eighteen

LATER VISIONS

T. S. ELIOT AND THE NEW ACADEMICISM

i

> "Saint-Beuve, as he grew older, came to regard all experience as a single great book
> . . and it seemed all one to him whether you should read in Chapter XX, which is the
> differential calculus, or in Chapter XXXIX, which is hearing the band play in the
> gardens."
>
> R. L. *Stevenson: An Apology for Idlers.*

IT will have become clear to readers of this book that my interest is in common phenomena rather than in æsthetic principles. To scholars this will seem a fault. I do not write for scholars. To me, as to Sainte-Beuve as reported by Stevenson, all experience is a single great book; and every form of knowledge, the domestic as well as the biological and astronomical and psycho-analytical, is capable of enriching the mind and imagination and increasing the interest of life. I represent the ordinary unlearned reader. He has few friends among the modern literati.

This is for the reason that literary fashion constantly changes. When it was first the rule to condemn such writers as Zola (I do not mean upon the ground that we have quite enough of the ugly in real life, etc., but more reasonably) because their work was not pastoral in character, it was pointed out that men had taken to living in cities, and that the novel and the play had both become urban. Where rural realism had its compensations of open-air liberty and beauty, urban realism was bounded by walls and a smoky sky. In the same way, this simple realism lost its importance as the general life became more and more complex. You could no longer suppose that men and women led an entirely animal life; but were forced to allow that they had thoughts and emotions which did not immediately reveal themselves. Subtlety entered the realistic novel, which dealt with emotional suffering, and not only with social conditions. But while the realistic attitude satisfied some writers, others pressed on to still further developments in the art of writing. They were struck by the discovery that the individual life is affected by all sorts of apparently unconnected but simultaneous events (Jules Romains illustrated this view in a tremendously long novel called in the English translation "Men of Good Will") and by the rhythm of life. Some of them, no doubt

370

influenced by the scientific and psychological ideas of the time, realized that there is an incessant activity of jumbled thought in every individual at every moment of the day. Endless emphasis upon this is the contribution of James Joyce to the novel. Others, such as Proust, found that one thought can be made to open a great pathway into memory, or that clever persons of low vitality enjoy, as Virginia Woolf's characters enjoy, a sort of twittering reverie which they suppose to be vivacious contact with life. With all these steps, authors have believed that they were approaching nearer to the essential, to the heart of man.

I have not hidden my conviction—I hope I have not been too sturdy, but one does what one can—that the later developments have over-subtilized the novel and taken it past reality into confusion. I mean that I think the objective novel capable of greater subtlety, and greater variety, than psychological explorers, infatuated with their own ingenuity, would allow. But even if these developments have done what I suggest, they have done it without doubt in obedience to the spirit of the hour. I happen not to approve: to me, these experiments, which are not entirely outside the range of my intelligence, are calculated clevernesses which those less clever than myself suppose to be works of genius. That may be mere jealousy on my part; if not personal jealousy, then jealousy for my own conception of the nature of originality, which to me has nothing whatever to do with purposeful novelty:

"Originality is any conception of things, taken immediately from nature, and neither borrowed from nor common to others . . . It is feeling the ground sufficiently firm under one's feet to be able to go alone. Truth is its essence; it is the strongest possible feeling of truth; for it is a secret and instinctive yearning after, and approximation towards it, before it is acknowledged by others, and almost before the mind itself knows what it is. Paradox and eccentricity, on the other hand, show a dearth of originality, as bombast and hyperbole show a dearth of imagination; they are the desperate resources of affectation and want of power."

Deliberate originality, that is, can only be a contradiction in terms, both for Hazlitt and myself. Whether, in these self-conscious days (I use the word 'self-conscious" without implicit blame), any writer can fail to know what he is doing before he does it, I cannot say. We are too much cluttered with æsthetic theory for most men to be other than dilettanti; but genius finds its own ways, no doubt.

These remarks, as I hope it has been clear, have their relation to modernity. The world is a very different place from what it was in the nineteenth century; and, in spite of Chesterton's claim, it is not possible to put the clock back. We have great speeds, great complexities, many new knowledges or at any rate theories concerning our bodies, our minds, the universe, light, and the future life. We are—still in the good sense—much more self-conscious than our fathers were. Inevitable that the self-consciousness and the complexities should fly together and provoke literary explosions! It could not have been expected that either would refrain. And although I have chosen to speak of the novel, because that is the form of art which most interests me, parallels—not exact, but relative—could be found in painting and poetry; in all knowledge and all human activity. Some men hate the fact, and would resist it; others exult, not so much in a sense of new life, as in a sense that they are offending the old boys; others, like myself, half-echoing E. M. Forster on another occasion, say: "Yes—oh dear yes—nothing stands still. I wish it would."

Now it will not be forgotten that the Post-Impressionists, who were introduced into England at the beginning of the Georgian age, derived from those Whistlerian impressionists who claimed to deal in Pure Art. They went much farther away from representational painting than the Impressionists; and in turn they were succeeded in France by painters who became more and more and more primitive, until the very nadir of human intelligence seemed to have been reached. These painters were reaching down below mind, down below the recognizable, down, down—they said—to purity. We thought, to the inane. And just as the symbolist poets —also of France—had sought to find pure poetry, unalloyed by ideas or worldly concepts, these painters tried to suggest the simplicities of nature by the simplest of means. The paradox of such activity seems to me to lie in the fact that the effort after nullity is made deliberately; that it arises, not from impulse, but from a plan consciously formed by the intellect; while the aim is at something outside intellect.

In thus reaching for the unknown, it has followed that poets and artists alike have discovered the incommunicable. Some of them, accordingly, have made a virtue of necessity, and have announced that they abjure communication. They are like the little boy in one of Talbot Baines Reed's school stories who said that in future he was going to mark his exercises "Private," for the master had such a vulgar habit of looking to see what he was doing. This seems to me to be another paradox; for I see no reason to publish what cannot be understood. However, there are always critics who can elucidate the meaningless in the finest phrases; and these have not been wanting.

But what has happened is that old-fashioned people (I use the phrase without approval or disapproval) have been inclined to snort. The gnomic offers such opportunity for the charlatan! And

those of us who stand four-square for Life As It Is have a certain
kinship with the stupid bird in Andersen's tale who, because she
could not understand something, said "That's the fault of the
thought." Feeling has run a little high. It has been retaliatively
suggested that all who are not modern are what Aldous Huxley's
girl called "rather second-rate." Just as if they were wearing last
season's clothes at a smart party.

Some of this insistence that the modern writer, being not quite
easily intelligible to others, is somehow of better *class* than they, is
probably defiant. But not wholly so. Nor is the matter solely one
of fashion, although fashion plays a strong part. There is certainly a
world-wide dissatisfaction with everything that was admired by
older generations—including democracy. Everywhere, younger
men and women are agitating for dictatorial government (either by
an individual or by camarilla); everywhere they are conscious of a
new and, they think, improved morality, a new and threatening fear
of the future, a disbelief in stability of any kind. And, since the world
is topsy-turvy, everything rushing at headlong speed to the unknown, many voices shouting, shouting in conflict, life really
presents itself to the modern mind in the form of a kaleidoscopic
terror.

To older people, who have the mental and spiritual anchor of
habit and order and quietness of mind (however sensitive they
may be to the chaos about them), the bits and pieces of the newer
art can give little satisfaction. To myself, many of them give no
satisfaction at all. But I feel decidedly doubtful about condemning
out of hand what is unintelligible to me. For this reason I will only
say that modern poetry, which I have particularly in mind in this
chapter, seems to me to be altogether too literary in everything
except its language. It is self-conscious in a bad sense, as well as in
a not so bad sense. It is also arrogant in tone, and I am inclined to
think pretentious in object.

Moreover, while aiming at the expression of what is called the
modern mind, it expresses only the thoughts of an approved small
circle of modern minds, so small, and so exclusive, that this circle
tends to crystallize itself into a new arbitrary mandarinate. Being
satisfied that the only knowledge worth having is within its grasp,
this circle claims to care solely for the best in art and literature; it
claims personally to represent the best artistic and literary effort of
the time, high above the town and the mob, high above sense and
sympathy, enthroned in the first-rate. I doubt if the claim is justified
or justifiable. We can all see the slight ridiculousness of E. M.
Forster's Cockney clerk whose happiest hour arose from contact
with a decent-mannered Cambridge undergraduate; some of us can
see the similar ridiculousness of Rosamond Lehmann's story of two

young creatures who dazzled some frumps with their wonderful modernity; but are not the severely elaborate scrutineers of genius who bring out their test-tubes and crucibles in order to discover that Swift was possessed of great power equally absurd? Are they not taking themselves, I mean, altogether too seriously? Because anybody who had ever read a line of Swift would have reached the same conclusion by a less pretentious route, and said nothing about it.

It is against this assumption that what the moderns are interested in—and the way in which they are interested—is the only good that I should protest. Many things interest me which do not interest the most academic students of literature; many things interest them which do not interest me. Our ways have been different; our minds are different. If the moderns make no concessions to the non-moderns (the contrary cannot possibly arise, for the great complaint of the moderns is that the non-moderns have conceded everything for the sake of shekels), but persist in remaining exclusively obscure, they will remain a faction. And since a newer modernity is usually a swing to reaction, I look to see a great revival in critical esteem for the unpretentiously explicit.

Would that be a bad thing? If the world could settle down to peace and goodwill, most of us think it would be a happier place for all. But in order that it should settle down, understanding would have to be the order of the day. Not exclusiveness, but at least a little cordial expansiveness. Tolerance, in fact. It will be said firmly that in art there must be no paltering. So say the fire-eating militarists in politics. Do we think them the wisest of men? My own view is that as the economic difficulties from which we now suffer gradually disperse (as according to orthodox economists of distinction they will do when the world inevitably resumes its normal swing), the pessimism of our day will give place to something more hopeful.

Before parting from the moderns, let us glance for a few moments at the one of them who has not yet been discussed in this book; whose poetry and criticism have alike had the strongest possible influence upon juniors, and whose influence, after a decline, is being acclaimed as he receives the highest State and academic honours possible to a literary man. I mean, of course, T. S. Eliot, who is, he says, "classicist in literature, royalist in politics, and anglo-catholic in religion."

ii. Thomas Stearns Eliot

"That critical discernment is not sufficient to make men poets is generally allowed. Why it should keep them from becoming poets is not perhaps equally evident; but the fact is, that poetry requires not an examining but a believing frame of mind. Those feel it most, and write it best, who forget that it is a work of art."

T. B. Macaulay: Essay on Dryden.

T. S. ELIOT was born in St. Louis, Missouri, in 1888. He was educated at Harvard, the Sorbonne, and Oxford University. When he first began to write I do not know. It is said by Alida Monro in the preface to her anthology, "Recent Poetry, 1923–1933" that "The Love Song of J. Alfred Prufrock" was first published in the Catholic Anthology in 1914; I first saw it in 1917, as a small book which was a sensation among those who watch for literary dawns. Then after the First World War Eliot contributed to *The Athenæum* when that paper was edited by Middleton Murry, and when Murry and Eliot seem to have been involved in curious argument of which the merest echoes found their way into Murry's *Athenæum* reviews of Eliot's early books of poems and which are referred to in Eliot's essays upon critical principles. It was in 1922 that "The Waste Land," which is not a single poem, but a collection of shorter poems woven into a whole, was published; and from that time others besides the eager young knew that a poet of powerful influence was abroad in the world. With "Prufrock," "The Waste Land" had a greater effect upon the course of modern English poetry than any other poems have done.

It is said that these poems are obscure. I think they are obscure. But long ago poems by Robert Browning and George Meredith were also found absolutely unintelligible; so it is not a damning charge against Eliot as a poet that his poems are obscure. What is of importance—far greater importance, I think, than the line-by-line gloss of those enthusiasts who exclaim at profundities—is that in these poems there is a lovely and secret melancholy music to which the ear responds with rapture. I know of nothing quite like this in English poetry; it has great beauty. Some of the shorter poems by Eliot have their similar extraordinary attractiveness—for example, "Gerontion." Others have what for me is an adolescent touch; several are elongated epigrams; one, "Hysteria," which is a prose piece, is no more than a clever cruelty—"I concentrated my attention with careful subtlety to this end." "Careful subtlety!" A terribly revealing phrase. A phrase into which the whole of an adverse criticism of Eliot's poetry might be condensed. But the enchantment of the poems under the three titles I have given is perfect.

N

One can understand quite well even now with what a shock of joyous discovery young poets who were already experimenting for themselves with the object of escaping from over-familiar rhythms and verse forms seized upon "Prufrock" and "The Waste Land." And it should be said punctually that Eliot is as far as possible from the further eccentricities of many who derive from him. He must often enough have sighed over both his imitators and his expositors. But two points arise from our reading of his poems. Such is the concentration of their form and the fewness of their numbers that in the midst of our admiration of a new and very striking talent we are called upon by some impulse to reflect upon the extremely meagre material given us for any estimate of the poet's full powers. We know that he is much lauded, and that books have been written about him; but we wonder (in the absence of consultation) how the authors of the books ever managed to make a great man of Eliot. A hint, a suggestion, yes; but the perfect picture? Not wholly, perhaps, in the poems, save by act of faith. At any rate, the poems, so few, so small (I mean, most of them so essentially small, un-ambitious in theme, little versicules in which banalities such as "the damp souls of housemaids" occur as if they were jewels), are surprisingly, however compact, trivial. Ah, but I have missed, you say, the notes to "The Waste Land." I have missed the profound significance of that poem, or that series of poems, so expressive of the mind and temper of the age.

No; I have not missed those notes, and I believe Eliot admitted them to be bogus. There are ten pages of them, and their ob-ject is to gather together, in comment upon line by line of "The Waste Land," all the literary sources of the poems, from Jessie L. Weston's "From Ritual to Romance" to Dante, Ovid, and St. Augustine. It is of their significance and therefore, perhaps, of the significance of "The Waste Land" that I am in doubt. Just as I have never understood why it was of such artistic importance in the case of "Ulysses" that Joyce had built his book on the framework of the "Odyssey," so I do not understand why it is so important to "The Waste Land" *as poetry* that it should have been based upon not especially esoteric reading. It is of course interesting, or it would be interesting if the notes seemed to add anything to the poem, to know why certain associations occurred to Eliot's mind when he was creating a poem, or after he had created it, and as he came to read it with a cooler mind. It is true, also, that Coleridge and other poets have in a similar way annotated their poems, showing sources and meanings which might have been missed by readers unacquain-ted with a variety of considerations peculiar to the poet's nature. But is there not, in these notes of Eliot's, some ostentation? Would it not be open to you, or to me, both of us so widely read, likewise to annotate our works with impressive references? We, too, could proudly say of certain collocations that they are "not there by accident." But we should only do this if we wished to *impress*.

But Eliot, besides having great influence as the most remarkable innovating poet of his day, was also a critic; and his criticism had as great an influence in forming the judgment of other, younger, men, as his poetry had in arousing them to the possibilities of highly complex modern verse. That they have gone beyond his word, which is always interesting and deeply sincere, may be allowed. It is not the purpose of this book to deal with the writing of critics; and I must reluctantly pass over a very important aspect of Eliot's work without detailed examination. Criticism of criticism, save in the most general terms, is impossible. Eliot was one who affirmed the need of critical method, as opposed to the person who claims to be able to judge all things by an inner light; and he was extremely sarcastic at the expense of those who believe in the inner lights of both artist and critic. He also had a strong belief in the craftsman-critic ("the critics who have practised, and practised well, the art of which they wrote"), providing always that such critic had what he called a highly developed sense of fact.

Setting aside a first doubt of the precision of that cautious "practised *well*," I should agree with him in this respect for the craftsman-critic, whose even wrong words often have interest if he has given his mind to the subject in hand. But when Eliot pins his faith to fact I think he rides off without providing us with a definition of the essential principle from which criticism must start. The nature of fact may have been well understood by Eliot; and I think I grasp what he meant. But I greatly doubt whether what Eliot regarded as a highly developed sense of fact is anything more than what I regard as imaginative candour. That is, he had a respect for his own integrity, and could perhaps appreciate the integrity of another critic, even though he disagreed with him; but he did not provide any common basis for judgment which shall be intelligible and acceptable to all parties. Having, as is the way of critics with a metaphysical bent (e.g. Coleridge), roused us to a belief that he is going to develop a great general theory of æsthetics, Eliot tired, or shrugged his shoulders, and his wisdom remains fragmentary. He was better in his inquiries into specific talents; for here he gave chapter and verse. We can follow him and agree or disagree with the facts presented.

However, what I wished to say in his connection is that just as Eliot's reputation is partly based upon his criticism, so he was in his character quite half critic. He was so much a critic that his poetry is the poetry of a critic. I mean, not that it is deficient in poetry, although I think it deficient in ardour, but that his critical sense was too active to allow of his poetry being other than meagre in quantity and restricted in range of emotion. In this respect he is of his age. Admirers of the age will say, properly; doubters will question contemporaneity as a virtue. Eliot argued for it as a virtue. The age is not, for the sincere, an age of fluency. Is it, possibly, an age, for poets, of costiveness?

I use that word in relation to something more than quantity. I use it as an adverse comment upon what some modern poets claim as a peculiar excellence. We all justify ourselves. It may be true that Swinburne and Tennyson would have done well to blot a few thousand lines of their writing; but if it was true, as a number of dramatic authors said in evidence before the Dramatic Censorship Committee, that awareness of the Censorship prevented them from writing with a sense of proper and dignified freedom, I think it is quite as true that respect for his own judgment prevented Eliot from giving his poetic inspiration its complete fulfilment. He did much to discipline modern poetry, as well as to give it a new direction; and he did much to lead younger poets to explore their own minds with what I hope is scrupulous exactitude, although I fear otherwise. But between over-fluency such as we have seen in certain modern poets whom I will not name and the small— Aldington's "hard or marble-like"—potatoes which come from poets of the too self-conscious school of to-day, there is a valuable mean which still requires a prophet. Eliot, more than any other man, has been responsible for the justification of literary frigidity (he was but a leader in the direction taken by all the most elaborately cultured poets and critics of the age); and I wonder whether, the lovely rhythm of his best poems apart, he did not do more harm than good by encouraging a tribe of arid sciolists to imagine themselves *esprits superieurs*.

A SHORT READING LIST OF CHARACTERISTIC BOOKS BY AUTHORS MENTIONED IN THE PRECEDING PAGES

Titles are marked 'n' (novel); 'p' (play); 's' (short stories); 'b' (biography or autobiography); 'v' (verse); 'e' (essays); 't' (book of travel). Where books are not summarily describable in this way no letter has been set against them.

CHAPTER TWO: HENRY JAMES:
    Roderick Hudson, 1875. *n.*
    Daisy Miller, 1879. *s.*
    The Portrait of a Lady, 1881. *n.*
    The Lesson of the Master, 1892. *s.*
    The Spoils of Poynton, 1897. *n.*
    The Ambassadors, 1903. *n.*
    The Golden Bowl, 1905. *n.*
    A Small Boy, and Others, 1913. *b.*
    Notes of a Son and Brother, 1914. *b.*

CHAPTER THREE: BERNARD SHAW:
    Plays, Pleasant and Unpleasant, 1898. *p.*
    Three Plays for Puritans, 1900. *p.*
    Man and Superman, 1903. *p.*
    John Bull's Other Island, 1904. *p.*
    Dramatic Opinions and Essays, collected 1907. *e.*
    The Shewing-up of Blanco Posnet, 1909. *p.*
    Back to Methuselah, 1921. *p.*
    Saint Joan, 1924. *p.*
    The Apple Cart, 1930. *p.*

H. G. WELLS:
    The Time Machine, 1895. *n.*
    The Stolen Bacillus and other stories, 1895. *s.*
    The Wheels of Chance, 1896. *n.*
    Love and Mr. Lewisham, 1900. *n.*
    The First Men in the Moon, 1901. *n.*
    Anticipations, 1901.
    A Modern Utopia, 1905.
    Kipps, 1905. *n.*
    Tono-Bungay, 1909. *n.*
    The History of Mr. Polly, 1910. *n.*
    The New Machiavelli, 1911. *n.*
    The Undying Fire, 1919. *n.*
    The World of William Clissold, 1926. *n.*

CHAPTER FOUR: HILAIRE BELLOC:
    The Bad Child's Book of Beasts, 1896. *v.*
    Danton, 1899. *b.*
    Robespierre, 1901. *b.*

The Path to Rome, 1902. *t.*
Emanuel Burden, 1904. *n.*
Esto Perpetua, 1906. *t.*
The Servile State, 1912.

G. K. CHESTERTON:
Greybeards at Play, 1900. *v.*
Robert Browning, English Men of Letters, 1903. *b.*
The Napoleon of Notting Hill, 1904. *n.*
The Innocence of Father Brown, 1911. *s.*
The Ballad of the White Horse, 1913. *v.*
The Flying Inn, 1914. *n.*
A Short History of England, 1917.

CHAPTER FIVE: J. M. BARRIE:
Auld Licht Idylls, 1888. *s.*
A Window in Thrums, 1889. *s.*
Sentimental Tommy, 1896. *n.*
Margaret Ogilvy, 1896. *b.*
Quality Street; The Admirable Crichton; Little Mary; all 1903. *p.*
Peter Pan, 1904. *p.*
What Every Woman Knows, 1908. *p.*
Dear Brutus, 1917, *p.*
Shall We Join the Ladies?, 1922. *p.*

A. A. MILNE:
The Day's Play, 1910. *s, e,* etc.
Belinda, 1918. *p.*
The Red House Mystery, 1921. *n.*
Mr. Pim Passes By, 1919. *p.*
The Truth About Blayds, 1921. *p.*
Success, 1923. *p.*
When We Were Very Young, 1924. *v.*
The Fourth Wall, 1928. *p.*

JAMES STEPHENS:
The Charwoman's Daughter, 1912.
The Crock of Gold, 1912.
Here are Ladies, 1913. *s.*
In the Land of Youth, 1924.

CHAPTER SIX: R. B. CUNNINGHAME GRAHAM:
Mogreb el Acksa; Journey in Morocco, 1898. *t.*
Thirteen Stories, 1900. *s.*
Success, 1902. *s.*
Hernando de Soto (Life of), 1903. *b.*
Faith, 1909. *s.*
Hope, 1910. *s.*
Charity, 1912. *s.*
A Hatchment, 1913. *s.*

W. H. HUDSON:
  The Purple Land, 1885. New ed., 1904. *n.*
  A Crystal Age, 1887. Revised new ed., 1906. *n.*
  The Naturalist in La Plata, 1892. *e.*
  Idle Days in Patagonia, 1893. *e.*
  Nature in Downland, 1900. *e.*
  El Ombú, 1902. *s.*
  Green Mansions, 1904. *n.*
  Far Away and Long Ago, 1918. *b.*

JOSEPH CONRAD:
  Almayer's Folly, 1895. *n.*
  An Outcast of the Islands, 1896. *n.*
  The Nigger of the "Narcissus," 1897. *n.*
  Tales of Unrest, 1898. *s.*
  Lord Jim, 1900. *n.*
  Youth, 1902. *s.*
  Typhoon, 1903. *s.*
  Nostromo, 1904. *n.*
  The Mirror of the Sea, 1906. *e.*
  Chance, 1914. *n.*

H. M. TOMLINSON:
  The Sea and the Jungle, 1912. *t.*
  Old Junk, 1919. *e.*
  Gallions Reach, 1927. *n.*
  All Our Yesterdays, 1930. *n.*

NORMAN DOUGLAS:
  Siren Land, 1911. *t.*
  Old Calabria, 1915. *t.*
  South Wind, 1917. *n.*
  Alone, 1921. *e.*
  In the Beginning, 1928. *s.*
  Looking Back, 1932. *b.*

CHAPTER SEVEN: GEORGE MOORE:
  A Modern Lover, 1883. *n.*
  A Mummer's Wife, 1884. *n.*
  A Drama in Muslin, 1886. *n.*
  Confessions of a Young Man, 1888. *b.*
  Esther Waters, 1894. *n.*
  Evelyn Innes, 1898. *n.*
  The Untilled Field, 1903. *s.*
  The Lake, 1905. *n.*
  Memoirs of My Dead Life, 1906. *b.*
  Hail and Farewell: Ave, 1911. *b.*
                      Salve, 1912. *b.*
                      Vale, 1914. *b.*
  The Brook Kerith, 1916. *n.*
  Héloïse and Abelard, 1921. *n.*
  In Single Strictness, 1922.

JOHN GALSWORTHY:
  Jocelyn, 1898. *n.*
  Villa Rubein, 1900. *n.*
  The Man of Property, 1906. *n.*
  The Silver Box, 1906. *p.*
  The Country House, 1907. *n.*
  Strife, 1909. *p.*
  Justice, 1910. *p.*
  The Patrician, 1911. *n.*
  Five Tales, 1918. *s.*
  The Skin Game, 1920. *p.*
  Loyalties, 1922. *p.*

ARNOLD BENNETT:
  A Man from the North, 1898. *n.*
  The Grand Babylon Hotel, 1902. *n.*
  Anna of the Five Towns, 1902. *n.*
  The Truth About an Author, 1903. *b.*
  A Great Man, 1904. *n.*
  Whom God Hath Joined, 1906. *n.*
  The Grim Smile of the Five Towns, 1907. *s.*
  Buried Alive, 1908. *n.*
  The Old Wives' Tale, 1908. *n.*
  Clayhanger, 1910. *n.*
  The Card, 1911. *n.*
  Hilda Lessways, 1911. *n.*
  The Matador of the Five Towns, 1912. *s.*
  The Price of Love, 1914. *n.*
  These Twain, 1916. *n.*
  Books and Persons, 1917. *e.*
  Riceyman Steps, 1923. *n.*
  Lord Raingo, 1926. *n.*

W. S. MAUGHAM:
  Liza of Lambeth, 1897. *n.*
  Mrs. Craddock, 1902. *n.*
  A Man of Honour, 1903. *p.*
  The Explorer, 1907. *n.*
  Lady Frederick, 1907. *p.*
  Smith, 1909. *p.*
  The Land of Promise, 1914. *p.*
  Of Human Bondage, 1915. *n.*
  The Moon and Sixpence, 1919. *n.*
  Home and Beauty, 1919. *p.*
  The Circle, 1921. *p.*
  The Trembling of a Leaf, 1921. *s.*
  The Painted Veil, 1925. *n.*
  Ashenden, 1928. *s.*
  The Gentleman in the Parlour, 1930. *t.*
  Cakes and Ale, 1930. *n.*

CHAPTER EIGHT: H. GRANVILLE-BARKER:
    The Marriage of Ann Leete, 1901. *p*.
    The Voysey Inheritance, 1905. *p*.
    Waste, 1907. *p*.
    The Madras House, 1910. *p*.
    The Secret Life, 1923. *p*.
    Prefaces to Shakespeare, 1923–5. *e*.

ALLAN MONKHOUSE:
    Love in a Life, 1903. *n*.
    Mary Broome, 1911. *p*.
    The Education of Mr. Surrage, 1913. *p*.
    Men and Ghosts, 1918. *n*.
    True Love, 1919. *n*.
    My Daughter Helen, 1922. *n*.
    The Conquering Hero, 1923. *p*.

ST. JOHN ERVINE:
    Mixed Marriage, 1910. *p*.
    Jane Clegg, 1911. *p*.
    Mrs. Martin's Man, 1911. *n*.
    John Ferguson, 1914. *p*.
    The Wayward Man, 1927. *n*.
    The First Mrs. Fraser, 1928. *p*.

CHAPTER NINE: E. V. LUCAS:
    The Open Road (anthology), 1899.
    Highways and Byways in Sussex, 1904. *t*.
    Life of Charles Lamb, 1905. *b*.
    A Wanderer in London, 1906.
    Over Bemerton's, 1908. *n*.
    Mr. Ingleside, 1910. *n*.
    The Vermilion Box, 1916. *n*.
    The Colvins and Their Friends, 1928. *b*.
    Reading, Writing and Remembering, 1932. *b*.

EDWARD GARNETT:
    The Breaking Point, 1907. *p*.
    Turgenev, 1917. *b*.
    Papa's War, 1919. *s*.
    Friday Nights. *e*.

FORD MADOX HUEFFER (*now* FORD MADOX FORD):
    The Brown Owl, 1892.
    The Cinque Ports, 1900.
    The Fifth Queen, 1906. *n*.
    The Fifth Queen Crowned, 1908. *n*.
    Ladies Whose Bright Eyes, 1911. *n*.
    The Good Soldier, 1915. *n*.

C. E. MONTAGUE:
A Hind Let Loose, 1910. *n.*
Dramatic Values, 1911. *e.*
Disenchantment, 1922 (*essay on war psychology*)
Fiery Particles, 1923. *s.*

MAX BEERBOHM:
The Works of Max Beerbohm, 1896. *e.*
More, 1899. *e.*
Zuleika Dobson, 1911. *n.*
A Christmas Garland, 1913 (*parodies*).

KATHERINE MANSFIELD:
From a German Pension, 1911. *s.*
Bliss, 1920. *s.*
The Garden Party, 1922. *s.*
The Dove's Nest, 1923. *s.*

JOHN MIDDLETON MURRY:
Dostoevsky: a Critical Study, 1916.
The Evolution of an Intellectual, 1920. *b.*
Countries of the Mind, 1922. *e.*
Keats and Shakespeare, 1925.
Life of Jesus, 1926. *b.*
God, 1929.
Son of Woman, 1931. *b.* of D. H. Lawrence.

CHAPTER TEN: ROBERT BRIDGES:
The Growth of Love, 1883.
Prometheus the Fire-giver, 1883.
Nero, 1885.
Eros and Psyche, 1885.
The Feast of Bacchus, 1889.
October, 1920.
The Testament of Beauty, 1929.

W. B. YEATS:
The Wanderings of Oisin, 1889.
The Countess Cathleen, 1892.
The Celtic Twilight, 1893.
Ideas of Good and Evil, 1903.
The Winding Stair, 1929.
Collected Poems, 1933.

W. DE LA MARE:
Songs of Childhood, 1902. *n.*
Henry Brocken, 1904. *n.*
The Three Mulla-Mulgars, 1910.
The Return, 1910. *n.*
Collected Poems, 1920.

Memoirs of a Midget, 1921. *n.*
The Connoisseur and Other Stories, 1926. *s.*
Desert Islands, 1930.
The Fleeting, 1933. *v.*

JOHN MASEFIELD:
Salt Water Ballads, 1902. *v.*
A Mainsail Haul, 1905. *s.*
Captain Margaret, 1908. *n.*
The Tragedy of Nan, 1910. *p.*
The Tragedy of Pompey the Great, 1910. *p.*
The Everlasting Mercy, 1911. *v.*
Gallipoli, 1916.
Sard Harker, 1924. *n.*
Odtaa, 1926. *n.*
Collected Poems, 1923.

JAMES ELROY FLECKER:
Collected Poems, 1916.

J. C. SQUIRE:
Imaginary Speeches, 1912.
Steps to Parnassus, 1913. *v.*
The Three Hills and Other Poems, 1913. *v.*
Tricks of the Trade, 1917. *v.*
Books in General, 1918, 1920, 1921 (3 ser.). *e.*
Poems, First Series, 1918. *v.*
Poems, Second Series, 1922. *v.*
Grub Street Nights, 1924 *s*

CHAPTER ELEVEN: ROSE MACAULAY:
What Not, 1919. *n.*
Potterism, 1920. *n.*
Told by an Idiot, 1923. *n.*
A Casual Commentary, 1925. *e.*
Staying with Relations, 1930. *n.*

SHEILA KAYE-SMITH:
The Tramping Methodist, 1908. *n.*
Isle of Thorns, 1913. *n.*
Little England, 1918. *n.*
Tamarisk Town, 1919. *n.*
Joanna Godden, 1921. *n.*
The End of the House of Alard, 1923. *n.*

HENRY HANDEL RICHARDSON:
Maurice Guest, 1908. *n.*
The Getting of Wisdom, 1910. *n.*
The Fortunes of Richard Mahony, 1917 ⎫
The Way Home, 1925   ⎬ A trilogy. *n.*
Ultima Thule 1929   ⎭

OLIVER ONIONS:
  The Compleat Bachelor, 1900. *s.*
  Tales of a Far Riding, 1902. *s.*
  Little Devil Doubt, 1910. *n.*
  Widdershins, 1911. *s.*
  Good Boy Seldom, 1911. *n.*
  In Accordance with the Evidence, 1912. *n.*

J. D. BERESFORD:
  Jacob Stahl, 1911. *n.*
  The Hampdenshire Wonder, 1911. *n.*
  A Candidate for Truth, 1912. *n.*
  The House in Demetrius Road, 1914. *n.*
  House Mates, 1917. *n.*
  The Prisoners of Hartling, 1922. *n.*
  Writing Aloud, 1928. *e.*

GILBERT CANNAN:
  Peter Homunculus, 1909. *n.*
  Miles Dixon, 1910. *p.*
  Round the Corner, 1913. *n.*
  Young Earnest, 1915. *n.*
  Mendel, 1916. *n.*
  Everybody's Husband, 1917. *p.*

COMPTON MACKENZIE:
  The Passionate Elopement, 1911. *n.*
  Carnival, 1912. *n.*
  Sinister Street, Vol. I, 1913; Vol. II, 1914. *n.*
  Guy and Pauline, 1915. *n.*
  Sylvia Scarlett, 1918. *n.*
  Sylvia and Michael, 1919. *n.*
  Poor Relations, 1919. *n.*
  Vestal Fire, 1927. *n.*
  Extraordinary Women, 1928. *n.*
  Gallipoli Memories, 1929.
  First Athenian Memories, 1931.

HUGH WALPOLE:
  The Wooden Horse, 1909. *n.*
  Mr. Perrin and Mr. Traill, 1911. *n.*
  Fortitude, 1913. *n.*
  The Dark Forest, 1916. *n.*
  The Cathedral, 1922. *n.*
  The Old Ladies, 1924. *n.*
  Portrait of a Man with Red Hair, 1925. *n.*
  Anthony Trollope: English Men of Letters, 1928. *b.*
  Rogue Herries, etc., 1930–34. *n.*

FRANCIS BRETT YOUNG:
    Robert Bridges: a Critical Study, 1913.
    Deep Sea, 1914. *n*.
    The Dark Tower, 1914. *n*.
    The Crescent Moon, 1918. *n*.
    Marching on Tanga, 1918.
    Portrait of Clare, 1927. *n*.
    My Brother Jonathan, 1928. *n*.

CONSTANCE HOLME:
    Crump Folk Going Home, 1913. *n*.
    The Lonely Plough, 1914. *n*.
    The Splendid Fairing, 1920. *n*.

MARY WEBB:
    The Golden Arrow, 1916. *n*.
    Gone to Earth, 1917. *n*.
    The House in Dormer Forest, 1920. *n*.
    Seven for a Secret, 1923. *n*.
    Precious Bane, 1924. *n*.

CHAPTER TWELVE: CHARLOTTE MEW:
    The Farmer's Bride, 1916; enlarged, 1929. *v*.
    The Rambling Sailor, 1929. *v*.

WILFRED OWEN:
    Poems, edited Sassoon, 1920; enlarged, and with Memoir by E.
        Blunden, 1931. *v*.

ROBERT NICHOLS:
    Ardours and Endurances, 1917. *v*.
    Aurelia, 1920. *v*.
    Guilty Souls, 1922. *p*.
    Fantastica, 1923. *s*.
    Under the Yew, 1927. *n*.
    Fisbo, 1934. *v*.

EDMUND BLUNDEN:
    The Waggoner, 1920. *v*.
    The Shepherd, 1922. *v*.
    English Poems, 1925. *v*.
    Undertones of War, 1928 (*war experience*).
    Life of Leigh Hunt, 1930. *b*.

ROBERT GRAVES:
    Poems, 1914–16. *v*.
    Poems, 1926–30. *v*.
    Goodbye to All That, 1929. *b*.

Siegfried Sassoon:
   The Old Huntsman, 1917, *v.*
   Counter-attack, 1918. *v.*
   The Heart's Journey, 1928. *v.*
   Memoirs of a Fox-Hunting Man, 1929. *b.*
   Memoirs of an Infantry Officer, 1930. *b.*

Edith Sitwell:
   Collected Poems, 1930. *v.*

Osbert Sitwell:
   Twentieth Century Harlequinade, 1916. *v.*
   Argonaut and Juggernaut, 1919. *v.*
   Triple Fugue, 1924. *s.*
   Before the Bombardment, 1926. *n.*
   Dumb Animal, 1930. *s.*
   The Man Who Lost Himself, 1929. *n.*
   Miracle on Sinai, 1934. *n.*

Sacheverell Sitwell:
   Southern Baroque Art, 1924.
   The Gothick North, 1929–30.

Chapter Thirteen: Bertrand Russell:
   German Social Democracy, 1896.
   Essay on the Foundations of Geometry, 1897.
   The Philosophy of Leibniz, 1900.
   Principia Mathematica (with A. N. Whitehead), 1910.
   Principles of Social Reconstruction, 1917.
   Mysticism and Logic, 1918. *e.*
   The Analysis of Mind, 1921.
   An Outline of Philosophy, 1927.

Roger Fry:
   Vision and Design, 1920. *e.*

Clive Bell:
   Art, 1914.
   Pot Boilers, 1918. *e.*
   Since Cézanne, 1922.
   Civilization, 1928.

Lytton Strachey:
   Landmarks in French Literature, 1912.
   Eminent Victorians, 1918. *b.*
   Queen Victoria, 1921. *b.*
   Elizabeth and Essex, 1928. *b.*

VIRGINIA WOOLF:
    The Voyage Out, 1915. *n.*
    Jacob's Room, 1922. *n.*
    Mrs. Dalloway, 1925. *n.*
    Orlando, 1929. Imag. *b.*
    A Room of One's Own, 1929. Feminist. *e.*

CHAPTER FOURTEEN: MAY SINCLAIR:
    Audrey Craven, 1897. *n.*
    The Divine Fire, 1904. *n.*
    The Three Brontës, 1912. *b.*
    The Life and Death of Harriet Frean, 1922. *n.*

DOROTHY RICHARDSON:
    Pointed Roofs, 1915. *n.* ⎫ These are the
    Backwater, 1916. *n.*   ⎬ first 3 vols. of
    Honeycomb, 1917. *n.*   ⎭ Pilgrimage.

REBECCA WEST:
    Henry James, 1916. *b.*
    The Return of the Soldier, 1918. *n.*
    The Judge, 1922. *n.*
    The Strange Necessity, 1928. *e.*

E. M. FORSTER:
    Where Angels Fear to Tread, 1905. *n.*
    The Longest Journey, 1907. *n.*
    Howard's End, 1910. *n.*
    A Passage to India, 1924. *n.*
    Goldsworthy Lowes Dickinson, 1934. *b.*

D. H. LAWRENCE:
    The White Peacock, 1911. *n.*
    Sons and Lovers, 1913. *n.*
    The Rainbow, 1915. *n.*
    The Lost Girl, 1920. *n.*
    Aaron's Rod, 1922. *n.*
    Fantasia of the Unconscious, 1923.

JAMES JOYCE:
    Dubliners, 1914. *s.*
    Portrait of the Artist as a Young Man, 1916. *n.*
    Ulysses, 1922. *n.*

CHAPTER FIFTEEN: EDGAR WALLACE:
    Songs, 1895. *v.*
    Writ in Barracks, 1900. *v.*
    Smithy, 1905. *n.*
    The Four Just Men, 1906. *n.*

Dorothy L. Sayers
Op. I, 1916. *v*.
Catholic Tales and Christian Songs, 1918. *v*.
Whose Body? 1923. *n*.
The Unpleasantness at the Bellona Club, 1928. *n*.
The Five Red Herrings, 1931. *n*.
The Nine Tailors, 1934. *n*.

Chapter Sixteen: Aldous Huxley
The Burning Wheel, 1916. *v*.
Limbo, 1920. *s*.
Leda, 1920. *v*.
Crome Yellow, 1921. *n*.
Mortal Coils, 1922. *s*.
Those Barren Leaves, 1925. *n*.
Point Counter Point, 1928. *n*.
Brave New World, 1932. *n*.

Noel Coward
Three Plays: Home Chat, Sirocco, This Was a Man, 1928. *p*.
Bitter Sweet, 1929. *p*.
Private Lives, 1930. *p*.
Design for Living, 1933. *p*.

Richard Aldington
Latin Poems of the Renaissance (trans.), 1915. *v*.
Images, 1916. *v*.
Images of Desire, 1919. *v*.
Death of a Hero, 1929. *n*.
The Colonel's Daughter, 1931. *n*.

Wyndham Lewis
Tarr, 1918; revised, 1928. *n*.
The Art of Being Ruled, 1926.
Time and Western Man, 1927.
The Childermass, Part I, 1928.
The Apes of God, 1931. *n*.

Chapter Seventeen: David Garnett:
Lady Into Fox, 1922. *n*.
A Man in the Zoo, 1924. *n*.
The Sailor's Return, 1925. *n*.
No Love, 1929. *n*.
The Grasshoppers Come, 1931. *n*.
Pocahontas, 1934. *b*.

J. B. PRIESTLEY:
  Brief Diversions, 1922. *e.*
  The English Comic Character, 1925.
  Benighted, 1927. *n.*
  The Good Companions, 1929. *n.*
  Angel Pavement, 1930. *n.*
  Dangerous Corner, 1932. *p.*

A. P. HERBERT:
  The Bomber Gipsy, 1919. *v.*
  The Secret Battle, 1919. *n.*
  The House by the River, 1920. *n.*
  Riverside Nights, 1926. *revue.*
  The Water Gipsies, 1930. *n.*
  Holy Deadlock, 1934. *n.*

P. G. WODEHOUSE:
  The Pothunters, 1902. *School story.*
  Something Fresh, 1915. *n.*
  Jill the Reckless, 1920. *n.*
  The Inimitable Jeeves, 1924. *s.*
  Bill the Conqueror, 1924. *n.*
  Sam the Sudden, 1925. *n.*
  Meet Mr. Mulliner, 1927. *n.*
  Very Good, Jeeves, 1930. *s.*

CHAPTER EIGHTEEN: T. S. ELIOT:
  Poems; and The Critic in Judgment, 1919. *v.*
  Ara Vos Prec, 1920. *v.*
  The Sacred Wood, 1920. *e.*
  The Waste Land, 1922. *v.*
  Poems, 1909–1925, 1925.
  For Lancelot Andrewes, 1928. *e.*
  Selected Essays, 1932.

INDEX